'This book will be quite valuable for clinicians
apeutic modality. Incorporating compassion-foc
individuals who suffer from undue self-criticism

Juaitn S. Beck, Ph.D.

'Cultivating Compassion for the self is a crucial change process. This book will
help you help clients cultivate this essential ingredient of healing."

Leslie Greenberg, Ph.D.

'This book is an exceptional and invaluable resource for therapists looking to
deeply engage with the transformative power of compassion in therapeutic
settings."

Steven C. Hayes, Ph.D.

'This is an incredibly practical and useful tool for therapists to help their clients
learn to be more self-compassionate using the CFT approach."

Kristin Neff, Ph.D.

'In this long-awaited volume, authors integrate the key elements of CFT into a
well-organized, comprehensive treatment manual. Innovative, practical, and
inspiring, I hope it lands on the desks of all clinicians!"

Christopher Germer, Ph.D.

'There is a lot to like about this book. It is a wonderful resource that makes the
depth and complexity of CFT engaging and accessible."

Stefan G. Hofmann, Ph.D.

Essentials of Compassion Focused Therapy

This book presents a comprehensive, 12-module transdiagnostic program to deliver Compassion Focused Therapy (CFT) in group and individual settings.

Offering an accessible step-by-step guide to the essentials of CFT and its application to a range of contexts, this book provides clinicians with clear guidelines to deliver the modules and adapt them to the specific needs of target groups/individuals. Each module focuses on a theme, which is explained through an introductory basic science for the clinician and then developed and explored through psychoeducation for the client, followed by a variety of experiential exercises. Also included are examples of CFT case formulations, therapist scripts, and client handouts. As an additional resource, clinicians are provided access to www.cftmanual.com, an online platform with downloadable support material such as guided audio meditations, videos of brief Yoga sessions, educational videos, and supplementary handouts.

This practice guide will be the authoritative resource in CFT for clinicians, trainers, supervisors, researchers, and clients with previous CFT experience who wish to deepen their practice.

Nicola Petrocchi, PhD, PsyD, is a psychotherapist, researcher, adjunct professor of psychology at John Cabot University (Rome), the founder and director of Compassionate Mind Italia, and an international trainer of CFT.

James Kirby, PhD, is a clinical psychologist, researcher, and Co-Director of the Compassionate Mind Research Group at the University of Queensland. In 2022, he authored *Choose Compassion*. He is an international trainer of CFT.

Beatrice Baldi, PhD scholar, is a clinical psychologist, 500H-certified Yoga teacher certified in Trauma-Sensitive Mindfulness, and a trainer in CFT. She has been collaborating for several years with Dr. Nicola Petrocchi in spreading a Compassion-focused approach to Yoga.

Essentials of Compassion Focused Therapy

A Practice Manual for Clinicians

Nicola Petrocchi and James Kirby with Beatrice Baldi

Nicola Petrocchi and James Kirby are co-first authors

Routledge
Taylor & Francis Group

LONDON AND NEW YORK

Designed cover image: © Alessia Auricchio [https://alessiaauricchio.carbonmade. com and https://instagram.com/alessia_auricchio_art]

First published 2025
by Routledge
4 Park Square, Milton Park, Abingdon, Oxon OX14 4RN

and by Routledge
605 Third Avenue, New York, NY 10158

Routledge is an imprint of the Taylor & Francis Group, an informa business

© 2025 Nicola Petrocchi and James Kirby with Beatrice Baldi

Access www.cftmanual.com

Disclaimer: This website which makes support materials for this book available is an author-hosted website and Routledge does not take responsibility for its contents.

British Library Cataloguing-in-Publication Data
A catalogue record for this book is available from the British Library

Library of Congress Cataloging-in-Publication Data
Names: Petrocchi, Nicola, 1979- author. | Kirby, James, 1984- author. | Baldi, Beatrice, 1994- author.
Title: Essentials of compassion focused therapy : a practice manual for clinicians / Nicola Petrocchi and James Kirby with Beatrice Baldi.
Description: Abingdon, Oxon ; New York, NY : Routledge, [2024] | Includes bibliographical references and index. |
Identifiers: LCCN 2023042289 (print) | LCCN 2023042290 (ebook) |
Subjects: LCSH: Emotion-focused therapy. | Compassion. |
Compassion--Psychological aspects. | Self-acceptance. | Self-defeating behavior. | Mindfulness-based cognitive therapy.
Classification: LCC RC489.F62 P48 2024 (print) | LCC RC489.F62 (ebook) | DDC 616.89/147--dc23/eng/20231215
LC record available at https://lccn.loc.gov/2023042289
LC ebook record available at https://lccn.loc.gov/2023042290

ISBN: 978-1-032-56553-8 (hbk)
ISBN: 978-1-032-56554-5 (pbk)
ISBN: 978-1-003-43605-8 (ebk)

DOI: 10.4324/9781003436058

Typeset in Calibri
by Taylor & Francis Books

Printed and bound by CPI Group (UK) Ltd, Croydon, CR0 4YY

Contents

Figures

Tables

Acknowledgements

I was looking forward to writing these acknowledgments! First, because this means that we are at the end of this revealing, inspiring, and wonderful long … long journey; second, and most importantly, because I can reconnect with all the incredibly generous souls that have made this possible. Thank you, James and Bea, for being not only creative, sensitive, and dedicated co-authors, but also for your constant compassionate presence. I will miss our Wednesday mornings, 8am Italian time! Thank you, Paul, for the gift of Compassion Focused Therapy, for your generous heart, profound mind, and for trusting and supporting me all these years. Thank you, Louise, wherever you are, for initiating me on my journey through healing. To Mum Carla, Dad Vitto, Samu, Leti, Mal, thank you for loving me and embracing all my transitions. To Roberto e Annarita, thank you for setting me free. To Grace and the team at Routledge, thank you for believing in us! To my clients, thank you for sharing your path with me – may we all remember that we are never alone, and that we can only heal together.

Niki Petrocchi

Niki and Bea, what a wonderful journey it has been, thank you for the support, fun and connection we have formed whilst writing this manual. It has been an absolute joy. Thank you Paul Gilbert for your constant support, wisdom and compassion. You have given the world a gift in Compassion Focused Therapy and thank you so much for letting us make our contribution with this manual. To our colleagues around the world thank you for your patience, understanding and encouragement with us as we wrote this manual which we hope will be of help. Thank you Grace and the team at Routledge. And finally thank you to my wonderful family, Cassie, Fletchy and Sofia who were so patient as I spent my Wednesday afternoons and evenings for what seemed like forever with my Italian family as we worked on this manual.

James Kirby

Giving thanks is something I try to do daily, for, as we also write in this book, a gratitude practice can be transformative. However, practicing gratitude at the end of writing a book is a whole new experience for me, one for which I wish to thank first of all my partners in this incredible journey: my two co-authors, Niki Petrocchi and James Kirby. Learning from you both has been invaluable and feeling your deep trust in me has been helpful and supportive beyond measure. I hope to one day be as inspiring to others as you have been to me. At this point, though it might be slightly expected, I also wish to thank all those creatures (I use this word as I include close family, friends, mentors, animals and compassionate images!) that up to this day have believed in me and given me the material and emotional support needed to face the hardships and to celebrate achievements in my life – this is certainly one big achievement that I would like to share with you! Finally, as I often do, I would like to acknowledge life itself: know that I never for one day took you for granted. I hope to honour you to the best of my abilities, as I attempt to create compassionate ripples into the world.

Beatrice Baldi

Foreword

CFT Essentials

The benefits of practising compassion have been known about for thousands of years, particularly in contemplative and spiritual traditions. A compassionate approach to life has long been suggested as a way to cope with the realities of life that include hardships, setbacks and losses. In addition, our minds are full of conflicts that can create turmoil and emotional pain. Depending on where our mind is at, we can behave harmfully or helpfully to ourselves and others. In many ways Compassion Focused Therapy (CFT) is a modern update of these basic principles using scientific insights allied with western therapeutic techniques. This is not a book for extensive references and complex science discussion, rather it is a book focused on the ideas of *how to do CFT*. Importantly, however CFT draws on the basic sciences as well as a variety of psychotherapeutic approaches.

A brief background in terms of the journey of how CFT came into being, and how it seeks to be an integrative evolutionary informed biopsychosocial approach. I can note that its origins go back over 40 years (see Gilbert et al., 2022 for details). Following on from my PhD studies in the 1970s, my first book called *Depression: From Psychology to Brain State* explored how psychological and social processes affect brain mechanisms. Psychotherapy involves not just understanding the content of a person's mind, but also what generates its *processes*. The focus on understanding biopsychosocial processes has been at the heart of research in CFT.. During the 1980s I worked on motivational theory to explore the interactions between biological, psychological, and social processes, and the differences between non-social and social *motives, after all compassion is care-focused social motive* (see Gilbert, [1989] 2016).. Emotions, cognitions, and behaviours are in the service of motives, because without a motive for something why would you have any emotions or thoughts about it. These, along with Buddhist interests and practices are the foundations of CFT.

It is one thing having scientific insights and theories about mental processes but the issue was how to translate these into therapeutic insights and practises.

There are many strands to this story - including many colleagues who have been involved in this endeavour. One key strand was during the late 1980s and early 1990s, when I was working with chronic and severe depressions using Cognitive Therapy. While some clients could identify depressogenic thinking and could stand back and generate more balanced forms of thinking, there were also individuals for whom this was not helpful. Stott (2007) has discussed this as the 'head-heart lag'; that is, cognitive change may not produce emotional change. One day I asked a particularly chronically depressed client, who was very good at generating helpful thoughts, to actually speak them out loud, so that we could explore how they were being experienced. To my surprise, the emotional tone of her thinking was very hostile. So, although the cognitive content was helpful, her emotional tone and motivation was not.

Exploring further I was very surprised by some of the emotion-hostility in people's supposedly self-supporting thoughts. I discovered that it wasn't only *what* they were thinking but *how* they were thinking that was the issue. So, the obvious solution was to invite people to generate a compassionate and helpful inner-voice and thought tone, and focus on a motivation to be helpful, understanding and validating. Simple you might think; but not really because this gave rise to a second surprise (if not shock). Some clients absolutely *did not want to do this*. They showed what we now call CFT fears, blocks, and resistances to compassion. Sometimes these were based on a misunderstanding of what compassion is, for example that it is weak, soft, or just being nice. This is why today we spend a lot of time using guided scenarios to help clients understand that the essence of compassion is the development of courage and wisdom to address suffering. Using examples help clients recognise that there are different types of wisdom and different types of courage that are needed for different types of suffering (e.g., emotional, physical). When addressing our own suffering it is important for us to recognise this too. Sometimes we need to develop more empathic skills, at other times emotion tolerance skills and at other times assertiveness skills, all of which are covered in this manual.

Another issue that arose in the early stages of CFT was that when you stimulate any emotion or motive you will also stimulate emotional memories in that motive or emotion system. This is called triggering. It turned out that when I started to guide people into compassion motivation, I was at times triggering unprocessed trauma memories embedded in their care system. If the people that we turn to for care and help don't provide care, but instead they neglect or hurt us (especially as children), then the care seeking motivation will be textured by those fears. So, when we begin to explore becoming more compassionate for the self, this opens up care systems and can trigger difficult emotions. For example, some clients who had felt let down and forced into self-reliance, might re-experience anger towards those who had let them down. Sometimes, for a child whose anger was punished or rejected, then beginning to acknowledge anger can also trigger feelings of being vulnerable to punishment, of feeling unlovable and rejectable. Sometimes people who were frightened of or neglected by their caregivers may start to experience grief as they begin to acknowledge a yearning to feel loved, wanted and supported, or yearning to be of value to, and appreciated by, others. An early client of mine noted that as she entered into her therapeutic journey of compassion, the more deeply in touch with her lived experience and unmet needs she became, the more accentuated the feelings of loneliness and grief became and it was developing the compassionate courage and focus to work them they helped her change.

CFT works with these emerging experiences on the compassion journey, including fears, blocks, and resistances, by validating, and by building the courage and wisdom to engage with them. One of the key issues for CFT is it provide what is necessary to help people rebalance their minds by making available a range of biopsychosocial processes that may have become dysfunctional during life. In figure 2.1 the authors use one of the standard CFT diagrams to help therapists understand this process.

We have a very tricky brain, that was designed for us (by evolution), not by us. Hence, we help clients understand that the brain carries potentials for a range of difficult emotions such as anger, anxiety, as well as states like depression. We can also be very self-focused and self-judgmental because our brain has evolved to do this, but these potentials are not our fault. Helping clients take an observational approach to how their tricky brains are working, and how to become more mindful of what arises in their minds as it arises, helps to depersonalise and de-shame the self for difficult emotions. This is fundamental to a compassionate orientation to our minds. However, with growing awareness and observation also comes the process of responsibility for guiding ourselves to be helpful not harmful which is a core motivation for compassion. These are key themes that Nicola, James and Beatrice guide readers through in this manual.

The book

This book is derived from a much larger manuscript that I have worked on for many years with many different versions and that James Kirby and Nico Petrocchi have contributed to. Their aim for this book is to give readers an easy, slimmed down opportunity to explore how to apply some of the basic science of CFT. Focused on the prevention of harm not just the alleviation of harm at any particular time, the book helps to look forward and to take actions that are going to prevent harm in the future. In addition, precisely because compassion is also concerned with the prevention of suffering it also seeks to the create the conditions for flourishing and helping others.

To sum up, this book reflects a long history of efforts to translate science into intervention. Here you will find much information on these endeavours brought together by three experts in CFT. It is full of clear guidance and recommendations with a library of carefully designed handouts, worksheets, and practises to explore and develop. I, like them, hope this book will be a way of getting familiar with CFT and excited to learn more about it and to research its effectiveness and therapeutic developments.

by Professor Paul Gilbert, OBE, Author of The Compassionate Mind

References

Gilbert, P. ([1989] 2016) *Human Nature and Suffering*. Routledge Mental Health Classic Edition. London & New York: Routledge.

Gilbert, P. (2022a). Compassion focused therapy as an evolution informed, biopsychosocial science of the mind: History and challenge. In, P. Gilbert & G. Simos. (eds). *Compassion Focused Therapy: Clinical practice and applications*. (chap 2. 24–89). London. Routledge

Stott, R. (2007). *When the head and heart do not agree: A theoretical and clinical analysis of rational-emotional dissociation (RED) in cognitive therapy. Journal of Cognitive Psychotherapy: An International Quarterly*, 21, 37–50. doi:10.1891/088983907780493313.

A. Introduction

Aims

- To provide a brief introduction to Compassion Focused Therapy
- To illustrate how to use the modules in this manual with creativity and flexibility
- To suggest potential measures that could be used to assess outcomes
- To provide a brief guide of how to read this manual

 Deepen your knowledge

In the book Gilbert, P., & Simos, G. (Eds.). (2022). Compassion focused therapy: Clinical practice and applications. Routledge, please refer to:

Chapter 1 – Setting the scene: psychotherapy at a crossroads and a compassionate way forward
Chapter 2 – Compassion focused therapy: an evolution-informed, biopsychosocial approach to psychotherapy: history and challenge

In the book Gilbert, P. (Ed.). (2017). Compassion: Concepts, research and applications. Routledge/Taylor & Francis Group.

Chapter 1 – Compassion: definitions and controversies
Chapter 15 – The emergence of the compassion focused therapies

DOI: 10.4324/9781003436058-1

What is Compassion Focused Therapy (CFT)?
A Brief Overview

Compassion Focused Therapy (CFT) is a process-based, evolutionary-informed, biopsychosocial therapeutic approach that cultivates compassionate motivation for ourselves and others. CFT defines compassion as, *"the sensitivity to suffering in self and others, with a commitment to try alleviate and prevent it"* (Gilbert, 2014). In fact, CFT uniquely promotes the flows of compassion (other-to-self, self-to-other, and self-to-self) to help face and alleviate suffering, treat mental health problems, and increase well-being. The core of compassion in CFT is the courage and wisdom to both engage with suffering and work out what to do that would be helpful. Multiple systematic reviews and meta-analyses evaluating CFT have found good evidence for the science underpinning the model, as well as the effectiveness of the therapy (see for example, Craig et al., 2020; Leaviss & Uttley, 2015; Millard et al., 2023; Vidal & Soldevilla, 2022).

The primary theoretical model underpinning CFT is social mentality theory, which emphasises the importance of motivational switching, with CFT focusing on deliberately switching and cultivating a compassionate motivation. To learn more about this integrative and complex theoretical model underpinning CFT, we highly recommend reading, "Compassion Focused Therapy: Clinical Practice and Applications" (Gilbert & Simos, 2021). Throughout this manual we will refer to this book and others for background reading of key theoretical topics and themes to help deepen your understanding of the processes that are fundamental to CFT. The primary aim of this practice manual is to provide a step-by-step approach for CFT clinicians to deliver CFT in their clinical work with clients in both individual and group setting, or in person or via telehealth.

Who Should Use this Manual?

No therapy can be learned through a book, and CFT is no exception. Therefore, this manual should not be taken as a way to learn CFT. Rather it should be understood as a guide that therapists who are already trained in CFT can use in implementing this therapy in groups or with individual clients. In a sense, it is like a map for those who already know how to drive. Please go to www.compassiona temind.co.uk for further information about the basic training and the various advanced training programs offered by the Foundation.

How to Use this Manual

The Essentials of Compassion Focused Therapy: A Practice Manual for Clinicians presents a comprehensive, 12-module transdiagnostic program to deliver CFT in group and individual settings. We have provided a 12-module guide, but how the modules are used and implemented can be flexible, depending on the target problems, as well as other pragmatic factors such as time. For example, you could choose to deliver the manual as 12 modules with each module being a single 2-hour session. Thus, you would deliver 24 hours of total intervention (12 sessions of 2 hours each = 24 hours). However, each module can also be split into two one-hour sessions, making it 24 one-hour sessions. Moreover, you might decide to go through the manual modules with your clients in chronological order the first time, then, in the subsequent sessions, you could return to key modules that might be beneficial, based on the client's need and your CFT formulation.

Thus, the modular nature of the manual allows for a flexible approach, providing clinicians with guidelines to deliver the modules, while at the same time enabling adaptations according to the specific needs of the target groups or individuals in the therapy. Examples of how the modules could be delivered are provided below in Figure A.1. If you are a researcher using CFT, the key is to

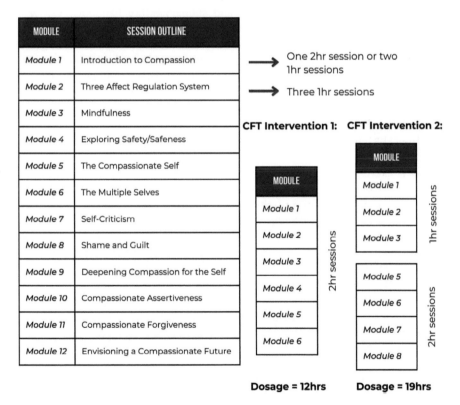

Figure A.1 The 12 Modules with Possible Variations.

ensure you are clear with the protocol regarding what modules were used and over how many sessions those modules were delivered. To help support researchers with the implementation fidelity of this manual, we have provided a "Summary of Key Processes" form for each module, including the key components of each module, which can be used as a checklist.

Throughout the modules we have provided ideas on how as a clinician you might present the material in either a group or individual format, or in-person or using digital technology (e.g., Zoom). Each module focuses on a specific theme, which is explained through a brief introduction of the basic rationale underpinning the module for the clinician, and then developed and explored through psychoeducation for the client, followed by a variety of experiential exercises. Each module includes therapist scripts, to help the clinician become more confident in delivering the practices, and client handouts to be used during the sessions and as home exercises.

As an additional resource to this book, clinicians have access to an online platform to further support their implementation of the CFT manual. This platform includes useful resources such as guided audio meditations, videos of brief yoga sessions to promote the embodiment of the concepts addressed throughout the modules, educational videos, and supplementary handouts. We will continue to add resources to this online platform over time.

As is well known, CFT can be used as a stand-alone intervention, or alongside other techniques and therapies with the aim of enhancing them. Indeed, blocks and resistances to developing compassion for self and others, and in particular the phenomenon of self-criticism and shame, are trans-diagnostic elements that decrease the effectiveness of many therapies.

In individual therapy, you can use this manual to reinforce basic skills that can then be implemented to improve the efficacy of other techniques offered (somewhat like basic athletic training that provides crucial preparatory exercises for whatever activity will be done next). By way of example: I work with a client who has Obsessive Compulsive Disorder to develop soothing rhythm breathing and build a compassionate image to stand beside him as I guide him through exposure with response prevention to touching the trash can. If you are a therapist who works only in individual settings, you might devote part of your session (e.g., at the beginning, as a warm-up) to the gradual application of these concepts and techniques, and then proceed with your standard procedures.

If you are a therapist who sees individual clients but also works with groups, you could create a weekly group in which, while respecting privacy and confidentiality, all your clients, irrespective of the problems presented, meet to train these compassionate skills, which will then be useful to them in the work they do with you during their weekly therapy sessions. Of course, this CFT group could be led by another CFT therapist. This would become a perfect example of a trans-diagnostic CFT group in which the principles of therapy are coached regardless of the issues the client reports, on the basis that working on these trans-diagnostic processes will strengthen the outcome of therapy. In fact the manual, as it is presented here, is designed for clients who do not report specific issues, so that a variety of clients with different issues may still feel that the practices, examples, and metaphors provided are useful.

If, on the other hand, you are a therapist working solely with individual clients, or a group therapist who is intending to work with clients who share the same issue, you may choose either to use this manual as is, or to adapt it to the specific issues presented by that group. The kind of examples and metaphors you will provide, the kind of discussions you will direct after each practice, variations of the proposed exercises or even additional exercises you might devise, will thus be guided by your knowledge of the typical processes that characterise that particular diagnostic group. For example, if you find yourself working with a group of clients with difficulties in the domain of eating, LGBT+ clients, or clients with specific disabilities it might be helpful to give examples of typical triggers that activate the threat system in these clients, or typical compensatory drive system mechanisms that they present. However, it is crucial for clinicians to remember the heterogeneity that distinguishes any group; therefore, attention to case formulation that we will discuss in the next section, is crucial.

Throughout the book, you will see several terms being used interchangeably; this was a deliberate choice, made to speak to the wide audience that we are addressing. We have chosen to use terms such as therapist and clinician to capture the diverse range of mental health professionals that exist internationally; in fact, we are aware that different countries follow different regulations regarding mental health professions and wanted to be as inclusive as possible. That being said, any professional who wishes to use this manual should have received solid training in CFT. You will also find terms such as patient/client being used interchangeably; this is again to capture the different ways of addressing the recipient of a psychological intervention that has been adopted in different countries. Finally, the choice of using both the terms participant and individual is to reinforce the idea that the manual can be applied to both group and individual therapy; furthermore, the word "individual" serves as a reminder that the client is, first and foremost, an individual.

CFT Case Formulation

Regardless of whether you are delivering the manual individually in one-on-one sessions or in a group setting, we think case formulation is critical to good therapy. Like all therapy models there are a number of ways to develop a CFT case formulation. In Chapter 2 we have provided some examples and templates on how you might like to develop your own case formulation. There are two specific case formulations often used in CFT: 1) case formulation according to the three-affect regulation model (The Three Circles); or 2) A CFT based formulation that is focused on past experiences, key fears/threats (external and internal), safety behaviours (external and internal), unintended consequences (external and internal), and self-to-self relating style. In therapy, you can apply these case formulations to your work with your client, and then collaboratively determine which modules might be key to shifting clients to a more compassion focused motivation.

Was my intervention helpful?

To help both aid case formulation, as well as to evaluate whether CFT has been helpful, we recommend administering key CFT measures before therapy. These suggested measures aim to assess underlying motives in accordance with social mentality theory. There are many motives that can cause difficulties, but two of the major motives of focus in CFT are competitive and compassionate motives (see Module 5: Social Mentality Theory and Fears).

In CFT our aim is to help with motivational shifting; as a result, the measures used to assess for competitive motives include:

> **Social Comparison Scale:** Allan, S. & Gilbert, P. (1995). A social comparison scale: Psychometric properties and relationship to psychopathology. *Personality and Individual Differences, 19*, 293–299.
> **Others as Shamer Scale:** Goss, K., Gilbert, P., & Allan, S. (1994). An exploration of shame measures–I: The 'Other As Shamer' scale. *Personality and Individual Differences, 17*, 713–717.
> **Strive to Avoid Inferiority Scales:** Gilbert, P., Broomhead, C., Irons, C., McEwan, K., Bellew, R., Mills, A., Gale, C. & Knibb, R. (2007). Striving to avoid inferiority: Scale development and its relationship to depression, anxiety and stress. *British Journal of Social Psychology, 46*, 633–648.
> **The Forms of Self-Criticising/Attacking and Self-Reassurance Scale:** Gilbert, P., Clark, M., Hempel, S., Miles, J. N. V., & Irons, C. (2004). Criticising and reassuring oneself: An exploration of forms, styles and reasons in female students. *British Journal of Clinical Psychology, 43*, 31–50.
> **The Defeat Scale:** Gilbert, P. & Allan, S. (1998). The role of defeat and entrapment (arrested flight) in depression: An exploration of an evolutionary view. *Psychological Medicine, 28*, 585–598.

Equally, it is also important to gauge the client's compassionate motivation. Possible measures you could use to assess compassion include:

> **The Compassionate Engagement and Action Scales:** Gilbert, P., Catarino, F., Duarte, C., Matos, M., Kolts, R., Stubbs, J., Ceresatto, L., Duarte, J., Pinto-Gouveia, J., & Basran, J. (2017). The development of compassionate engagement and action scales for self and others. *Journal of Compassionate Health Care, 4(1)*, 4.
> **The Compassion Motivation and Action Scales:** Steindl, S. R., Tellegen, C. L., Filus, A., Seppälä, E., Doty, J. R., & Kirby, J. N. (2021) The Compassion

Motivation and Action Scales: a self-report measure of compassionate and self-compassionate behaviours. *Australian Psychologist, 56*, 93–110.

Fears of Compassion Scales: Gilbert, P., McEwan, K., Matos, M., & Rivis, A. (2010). Fears of compassion: Development of three self-report measures. *Psychology and Psychotherapy: Theory, Research and Practice, 84*(*3*), 239–255.

Three Types of Positive Affect Scale: Gilbert, P., McEwan, K., Mitra, R., Franks, L., Richter, A., & Rockliff, H. (2008). Feeling safe and content: A specific affect regulation system? Relationship to depression, anxiety, stress, and self-criticism. *The Journal of Positive Psychology, 3*, 182–191.

Social Safeness and Pleasure Scale: Gilbert, P., McEwan, K., Mitra, R., Richter, A., Franks, L., Mills, A., ... Gale, C. (2009). An exploration of different types of positive affect in students and patients with a bipolar disorder. *Clinical Neuropsychiatry, 6*(*4*), 135–143.

These scales, including other measures that are important to CFT, can all be found on the Compassionate Mind Foundation website. In addition to these measures, clinicians and researchers may wish to include a measure of early life events or attachment. Finally, depending on your target population there might be specific outcome measures you will want to include, such as a specific depression scales or traumatic symptom measures.

Over the period of the intervention you can then assess your clients at Time 1 (before CFT intervention) and at Time 2 (after CFT intervention). During the modules, we also provide examples of in-session measures (visual analogue scales, 1 to 10 rulers) you can use, including the "Three Circle Check-In". These measures can help aid in the further development of case formulation, but also provide important feedback on how the therapy is progressing.

In-Person and Telehealth Tips

Finally, the chapter offers some practical tips on how to adapt the practices offered in the modules for teletherapy, which has become an integral part of clinical work for many therapists.

Group Tips

When delivering CFT in groups be aware that the most important ingredient for any group therapy to work is developing the alliance between the therapist and members, as well as among members. Therefore, creating a supportive, cohesive group is extremely important. Make sure that, as the therapist, you facilitate the development of group behaviour and interactions, allowing opportunities for the group to 'tell their story' and 'be heard', with the aim of cultivating a compassionate group norm. This enables: 1) members to experience compassion from others in the group; and 2) gives group members the opportunity to be compassionate to others in the group. These are examples of compassionate flow, which groups are ideal in helping support. Thus, a major advantage of groups is that it allows for compassionate flow, shared learning, and shared humanity (universality; Yalom & Leszcz, 2005) to be experienced constantly. However, there are also some other important considerations for group work:

- Don't rush, allow space and time, but remember there is limited time for each person
- The depth of formulation may not be to the same extent as it would be for individual clients
- People in groups can go at different paces, thus, be mindful on how group members are progressing (for example, at the end of a practice, it is important to ask who found it helpful but also who did not, so as to avoid the "I'm the only one who did not benefit from this" shaming effect that some successful sharing can generate)
- Some people can be very talkative and others quiet, so creating opportunities for shared input is important
- If possible, it can be very helpful to determine an eligibility to group criteria, that way the group has a shared connection, as opposed to some having severe symptoms being placed with others with minimal difficulties
- Logistics: make sure the room is big enough, there are breaks for tea/coffee, name tags, flip charts and white boards

Attending to Yourself On Your CFT Journey

As therapists we are focused on expressing compassion to our clients and helping them be open to receiving our compassion while developing their own compassionate skills. However, it is critical as a therapist that you also attend to yourself on the CFT journey. Therapy can be challenging at times, and we can experience moments of setback and difficulty. Thus, it is important we are self-compassionate during these periods. Here are some things to consider:

- Do you warm up and warm down between clients or to start and end each day?
- Do you do your own three-circle check-in?
- Are you connecting with other CFT therapists and getting peer support, encouragement and supervision?
- Do you savour and celebrate the therapy successes you have?
- Have you developed your own compassionate coping strategies?

There is no one or right way to take care of yourself as a CFT therapist, the key is to be aware of your own needs and be compassionate to them. To help you with your own self-care as you implement CFT, we would highly recommend that you consider experiencing 'CFT from the inside-out'. This might mean completing a three-day CFT experiential workshop. There is research showing that if you experience the CFT exercises themselves, not only does it help with your own self-care, it actually helps deepen your knowledge of the CFT approach, and leads to better implementation of CFT, which helps the client.

Be Culturally Competent When Using this Manual

It is important for any psychotherapist of any approach to develop cultural knowledge of self and clients, and cultural competence in assessing and using interventions with clients. This sensitivity is especially important for a therapist who wants to teach something as potentially culturally loaded as compassion. The evolutionary approach underlying CFT helps to culturally "unload" the concept of compassion, referring it back to a biologically based motivational system that precedes our culture, our value structure, and our religion. However, it is important that the approaches and techniques that a psychologist uses to improve a client's life are consistent with the values and life experience of that client. "Talk therapy" may be suitable for some cultures, which might also place great value on "insight". Clients from other cultures may respond much more positively to action-based therapies, or artistic or musical expression, rather than self-discourse and emotional writing. Clients from collectivistic cultures may not find calm in the classic visualisation of the "safe" place where the subject is typically asked to imagine themself being alone. It is for this reason that throughout the manual we have suggested various versions of the meditations offered, as well as different expressive modalities to gather feedback on the process – each therapist will, however, need to adapt these suggestions to their specific group of clients, being sensitive to, for instance, ethnicity, neurotype, disability, or LGBT+ identity.

We hope you find this manual helpful as you deliver CFT to your clients.

A Quick Guide to Reading this Manual

Throughout this manual you will find several colour-coded boxes and texts that provide different kinds of useful information as you read and deliver the modules. Below you can find a brief summary of what each of these mean.

Aims: at the beginning of each module you will find a bulleted list of the aims of the module; use this to help you navigate the main concepts you should be sure to cover when delivering it.

Deepen your knowledge: at the beginning of each module, you will find references to other books that you can use to deepen your knowledge of the theory underlying the topics covered in that module.

The **Summary of Key Processes** table is a useful starting point both for planning and executing your sessions; here you will find the five phases into which each module is divided, the main touch points for each phase, as well as references to the therapist scripts and client handouts. The scripts provide guidance to the therapist delivering practices; the client handouts can be photocopied and given to clients to support them during and between sessions. Remember that it is not mandatory to do all the practices listed for each module in one session.

Therapist Background Knowledge: these sections provide some basic theoretical knowledge that is useful to keep in mind when delivering the sessions. This information does not necessarily have to be shared with clients, but is important for the therapist to know; it is by no means exhaustive, which is why additional reading is suggested at the beginning of each module.

Therapist Task: these sections provide guidance in terms of what the therapist should do during the session; suggestions are given for activities, prompts to offer, and the general flow that should be followed during the sessions.

Therapist Tips: these provide additional guidance to the therapist delivering the module. They aim to answer frequently asked questions, to point out possible difficulties that therapists may encounter, and support them in the process.

Optional Practices/Exercises/Ideas: these are practices and exercises that are optional and can be added to the program if time allows; alternatively, they can be offered as prompts for reflection at home.

(xx minutes) Next to each therapist's script, you will find an indication of the approximate duration of the practice; we suggest that you try to stick to these durations in order to provide sufficient time for the clients to experience the practice, while at the same time, not making it too long, thereby running the risk of not being able to finish the program in your sessions.

Three Circle Check-Ins: these are moments in which clients are asked to briefly assess the size of their three circles, usually through drawing. Three Circle Check-Ins are usually recommended at the beginning and end of each sessions, and sometimes even before and after specific practices, with the aim of helping clients to see the effect that these practices have. The therapist can be creative in using these moments as they see fit.

B. CFT Formulations

Aims

- To introduce several ways to develop tailored Compassion Focused Therapy formulations for your clients
- To illustrate the Three-Circle Formulation
- To illustrate the Three-Circle Formulation applied to a specific episode
- To illustrate the Three-Circle Formulation applied to the therapeutic relationship
- To illustrate the Biopsychosocial and Evolutionary Focused Case Formulation

 Deepen Your Knowledge

In Gilbert, P. & Simos, G. (Eds). (2022). *Compassion Focused Therapy: Clinical Practice and Applications*. Routledge, please refer to:

Chapter 6 – Formulation and Fears, Blocks and Resistances

In Gilbert, P. (2010). *Compassion Focused Therapy: Distinctive features*. Routledge/Taylor & Francis Group, please refer to:

Chapter 9 – Formulation

DOI: 10.4324/9781003436058-2

There are many ways to approach case formulation in Compassion Focused Therapy (CFT). Although this manual provides a modularised intervention model, case formulation offers the key approach in tailoring this manual to an individual client and their major difficulties.

The most important aspect to remember when approaching CFT formulations is the focus on **motivation** (which social mentality does the client typically adopt in the interaction with others and with themselves?), how motivation impacts on the three emotion regulation systems, and **motivational shifting**, specifically, helping individuals to shift from a dominant competitive social mentality to a compassionate social mentality. This is discussed in-depth in Gilbert's Chapter 6: Formulation and Fears, Blocks and Resistances.

For the clinician, case formulations can be structured in many ways, and we suggest these two approaches to begin with 1) Three-Circle Formulation (in general, in a single problematic episode, in the therapeutic interaction); and 2) Biopsychosocial and Evolutionary Focused Case Formulation. Based on these case formulations, therapists can then determine which exercises and modules from this manual are critical to help shift the client from dominant competitive motives to compassionate motives.

Formulation should be based on the assessment with the client, which is based on social mentality theory. See Figure B.1 below, indicating the mentalities and associated measures that can be used.

The Three-Circle Model Formulation

The most intuitive and client friendly formulation is to use the "Three-Circle Model" formulation. The Three-Circle Model will need to be explained to the client via psychoeducation, which is outlined in Module 2, and presented below as a figure. This formulation of the client's suffering based on the possible imbalance of the three systems of emotional regulation is usually the first one to be conducted in the therapeutic process and refers to the "general period" that the patient is going through and that brought them to therapy.

Using this formulation to frame the patient's difficulties easily allows the patient to understand three main elements that will help in future CFT intervention: 1) mental difficulties are usually due to an imbalance of the three emotional systems, with a prevalence of the threat system and drive system, and a more or less chronic hypo-activity of the soothing system; 2) both external factors (threats in the environment or lack of safety in the environment) and internal factors (rank-focused motivational style and self-criticism) can produce an imbalance of the three systems; and 3) it is possible to generate a balancing force for the three systems by repeatedly and intentionally shifting into a compassionate motivation toward the self and others.

These examples below show how two recurring factors that are commonly reported by clients (an excessive focus on a competitive motivation style and self-criticism) modulate the three systems.

THE PATH OF CFT

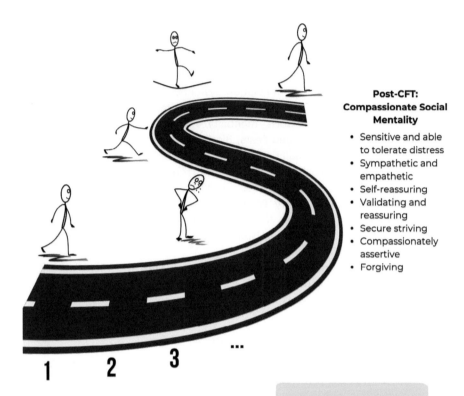

Post-CFT:
Compassionate Social
Mentality

- Sensitive and able to tolerate distress
- Sympathetic and empathetic
- Self-reassuring
- Validating and reassuring
- Secure striving
- Compassionately assertive
- Forgiving

Pre-CFT:
Competitive, Threat-
based Social Mentality

- Social comparison (inferior/superior)
- Shame (external/internal)
- Humiliation
- Submissive/Aggressive
- Insecure striving
- Self-critical attacking

Motivational shifting
from Competitive,
Threat-based to
Compassionate social
mentalities

Figure B.1 The CFT Path (which continues well past the 12-module training) Encourages a Motivational Shift from a Threat-based, Competitive Mentality to a Compassionate Mentality.

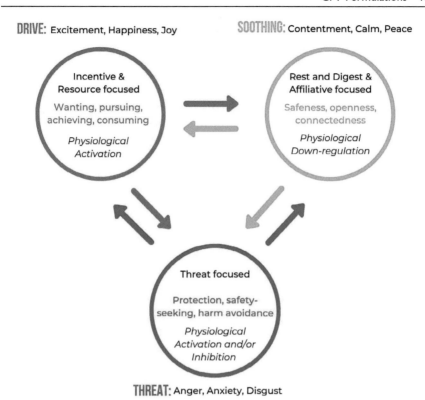

Figure B.2 The Three-Circle Model. Adapted from Gilbert, P. (2005). *Compassion and Cruelty.* Source: Gilbert, P. (Ed.). (2005). *Compassion: Conceptualisations, Research and Use in Psychotherapy.* Routledge.

Figure B.3 Competitive Motive Shaping the Three Circles.

Here, the clinician is emphasising that a competitive motive can shape the three circles into a configuration which has a dominant threat-drive balance, see Figure B.3 on the left. When in a competitive motive, when it comes to self-relating style, if the person is focused on drive (blue circle) and experiences set-back, disappointment or failure, the person is then vulnerable to a self-relating pattern, that is threat based (i.e., self-criticism with emotions towards the self of anger, disgust, and contempt). See Figure B.4.

When caught in a competitive motive, the client regulates predominantly through drive and threat – which means they 'simply' have to work harder to prevent failure or overcome failure, this can lead to all kinds of mental health difficulties, such as over-compensation and perfectionism, insecure striving, depression, and anxiety.

Thus, the key is helping the client realise that voluntarily shifting their motive from a competitive to a compassionate one, will help them bring the three circles back into balance, see Figure B.5 below. The therapist should aim to include the client's narrative and experiences in the three circles, so that it is tailored to them. A key feature of the intervention plan, therefore, is to shift to a compassionate motive and begin to strengthen and develop the soothing system (green circle). The therapist can also choose to explain to the client how this links with physiology.

The Three-Circle Model can also be applied to interpersonal difficulties, such as those in a work context, for example boss-employee, or in other roles, such

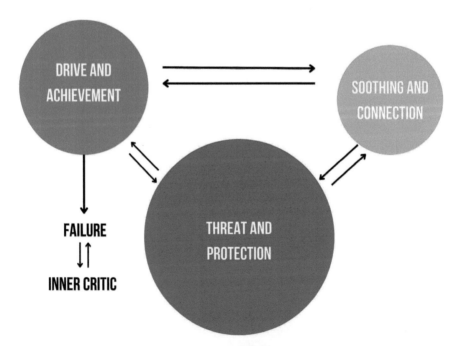

Figure B.4 Self-criticism as Expressed by the Three Circles.

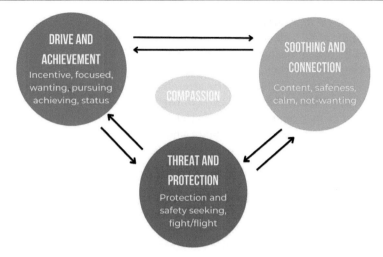

Figure B.5 Compassionate Motive Balancing the Three Circles.

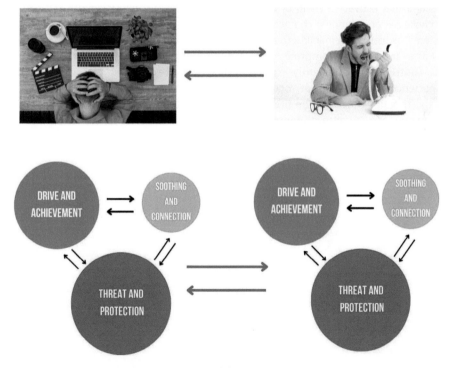

Figure B.6 Competitive Motives dominated by a Large Threat System Regulating Interpersonal Relationships

as in romantic relationships, friendships, parent-child relationships, and so on. An example of three-circle interpersonal regulation using the Three-Circle Model is provided below between a toxic boss and an employee.

In this example, the clinician aims to demonstrate how the client's three circles can be 'moved' or 'influenced' by external factors, such as other people or even the context itself. Thus, the key is to begin to determine how to regulate oneself when in that context or with that person, or whether other options are more helpful (e.g., leave a relationship or find another job, etc).

The Three-Circle Model Applied to a Specific Episode

The Three-Circles Model can be used to conceptualise a specific problematic episode that the client brings to the therapy session.

In this case (refer to Figure B.7), the overall imbalance of the three circles (described in the previous paragraph) is represented on the left (described as client background). This imbalance (at the macro level) characterises the vulnerability that the client presents at this time in their life. However, what we commonly observe is that this imbalance manifests itself in the micro level too. This impacts how the patient reacts to and handles specific triggers or prompting events that occur in daily life, and that activate a chain of events (emotions, actions, physiological reactions, motivational orientations) characterised by the dominance of the threat and drive systems, as well as an inability to activate the soothing system.

For example: the prompting event may be my colleague telling me that I am not contributing sufficiently to the project we are working on together. I experience an initial threat focused reaction, characterised by anxiety related to the thought that I will be fired if she tells the boss, a feeling of constriction in my stomach, a sense of general paralysis, and a desire to curl up into a ball.

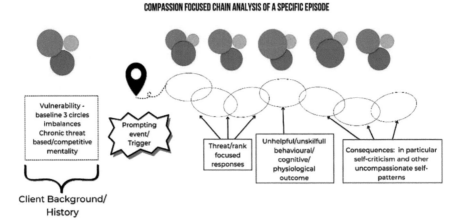

Figure B.7 Compassion Focused Chain Analysis of a Specific Episode.

I can then experience a subsequent threat-focused reaction (I can't tolerate this state of anxiety and have to get it off my chest, I criticise myself, get a drink at the bar under the office, or drink half a bottle of the anti-anxiety medication I have in my purse), or a "drive-focused" reaction (I go out and buy that slightly expensive sweater that I wanted so badly) or a rank-focused reaction (I point out to my colleague a typo in the document they just sent me, reiterating how frustrating it is for me to work with someone who does not speak English as their first language; or pointing out how hard it must be for them, being single, to live so far from downtown and having to commute every day, and how convenient the apartment that my partner and I just bought for ourselves is, being right next to the office). These strategies can be followed, like other links in the chain, by other threat or drive focused reactions, which, however, tend to produce fewer and fewer functional outcomes (I end up criticising myself more and more, or creating open conflict in the workplace, only to come home to attack my partner, and further criticising myself for doing so).

This conceptualisation of a problematic episode helps the clinician and client hypothesise and test possible "compassion-focused exits" that allow the activation of the green system and the balancing of the other two systems, and thus the interruption of typical loops that exacerbate mental suffering. For example, in response to my colleague's first comment and the anxiety that immediately ensues, I may decide to activate my compassionate mind: I slow my breathing, modify my posture, activate my compassionate tone of voice, and tell myself that I recognise fear and that it is normal to feel this way. I then try to imagine my compassionate image next to me, and to feel its understanding and support. Or I might activate my compassionate self and try to respond with compassionate assertiveness, asking for clarification about the feedback, trying to understand where it is coming from (perhaps, from this perspective, I notice that my colleague seems very stressed at this time). I remind myself that it is normal not to be performing at 100 percent all the time, given also what I am going through (compassionate validation). This kind of conceptualisation of specific episodes, therefore, allows us to understand which interactions are most problematic for the client and to apply the usefulness of compassionate shifts to everyday life and interactions that constantly occur.

The Three-Circles Model Applied to in Session Client/Therapist Interaction

What happens in the session lends itself well to observation through this conceptualisation. There are three types of simultaneous "interactions" that can generate a balance or imbalance of the three systems: the first is the interaction between client and therapist (interpersonal dimension) and the other two are the interactions that both client and therapist have with themselves (intrapersonal interactions). The interaction between the patient and me could be, for example, that the patient willingly agrees to do a visualisation practice, feels safe with me, "we are on the same team" and we are working toward the same goal (interpersonal dimension).

However, at the intra-personal level, the patient's inner dialogue may be dominated by self-criticism and threat: "What if I can't do it right? What if I'm doing it all wrong? This therapist is so nice, I can't let them down! That's it, I'm overthinking as usual and ruining everything! This won't work either! And if this doesn't work, nothing will work! Come on, don't get distracted!"

In addition, the therapist's inner dialogue may also be dominated by a threat focused rank/competitive motivational style. The therapist may say to themselves: "Surely I'm not doing it right! The patient will lose confidence and be disappointed! Am I going too slow? I will never become a good compassion focused therapist!" Or: "What did I just say! How could I be so stupid! I wonder if this is the right time to do this practice, I wouldn't want it to harm them!"

Therefore, the formulation of the therapeutic interaction itself (what is happening in the here and now of the session) which sets out to regulate the imbalances of the three systems, can shed light on which social mentality is most often activated at the interpersonal level, and which one is activated at the intra-personal level, both in the patient and the therapist. Insights derived from this type of analysis of therapeutic interaction can be very useful in facilitating compassionate shifts both in and out of session.

Figure B.8 The Three-Circle Model Applied to Client/therapist Interactions.

Biopsychosocial and Evolutionary Focused Case Formulation

Beyond the Three-Circle Model we can also use the standard CFT formulation developed by Gilbert, which is focused on historical influences and key fears (external and internal) that can give rise to safety behaviours that cause inadvertent consequences, which, in turn, shape the way we self-relate.

This kind of case formulation answers broader questions beyond those related to the client's actual functioning: how did the client come to develop this kind of hyper-activation of a particular social mentality? How was the typical imbalance of the three systems that they present at this time functional for them? What historical events produced it?

This is, therefore, a formulation that not only makes the clinician understand what areas can be the subject of further investigation and intervention (including the past, for example with specific compassion focused imagery rescripting or compassion focused EMDR interventions) but also stimulates a deshaming interpretation of the history of the person in front of us. Thus, this case formulation, helps both us and the client to adopt a compassionate and validating narrative of the various attempts that we have all made, as human beings, to protect ourselves from threats.

Below is an example of a **Biopsychosocial and Evolutionary-focused** formulation for a parent struggling in their role, a parent who is highly self-critical of their own parenting, with fears of being judged as a bad parent. Linking parenting to a past experience of what it was like to be parented, how they experienced their own

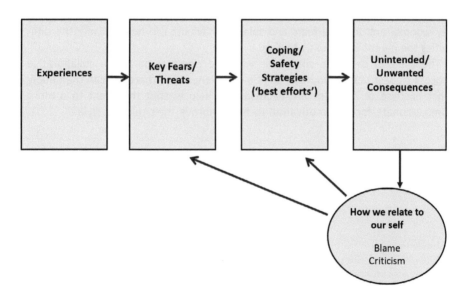

Figure B.9 A Wireframe for a Biopsychosocial and Evolutionary-focused Case Formulation. Source: Adapted from Gilbert, P. (2007). Advanced Clinical Skills workshop handouts

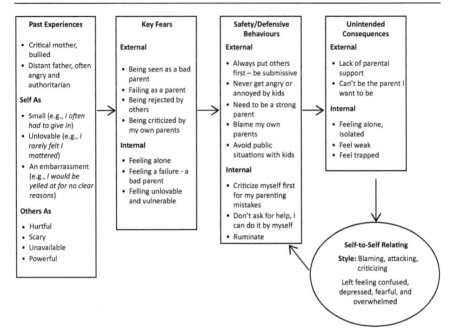

Past Experiences	Key Fears	Safety/Defensive Behaviours	Unintended Consequences
• Critical mother, bullied • Distant father, often angry and authoritarian **Self As** • Small (e.g., *I often had to give in*) • Unlovable (e.g., *I rarely felt I mattered*) • An embarrassment (e.g., *I would be yelled at for no clear reasons*) **Others As** • Hurtful • Scary • Unavailable • Powerful	**External** • Being seen as a bad parent • Failing as a parent • Being rejected by others • Being criticized by my own parents **Internal** • Feeling alone • Feeling a failure - a bad parent • Felling unlovable and vulnerable	**External** • Always put others first – be submissive • Never get angry or annoyed by kids • Need to be a strong parent • Blame my own parents • Avoid public situations with kids **Internal** • Criticize myself first for my parenting mistakes • Don't ask for help, I can do it by myself • Ruminate	**External** • Lack of parental support • Can't be the parent I want to be **Internal** • Feeling alone, isolated • Feel weak • Feel trapped

Self-to-Self Relating

Style: Blaming, attacking, criticizing

Left feeling confused, depressed, fearful, and overwhelmed

Figure B.10 An Example of a Shame-based CFT Formulation for a Self-critical Parent. Source: Adapted from Gilbert, P. (2007). Advanced clinical skills workshop handouts

parents, connecting to possible past shame-experiences, and understanding the key external and internal fears and safety behaviours can help validate the difficulties the parent is presently having.

The clinician can then share this with the client as part of a collaborative process to best understand the client's experience. The therapist can then apply what exercise or modules are necessary to help in shift the client to a more compassionate focused motivation to help improve their relating style.

Chapter 1

Module 1

Introduction to Compassion and the Tricky Brain

Aims

- To introduce the evolutionary model that underpins Compassion Focused Therapy and the distinction between 'it's not your fault' and the ability to 'take responsibility' through the wisdom of how our minds work
- To encourage discussion, establish the importance of ground agreements for creating both safeness and safety, such as confidentiality
- To be able to respond to potential difficulties within the group, including risk assessment
- To begin the process of understanding what compassion is and isn't and begin to elicit and work with key fears, blocks, and resistances
- To begin the process of understanding compassion as a 'flow' (self-to-self, self-to-other, other-to-self) and how this connects to a compassionate self

 Deepen Your Knowledge

In Gilbert, P. & Simos, G. (Eds). (2022). *Compassion Focused Therapy: Clinical Practice and Applications*. Routledge, please refer to:

Chapter 1 – Setting the Scene
Chapter 2 – Compassion Focused Therapy: an Evolution-Informed Biopsychosocial Approach to Psychotherapy – History and Challenge

DOI: 10.4324/9781003436058-3

Summary of Key Processes

Table 1.1 Module 1: Introduction to Compassion & Tricky Brain

Phase		Main Touch Points	Therapist Scripts	Client Handouts
1	Welcome the Group	**1a)** Friendly welcome **1b)** Elicit participants' own ground agreements **1c)** Facilitate collaborative enquiry into goals and "What brings you here?" **1d)** CFT Forecast	☐ **Script 1.1:** What brings you here	☐ **Handout 1.1:** Handout of Ground Agreements for Working Together
2	CFT definition of compassion	**2a)** Introduce compassion definition according to CFT **2b)** Imagery: Compassion to Others		☐ **Handout 1.2:** What compassion is and is not
3	Evolved Tricky Brain	**3a)** Realities of Life **3b)** Psychoeducation of core principles of CFT	☐ **Script 1.2:** Realities of Life Meditation ☐ **Script 1.3:** Examples for introducing the CFT Reality Check ☐ **Script 1.4:** Examples for generating changes in body feelings	☐ **Handout 1.3:** The Core Principles of CFT ☐ **Handout 1.4:** The Tricky Brain
4	Loops in the Mind	**4a)** Old and new brain loops **4b)** Exercise: Our own loops in the mind **4c)** Emotion brain: External/Internal creations		☐ **Handout 1.5:** Loops in the mind ☐ **Handout 1.6:** Mind Body Connections
5	Preparation for the Compassionate Path & Wrap-Up	**5a)** Summary of the Session **5b)** Preparation for the Compassionate Path	☐ **Script 1.5:** Preparation for the Compassionate Path	☐ **Handout B:** Personal Practice Diary

Phase 1: Welcome the Group

The goal of this phase is to create a connection among the group members. In this first module you will be spending quite a lot of time getting to know the participants and allowing space for introductions and initial sharing of background and intentions.

Main Touch Points

1a) Friendly welcome

 Therapist Task

If you find it useful, provide sticky nametags. Invite participants to introduce themselves to the people around them (left and right) and then possibly to the group. Begin by presenting yourself. Alternatively, you can also ask them to get into pairs and briefly introduce each other; then, coming back to the large group, each person will introduce their partner to the others.

1b) Elicit participants' own ground agreements to create a safe environment

 Client Handout 1.1 – Ground agreements
Therapist Script 1.1 – What brings you here?

 Therapist Task

Ask participants to reflect on what ground agreements would be helpful to them during the therapy, as this will help them to feel more engaged and part of the process. Be sure to bring their attention to the function of the agreements they formulate: to be of help and support.

> *"In order for us to work together here we need to create an understanding of how we are going to support and respect each other and make this a friendly safe and sharing space. Let's first discuss how we would like to work together so we feel safe with each other".*

To help create a sense of safeness and openness you could write the ideas on a flipchart/whiteboard. During the early stages of Module 1 it will be important to validate that coming to the group or individual therapy can be anxiety provoking and they are already showing courage by coming; this is precisely why we wish to establish these ground agreements. Highlight that we are here to help each other as well as ourselves.

1c) Facilitate collaborative enquiry into goals and "What brings you here?"

 Therapist Task

After ground agreements have been established, you can then deepen the process of connection by going around the group, inviting people to express a **goal** for them to achieve in coming to the session, as well as an optional worry that they may have about coming to the group. Write these on the flipchart/whiteboard to help participants realise that many of their goals and worries are most likely shared – increasing the connection yet again. In online settings you can invite them to use the chat function, where everyone can write what they feel, which is then read aloud by the therapist.

A practice that can be used to focus and share goals is the practice "What brings you here?" (**Therapist Script 1.1**), which can be done as a self-reflection followed by group discussion or as a practice in pairs.

 Therapist Tips

Watch out for people whose goals are *to get rid of things* and discuss this early: the therapy is about learning how to work with difficulties rather than get rid of them per se. Their concerns or problems may well lose their power and intensity, but you should highlight the fact that if they focus on getting rid of something it will start a process of over monitoring and that it's not helpful to them. Use the example of sleep: if we constantly monitor whether or not we are asleep, the monitoring itself can get in the way of actually falling asleep. So, therapy is about focusing on building and developing rather than getting rid of, and exploring this process with curiosity.

1d) CFT Forecast

 Therapist Task

Provide an overview of the nature of the 12 modules.

> *"In each session we'll be spending a little time learning some important things about CFT. But mostly, we will learn and practice skills that can help us handle stressful internal and external challenges and emotions. In the sessions we want to hear from you. About how CFT is working or*

not working for you. So, our group is as personally relevant to you as possible. Today we're going to learn what compassion is and is not, and introduce three core qualities of compassion – wisdom, strength, and commitment – which we'll continue to use throughout our group sessions. We are also going to learn the 6 core principles of CFT and spend time on this important point regarding how we have a very tricky brain. We'll end by doing a closing practice to prepare us for this compassionate path".

Phase 2: CFT Definition of Compassion

In this phase, it is important to define what compassion is according to Compassion Focused Therapy.

Main Touch Points

 Client Handout 1.2 – Defining Compassion

2a) Introduce the definition of compassion according to CFT

 Therapist Background Knowledge

In CFT, the definition we use for compassion is, *"the sensitivity to suffering in self and others, with a commitment to alleviate and prevent it"*. This definition emphasises two key aspects, first, to engage with suffering, and then secondly to start to try and do something to help alleviate or prevent suffering. As a result, there are six competences that are engagement focused, and six competencies which are action focused. This is depicted in the figure below.

It is important for the CFT therapist to remember that some clients will have difficulties with some of these competencies, while others will have strengths. Our aim as therapist is to validate, whenever possible, both the client's strengths and their difficulties. The 12 modules of this manual are focused on developing knowledge and skills across all 12 of these competencies.

We don't often explicitly describe the 12 competencies of compassion with clients (although you may like to do this), rather we focus on building 1) wisdom; 2) courage; and 3) commitment. Although not emphasised in the figure, another key quality that is useful in the development for compassion is warmth. Some clients will have fears, blocks, and resistances (FBR) to warmth;

COMPASSION

Main qualities

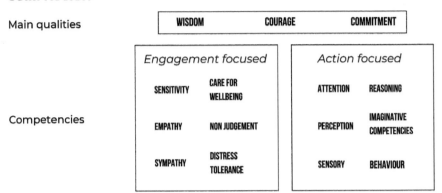

Competencies

Figure 1.1 The competencies of compassion.
Source: Adapted from Gilbert, P. (2010). Compassion Focused Therapy: Distinctive Features (1st ed.). Routledge.

however, it is important to understand and validate what those FBRs are, as well as help begin to generate the quality of warmth. Indeed, as the therapist, we can role-model these compassionate qualities in the therapeutic relationship.

It is also important to recognise how compassion is contextual to the suffering encountered, and as such the compassionate responses may differ depending on the emotional suffering (e.g., anger, anxiety, sadness), physical suffering (e.g., pain or an injury), or resource-based suffering (e.g., lack of food or shelter) experienced. Clients may be very good with some of these forms of suffering (e. g., physical injuries), but struggle with emotional suffering (e.g., sadness). This is also emphasised throughout the 12 modules.

   Therapist Task

The therapist can provide an introduction such as "As we are going to be focusing on compassion during this training let's explore what compassion means to you. What comes to mind when you think of compassion?"

- Write the participants' ideas of compassion on the flipchart/whiteboard and then see if there are things they like or don't like about it
- Discuss what compassion is and is not; define it. You can refer to **Client Handout 1.2**
- Focus on the two parts of the definition of compassion, and its three qualities.

Therapist Tips

Try to link the qualities the clients have listed to the qualities of wisdom, strength, and commitment. That way, you can validate their intuitive wisdom on how they already know what compassion is.

 Optional Ideas on Introducing Compassion

- Using examples and stories to show compassion (you can take inspiration from movies, books, online videos, recent news), highlighting the two psychologies of compassion (engagement/action)
- You could give the CFT example of a friend you care about who needs to go to hospital for tests on a health concern but is scared to go and doesn't want to. The friend shares this with you. At this point, try asking the group: "What do you do?". Go around the group getting ideas on what they would do for the friend. Connect their responses to the definition of compassion. Keep going until somebody says, "I would go with them", validating the wisdom that doing something scary with someone is easier than alone, and how they were committed to taking action to help the friend
- You could also highlight the two psychologies of compassion by using other examples, such as the *"child with the wounded knee"* (kids need comforting and a band-aid), *"the doctor"* (only validating doesn't heal a broken arm – they will need to have been trained and gained the wisdom to know what to do), or *"the river"* (you can't save someone from drowning by jumping into the river if you can't swim yourself). This is to highlight that sensitivity to suffering is not enough, but the desire and commitment to help (and to help skilfully) is also crucial
- Guide the group towards the realisation that compassion is not stupid or passive or weak, but actually uses wisdom, strength and courage, and commitment to try to be helpful

2b) Imagery: Compassion to Others

 Therapist Task

In order to help participants relive moments in which they have experienced compassion, you can use the aid of imagery.

You might ask: *"I invite you to close your eyes and think of a time when you tried to help somebody who was having difficulties. Don't focus too much on their distress, but on what was happening in you".*

During the guided meditation, try exploring these questions:

- What qualities do you notice in yourself in this moment?
- What were you focused on?
- What were you feeling?
- What were you thinking?
- And what were you doing?

Therapist Tips

Link the responses from the participants to the definition of compassion. Make sure it is clear that compassion is a motivation that involves noticing suffering, followed by a response to alleviate suffering. The feelings we experience and the actions we take will all depend on the suffering we encounter. You can use examples of compassion towards somebody who is sad, anxious, or angry; how we are compassionate to each of these people and their corresponding emotions and actions will vary slightly. Allow sufficient time to allow group members to explore their own understanding of compassion. Indicate how these fit with the three qualities of wisdom, strength and commitment.

 Optional Ideas

- You can also look at the flipchart/whiteboard of the fears and worries people generated about attending the group at the beginning of this module. You could then ask the group: *"if we were at our most compassionate, how would we like to help each other with these fears and worries?"*
- You could consider doing an imagery exercise on compassion from others (see below), however, this could be distressing for some populations. It is up to your therapeutic experience and understanding of the population you are targeting in the intervention as to what is most appropriate. We suggest compassion to others is always best as the first imagery exercise. For more general populations you could do compassion from others.

 Optional Imagery: Compassion from Others

Ask: *"What we will do here is take a moment to imagine what it would feel like to have somebody in your life that is committed to supporting you, is willing to help you, and is compassionate towards you. Begin by bringing to mind somebody who has been compassionate to you in the past".*

Try guiding them through the following self-reflections during meditation:

- What qualities do you notice in yourself in this moment?
- What were you focused on?
- What were you feeling?
- What were you thinking?
- And what were you doing?

Phase 3: The Evolved Tricky Brain and Realities of Life

In this phase you will try to answer the question: "Why do we need compassion?". The answer lies in the complexities of our evolved tricky brain, which often makes it difficult to cope with the inevitable ups and downs of life.

Main Touch Points

 Client Handout 1.3 – The core principles of CFT
Client Handout 1.4 – The tricky brain
Therapist Script 1.2 – Realities of life meditation
Therapist Script 1.3 – Examples for introducing the CFT reality check
Therapist Script 1.4 – Examples for generating changes in body feelings

3a) Realities of Life

 Therapist Task

Guide the group through this meditation, included in **Therapist Script 1.2**. The exercise itself should take about 10–15 minutes. You can audio record the practice during the session (using your phone); inform participants that this is a possibility and that you can email them the recording. Alternatively, create pre-recorded audio files of these practices so that participants can continue to practise them outside of formal group sessions.

 Therapist Tips

Pace it slowly, don't rush the meditation. Allow time after the exercise to reflect on the experience. Ask the participants to comment on how the exercise felt, what was experienced. Noticing both the good things, but also some of the difficulties, possibly fears or resistance they had to it. Explore these reactions as a group.

After the exercise, direct the group to the Handouts. In particular **Client Handout 1.3: The core principles of CFT** and **Handout 1.4: The Tricky Brain,** highlighting how the meditation brought them into contact with these core principles of CFT.

The 6 core principles include: 1) Genes we did not choose; 2) Social construction: 3) the Tricky brain; 4) It's not your fault; 5) Compassionate wisdom; and 6) Compassionate cultivation.

3b) Psychoeducation of core principles of CFT

  Therapist Task

Make space for a group discussion about the core aspects of each component of CFT, highlighting how the meditation brought them into contact with these core principles of CFT.

You can use the **Client Handouts 1.3** and **1.4** as guides. The key is to open up each point of discussion as part of the group.

Point 1: Genes we did not choose

You can ask: *"Who here chose to be born, chose the parents they have, the gender they have, chose to be human? To have the skin colour, height etc they have? To have the emotions they feel?"*

Alternatively, you can focus on the body and invite participants to stand up, walk around, flex their fingers, and arms, and notice subsequent feelings: *What is it like when we realise that these have been built for us by our genes?*

Point 2: Socially constructed

"Imagine I had been kidnapped as a three-day-old baby by a very violent drug gang. In this case, this version of me as your therapist would not be here. Who do you think I would have become?"

Expand the idea to the participants' own experience: *Imagine being raised by the neighbour next to you; would you have become the same you?*

Invite participants to think about the following points:

- There are many thousands of potential versions of us that will never have a chance to live and/or would never wish to live (remember a trip that you have done in a very different culture; have you ever thought: "What would my life be like if I were born here?")
- Even in daily life, there are many versions of the self (emotions and social roles as different selves).

- *How many versions of you have you been today (working self, mother/father self, son/daughter self, self/partner self...)?*
- We can use this fact to train our minds to work in new ways. We can cultivate new versions and patterns in our lives – one of these is the compassionate self.

Point 3: The Tricky Brain

Introduce the fact that human brains and emotions are much more difficult to regulate than we think. You can use the zebra example (**Therapist Script 1.3**) to elicit the following point:

As humans are a form of life on the planet, we share similarities with other forms of life, in particular with other animals. For example, the brains of mammals (e.g., chimpanzees, or kangaroos) are very focused on avoiding harm and seeking food, company, and reproduction. But in your opinion, do other mammals struggle less with mental difficulties than us? What is the thing they don't have?

Uniquely, humans have cognitive capacities of self-awareness, which enable us to internally judge and comment on how we are doing, and this often means we can be self-critical. This self-awareness also allows us to be creative and anticipate the future for the better but also for the worse, resulting in rumination, worry, self-consciousness. We have a type of self-awareness and knowing awareness that allows us to do things that animals cannot do. For example, we can choose not to eat in order to lose weight, or we can choose to exercise to get fit. But you will never see zebras doing their training in the morning to get fit to better avoid the lions. Nor are you likely to encounter lions choosing to change their diet into vegetarianism so they don't have to hunt zebras.

This means humans can choose to practise certain skills so that we can begin to lead a different life. And the more we practice, the greater our skills become. Importantly, we know that our brains and our bodies change with practice too. If you learn to play the piano, over time the part of your brain that controls hand movements would literally get bigger. So, practicing can change our brains – this is known as neuroplasticity.

Point 4: It's not your fault

Connect the previous facts to the compassionate wisdom that all these facts cause us pain, but we didn't choose this, it is not our fault. We did not design the versions of ourselves we have become. We didn't build our brains. We still have the responsibility to learn how to work with these tricky brains. You can use basic hygiene as an example:

"We would not blame ourselves for needing to go to the toilet, but our responsibility is to make sure that we use the toilet properly and hygienically –

in fact, it's something we learn to do – a skill we spend time practising and developing!"

Point 5: Compassionate wisdom

Even though, as we shall see, blaming ourselves is an automatic defence reaction, it doesn't lead anywhere, even if we did something to worsen the situation. Use the car park and alcohol examples in the **Therapist Script 1.3**.

Compassionate wisdom is moving away from blaming and shaming ourselves, and simply recognising that, for whatever reason, we are struggling, but we want to find ways to help ourselves and others because, at the very core, it is not our fault if we are suffering.

Invite participants to think about something in their life that was clearly not their fault but for which they took responsibility and acted to help or repair or change.

Point 6: Compassion cultivation

Remind participants that we are here to learn skills to develop this compassionate motivation so you can be helpful and supportive towards yourself and others when distressed.

Introduce the idea that one of the properties of this brain, which we did not choose, is that we can use the mind to generate certain feelings and bodily states on purpose.

Use the ice-cream and lemon visualisations, as well as the "laughing and having an argument" visualisations to illustrate this point (**Therapist Script 1.4**). Emphasise that this ability can be used to train compassion.

You might want to expand these concepts by referring to the diagram below:

Phase 4: Loops in the Mind

In this phase you will be going over how our new brain competencies can cause serious trouble through no fault of our own.

Main Touch Points

Client Handout 1.5 – Loops in the Mind
Client Handout 1.6 – Mind Body Connections

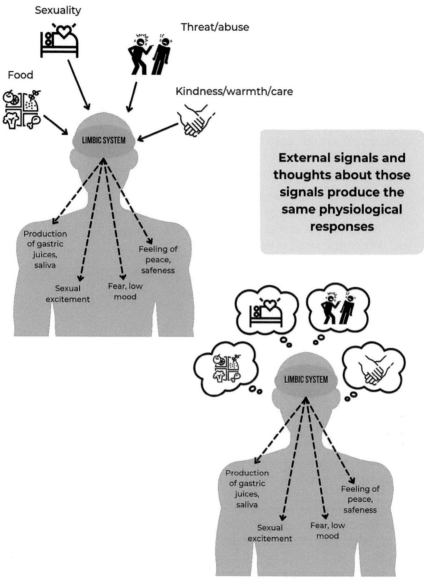

Designed using iages from flaticon.com

Figure 1.2 External signals (for example food) and thoughts about those external signals (thinking about food) produce the same physiological responses in human beings.
Source: Adapted from Gilbert, P. (2009) The Compassionate Mind. London: Constable & Robinson and Oaklands, CA: New Harbinger

4a) Old and new brain loops

 Therapist Task

We find ourselves here as part of the flow of life: a being, like all other beings on this earth. And we have all been shaped through a process of evolution. Although there are many things we share with other animals, there are also some things we don't share.

To explore old and new brain loops, try exploring these questions with the group:

- *What can you do that most other animals can't?*

    a   We can think and reason and work things out
    b   We can ruminate, run things over and over in our mind
    c   We can create images in our mind and fantasise
    d   We have a sense of self
    e   We can self-criticise
    f   We can try and think about what other people are thinking about us
    g   We can empathise with other people

These are examples of our **new brain.** We have these incredible cognitive capacities that allow us to imagine, think, reflect, and even think about the fact that we are thinking. But we also have an old brain, which allows us to do things, that almost all other animals can do as well, what might those be?

a   Motives like avoid harm (survival), seek food, seek shelter, protect our territory, seek sexual opportunities (reproduce), seek status, care for our children or offspring
b   Defensive behaviours such as fight/flight, as well as freeze and submit
c   Basic emotions such as anger, anxiety, disgust, sadness, joy

Unfortunately, what can happen, through no fault of your own is that we can get into new-old brain loops.

You can once again refer to the Zebra example to illustrate this point (**Therapist Script 1.3**).

 Therapist Tips

Make sure you have emphasised the uniquely human cognitive capacities of self-awareness, and the ability to think, judge, and thus self-criticise (we can be creative, anticipate the future for the better but also for the worst: ruminate, worry). Unfortunately, we did not choose this reality: the development of superior abilities has been accompanied by side effects that make us particularly susceptible to mental suffering.

4b) Exercise: Our own loops in the mind

 Therapist Task

Refer the group to **Handout 1.5: Loops in the Mind** so they can have the chance to draw their own loops. Get them to do their own loops by themselves, then share with the person next to them, then come back and share as group.

4c) Emotion Bain: External/Internal creations

 Therapist Task

Draw the Emotion Bain: External/Internal creations (e.g., meal, sex, bullying, and compassion) on a Flipchart/Whiteboard. Also use **Handout 1.6: Mind Body Connections.**
   This helps further emphasise how what we play out in the minds, plays out in our bodies. This is also why choosing to internally create a compassionate relationship with ourselves can be so important.

    Therapist Tips

Emphasise how our brains, quickly and without us asking them to, bring the external world into our internal worlds, which keeps our physiology active. Emphasise the mind-body connection.

Phase 5: Preparation for the Compassionate Path & Wrap Up

Emphasise how developing our own **Personal Practice** can help with the development of our compassionate minds.

Main Touch Points

    Client Handout B – Personal practice diary
   Therapist script I.5 – Preparation for the compassionate path

5a) Summary of the Session

 Therapist Task

Provide a summary of the session so far, trying to reconnect to the wisdom that we don't choose the environments we grow up in, that influence what we value, how we act, and what we do. Not only we can begin to realise that "it's not our fault", but also we can start to choose to do things differently, in ways that help us, in ways that are compassionate. We don't have to be stuck with the version of who we are now, it is possible to change. Attending this training is already an important manifestation of our ability to choose.

Developing our compassionate self begins with thinking about the version of the self we want to become, and how to work towards that. Emphasise the compassionate wisdom that comes with affirming: "It is not my fault, but it is my responsibility".

5b) Preparation for the Compassionate Path

 Therapist Task

Guide the group through this closing meditation, included in **Therapist Script 1.5**. The exercise itself should take about 5–10 minutes. Audio record it as well so you can send it to the participants as part of their personal practice.

Refer to **Handout B: Personal Practice Diary**, highlighting that in order to nourish compassion and promote a motivational shift, we must commit to practicing during the week. When going to the gym, we cannot expect our muscles to become conditioned if we workout only once a week with our personal trainer and then not use our muscles in everyday life; the same goes for building our capacity to shift toward our compassionate mind.

Practicing compassion can take many forms (in Module 2, we will introduce the difference between formal and informal practice). The important thing when planning our practice is to set wise goals. In fact, even though we may like the idea of practicing compassion during our regular weekly schedule, unless we set out a deliberate plan to execute, our tricky brain will make it difficult for us to stick to practicing consistently and over a longer timeframe.

Wise goals are goals that:

- We feel are sustainable for us in the long run
- Can be easily built into our lives without requiring massive changes to our routines
- Are specific and time-bound

Some questions you can use to help participants when they have to set their goals are:

- Am I being specific enough with my goals?
- Are my goals within my scope of reach?
- Why am I working towards this goal?
- How will I know I have reached my goal? How can I measure it?

When pursuing a goal, the concept of *implementation intention* is crucial. In fact, what we lack often isn't motivation, but clarity about our goals. For our meditation practice, implementation intention and wise goals can translate into something like:

> *I will practice with my guided audio meditation on Tuesday and Thursday before waking up the kids up for school.*

> *I will practice 1 minute of soothing rhythm breathing [refer to Module 2] every time I come back from my coffee break at work.*

> *If my meeting runs over and I don't have time to meditate before dinner, I will set my alarm clock 15 minutes earlier so that I can practice in the morning.*

Take some time to go over these principles with clients at the beginning of the training, as they will be crucial in implementing the practices in the subsequent stages.

Ask each person to decide what homework they would like to do for the week as they tap into their inner wisdom. Once they have decided what they want to do, ask them to share it with at least someone in the group (if you are in a group setting), as a way to show their commitment and stay accountable.

We will repeat this invitation at the end of each session, always asking the client what they wish to do during the week to continue cultivating compassion; if they are not sure or cannot come up with ideas, we will provide some suggestions based on what was covered during the session.

We suggest you always follow-up your sessions with an email to the group; this is an occasion to keep in contact, summarise once more the key points that were discussed during the session and reiterate the invitation to implement personal practice during the week. Feel free to structure this email as you feel is best, taking into account the characteristics of the group you are working with (you might want to create a WhatsApp or Telegram group to keep in contact during the week, or perhaps create a private Facebook group or a Google group).

Below you can find an example of an email script for Module 1:

Dear group members,

Thank you for coming along today and beginning your journey with compassion focused therapy. It has taken courage just to get here and so you have already started that journey. If at any time you have concerns about continuing, please talk to me as your therapist since it is my intention to support you in the best way I can through what can understandably be difficult and hard times. In Module 1 today we looked at what compassion is, our tricky brain and mind, and how it is easy for us to get caught in difficult painful and upsetting thoughts. The practices we shared today and that we will cover the coming weeks will help you develop ways of being compassionate in the face of difficulty and cultivating connection with yourself and others.

Once again thank you so much for coming along today and giving me the opportunity to working with you.

To continue your compassionate practice this week:

- *Try to aim for at least three practices. You can find attached to this email the audio recordings of the meditations we did – feel free to choose which recording to use as a guide for your personal practice.*
- *Fill out your weekly and/or daily diary – this is an occasion to reflect on your personal practice as well as what can help sustain you on your compassionate path or, on the other hand, represent an obstacle for you.*

Feel free to reach out this week if I can be of any assistance.

Wishing you well,

Therapist

Therapist Scripts*

* These are guides to be used flexibly, not necessarily word for word, but rather following your sensitivity, personality, and your clients' characteristics.

Therapist Script 1.1: What Brings You Here (10 minutes)

This practice is to be carried out in pairs (A and B). On Zoom, you can create breakout rooms and guide the process; in individual sessions, the therapist can ask the client.

Begin the practice with both people sitting in a comfortable position, facing each other, closing their eyes and taking a couple of breaths to land in the present moment.

Invite them to bring their attention to each point of contact with the seat beneath them. Invite them to bring their attention to their breathing, to the flow of air coming in and out of the nose, noticing how this enables them to establish some form of contact with the space around them, with the person in front of them.

Then, invite both participants to open their eyes again, and begin the exercise with A asking B "What brings you here?". B will have about one minute to answer A, saying everything that comes to mind without censoring it (the therapist can ring a bell to keep the time). A should only engage in active listening, without interrupting B at any moment, but acting as a vessel for everything that is shared. Once B has finished, A will ask B once again "What brings you here?". After giving B a chance to answer for one more minute, A will ask the same question one last time: "What brings you here?".

The exercise is then reversed, with B asking the questions and A answering. Always leave about one minute for each answer.

Once they have both finished, give some time for feedback between the two, so they can share whether they felt welcomed by the other, and how it felt to dive deeper into the real meaning behind their showing up to this training.

Therapist Script 1.2: Realities of Life (15 minutes)

Therapist Tips

Throughout this manual you will find many scripts to support you in delivering the practices of CFT. These scripts are to be used as guides and we invite each therapist to bring their personal touch to the practices. We suggest each therapist develop their own modality of delivering a meditation practice through repetition and by taking inspiration from the many meditation teachers who share their work. The scripts provided do not include indications for pauses to be taken between each section and invitation, however, these are fundamental and must be considered when delivering the practices. Be sure to provide longer pauses for key moments of the meditation (such as the "It's not your fault" awareness in this specific practice) so that participants can really connect with the message and let it settle.

To begin this meditation, I invite you to close your eyes, or if you wish you may keep them slightly open, with your gaze looking downwards at something non-distracting.

There is no need to do this practice perfectly, but rather just give yourself permission to explore whatever arises in the body and in the mind, to allow yourself to feel whatever you feel. There is no right or wrong way to do or experience this practice.

Try to connect to the rhythm of your breathing; let your breath slow down as it wishes, without forcing it. Give yourself permission to slow down the flow of your breath with ease.

Try to bring this friendly curiosity to your present-moment experience by bringing your hands to your knees with your palms facing upwards, or touching your arms or the area of your heart or the stomach. You may also wish to bring a slight smile to your lips – let these small actions remind you of your intention to simply be as you are in this moment.

Now try to imagine, as best you can, that you could step out of yourself and sit down in front of yourself, or, if you prefer, beside yourself; don't worry if the image that appears is blurry, if it comes and goes. Just try and get a sense of it.

Now, simply observe this being. Try to observe this person as it sits there. Try to observe how they are sitting, what posture they are holding. Try to observe this being as you would observe a friend.

Now begin contemplating some realities of life that this being has experienced.

This being did not choose to be born, to emerge on this planet, in a certain place, at a certain time, within a certain family. This is something that they did not choose. You can try whispering "It's true, you really didn't choose this".

Try to consider how many things this being did not choose: its gender, the color of its skin, its height, body shape...even the language it speaks. It didn't choose the country it was born in, and therefore, it didn't choose the laws, values and social stigmas of that place, and pressures it faces because of them.

If you look within the heart and the mind, of this being, you can also see that it didn't choose any of the emotions it feels. It didn't choose to feel anger, sadness, jealousy, or fear – rather these emotions just come with being human. We can learn ways to work with them, but we didn't choose them.

Try to contemplate how many difficulties this person has faced in having to live with these emotions in the past, emotions which, perhaps, were often hard to understand, and which no one had ever explained how to manage.

In the past this person might have tried to cope with these emotions in a way that wasn't very thoughtful, a bit clumsy maybe, but all they were trying to do - just like all other human beings, was simply to be OK, to be happy, and to not suffer.

*It's not **your** fault – you didn't ask for any of these things, and it has been difficult to know how best to deal with them; but it's not your fault.*

You might feel some gratitude, respect, for this being who has simply emerged into this life, trying to do their best to navigate through this journey.

This being, just like all others, will certainly go through hardships in the future. We might try to wish them well, to send them a compassionate message: may you have all the wisdom, courage, and strength that you need to face what life will bring you.

If it feels right to you at this moment, you can imagine touching the hand of this being, or maybe their arm or face. As if were offering them a sign of compassion. Is there any other phrase that you would like to tell them? Something that might really help them in this moment? Try saying this to them now...

Perhaps you can see them smiling; maybe you notice they like being caressed in this way, to receive this warm and compassionate message.

Take a moment just to be next to this being, to experience their presence.

Now, before ending this practice, try to come back into yourself and notice how it feels to be looked at with compassionate eyes.

Begin to connect with all the other beings in this group – connect your breath to theirs, and in doing so, recognise how they too have explored their vulnerabilities, they too are beginning this journey of self-discovery, they too simply wish to be well.

Imagine your next breaths are directed towards these beings, and you are sending them a genuine wish that they may be well.

As you extend these thoughts towards them, try to feel that they are also sending those wishes to you, their own wishes of well-being for you.

Then, when you feel ready, you may open your eyes again.

Therapist Script 1.3: Examples for Introducing the CFT Reality Check

Zebra Example

Let's consider a specific example. Imagine a zebra running away from a lion. Once it gets away and can no longer see, hear, or smell the lion, there is nothing to keep them feeling anxious; in fact, they settle down quite quickly. However, while a human will also be relieved to escape a lion, their new brain will continue to brood over things. "Can you imagine if I had been caught and what would it be like to be eaten by a lion?! (Horrid images pop into your mind!). Suppose there are two lions tomorrow, and suppose I can't get to the watering hole .... And suppose.... and suppose.... To the point we can start criticising ourselves for being a zebra!
    A zebra would never do anything like this!

Car Park Example

Suppose while your car is parked in the car park and somebody smashes into the back of it and drives off. Although this is completely unfair, and you may feel very angry, only you can phone the garage and get them to come and repair it. It is your responsibility – it has nothing to do with fairness. We do not like this idea, but unfortunately, it is a fact of life: bad things happen to us that are undoubtedly unfair. We can be very angry about that – quite understandably – but we must also begin to accept things and turn our attention to what we are going to do to help rectify the situation? This wisdom is captured in an ancient Chinese proverb: "Better to light one candle than to curse the darkness".

Alcohol Example

Let's consider of another example. As a result of early-life difficulties someone, who we will call Sam, abuses alcohol and becomes aggressive. He is deeply lonely on the inside. We can understand this without blaming him. But, at the same time, we can ask: how could we help Sam start to think about how to work with some of the things that are causing him to abuse alcohol and become aggressive? How can we help Sam take responsibility for addressing his pain, loneliness, and to encourage him to change his behavior? Blaming and shaming might drive him further into drinking, right?

Therapist Script 1.4: Examples for Generating Changes in Body Feelings

Ice-Cream and Lemon Examples

Sit comfortably and breathe in relaxed way – close your eyes or just look down with your eyes not focused on anything in particular.

Imagine it is a hot day in mid-summer; the sky is blue and the air warm – and maybe you are sweating a bit because it is hot. Now imagine buying your favourite ice cream – and gradually licking and eating it – feel its coolness and sweetness. Hold that image for a moment and notice what you are feeling in your body.

Okay, now imagine it is the same day and you walk into a friend's house and you see a bright yellow lemon on the kitchen counter. You cut out a wedge out and pick it up and bite into the juicy lemon. The acid of the lemon hits your tongue – hold that – now what is happening in your mouth and body?

How different are the two images' effects on the feelings in your mouth?

It is important to realise that, for most of us, it's not possible to create these physical reactions simply by choosing to do so: it is necessary to create images to activate our physiology.

Laughing and Argument Examples

This time we are going to pay attention to different memories and notice how they play out in our bodies. Once again, sit comfortably and breathe in a relatively relaxed way, one that you are comfortable with. Now call to mind a time when you were laughing; maybe somebody had told you a good joke, or you were with people you like. Just let the scenario play out in your mind – once again, notice what happens when you remember the joke.

Notice how you are feeling in your body right now.

Okay, let that image fade. Now bring to mind a memory of having a mild argument or disagreement with somebody. Remember what was said and how you felt. Just let stay in your mind for a few moments.

Notice what is now happening in your body.Are there other feelings different from the two memories?

Therapist Script 1.5: Preparation for the Compassionate Path (7 minutes)

We are going to conclude today's session with a practice to help us start to cultivate compassion. I will record this practice so you can do it again during the week as part of your personal practice.

Let's try to intentionally develop our compassionate mind. We'll start by closing our eyes or looking down at something non-distracting. Start to notice how you feel seated in your chair right now in this moment. Just connect with the rhythm of your breathing as it is now, gently inhaling and exhaling.

Now notice your compassionate body posture, one where your back is straight and shoulders back in line with your hips, chest open, allowing yourself to breath with ease.

Now, start to slow your breathing, gradually, with each breath getter slightly longer, slightly slower and slightly deeper. And just continue with this rhythm of breathing for the next minute or so.

As you are doing this you might say to yourself on the out-breath with a friendly inner tone of voice, "mind slowing down" and then with the next out-breath "body slowing down" – gradually, getting that feeling of grounding in the body, with a sense of slowing down but also keeping an alert mind..

Just notice yourself becoming more grounded. Allow time for this to settle in – maybe for the next minute or so.

Now tune into your inner compassionate mind, remembering the wisdom that you have developed today – that we all just find ourselves here with a very tricky brain and certain life experiences that have shaped how our minds and bodies work – the version of ourselves that we currently are. But we are also a mind that can learn how to change, and make choices so we are developing the strength and commitment to try to help ourselves and others to address and deal with life and our inner difficulties.

As we are sitting here, we also say to ourselves in a friendly and committed way:

I have come here today and will continue to come over the next few weeks in order to:

- *Work on ways to be helpful to myself*
- *Support others as best I can on their journey*
- *Be open to the helpfulness of others*

Now tune into your body once again. Feel your body in the chair in this moment, and slowly starting to come back into the room. When you are ready, open your eyes and come back into the room.

Thank you for your time and efforts today.
See you next week.

Client Handouts

Client Handout 1.1: Ground Agreements for Creating a Safe Space

 Respecting and supporting each other

We agree to respect each other and the courage of coming here.

We try to support each other as best as we can.

We try to avoid putting people down or criticising them. However, we will endeavor to offer accurate and helpful feedback. Furthermore, simply listening with honest curiosity is often much more helpful than giving advice.

 Sharing experiences

We can all learn from each other's experiences.

There is no pressure to talk if one doesn't wish to, yet we also recognise that we all will try to encourage each other with kindness to face things that we might find difficult.

If someone is feeling distressed about a topic, it is okay for us to pause and focus on that before moving on.

 Keeping confidentiality

All personal experiences we discuss are confidential.

 Being open minded

We all come from different places and have different experiences. So, we try not to think in terms of right or wrong, but rather we try to be open to the many and varied possibilities. We want to make new experiences, so we try to be open to learning.

 Personal Practice

The group is focused on creating new brain and body patterns, so the personal practices we learn and record are important for you to engage in.

We will begin each session with a check-in with how your personal practice went, celebrating successes and discussing challenges.

Your personal practice is going to help you engage and get the most out of this group. We suggest you try to aim for at least three practices per week as we progress through this training.

Any specific recommendation that came up for this group?

Client Handout 1.2: What Compassion is and is Not

For me, Compassion is:

For me, Compassion is NOT:

What compassion IS

Compassion can be defined as:

> *"A sensitivity to suffering in self and others, combined with the desire to alleviate and prevent that suffering"*

There are therefore two parts to compassion:

- Sensitivity to suffering
- Desire to alleviate suffering

The desire to alleviate suffering can manifest itself in many ways. It must however start from an **intention**: a **wish to alleviate suffering, a wish for wellbeing** in the other or in the self.

Often, it is this very intention that creates the fertile ground for compassionate action. In some situations, the wish to alleviate suffering cannot immediately manifest in the form of helpful actions. At other times, it can and must be paired with a committed, courageous wise action. A wise action is one that is within one's personal limits (if I see someone drowning and I dive in to help them, and only then realise that I cannot swim – this is not a helpful action).

Compassion does not mean avoiding suffering. Sometimes we are faced with difficulties that cannot be immediately solved, and obsessively searching for a solution to eliminate the pain is what causes suffering. Compassion gives us the space to sit with the uneasiness (or sometimes outright pain) in a way that is wise, brave, less self-critical, and ultimately more accepting and grounded, and it allows us to navigate pain with greater ease.

What compassion is NOT

- *Compassion is not just being nice*
- *Compassion is not just empathy*
- *Compassion is not avoiding pain*
- *Compassion is not just being polite*
- *Compassion is not just feeling sorry for people*
- *Compassion is not just being kind*
- *Compassion is not weak*
- *Compassion is not being submissive, in fact compassion can be quite assertive*
- *Compassion is not about liking everyone. Compassion simply means that we don't wish to cause people any harm. And if a person is suffering, we would try to help them, even if we do not particularly like them or want to be their friend or see them again.*

What do you usually do when you are faced with suffering? Think back to some difficult situations you have had to face in your life and write out how you reacted (remember that avoiding suffering is an animal instinct – so it is not your fault); what would a compassionate approach to those difficulties look like?

Notes/drawings/sketches

THE COMPASSIONATE SELF

Compassion is being sensitive to one's own and others' suffering, combined with a desire to alleviate and prevent that suffering.

Compassion encompasses several qualities; in Compassion Focused Therapy we focus specifically on three of these qualities:
1) wisdom; 2) strength; and 3) commitment.
These three qualities make up what we call the Compassionate Self.

 WISDOM

We just happen to find ourselves here as part of the flow of life, with a tricky brain that can get caught up in angry or worry loops, and this is not our fault

+

 STRENGTH

Strength comes from our compassionate body posture, our breathing, which allows us to cultivate a sense of groundedness.

+

 COMMITMENT

We try whenever we can to be kind and compassionate to the suffering we experience and that we see around us; we try to prevent and alleviate the suffering in a wise way - this is a journey which requires our commitment.

Figure I.3 The Compassionate Self.

Client Handout 1.3: Six Core Principles of CFT

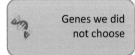 **Genes we did not choose**

- We all justfind ourselves here with gene-built bodies.

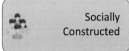 **Socially Constructed**

- The environments we find ourselves in influences the person we become. There are many thousands of potential versions of us that we will never have a chance to live.

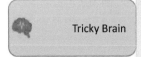 **Tricky Brain**

- Human brains and emotions are much more difficultto regulate than we think.

 It's not your fault

- Itis not your faultfor having the brains that we do, or that we are shaped by our life experiences, including family and cultures. We didn't choose anything ofthis, so itis not your fault! But we still have the responsibility of living with these things in helpful ways.

 Compassionate wisdom

- Moving away from blaming and shaming ourselves and simply recognizing that, for whatever reason, we are struggling, but we wantto find ways to help ourselves and others because, atthe very core, it's not our faultif we are suffering.

 Compassion Cultivation

- On purpose we can choose to cultivate compassion which shapes what we feel, how we think and what we do so that we can live a life of meaning.

Client Handout 1.4: The Tricky Brain

THE TRICKY BRAIN

FLOW OF LIFE
Like all living beings, we just happen to find ourselves here, now, part of the flow of life.

STEP 01

HUMAN BRAIN
We have a brain that we did not design, but which was developed through thousands of years of evolution.

STEP 02

NEW BRAIN CAPACITY
Our brains have the capacity to imagine, have complex language and be creative. But also the ability to ruminate and worry.

STEP 03

SHAPED
We are shaped by the family we are born into, which we did not choose. Ask yourself this: "Would the same version of me exist if I was kidnapped by the mafia as a 3 year old baby?"

STEP 04

NOT YOUR FAULT
So it is not our fault that our brains get caught up in anxious or depressive loops. The brain is a tricky thing. But we can take responsibility for it by using wisdom and compassion.

STEP 05

Figure 1.4 The Tricky Brain.

Client Handout 1.5: Old and New Brain Loops

To read the illustration begin at the "Start" point and then follow the black and red arrows – these form a loop. The "Compassionate Turn" allows us to move away from threat-based loops and into a sense of reassurance and intention to support and be helpful.

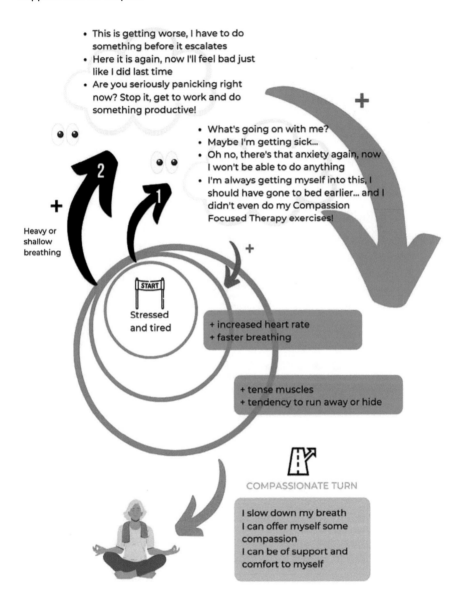

Figure 1.5 Old and New Brain Loops.

Client Handout 1.6: Mind–Body Connections

What we think and imagine has a great effect on our body. If we imagine eating our favourite meal it will stimulate stomach acid and saliva as if we were actu-

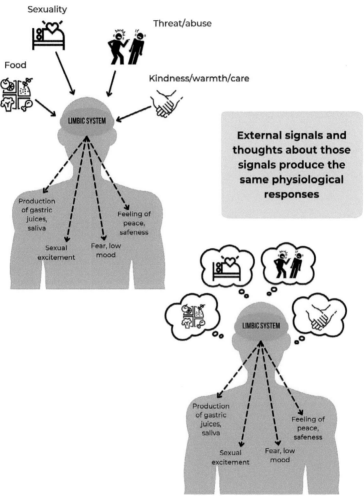

Designed using iages from flaticon.com

Figure 1.6 External Signals (for example, Food) and Thoughts About Those External Signals (Thinking About Food) Produce the Same Physiological Responses in Human Beings. Adapted from Gilbert, P. (2009) The Compassionate Mind. London: Constable & Robinson and Oaklands, CA: New Harbinger.

ally about to eat a meal. What we create in our mind will impact our body. That is why bully-threatening thoughts, images and emotions can make us feel agitated, just as if they were really happening. That is why it is so helpful to cultivate compassionate thoughts and images; they will create the physical reactions in our body that we would experience if we were really treated with compassion.

Chapter 2

Module 2

Three Types of Emotion

Aims

- To introduce an evolutionary functional analysis of emotion that orients clients to consider emotions in terms of basic forms and functions (how and why they work in their minds and bodies as they do)
- To illustrate the nature and function of threat-based emotions, drive and reward-based emotions, and emotions that are associated with soothing, grounding, settling and contentment
- To clarify that emotion systems can blend and co-regulate each other
- To clarify compassion as a motive
- To begin to develop the soothing system

 Deepen Your Knowledge

In the book Gilbert, P. & Simos, G. (Eds). (2022). *Compassion Focused Therapy: Clinical Practice and Applications*. Routledge, please refer to:

Chapter 2 – Compassion Focused Therapy: an Evolution-Informed, Biopsychosocial Approach to Psychotherapy – History and Challenge
Chapter 3 – The Evolved Functions of Caring Connections as a Basis For Compassion
Chapter 10 – Compassion Focused Therapy and the Body: how Physiological Underpinnings of Prosociality Inform Clinical Practice

DOI: 10.4324/9781003436058-4

Summary of Key Processes

Table 2.1 Module 2: Three Types of Emotion

Phase		Main Touch Points		Therapist Scripts		Client Handouts
1	Introduction	**1a)** Compassionate Landing **1b)** Revision of personal practice and recap of previous session **1c)** Fears, Blocks and Resistances	□	**Script 2.1:** Compassionate Landing	□	**Handout 2.1:** Compassionate weekly reflection
2	CFT flow of life	**2a)** Experiential exercise to connect with flow of life	□	**Script 2.2:** Flow of life meditation		
3	Three Circles	**3a)** Introduction to the three circles **3b)** Drawing the circles **3c)** Problems of threat and drive emotions **3d)** Distinguishing between a threat-fuelled drive system and a soothing-fuelled drive system **3e)** Soothing emotions and link to compassion	□	**Script 2.3:** Three emotional systems visualisation	□ □ □ □ □ □	**Handout 2.2:** The three circles **Handout 2.3:** Thoughts, Sensations, Behaviours **Handout 2.4:** Drawing the three circles **Handout 2.5:** The three circles in action **Handout 2.6:** Your personal smoke detector **Handout 2.7:** Reflecting on threat, drive and soothing emotions
4	Building our soothing system	**4a)** The difference between formal and informal practice **4b)** Working with the breath	□	**Script 2.4:** Soothing Rhythm Breathing	□ □	**Handout A:** Circle Check-In **Handout 2.8:** Formal and Informal Practices
5	Wrap-up	**5a)** Summary of the session and suggestions for personal practice **5b)** Closing practice	□	**Script 2.5:** Closing practice	□ □	**Handout 2.9:** Compassionate Compass **Handout B:** Personal practice diary

Phase I: Introduction

The goal of this phase is to give participants a chance to emotionally connect to the session through a short guided Compassionate Landing and to go through any experiences (good and not so good) they might have had during the past week of practice or personal reflection. This is also an opportunity to introduce the concept of Fears, Blocks, and Resistances that might have come up during their personal practice and that will be addressed in all subsequent modules of the training.

Main Touch Points

Therapist Script 2.1 – Compassionate Landing
Client Handout 2.1 – Compassionate Weekly Reflection

1a) Compassionate Landing

Therapist Task

The Compassionate Landing is a moment to guide participants into a space for reflection and practice, welcoming themselves as they arrive to the space, noticing any sensations, emotions, and thoughts that they might be carrying with them from the day.

It is also a recurring moment during the training, which gives structure and a sense of safeness to participants, something they can come back to time and time again; furthermore, it provides them with an opportunity to observe how different their state may be every time they land into a session.

This is a good moment for the therapist to connect participants once again to their compassionate motivation and intentions:

- To work on ways to be helpful to oneself
- To support others as best as possible on their journey
- To be open to the helpfulness of others

You may use the **Therapist Script 2.1** to guide participants through this first meditation.

1b) Revision of personal practice and recap of previous session

   Therapist Task

This is a moment to allow the sharing of experiences during the week. Participants may want to reference to their personal practice diary or just share about reflections they may have had during the past week on the topics explored together. Also ask them whether setting wise goals helped them in sticking to their plan and how they incorporated flexibility into their plan in the case of unexpected events.

The sharing can occur either in the large group or in small groups (this last option is particularly suggested for online trainings).

The therapist can provide a brief recap of the last session, in which the main points were:

- Setting the ground agreements
- Introducing what compassion is and what it is not
- Connecting to the realities of life
- Establishing a personal practice

This can also be a space to setting the scene for the current module; the main themes that are going to be explored are:

- The flow of life
- The three types of emotions that we call the Three-Circle Model
- Starting to build our soothing system

1c) Fears, Blocks and Resistances

   Therapist Task

When participants approach meditation and compassionate inquiry into their thoughts, sensations, and emotions, it is rather frequent for them to encounter fears, blocks and resistances (FBRs). Therefore, it is very useful to introduce them to the concept of FBRs from the very first sessions and to continue working on them throughout the entire training.

As a way to open the discussion, you might want to guide them through some questions in the group discussion, such as:

- *Which part of the suggested home practices did you do and why?*
- *Which part of the practices did you not do and why?*
- *Can you find the anxiety behind those reasons? Is there some part of you that feels anxious in some way about doing this exercise?*

You may encourage participants to explore this theme through a self-reflection or group reflection, using the exercise "Compassionate Weekly Reflection" (**Client Handout 2.1**).

 Therapist Background Knowledge

What are FBRs?

Motives can be viewed as stimulus-response algorithms of the kind *if A, then do B*, and they can be facilitated, or inhibited. The evolved algorithm of compassion involves suffering and distress as the stimulus and actions to alleviate the suffering as the response.

FBRs are examples of inhibitors to compassion, which reduce the likelihood of the motive being activated and can hinder all three flows of compassion. This means the individual will either not detect the signal of suffering or will not act upon the signal to try to alleviate the suffering. A lot of Compassion Focused Therapy (CFT) is about investigating fears, being open to them, and understanding them. Often, we need to acknowledge, understand and validate these fears, before moving on to develop compassion practices.

Fears of compassion refer to the avoidance or fear response that individuals can have to compassion; these may be related to seeing compassion as a sign of weakness, self-indulgence, self-pitying, or that compassionate efforts will be seen as incompetent, unhelpful or rejected. Individuals may also be afraid of being overwhelmed by distress or by the needs of others when engaging in compassionate acts. Another fear could be that of compassion being viewed as manipulative or for self-interest.

Here are some common examples of fears:

Being too compassionate makes people soft and easy to take advantage of.
If people are friendly and kind I worry they will find out something bad about me that will change their mind about me.
I fear that if I become kinder and less self-critical toward myself, then my standards will drop.

Blocks to compassion are present when an individual would like to be compassionate but is unable to do so due to environmental constraints, such as lack of time, resources, or availability.

Resistances to compassion refer to those situations in which an individual could be compassionate but is not. This is not due to fear but rather because the person sees no point to compassion or is focused on competitive self-advantage and therefore holds on to his/her resources rather than sharing them, and believes compassion will be unhelpful in securing their goals.

Therapist Task

We can ask participants to come up with different fears they have and/or complete the Fears of Compassion Scales (please see the Resources page on the Compassionate Mind Foundation website: www.compassionatemind.co.uk/resource/scales)

Then, a group discussion can be led on the following questions:

- *Do you feel anxious about cultivating compassion for the self?*
- *Do you feel anxious about cultivating compassion for others?*
- *Do you feel anxious at the idea of opening up to compassion coming from others?*
- *How does it feel knowing that others have the same or similar types of fear?*

The therapist might show the following picture to participants and guide them through the image starting from kindness (marked with a start flag below).

Now that we know the different types of fears, we should explore the possible origins of these fears. Start a brief group discussion:

- *Where do you think your fear come from?*
- *Who/what circumstances taught you to be anxious about this form of compassion?*
- *How did/does this fear help you?*
- *How did/does this fear impair your well-being? Why wouldn't you want more of it?*

 Therapist Background Knowledge

Where Do FBRs Come From?

We can imagine fears of compassion developing in those who have learned associations between prosocial actions and aversive outcomes. For example, a child might be punished by parents or other authority figures (such as teachers, coaches, or mentors) for being too kind, generous or compassionate – these qualities might be viewed as naïve or inappropriate by these adults. Additionally, a child might seek care from their parent and approach them while upset about something, but the parent again punishes them for being a nuisance, a pain or too needy. Here the association is between wanting care and punishment, resulting in avoidance and fear. Or the child receives care and affection, but in an inconsistent way, because soon after the parent becomes cold or distant, or abusive (thus feeling that they cannot trust that source of compassion).

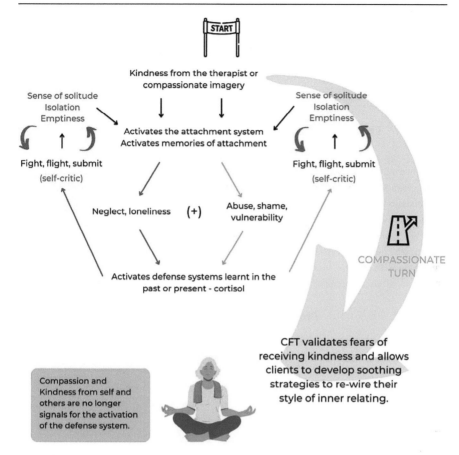

Figure 2.1 Possible client reactions to the kindness of therapist or the compassionate image.

Source: Adapted from Gilbert, P. (2009c) Evolved minds and compassion-focused imagery in depression. In L. Stopa (ed.), *Imagery and the Threatened Self: Perspectives on Mental Imagery and the Self in Cognitive Therapy* (pp. 206–231). London: Routledge

This is what conditioning is all about. Let's imagine that we like chocolate cake, but then one day we have some chocolate cake that makes us very sick. If I offer you a piece of chocolate cake you might go running to the bathroom to vomit instead of accepting it happily, which is certainly not what I would expect! This illustrates how a potentially positive signal can become toxic.

Our attachment system can be classically conditioned so that the feelings associated with warmth and compassion are experienced as a threat and toxic (see the diagram in Figure 2.1 above). The work in CFT, therefore, is to "detoxify" the system and enable patients to experience these aspects as they were designed to be experienced. Working with fears of compassion is not something that can be rushed. There will be a lot of work around grief, de-shaming, strengthening the capacity to tolerate very painful levels of negative emotions.

 Therapist Tips

Be sure to always address, acknowledge, and validate FBRs during the training. Participants will likely struggle with accepting that they have these FBRs toward compassionate action and thoughts, so it is extremely important to bring them to the table with a welcoming and curious attitude. Always remind participants that we are working to show compassion toward our FBRs too – our aim is not to eliminate them, but rather to get to know them better and to find helpful ways of working with them.

Phase 2: CFT Flow of Life

In this phase the focus shifts from realities of life to the flow of life. The therapist guides participants through contemplating the concepts of shared humanity and vulnerability.

MAIN TOUCH POINTS

 Therapist Script 2.2 – Flow of Life Meditation

2a) Experiential exercise to connect with flow of life

 Therapist Task

The Flow of Life Meditation is designed to help participants contemplate the "unchosen nature" of their emotional systems. Its aim is to encourage the discovery of our "common emotionality", which connects us to all mammals and all our ancestors. We want participants to realise that we did not choose our basic needs, and the basic functions of our bodies – our basic motivations – and maybe generate some insight into the unchosen nature of the emotions/motivations of our ancestors, too. In this way, it paves the way for the exploration of the three emotion regulation systems.

Potential questions for group discussion:

- *Which part of the meditation did you connect with the most?*
- *Which part was hardest for you?*
- *Which part was most useful for you?*

Phase 3: Three Circles

This phase is entirely dedicated to introducing the Three-Circles Model to explain our three different types of emotions. This model can be explained by using a blend of theoretical explanations, experiential practices, and self-reflection exercises.

Main Touch Points

Therapist Script 2.3 – Three Emotional Systems Visualisation
Client Handout 2.2 – The Three Circles
Client Handout 2.3 – Thoughts, Sensations, and Behaviours
Client Handout 2.4 – Drawing the Three Circles
Client Handout 2.5 – The Three Circles in Action
Client Handout 2.6 – Your Personal Smoke Detector
Client Handout 2.7 – Reflecting on Threat, Drive, and Soothing Emotions

3a) Introduction to the three circles

Therapist Background Knowledge

The Three-Circle Model, also called the tripartite model of affect regulation, is a basic, heuristic model which attempts to capture clusters of emotion in terms of three basic life tasks: harm avoidance and threat sensitivity, seeking resources for survival and reproduction and settling into states of rest and digest. Emerging from these three basic life tasks are three types of emotion that evolved primarily to:

- Detect and respond to threats and losses (fear, anxiety, anger, disgust, and 'shutdown')
- Detect and respond to opportunities for resource acquisition (excitement, awe, wonder, joy, pleasure, pride and humour)
- Detect and respond to opportunities to rest and digest (settling, calming, contentment, peaceful, playfulness, and social safeness)

Therapist Task

To begin introducing the Three-Circle Model and the three functions of emotion, the therapist can guide participants through a short visualisation that explores three different scenarios connected to the three circles, highlighting what differences are noticed (**Therapist Script 2.3**).

The therapist can also choose to refer to examples from the animal world, inviting participants to reflect upon the different types of behaviours they recognise in cats (resting, playing, seeking food, fight, or flight).

To explain the Three-Circle Model , feel free to refer to the **Client Handout 2.2** making sure to focus not only on the three circles, but also on the ways in which they influence and balance each other. You may want to use different methods to help explain the model, either using slides, a flipchart, or simply by discussing orally it with the participants.

Try eliciting the emotions, bodily feelings and action tendencies associated with the three circles (**Figure 2.2**). You may want to point out that emotions,

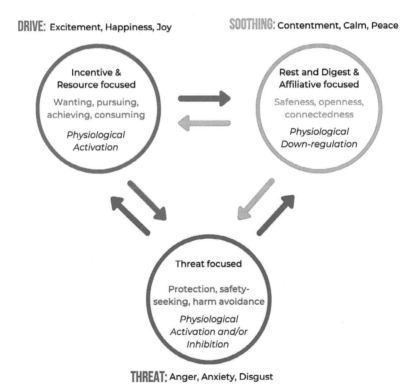

Figure 2.2 The Three-Circles Model.
Source: Adapted from Gilbert, P. (2005). Compassion and Cruelty. In P. Gilbert (Ed.). (2005). *Compassion: Conceptualisations, Research and Use in Psychotherapy.* Routledge

thoughts, bodily feelings and action tendencies turn up automatically, once a system is activated. All emotions have a function (alert for threats, stimulate our bodies, prepare for action). Invite reflection on negative emotions to, without them we would not survive.

You can use the **Client Handout 2.3** to invite participants to reflect upon their own thoughts, bodily feelings and action tendencies associated with each system.

 Therapist Background Knowledge

The body has two complementary nervous systems: the sympathetic (arousing) and the parasympathetic (calming). Both are needed not only for balancing different functions in our bodies, but also for psychological balance. Our different emotional regulation systems operate through both the Sympathetic (SNS) and Para-sympathetic (PNS) nervous systems. The SNS activates bodily processes that enable us to take actions such as run away, fight, seek food or reproduce. While the SNS can be thought of as our accelerator, increasing heart rate and getting more oxygen around the body when we are called to action, the PNS (also called rest and digest) can be thought of as our braking system, slowing the heart rate and bringing the system back into balance. The threat and drive circle are more linked to activation of the SNS. The soothing circle is more associated to PNS. However, when our sympathetic nervous system has kicked into overdrive, and fight or flight responses

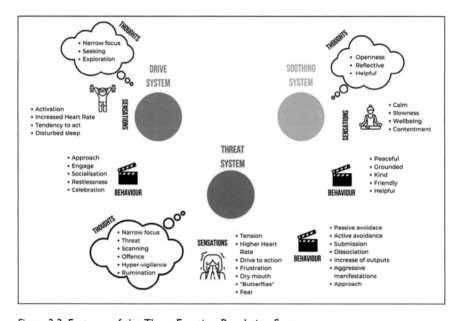

Figure 2.3 Features of the Three Emotion Regulation Systems.

do not work, the parasympathetic system can spike so strongly that it overwhelms the sympathetic arousal and sends the person into a state of freeze as a form of self-preservation (think of someone who passes out under extreme stress.). Shut-down states can manifest as full collapse, dissociation, or a more partial freeze, such as the inability to think clearly or access words or emotions, or to move parts of the body.

  Therapist Task

Unlike animals, the three systems get out of balance in humans – with a dom-inance of the threat system.

The soothing system is the one we find to be systematically underdeveloped, meaning people usually struggle to activate it. The aim of CFT is to strengthen the ability to turn on the soothing system via the three flows of compassion, in order to create flexibility among the three systems.

Cultivating a strong and well-developed green circle can be thought of as creating a safe and secure base that can optimally regulate the blue and red circles. Promoting a good balance between circles means you will be able to rely on a solid sense of groundedness and optimally shift through the circles.

We can encounter different types of imbalances (or configurations) between the three circles. You might want to discuss these with your clients, thinking about the situations in which it might be favourable to momentarily experience them.

For example, when we are playing a tennis match with our friend, it is func-tional to have a bigger blue circle, with smaller red and green circles. However, when you is preparing to lie down on a hammock on a Sunday evening with your favourite novel, it might be more functional to have a larger green circle, and smaller blue and red circles. If I'm having a fun dinner with a group of friends, it might be more functional for me to have a larger green and blue circle, and smaller red circles.

In fact, the same activity can be characterised by different proportions of the three systems, depending on the motivation with which I do it. If I go to the gym for the purpose of taking care of myself, having fun, and improving my health, then the blue and green systems will mainly be active. However, if I go to the gym because I want to become thinner than my roommate, or because, if I don't build more muscle, I'll continue to be ashamed of my body and afraid of being rejected by potential partners or not being accepted by my peer group, then my red and blue systems will mainly be active.

Remind participants not to fall into the trap of thinking that we never want our threat system to come online; try to reflect with them on some potential real-life situations in which having a large red circle and small blue and green circles might be favourable. If my house is on fire and about to collapse, it makes sense for my red system to be activated; it makes no sense at that moment to wonder what I could wear to look prettier than my neighbour, or to mindfully contemplate the newly bloomed orchid on the windowsill, or to relax and meditate.

You can come up with different settings to help them in this process of exploring the dynamic nature of our three emotional regulation systems, and even ask them to come up with their own examples.

In Figure 2.4 below, you will find some examples of possible imbalances we can come across; you might want to share these with participants or invite them to come up with the different possible configurations.

One example of the first imbalance is when I have just received a rejection letter or my partner has broken up with me, and I am in bed, depressed, in the grip of self-criticism and shame. I don't feel like doing anything, I don't feel like going out with friends or even watching a movie; I just feel anxiety, sadness and other negative emotions but no positive emotions. I am lying in bed, but I am not calm and relaxed.

An example of the second imbalance is when I crave strong feelings, drive my car at 300 miles per hour on the highway, feeling excited but without any sense of anxiety, and I have no awareness of the danger I am in. Or when, perhaps after a few too many drinks, I have unprotected sex without feeling the danger of what I am doing; I just feel sexual arousal and nothing else.

An example of the third imbalance is when I feel lonely and unloved because I don't have friends or a partner, I feel ashamed that I don't have them, and I "throw myself into my work" trying to make money, become someone important or famous, become obsessed with the perfection of my body to the point of taking steroids or resorting to plastic surgery. These coping strategies make me feel "better" or "better than others," but basically I still feel unlovable, and full of shame and fear; I continue to feel lonely and disconnected. Many addictive behaviours can be characterised by this imbalance.

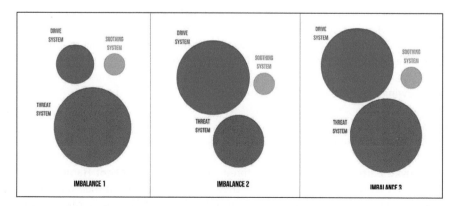

Figure 2.4 Examples of Possible Imbalances.

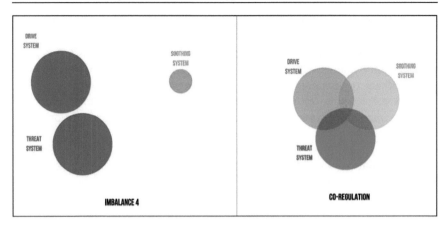

Figure 2.5 Co-regulation of the Three Systems.

You can take into account not only the relative dimensions of the three circles, but also the distance between them (as can be seen in imbalance 4): a green system that is not only underdeveloped but also considered inaccessible might be drawn very far away from the other two circles. On the other hand, when an individual is able to find a state of co-regulation, we can think of the three circles as merging and sustaining one another.

An example of this conformation (imbalance 4) is when we have an intense formal meditation practice in the morning, where we train our ability to be present and centered. We feel like we are doing a good job with our morning meditative practice, but then as soon as we walk through the office door we "become another person". We are immediately immersed in anxiety or perfectionism, maybe competition. We might think it's okay to experience compassion while we meditate, as an exercise, but then when we are at work, and we unable to, or perhaps don't want to, access the state we cultivated in the morning. In the middle of an argument, we are unable to resort to any of our self-regulating strategies. Another example is when we cultivate the green circle during long hours of mindfulness or long meditation retreats, but then, as soon as we return to our normal routine, we are unable to transfer that mind-state to our daily lives.

3b) Drawing the Three Circles

 Therapist Task

Next, invite participants to draw the three circles (using the **Client Handout 2.4**) in the size that reflects how much time they spend in each one in their daily lives. Then, put them into pairs and invite them to have a short discussion, offering the following points to explore:

- *Which system has been trained the most?*
- *Which experiences and activities are part of each system?*
- *Which memories are inside of each system?*
- *Which people in your life are inside of each system?*
- *Would you like the proportions [of each circle] to be different?*
- *What proportion of circles would you wish for someone you love?*
- *What do you notice by doing this?*

 Therapist Background Knowledge

What About Sadness?

When reflecting on their own three circles, clients will often ask about sadness and its place in the Three-Circle Model. Sadness has always been quite tricky as to whether it fits into the threat system or links best to the rest and digest soothing system. There are advocates for both positions. Sadness is slightly different from other basic threats in the sense that it emerges following a loss, not before it; however, because of our new brain, we can anticipate loss, and therefore, feel loss in an anticipatory way.

Two important distinctions must be made. Grieving is different to sadness because it is a process that can involve the threat emotions of anger and anxiety as well as sadness over time. Furthermore, we must distinguish anhedonia – the loss of feeling which is experienced in states of shutdown, helplessness and depression – from sadness.

Through the practice of compassion, and the increase in the feeling of safeness that it generates, we can facilitate moving people out of shutdown and numbness or anger and anxiety, and into sadness. In fact, the physical response of sadness, namely crying, is facilitated by a state of safeness: when we cry, we might feel particularly vulnerable because we are not able to see clearly, we can't breathe well, our muscles feel floppy.

 Therapist Task

Our three circles are constantly changing as we interact with others; we are a social species, and this means that we are co-regulating all the time. These co-regulations can lead us towards different three-circle configurations. When dysfunctional co-regulating patterns are repeated over time (for example in relationships in which the relational dynamic is not attuned to the needs of both parties) it can lead to getting "stuck" in one of the three-circle imbalances we have examined.

To help the group grasp this concept, go through the following examples together and focus on the dynamic nature of the three-circle configuration. After going through the examples (you can also provide examples that you feel might better resonate with the group you are working with), invite participants to come up with their own examples and have a group discussion.

You can also invite them to explore the three circles in action by thinking back to an argument they recently had with someone; they may use the prompt questions in the **Client Handout 2.5**.

3c) Problems with threat emotions

 Therapist Task

Negativity Bias

All types of emotions have evolved for a specific purpose. However, they can also become a problem when experienced in certain intensities or situations.

Figure 2.6 The Dynamic Nature of the Three-Circle Configuration (Example 1).

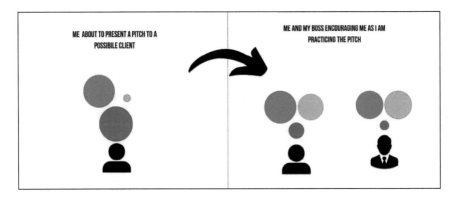

Figure 2.7 The Dynamic Nature of the Three-Circle Configuration (Example 2).

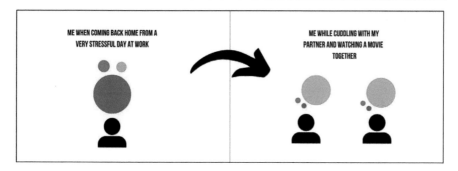

Figure 2.8 The Dynamic Nature of the Three-Circle Configuration (Example 3).

You can guide participants in the following reflection:

Imagine you are going Christmas shopping for all your friends and relatives. You visit ten different shops, looking for the perfect present. In nine of those shops, the sales clerks are very helpful and assist you in finding just what you need. However, in one shop, the sales-clerk is very rude, makes you wait a long time, and can't be bothered to help you, then tries to short-change you; when you leave this shop, you are feeling very annoyed.

Ask participants:

- *Who is the person you are likely to be focusing on when making your way home?*
- *Who is the person you are likely to talk to your partner about?*
- *What happens in our bodies and minds when we focus on that rude person and talk about our feelings to our partners?*

In a group discussion, help participants recognise that 90 percent of their interactions were positive, but they do not ruminate or focus on those. If they did, they would surely feel better, but the nature of the human brain brings us to focus on the negative. This phenomenon is called negativity bias and it is not their fault, they did not choose it.

Elicit the evolutionary functions of the negativity bias, i.e., how the threat emotions can be helpful and necessary or what it would be like if we did not have them. A classic example is the absence of any anxiety after having had a few too many drinks, which can lead us to drive in an altered state of consciousness; in this case, anxiety would protect us from a possible accident. Not having it can become a problem.

Negative Emotions and the Body

 Therapist Background Knowledge

Threat emotions are designed to significantly stimulate the body and they can appear when we encounter a source of worry and anticipation. They might come on quickly, with intense, automatic body experiences, with specific patterns of memory-thinking processes and attention styles, knocking out any positive emotions that might be present. As neuropsychologist Rick Hanson reminds us, threat emotions often act exactly like Velcro – they are sticky and become a focus for dwelling and ruminating on things.

Threat emotions are very prone to becoming conditioned – that is being associated with a stimulus. Whenever that stimulus appears again, we will tend to experience that same threat emotion.

Imagine you are on vacation. You wallet was stolen during your vacation. Now, every time you see an ad about going on vacation somewhere, you will feel threatened.

Most importantly, threat emotions are our default system. We have evolved to be set on threat mode and scour the horizon for possible life-threatening predators (or, in our modern-day world, yet another work-task to be added to our to-do list). This forms the basis of many of our cognitive biases, such as negativity bias and the "better safe than sorry" processing strategy. We tend to remember negative events more easily than positive ones.

Internal and External Threats

 Therapist Background Knowledge

Our threat system can be thought of as a very sensitive smoke detector, which, in humans, can be set off either by internal or external threats. Since it is so sensitive, it can easily hijack the other systems. This is why it is so important to always highlight that having a big red circle **IS NOT OUR FAULT**. It is, however, our responsibility to learn how to balance it with our other two emotional systems.

Discuss which are some of the common internal and external threats that set off our alarm system; be sure to highlight how the threats that set off our alarm system are very often similar in nature, in the way they formed and became conditioned, and, at the same time validate the unique experience of each individual.

You can have participants fill out the **Client Handout 2.6**, listing the internal and external threats that set off their very personal smoke detector.

Invite participants to reflect on how they act/think/feel when they are in their threat system by using the questions in **Client Handout 2.7**.

3d) Distinguishing between a "red-fuelled" drive system and a "green-fuelled" drive system

    Therapist Task

Drive emotions can be very helpful, for they form the basis of joy and positive relating. However, they can also become a problem. Drive emotions are often short-lived and can easily transform into disappointment or, when blocked, lead to frustration. Try to encourage reflection on this point by asking participants in which real-life situations they have experienced joy and excitement transform into disappointment and frustration.

There are situations in which our drive system is "fuelled" by our red circle, that is, by threat – we are constantly in doing mode, always keeping ourselves busy, achieving and proving ourselves, but we do so out of fear of rejection rather than for the sheer pleasure of seeking knowledge. Again, invite participants to come up with real-life examples of times when their drive system became overly active and brought them to lose sight of setting wise and realistic standards for themselves. *What was the threat behind their perfectionistic standards?*

It is important to cultivate a "healthy blue system"; this is when our drive system is "fuelled" by our green circle. For example, we wish to get fit and take care of ourselves, and we feel excitement and joy in our physical activity because we know it will help us in our goal. Or, we have decided to save and set aside money to help our beloved grandchild with his studies, and we feel happiness and pride when we realise that we are succeeding and that he will be able to go to college with the money we have set aside. We feel joy in helping people during our volunteer hours, as long as the motivation for volunteering is to be of help and alleviate suffering, and not to "be better than my neighbour". When the blue system is "in the service" of a compassionate motivation (helping others and ourselves to live a life that is fully and courageously respectful of our deepest needs and values) it is very often fuelled by a sense of grounding.

When we push ourselves feel we must achieve things and do things to prove our worth (a competitive mindset), failing to succeed can evoke feelings of worthlessness, of being a failure and activate a self-critical inner dialogue. We are no longer in a state of "secure striving", but have turned to threat-insecure striving, which locks the soothing system out of the equation. Working on strengthening our soothing system via compassion for ourselves and others will help us to regulate our threat system and our self-criticism (we will be addressing this in depth in Module 7) and create a healthy drive system.

Encourage participants to distinguish a time in which they were in a state of secure striving from a time in which they were in a state of threat striving.

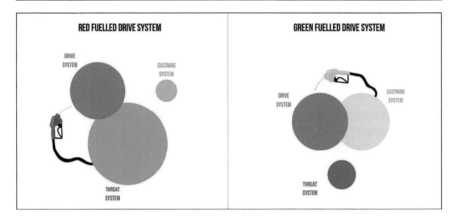

Figure 2.9 "Red-Fuelled" and "Green-Fuelled" Drive System.

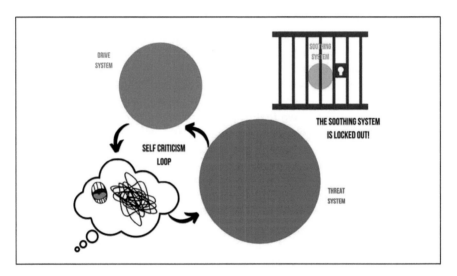

Figure 2.10 An Inaccessible Soothing System.

- *Which feelings arose in both situations?*
- *What was the real motivation behind the striving?*
- *Was the striving coming from a desire to avoid negative emotions, rejection or insecurities?*

Discuss the examples among the group.

Finally, invite participants to reflect on how they act/think/feel when they are in their drive system by using the questions in **Client Handout 2.7**.

3e) Soothing emotions and their link to compassion

 Therapist Background Knowledge

Soothing and settling are related to a general slowing down of the body and mind. We are content and more peaceful, and have a broader outlook on the world. All animals, including us, need opportunities to rest and just chill out. As we will see, this emotional state is characterised by increased activity in our parasympathetic nervous system. Soothing emotions help to balance the other emotions, make us feel safe, and allow for exploration and creativity.

 Therapist Task

Participants may wish to explore their soothing system and emotions using the questions in **Client Handout 2.7**.

At this point, it is important to clarify that compassion is not only the soothing system. The therapist should highlight the difference between an emotion and a motivation, reminding participants that compassion is a motive, not an emotion. Being compassionate can activate different emotional states. Even anger can sometimes be compassionate, if what lies behind that anger is a genuine desire to prevent, protect, and ultimately be helpful and alleviate suffering.

The reason we spend a lot of time stimulating the soothing system is that its physiological architecture and focus facilitates the cultivation of compassion: the sense of slowing down promotes connection with ourselves and others, grounding increases our ability to navigate the suffering without feeling unbalanced. It is this very state that fosters the compassionate intention to be helpful.

Spend time explaining how compassionate motivation can be used as a focus and intention to balance the different types of emotions we have. Being motivated by compassion gives us quite a lot of flexibility regarding the kind of emotions and behaviours we can experience. The emotions and behaviours that are most useful are quite context-dependent.

Phase 4: Building our Soothing System

In this phase, the group starts exploring how to build the soothing system and activate the parasympathetic system. The therapist should emphasise that our soothing system can help to balance the other two systems and spending time in a calm, connected, and peaceful state can promote greater physical and mental well being.

Main Touch Points

Therapist Script 2.4 – Soothing Rhythm Breathing
Client Handout A – Circle Check-In
Client Handout 2.8 – Formal and Informal Practice

4a) Working with the breath

 Therapist Background Knowledge

Depending on the kind of audience you are working with, you might want to delve a bit deeper into the theory of why and how breathing techniques enable us to tap into our soothing system.

The Physiology of the Soothing System

The soothing system is linked primarily to the parasympathetic nervous system (PNS), which acts as a brake to help regulate your heart. Without a parasympathetic system, your heart rate would be around 120 beats per minute. Therefore, the parasympathetic system is slowing it down all the time.

One important part of the parasympathetic nervous system is the vagus nerve, our tenth cranial nerve, which projects to many different body parts. Vagal tone predicts calm and affiliative behavioural states, the capacity to experience more positive emotional states, and parameters such as lower blood pressure.

A key measure of the parasympathetic nervous system function is heart rate variability (HRV). HRV is the variation in the time interval between heartbeats and it is measured in the variation beat-to-beat interval. HRV is in synchrony with our breathing: s we inhale the sympathetic nervous system (SNS) is activated and our heart rate (HR) increases, as we exhale the PNS is activated and our HR decreases, resulting in HRV.

 Therapist Task

The main breathing exercise we use in CFT is soothing rhythm breathing.

Before the practice, introduce the group to the concept of the "Circle Check-in" which we will be using from here on. This is a way to quickly and easily notice how our three circles change as we intentionally direct our attention in a certain direction, guided by a specific motive. Each time you find this box in the following modules, we suggest you take a Circle Check-in break; as always, feel free to insert these when you feel most appropriate for your group.

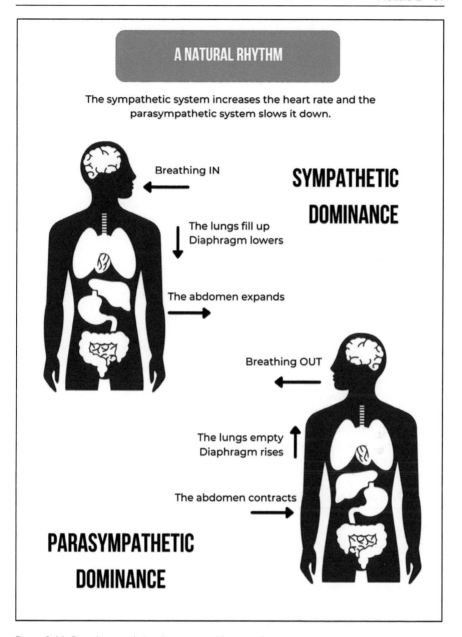

Figure 2.11 Breathing and the Autonomic Nervous System.

Using **Client Handout A** invite them to draw their three circles on the left side of the image, representing how they were feeling the moment they walked into the session today. Each time you see this box, you can pair it with this client handout.

Three-Circle Check-In

Follow **Therapist Script 2.4** to guide participants through the Soothing Rhythm Breathing practice; then bring them back to their circle check-in and invite them to fill in the right side of the image.

4b) The difference between formal and informal practice

 Therapist Task

This is a good opportunity for the therapist to focus on the benefits of having different strategies to cultivate your soothing system. Participants should become familiar with the differences between formal and informal practice and what the benefits of each are. In the table below you can find some examples of formal and informal practices – please note that this is by no means an exhaustive list of the different practices; invite clients to come up with their own examples of formal and informal practices and add them to **Client Handout 2.8**.

Table 2.2 Formal and Informal Practices in Compassion Focused Therapy

FORMAL PRACTICE	INFORMAL PRACTICE
→ proactive decision to do a practice, intentional time commitment for the practice	→ reactive, opportunity to bring a compassionate motivation to everyday lives
Soothing Rhythm Breathing	Practicing Loving Kindness for strangers on the bus
Imagery exercises	Softening your gaze when you look at yourself in the mirror in the morning
Soothing touch and compassionate posture	Stopping to connect and chat with the barman who is notably feeling sad today

Phase 5: Wrap-Up

The final phase of the module is a wrap-up of the theme that has been explored. Emphasise how continuing to work on your **personal practice** (whether formal or informal) can help with the development of your compassionate minds.

Main Touch Points

Therapist Script 2.5 – Closing practice
Client Handout 2.9 – Compassionate Compass
Client Handout B – Personal practice diary

5a) Summary of the session and suggestions for personal practice

 Therapist Task

Take 5–10 minutes to briefly summarise the points that you have gone through in this module. Repetition is important to help fix the main concepts that you wish participants to focus on and take with them into the following modules.

You may want to provide participants with some suggestions for personal practice and self-reflection:

- Read **Client Handout 2.2**
- Practice at home by choosing which homework you would like to do; if you are not sure, you can begin by listening to the audio track for soothing rhythm breathing
- Complete **Client Handout 2.9** to help orient your practice and daily actions
- Complete the practice diary in **Client Handout B**

 Therapist Tips

Using the words "invitations" or "suggestions" or "prompts for personal practice" instead of "homework" will help you deliver the message that these personal practices are not merely another thing to be added to our to-do list, but rather deliberate choices that each of us makes to cultivate the compassionate mind and motive. When clients start to see their home-practice as homework, they might switch from a joyful drive to threat-based drive, especially they do not manage to follow their practice plan exactly as they said they would.

5b) Closing practice

 Therapist Task

It is important to always take a moment at the end of the session to acknowledge anything and everything that has come up for participants while exploring the themes offered. Try to focus their attention by inviting them to share in one sentence:

What can I take home from today's session (because I feel it's going to be helpful)?

Guide participants through a short closing practice using **Therapist Script 2.5**.

Therapist Scripts

Therapist Script 2.1: Compassionate Landing (7 minutes)

(We will use this meditation from now on to open all sessions with small variations that recall some key elements of the previous session or introduce elements that will be covered in the current session – from now on, we will not repeat this script, but merely suggest possible variations to be included).

To begin this practice, close your eyes or, if you prefer, keep them half-closed with your gaze downward. Adopt an upright, but not rigid posture – try to find a posture that facilitates breathing and a relaxed curiosity about what is going on inside you.

Start by simply bringing your attention to your breathing, without changing it, and keep your attention there for a few moments, listening. Give yourself a chance to simply observe the natural rhythm of your breathing for a few moments.

Now do a brief scan of your body, with the sole intention of observing with curiosity what is present in this moment – if you feel particularly tense areas, try whispering to them: "I feel your tension... thank you for trying to protect me... we are safe now".

Imagine welcoming the main areas of the body to the best of your ability today– starting with your feet, try to say hello to that part of your body and, even if it feels a little strange, imagine this part feeling pleased to be seen and acknowledged, and connected to the whole.

Move on to your pelvis, say hi and welcome this body part here today...move on to your torso and all the vital organs it contains, greet them and welcome them...imagine them feeling pleased to be seen and acknowledged.

Now extend this welcoming attention to your heart, shoulders, arms, and hands...and then to your neck and the muscles of your face...which if you want you can soften into a slight smile...as if we have just seen a friend or a being that naturally makes you smile...and then bring your attention to your head.

Now imagine the people around you, maybe in this group, that you met in the previous session, or in this building or this city...How many of the worries and tensions that you are experiencing at this moment are probably also theirs... we have all found ourselves immersed here in this flow of life....

Try to formulate a compassionate intention: "may I be of help to these people and not harm them; may I be of help to myself and not harm myself; may I be open to the compassionate intentions of others".

Allow yourself a few moments now to listen to whatever feelings have arisen...

Then, when you feel ready, gently open your eyes again.

Therapist Script 2.2: Flow of Life Meditation (20 minutes)

In this guided meditation we will use a visualisation to get in touch with the flow of life. Let the images come spontaneously, without forcing them in any way.

To begin, get into a comfortable position, sitting on the floor or in a chair, your sit bones well rooted, your spine stretched out, your shoulders soft, your chin slightly down... give yourself a few moments to find your most comfortable position today and then gently close your eyes or, if you prefer, keep them slightly half-closed with your gaze downward.

We begin by rooting ourselves to our breathing, following the smooth flow of air coming in and out of our body. We feel the body expand with each inhalation and soften with each exhalation.

Now, as best as we can, let's begin to use our mind's eye to paint a picture of the universe in the moment before the Earth was born; we were not here yet, the planet had not yet taken shape; let's try to imagine the feeling of silence... perhaps of darkness or perhaps of a strong light enveloping us....

Now let's take a small step forward along this path and imagine the new-born Earth... still in its infancy... let's imagine the sound of the first seas, maybe of storms in the first oceans... a blue globe in continuous movement and evolution... slowly the first green elements begin to emerge beneath and above the surface of the water... from algae, to the first soft mosses, ferns unfurling in the warm sunlight, the first shrubs and then trees with their increasingly thicker and more luxuriant foliage... a powerful sprouting of a thousand green life forms.

Now let's move on to imagine the first animals being born and beginning to inhabit this Earth, which is getting more and more complex. Try to get in touch with what this vision awakens within you: perhaps a slight sense of wonder at life unfolding in this way.

In its life, each of these animals has experienced a sense of threat in the face of danger, has sought out the resources in his environment to survive as best it could, has experienced moments of peace while resting in the warmth of the sun's rays.

Among these animals, the first human beings also appeared... millions of years ago... let's try to get in touch with what their primary needs were ... What did they need?... What did they fight for?... What were they afraid of?... What made them feel safe? We begin to notice something in common with those early humans... their need for friends and connection... their need to protect each other... their desires... their lusts.

Let's continue this journey... let's imagine humans in the various eras. Let's observe their behaviours from the outside... moving to distant lands, wars... what drives them to act this way? Let's imagine that we get in touch again with their deepest needs and motivations... and maybe we can also see their need for friends and connection... their need to protect each other... their desires... their lusts.

If you feel comfortable and safe doing so, let us imagine our grandparents... even if you never met meet them... let us also observe them and how they act, as they have to make difficult decisions, as they try to navigate through their emotions... let's recognise in them the same motivations, the attempt to protect themselves, their insecurities, their dreams, their need for friends and connection ... maybe just the intention to be happy and not to suffer...

And now, if and how you feel comfortable and safe doing so, let us look at our parents. If you did not meet them, try, if you want, to create an image of them, even if it is not clear. They, just like you, will have gone through happy moments, difficult moments, and they will have overcome some things and lost others... maybe you can see also in them the same motivations, the attempt to protect themselves from threats, to seek their own security and stability, to be able to experience a sense of good and to be able to share it with others.

Let us now try to bring to mind the moment of our birth... we did not choose it; this being did not choose when to be born, did not choose its parents... it did not choose its feelings, its physical characteristics...it did not choose its sexual gender.... It did not choose to be so exposed to what is going on around them. It doesn't yet know how influential its environment will be in its life...

Nevertheless, this child, like so many others, is driven by the same emotions – they feel fear in the face of danger, cry out for care and help, explore their space to gather information about their surroundings, and seeks reassurance.

Now imagine that this child is beginning to grow up; they are now 5–6 years old. Observe this child as they play, as they interact with others...what emotions do they have? What fears? What desires?

Maybe you can see how much their fears, their desires, and what they believe about themselves, are shaped and influenced by their past, by everything that happens around them...they did not choose. It is not their fault...

Let's take one more step forward and imagine ourselves now in school...and the child has grown up and become an adolescent ...maybe when they fell in love for the first time...and maturing into a young adult, the tough decisions we have to make...the insecurities....and yet let's recognise in them the same motivations, the same attempt to protect themselves, their insecurities, their dreams, their need for friends and connection...maybe just the intention to be happy and not to suffer that has accompanied this whole journey.

Then, slowly, we land here, right here, right now. In this room, maybe surrounded by other people who are on the same journey ... let's try to see ourselves from the outside, with the friendly curiosity that we would have toward someone who has been on a great journey ... how is this person feeling? What are their emotions now? What moves them?... Perhaps even in this being we can see the same motivations, the same attempt to protect themselves, their insecurities, their dreams, their need for friends and connection...maybe just the intention to be happy and not to suffer...

We are about to conclude this journey now... let us feel rooted in our posture, back relaxed, shoulders soft, heart open... and then when you are ready, you can open your eyes again, taking a few moments to feel whatever sensation may have emerged and reconnect with the room around you.

Optional (the journey continues – choice to be evaluated based on time and characteristics of the population we are working with)

Now let our minds take us to a future time, ten years from now...what kind of person are we? Perhaps this person also still has that same desire to protect themselves from threats, to fulfil their plans, to nurture their affections, to experience a sense of peace. What does this person wish for? Maybe you can see in them the same intention to be happy and not to suffer...

And then let's take it one step further. Let's imagine ourselves as old people, our skin no longer taut, now with wrinkles, hair that has turned gray... what desires does this person have? What is really important to this person? What do we feel for this person? What do we wish for them? What can this person teach you right now?

Finally, we come to the moment of departure from this life; we, along with the millions and millions of people who are leaving this planet with us on the same day... let's try to notice if the sense of this incessant flow of life comes to us, we did not choose all this, we are not alone in going through it...

And now let our mind retrace all this journey... there have been so many changes, so many transformations... and at the same time so many threads that unite us even to the very first life forms emerged on this planet... let's try to stay in touch with the feelings that this flow of life awakens in us... what emotions live in us at this moment...and let them be, exactly as they are...

Then, slowly, we turn our attention back to the form we are in today, right here, right now. Let us once again allow our breath to cradle us with its calming rhythm... let us feel rooted in our posture, back relaxed, shoulders soft, heart open... and then when you feel up to it, you can open your eyes again, and take a few moments to reconnect with the room around you.

Therapist Script 2.3: Three Emotional Systems Visualisation (7 minutes)

When you feel ready, gently close your eyes and take a couple of moments to land into your body and breath.

Now try to bring to mind a recent situation or event in which you've experienced a small conflict with someone, or maybe a situation in which you felt anxious... let your mind recreate the scene... what is happening? What thoughts are emerging? What do you feel in your body? What changes do you notice in your breathing? What is your body asking you to do?

Now, gently let go of this first scene and imagine a situation in which you've experienced an achievement or a sense of pride... maybe a success at work, a competition you've won, maybe you won the lottery. What thoughts are emerging? What do you feel in your body? What changes do you notice in your breathing? What is your body asking you to do?

Now imagine coming back home or wherever you feel safe, somewhere you consider to be your nest… close the door and leave the world outside… you are safe here… you don't have to do or achieve anything, you can simply relax here… maybe you lie down on the couch or on the floor or on the grass… maybe there's someone with you (even a dog or a plant) that you feel by your side and to whom you don't owe any explanation… they simply want to be there with you, by your side. What thoughts are emerging? What do you feel in your body? What changes do you notice in your breathing? What is your body asking you to do?

Gently let go of this third image, come back to your breathing and when you feel ready, open your eyes.

Therapist Script 2.4: Soothing Rhythm Breathing (8 minutes)

To begin this practice, take a comfortable position, sitting on the floor or in a chair…we will start by closing our eyes or looking down at something non-distracting. Now, gently create a compassionate body posture, one where your back is straight and shoulders back, in line with your hips, your chest open, allowing yourselves to breath with ease.

Now turn your attention to your breathing; with curiosity, try to notice the rhythm of the breathing…if it is free or constricted, if it is deep or shallow, if there are particular points of the body where you feel it most. Notice how we did not choose this process of breathing…which nourishes our cells from the moment we were born.

Now, let's try to create a slightly slower breathing rhythm. We can start by slowing our breathing to a level that is comfortable today. Then, we can help ourselves by counting: we start by counting to 3 on the inhale, and again to 3 on the exhale, then to 4…, then to 5….

If we realise that counting doesn't help us right now, we can simply cultivate the intention to make our exhalation a little longer.

If we wish, we can add to our calming breath:

- *A mantra: inhale…mind slowing down…exhale…body slowing down*
- *An image: the breath caressing me inside (breath nourishing with its oxygen); waves of the sea "coming in and out"*
- *An image: I am a large tree, rooted and flexible, breathing calmly…absorbing energy through the sun, releasing energy through oxygen in a continuous exchange with the outside world*

Remember that if distracting thoughts come up during meditation, this is completely normal; it is the nature of our mind, which we did not choose… whenever we notice that the mind has gone elsewhere, we simply bring it gently back to our breathing.

After 5–8 minutes, we gently let go of our attention from our breathing and when we feel like it we can slowly open our eyes again, giving us time to get back in touch with the room around us.

Therapist Script 2.5: Closing Practice (5 minutes)

(We will use this meditation from now on to close all sessions with small variations that recall some key elements of the session that has just ended – from now on we will not repeat this script, but only suggest possible variations to be included).

To close our session for today, let's consciously re-visit our intention to develop our compassionate mind and pattern. We will start by closing our eyes or looking down and feeling how we are sitting on our chair right now.

Notice your compassion posture with your back straight and shoulders in line with your hips with an open diaphragm. Now invite your breathing to slow down, and with each slower and deeper breath say, in a friendly tone, slowly, alternatively "mind slowing down" and then "body slowing down" – gradually getting that feeling of grounding with a sense of stillness/slowing but also with an alert mind. Notice yourself becoming more grounded.

Allow time for this to settle in.

Now, tune into your inner compassionate mind and pattern ... remember the wisdom that you have been developing in the course so far – that we all just find ourselves here with a very tricky brain and certain life experiences that have shaped how our minds and bodies work – the version that we are.

But we are also a mind that can learn how to change, to make choices so we are developing the strength and commitment to try to help ourselves and others to address and deal with life and our inner difficulties.

We now know that nature has endowed us with an emotional system, the soothing system, that helps us feel grounded, calm and present, able to navigate life to the fullest ...and that can be trained with compassion for ourselves and others.

As we are sitting here, let's try to remind ourselves in a friendly and committed way:

I am here today, and the next few weeks, to:

- *Work on ways to be helpful to myself*
- *Support others as best I can on their journey*
- *Be open to the helpfulness of others*

Thank yourself for showing up today, exactly as you are.
When you feel ready, gently open your eyes and come back to the room.

Client Handouts

Client Handout 2.1: Compassionate Weekly Reflection

Let's do a curious, friendly reflection on this past week:

Which part of the self-practice did I do and why?

Which part of the self-practice did I not do?

Was this due to any anxieties or block regarding the practice or the path? Which ones can you identify?

We extend gratitude, respect, and compassion to resistances. What would make you and your resistances feel safer in going forward on this path?

Client Handout 2.2: The Three Circles

THE 3 CIRCLE MODEL

Each emotional system is important.
Depending on our motivation, our emotional systems will function differently.

THREAT SYSTEM (RED)

The threat system is focused on the protection, safety-seeking, escape/attack response. Emotions related to this system include anger, disgust, fear, anxiety. The red circle is essential to our survival. However, we often let it guide us without realizing it.

DRIVE SYSTEM (BLUE)

The drive system is focused on incentives and resources. It directs us toward what we want, desire, or seek to achieve. The emotions connected to this circle are enthusiasm, vitality, and determination. We often use the blue circle to manage the emotions of the red circle.

SOOTHING SYSTEM (GREEN)

The calming system has to do with grounding, connection, and security. Emotions connected to this circle include calmness and contentment. It helps us rest and metabolize and cultivate open awareness. It regenerates us.

COMPETITIVE MOTIVATION

When we have an active competitive motivation our emotional systems are more likely to be in a state of imbalance, both when the goal is achieved and not achieved. Our red circle is often predominant. We often attempt to prove our worth to ourselves and others. When we adopt this mindset, we become self-focused and can be very fearful, critical, and hostile toward ourselves and others.

COMPASSIONATE MOTIVATION

Our compassionate motivation helps us bring balance to our emotional systems. It helps us connect to wisdom, courage and commitment so that we can be supportive of ourselves and others.

Figure 2.12 Different Configurations of the Emotion Regulation Systems.

Client Handout 2.3: Thoughts, Sensations, Behaviour

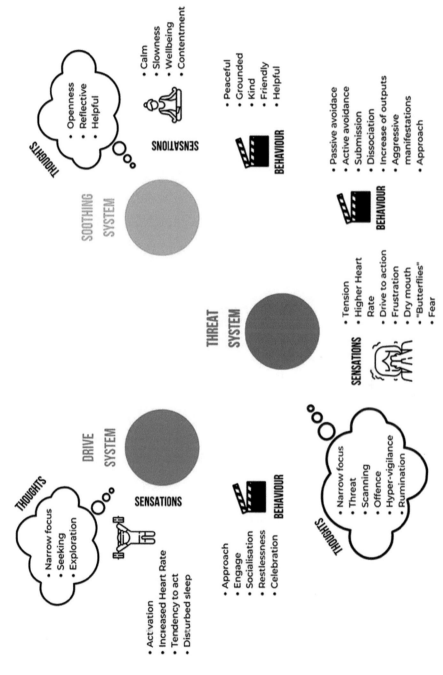

Figure 2.13 Elements of the Three Emotion Regulation Systems.

THOUGHTS, SENSATIONS AND BEHAVIORS

For each system, try listing the sensations, emotions, thoughts, attention
pattern and behaviours or action tendencies that you experience.

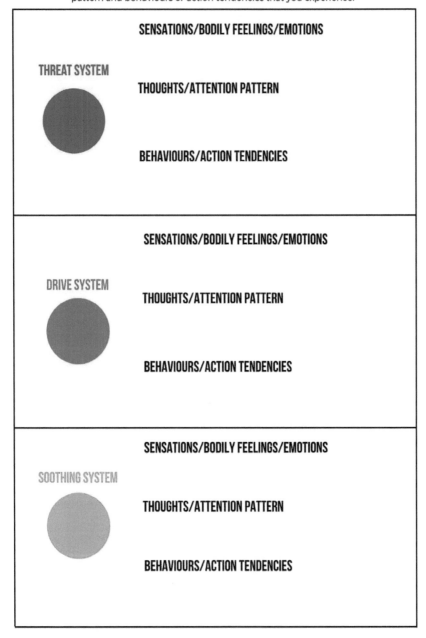

Figure 2.14 Your Three Emotion Regulation Systems.

Client Handout 2.4: Drawing the Three Circles

Consider the following possible three-circle configurations, then draw your own three circles.

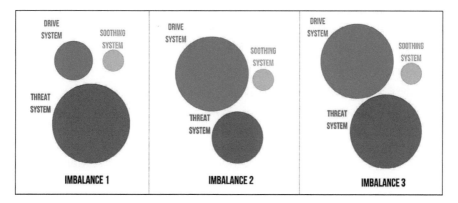

Figure 2.15 Three-Circle Imbalances.

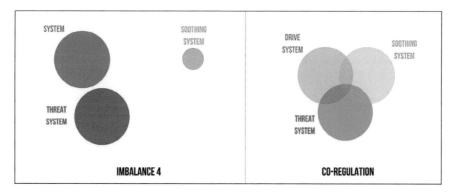

Figure 2.16 Three-Circle Co-Regulation.

YOUR THREE CIRCLES

Try representing in the space below your three circles.
Draw the circles, assigning them the correct "proportion" to
your life right now.

Inside each circle try writing:

- What current experiences and events are part of each of them
- What activities are part of each one
- What memories you have within each one
- How are they related to each other. Do they offset each other? Do
  they regulate each other?
- What people would you place within each?

Points for reflection:

- Was there a time when their conformation changed?
- Do you wish the proportions were different at this time?
- What do you wish for yourself from now on? What would you wish
  for another person you care about and cherish?

Figure 2.17 Exploring Your Three Circles.

Client Handout 2.5: The Three Circles in Action

Consider the following three-circle dynamics, then reflect on your own experience.

Figure 2.18 The Dynamic Nature of the Three-Circle Configuration (example 1).

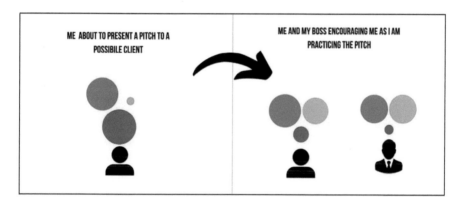

Figure 2.19 The Dynamic Nature of the Three-Circle Configuration (example 2).

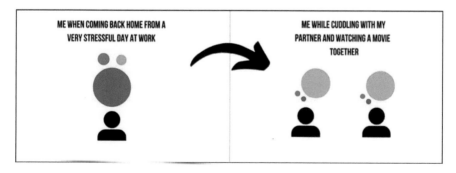

Figure 2.20 The Dynamic Nature of the Three-Circle Configuration (example 3).

© Petrocchi, Kirby and Baldi (2025), *Essentials of Compassion Focused Therapy*, Routledge

Call to mind a discussion you recently had. Take a few moments to paint the scene, considering what you see, the sounds and smells that are there. Get in touch with the physical sensations you feel about being in that situation again, in front of that person or people.

Now take up the three-circle diagram again; which circles have been activated in this situation?

What would you place within each circle *in this specific situation*?

Now try to think about how these three circles interacted with each other. Do you have the impression that one of the circles was activated to compensate another?

Client Handout 2.6: Your Personal Smoke Detector

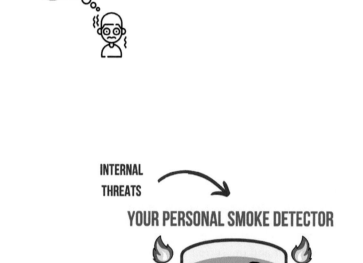

MY INTERNAL THREATS ARE:

MY EXTERNAL THREATS ARE:

Figure 2.21 Internal and External Threats.

Client Handout 2.7: Reflecting on Threat, Drive, and Soothing Emotions

Red Circle (Threat)

- What are my external/internal threats?
- In my threatened state, what automatic thoughts or behaviours do I notice?
- How do I recognise that I am in my threatened state? What physical signals do I notice? What mental signals?
- What other defensive processes do I notice in myself?
- What are the "nurturing" things I stop doing when my threat system is active?

Blue Circle (Drive)

- Where does the main source of well-being in my life come from?
- How much comes from my achieving goals? From being better than others?
- How do I recognise that I am in my "drive state"? What physical signals do I notice? What mental signals?
- What success/goals/achievements do I consider crucial to my well-being?
- What does this system contain for me?
- What do I need to achieve to feel good?

Green Circle (Soothing)

- What elicits a sense of contentment and slowing down in me?
- In what situations do I feel most present, without the urge to go elsewhere, connected to myself and my surroundings?
- How do I recognise that I am in my "soothing state"? What physical signals do I notice? What mental signals?
- What thoughts do I tend to have when I am in this state?
- What actions do I want to take when this system is active?

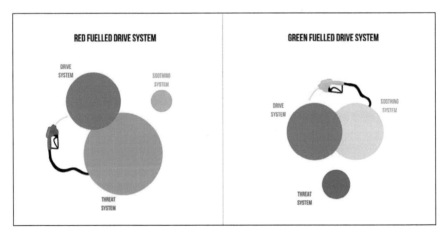

Figure 2.22 Red-Fuelled and Green-Fuelled Drive System.

Can you think of any times when your drive system has been fuelled by your threat system?

Can you think of any times when your drive system has been fuelled by your soothing system?

Can you think of any times when your self-criticism created a "red-blue" loop, and you felt that your soothing system was inaccessible?

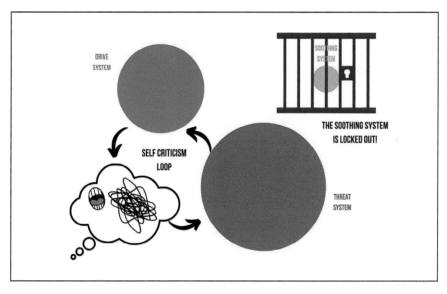

Figure 2.23 The Soothing System is Inaccessible.

Client Handout 2.8: Formal and Informal Practice

In this table you can find some examples of formal and informal practice.

Feel free to fill in the empty spaces in the table with your own favourite forms of formal and informal practice!

Table 2.3

FORMAL PRACTICE → proactive decision to do a practice, intentional time commitment for the practice	INFORMAL PRACTICE → reactive, opportunity to bring a compassionate motivation to everyday lives
Soothing Rhythm Breathing	Practicing Loving Kindness for strangers on the bus
Imagery exercises	Softening your gaze when you look at yourself in the mirror in the morning
Soothing touch and compassionate posture	Stopping to connect and chat with the barman who is notably feeling sad today

Client Handout 2.9: Compassionate Compass

There are moments in our days or weeks in which we might feel like we have lost our direction; at times we are not fully aware of it, rather it comes as a feeling of distress, discomfort, irritation, or disconnection.

How can we re-orient ourselves?

You might think of having a compassionate compass with you, that you can take out of your back-pocket and use to still your mind, slow down your breathing and root yourself in your compassionate motivation.

Figure 2.24 The Compassionate Compass.

You might want to practise using your compass first thing in the morning. Instead of absent-mindedly jumping out of bed as soon as the alarm goes off, picking up your phone or switching on the TV, you can spend a moment orientating yourself within this new day.

While still under the duvet, you can engage in soothing rhythm breathing, welcome yourself to the day with a friendly voice whispering *"Good morning"*, and set your compassionate intention for the day – imagining what it would be like if you were at your compassionate best, how would you feel, how would you connect with others, how would you act. And then, begin your new day.

Try this practice for a couple of days and then write down what you notice when you start the day in this way; remember, you can take out your compassionate compass at any moment of the day to re-orient yourself.

Chapter 3

Module 3
Mindfulness

> **Aims**
>
> - To introduce the nature and function of attention
> - To illustrate the connections between attention and how it helps track motivation and goals, as well as influence physiological systems
> - To introduce the concept and experience of mindfulness
> - To illustrate different forms of mindfulness, how they can be guided by different motives, and how we can have fears of mindfulness
> - To guide mindfulness exercises using a compassionate lens

> **Deepen Your Knowledge**
>
> In Gilbert, P. & Simos, G. (Eds). (2022). *Compassion Focused Therapy: Clinical Practice ad Applications*. Routledge, please refer to:
>
> Chapter 7 – Compassionate Mind Training: Key Themes
>
> In Gilbert, P. (2010). *Compassion Focused Therapy: Distinctive Features* (1st ed.). Routledge, please refer to:
>
> Chapter 17 – Preparing and Training One's Mind: Mindfulness and Soothing Breathing Rhythm

DOI: 10.4324/9781003436058-5

Summary of Key Processes

Table 3.1 Module 3: Mindfulness

Phase		Main Touch Points	Therapist Scripts	Client Handouts
1	Introduction	**1a)** Compassionate Landing **1b)** Revision of personal practice and recap of previous session	□ **Script 3.1**: Compassionate Landing	□ **Handout 3.1**: Compassionate Weekly Reflection
2	Attention	**2a)** Attention as a spotlight and an amplifier	□ **Script 3.2**: Attention as a spotlight	□ **Handout 3.2**: Spotlight of my day: three compassion episodes
3	Mindfulness	**3a)** Definition of mindfulness **3b)** Basic mindfulness practices	□ **Script 3.3**: Mindful breathing □ **Script 3.4**: Compassionate Labelling □ **Script 3.5**: Mindful Walking	□ **Handout 3.3**: The cycle of mindfulness
4	Widening and deepening your mindfulness	**4a)** Fears of Mindfulness **4b)** Advanced mindfulness practices	□ **Script 3.6**: Mindful eating □ **Script 3.7**: Mindful listening	□ **Handout 3.4**: Fears of Mindfulness □ **Handout 3.5**: Mindful Café
5	Wrap-up	**3a)** Summary of the session and suggestions for personal practice **3b)** Closing practice	□ **Script 3.8**: Closing practice	□ **Handout B**: Personal practice diary

Module 3: Mindfulness

Detailed Module Outline

Phase 1: Introduction

Main Touch Points

Therapist Script 3.1 – Compassionate Landing
Client Handout 3.1 – Compassionate Weekly Reflection

1a) Compassionate Landing

 Therapist Task

Compassionate Landing is a moment that is repeated in every session to guide participants through entering a space for reflection and practice.

This is a good moment for the therapist to connect participants once again to their compassionate motivation and intentions:

- To work on ways to be helpful to oneself
- To support others as best as possible on their journey
- To be open to the helpfulness of others

It is also advised to include in each landing a link to the themes of the previous modules. This creates coherence throughout the entire training. In the Compassionate Landing of Module 3 you might want to include some parts that refer to the unchosen nature of our tricky brains (Module 2). See **Therapist Script 3.1 for** some suggestions on how to lead the compassionate landing.

Before the landing, offer a moment for a Three-Circle Check-In; we encourage the therapist to repeat this moment at least once during the session, either after a key practice or before the closing, to clearly show that we can influence the balance between circles thanks to our practice.

Three-Circle Check-In

1b) Revision of personal practice and recap of previous session

 Therapist Task

Right after the compassionate landing, encourage participants to do a little bit of self-reflection on their experiences during the week. If they have not filled out their personal practice diary, encourage them to do this now, just so they can jot down some "compassionate moments" they can recall from the past week.

You may want to encourage the use of **Client Handout 3.1** to facilitate the self-reflection.

 Therapist Tips

In these first sessions (and often up until the last) you will likely have to gently open up a discussion around the emotions of guilt and shame that surrounds the theme of personal practice at home throughout the entire process of the training. See, again, **Client Handout 2.2 for suggestions.**

Following self-reflection, have participants get into pairs and share whatever they would like to share regarding their past week, including any compassion episodes or any fears, blocks, and resistances (FBRs) they might have experienced. If needed, briefly revise the concept of FBRs, linking to what was discussed in Module 2.

Invite them to notice the change in their tone of voice, facial expression, posture and overall physical sensations when they speak of their compassion episodes – both in themselves and in their partner.

 Therapist Tips

We will be suggesting this kind of reflection in pairs for all the following modules. It is a space in which participants have the opportunity to find intimacy, choose to what degree they are willing, or they feel it is helpful to open up, as well as connect on a deeper level with the other participants. We suggest you rotate the pairs, always inviting participants to find a new partner to work with. This creates an opportunity to connect with more people and to experiment with what communication is like with someone we find ourselves more or less in tune with.

Following this work in pairs, you may choose to spend some time de-briefing to the group at large.

A key component of Compassion Focused Therapy (CFT) when delivering it in a group context is helping facilitate discussions between participants. You, the therapist, help group members notice spontaneous instances of one of the three flows of compassion (or maybe the lack thereof).

You can stimulate mentalisation in the participants by having them think about what might be happening to one particular participant who has shared his/her struggles around a practice. Does anyone else resonate with this difficulty? How do we feel if we remind ourselves that we did not choose these difficulties, that they are connected to our tricky brains?

Then, you can motivate them to switch towards compassion and, without providing any advice, notice if there is something that we would like to say to this person that might be helpful – maybe just "I understand how you are feeling, I've also felt that way at times".

Some questions you can use for open-ended group inquiry are:

- *How are you feeling when we face the difficulties of your mind?*
- *How are you feeling about the difficulties this particular person has?*
- *Then, turning to the person (if appropriate): how do you feel in this moment, receiving the compassionate attention of the group?*

Before moving on, the therapist can provide a brief recap of the last session, in which the main points were:

- The flow of life
- The three-circle model of emotional regulation
- Compassion as a motive
- Starting to build a soothing system

This can also be a space to set the scene for the current module; the main themes that are going to be explored are:

- The nature of attention
- Mindfulness and its applications

Phase 2: Attention

Main Touch Points

 Therapist Script 3.2 – Attention as a Spotlight
Client Handout 3.2 – Spotlight of My Day: Three Compassion Episodes

2a) Attention as a spotlight and amplifier

 Therapist Task

In CFT, we always precede mindfulness with attention training, inviting people to reflect on what attention is and how we can *willingly move it to different aspects* of our experience, such as sensations within the body, specific thoughts, emotions, or desires. In addition, *we know* we are paying attention to something: this is what we call knowing awareness.

Not only can attention be moved on purpose, but it can also be used as an *amplifier*. Whenever we pay attention to something, it tends to become more present, somehow "bigger" in our perception; this means our attention acts just like a magnifying glass or a zoom lens. This is true whatever the object of our attention is: we have probably all experienced a situation in which focusing on a small niggle in our body has made it seem much more painful than it actually was.

Attention also acts as a *spotlight*; whenever we focus our attention on a certain concern, other things we were thinking about tend to disappear from our mind.

Guide participants through the short experiential exercise "Attention as a Spotlight" (**Therapist Script 3.2).**

This exercise consists of three parts: in the first part, we will focus on shifting our attention between bodily sensations, in the second we will shift our attention between memories. The last part is dedicated to focusing on kind and compassion episodes. In this part, you will invite participants to focus on situations in which they received or offered kindness and compassion and how that made them feel.

 Therapist Tips

When we guide clients through recollecting positive memories, we are not looking for moments of complete joy. The emotional intensity experienced by the participants might be very low, especially if clients are experiencing depressive episodes; highlight that the chosen moments can just be a feeling of being OK.

Some people might still not be able to think of a moment in which they experienced being OK; in this case, you can invite them to switch perspective: *was there less of something negative? What there anything that helped you feel even just a little less bad?* Remind them **it's not their fault.** "*Notice if there are thoughts about this being your fault – remember this is just your threat system hijacking your attention*".

When conducting this practice with a clinical population, be aware that it might be harder for people to recall moments in which they received compassion, it might even be distressing for them because they can't think of anyone being kind to them. In this case, remind them that it is the effort of finding something positive that is at the heart of this training, even if we do not initially feel the way we were expecting to. In these first phases, it is important to simply orient our intention to the best of our ability.

After the experiential exercises, you might want to give space to open reflection and sharing, following it up by a brief summary of the main points:

- We can shift attention not only to our surroundings (external) or the moment, but also towards memories, emotions, and thoughts (internal)
- When we shift attention, our body and mind change accordingly
- Being caught in our threat system can cause a lot of stress and we might need to practise noticing and switching to a compassion focus (using one of our learned strategies, such as soothing rhythm breathing)

You might also wish to encourage some reflection in pairs. Invite clients to do some self-reflection using **Client Handout 3.2** and then to share what they have identified to be their compassion episodes.

Phase 3: Mindfulness

In this phase, we begin to introduce and experience the concept of mindfulness. Mindfulness skills are important for remembering to notice what we are experiencing in the moment and helping bring ourselves back into balancing emotions, perhaps by using one of our CFT practices. If we do not notice the 'moment' we go on auto-pilot (our impulsivity or distractions), then we get lost in thoughts and emotions, making it very difficult for us to steer our minds in the direction of our intentions.

In this phase, we will explore the different types of mindfulness and how they can be harnessed to cultivate our compassionate motive and our soothing system.

Main Touch Points

Therapist Script 3.3 – Mindful Breathing
Therapist Script 3.4 – Labelling Emotions
Therapist Script 3.5 – Mindful Walking
Client Handout 3.4 – The Cycle Of Mindfulness

3a) Definition of Mindfulness

   Therapist Background Knowledge

In CFT, as in other forms of psychotherapy, we use mindfulness to explore the workings of our tricky brain, as well as the content and patterns of our minds. This is crucial if we are to live to be helpful and not harmful, and, therefore mindfulness is a way to help support and cultivate our compassionate motivation.

Typically, mindfulness is embedded in three basic processes which are *intention, attention and orientation*. We develop an intention to become mindful. We practise attention and realise whether we are moving away from that intention (for example if we are experiencing mind wandering); finally, we choose how to orient toward the process. In CFT, we encourage the adoption of a friendly, compassionate orientation or attitude towards the processes in our minds that we observe, rather than a self-critical, harsh, or forceful way of practicing.

Through mindfulness, we are able to bring wisdom to two types of automatic reacting we are all biologically wired for: **impulsive reacting** and **distracted reacting**.

In impulsive reacting, we are triggered by internal or external stimuli which can switch on our threat system. When lost in loops between old and new brain processing (refer back to Module 1), worries and fears can manifest as a clouded mind.

Distracted reacting is sometimes referred to as automatic pilot – that is, automatically run behaviour programmes (for example habits or deeply ingrained behavioural routines). For example, once you have learned to ride a bicycle you don't tend to think that much about it. In this case there is no threat to which our mind is reacting, our mind has simply entered the brain's default system for thinking, daydreaming, and ruminating.

When we realise that the mind has gotten distracted, we become mindful of the possible consequences and can respond helpfully.

   Therapist Task

Before taking participants through the first mindfulness practice which focuses on breathing, (**Therapist Script 3.2**), you might want to spend some time high-lighting the intention that lies behind mindfulness.

You can use Figure 3.1 below (or even draw it on a whiteboard as you speak) to explain this concept (clients can find it in **Client Handout 3.4**).

In the first few moments of any formal mindfulness practice, perhaps while focusing on our breathing, the mind might appear rather calm and quiet (this is

MOTIVES THAT SUSTAIN MINDFULNESS

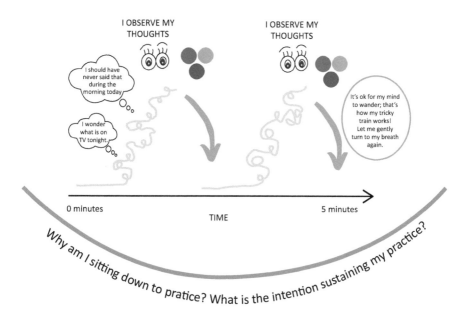

Figure 3.1 Motives That Sustain Mindfulness.

the horizontal part of the yellow line). As we sit for a while (usually a few seconds!), our mind will inevitably start wandering – as we have previously discussed, this is the nature of our tricky brain and it is not our fault. As the mind wanders, we will begin observing all kinds of thoughts: they might be thoughts about the future, about something that has happened, they might be neutral thoughts, judgemental thoughts, or anxious thoughts. Whatever their nature, they capture our attention and distract us from our breathing, which we were focusing on. The mindfulness practice is all about noticing what happens and then bringing our attention back to the breathing (or whatever anchor we had previously chosen).

One possible (and rather frequent) scenario we encounter is that, upon noticing that our mind has wandered elsewhere, we get frustrated and upset with ourselves (activating the threat system), we start criticising ourselves for not being able to focus on the breathing, for not being able to do the practice, for messing up once again. And our inner self-critical dialogue can quickly follow leading to a downward spiral. In this case we might end up finishing the practice with a sense of irritation, frustration and maybe even unworthiness.

What we wish to encourage instead is a compassionate switch of attention-focus – whenever we notice that our mind has wandered elsewhere, we wish to normalise it as part of the way the human brain works. Indeed, we can thank our mind for manifesting its ability to wander, and we can praise ourselves for noticing when this process takes place. We practise observing our mind-wandering with respect and gratitude (it can often be a source of creativity!). Then, we can gently accompany our attention back to our breathing, ready to be curious about where and what it will move on to next. This will leave us feeling deeply connected to our experience and to our compassionate motive and more likely to come back to our practice.

Therapist Tips

In our modern-day world which promotes and rewards the maximisation of productivity, mind wandering is often perceived as something bad. However, research has shown that mind wandering is not all bad; when differentiated from perseverative cognition (such as rumination and worry), mind wandering can actually facilitate creative problem solving by helping to integrate past and present experiences.

Also, we should consider that sometimes, we do not really want to be overly mindful! Think about going to the movies: you certainly would not go there to be mindfully aware of what is going on in the cinema, of the breathing of the person sitting next to you, or the texture of the seat you're sitting in; you are there to fully immerse yourself in the movie. When you go to the movies, what you are looking for is absorption, not mindfulness. Or imagine being stuck in traffic for several hours; it can be helpful to be absorbed in the music you are listening to, or let your mind wander and start dreaming about your next vacation, while it is less helpful to be mindful, moment by moment, of the traffic jam you are stuck in.

3b) Basic Mindfulness practices

   Therapist Task

Once we have explored the basic definition and functions of mindfulness, we can now begin to experience it first-hand. CFT offers several mindfulness practices, each being an opportunity to connect with a different aspect of our existence.

We suggest you begin with the practice of Mindful Breathing (**Therapist Script 3.3**), in which the anchor for our attention is the breathing itself. The Mindful Breathing practice involves pausing, observing our breathing, and noticing when our attention leaves our breathing (for example, because we get lost in thoughts, distracted by a sensation inside or outside ourselves, or caught up in an emotion).

We then move on to the practice of Compassionate Labelling (**Therapist Script 3.4**). Labelling (assigning a name) helps us to distance ourselves from disturbing thoughts and the experiences that follow and facilitates the process of dis-identification: thoughts, emotions, and moment-to-moment experiences do not define who we are but move through the body and mind. This is very helpful, especially when working with threat-based emotions.

Three-Circle Check-In

Finally, you can teach participants the practice of Mindful Walking (**Therapist Script 3.5**). This practice can be done indoors, but if you have the opportunity, it can also be wonderful to experience outdoors. You can choose whether to lead this practice during one of your sessions in-person or to leave it as an audio recording for participants to practise in their own time.

Phase 4: Widening and Deepening Your Mindfulness

Once we have become more familiar with the basic mindfulness practices and get a better idea of a mindful, compassionate attitude, we can begin bringing that mindful attitude into other kinds of activities, such as eating. As we continue to explore different aspects of mindfulness, we could also come across some fears of mindfulness – it is important to address those and start making them feel welcome and a normal part of this process.

Main Touch Points

Therapist Script 3.6 – Mindful Eating
Therapist Script 3.7 – Mindful Listening
Client Handout 3.5 – Fears of Mindfulness
Client Handout 3.6 – Mindful Café

4a) Fears of Mindfulness

 Therapist Background Knowledge

Mindfulness is often accompanied by many misinterpretations, which can make it difficult, and even scary, for people to experience it.

It is rather common to come across fears of mindfulness. For some people, these manifest as a resistance towards the practice itself, perhaps spurred on by the thought of it being useless, pointless, or just a waste of time. For others, they may present as a more outright fear of what could emerge once they give themselves a chance to slow down and be in closer contact with their feelings and thoughts.

While referring to FBRs is certainly useful to address fears of mindfulness, it can also be helpful to take some time to underline what mindfulness is not.

 Therapist Task

Mindfulness is a way of paying attention and knowing that one is paying attention, in a non-judgemental way. Mindfulness is not trying to push things away, emptying the mind of thoughts or making the mind settled. The moment consider mindfulness as an activity with a desired outcome, it becomes a task. This will bring us into a state of self-monitoring, in which we ask ourselves whether we are doing it correctly, or if others are doing it better, and so on. Mindfulness is a process which unravels moment by moment, where we give direction but do not focus on expectation.

Remind participants that mindfulness is a process, not an outcome.

You may wish to use Socratic questions to illuminate their difficulties:

- *What do you think mindfulness might help us with?*
- *What do you think is the most difficult thing with mindfulness?*
- *What might get in the way of becoming more mindful and aware of what is going on in our minds as we live our lives?*

Clients can write down or draw any FBRs to mindfulness that might have emerged during the practice or discussion in **Client Handout 3.5**.

4b) Advanced Mindfulness Practices

 Therapist Task

As previously mentioned, mindfulness is a state that we cultivate through practices, so that we may begin entering that state more often as we go about our daily lives.

This is why it can be interesting to experiment with adopting this mental (as well as physical) attitude in different situations and in different exercises.

One very insightful practice is that of Mindful Eating (**Therapist Script 3.6**). You may choose to leave this as a practice script that participants can experiment with on their own time, or you may wish to lead them through the exercise by using a small piece of food (a raisin is commonly used).

Two other practices that can be introduced are Mindful Listening (**Therapist Script 3.7**), which promotes developing mindfulness in interpersonal dynamics, and Mindful Café (**Client Handout 3.6**), that can be suggested as something to do during the week, in between sessions.

There are also many other ways to be mindful; for example, you may encourage participants to try painting or drawing in a mindful way (there are now many adult colouring books available for this purpose), listening to the same piece of music in a mindful and non-mindful way, and noticing what differences arise.

It might be fun and enriching to have each participant suggest one alternative way in which to bring mindfulness into their lives – a way to build a shared catalogue of mindfulness exercises.

Phase 5: Wrap-Up

The final phase of the module is a wrap-up of the theme that has been explored. Emphasise how continuing to work on your personal practice (whether formal or informal) can help with the development of our compassionate minds.

Main Touch Points

Therapist Script 2.5 – Closing Practice
Client Handout B – Personal Practice Diary

5a) Summary of the session and suggestions for personal practice

 Therapist Task

Take 5–10 minutes to briefly summarise the points that you have gone through in this module. You may want to provide participants with some suggestions for personal practice and self-reflection:

- Complete the **Client Handouts**
- Practise at home, choosing which homework you would like to complete (which practice and how often)
- Complete the practice diary (**Client Handout B**)

5b) Closing practice

 Therapist Task

It is important to always take a moment at the end of the session to acknowledge anything and everything that has come up for participants while exploring the themes introduced.

As in previous sessions, invite them to share their experience, in a sentence or two.

- What do I take home from today's session (because I feel it's going to be helpful)?
- What are some key things that I would like to share and tell other people about?

Facilitating the sharing of ideas and personal reflections can be very helpful on many levels: it helps to integrate what they have learned and fosters a process of group bonding.

Invite participants to bring their attention to their intention to be helpful to self and others rather than neglectful. To do so, it can be useful to anchor our memory; we could take a stone and carry it in our pocket or handbag, find a colourful bracelet that triggers our memory to be compassionately mindful. It is very useful to invite participants to think about how they can creatively remind themselves to orient themselves towards their intention.

Finally, guide clients through a short closing practice; you may wish to use **Therapist Script 2.5**, but feel free to make your own closing compassionate practice.

Therapist Scripts

Therapist Script 3.1: Compassionate Landing (8 minutes)

Use the Compassionate Landing script in Module 2 (**Therapist Script 2.1**) and integrate some references to what was addressed in the previous module.

Here is an example of how you could do this:

"[…] Allow your breathing to land here with you, recognising its patterns, as best as you can without any judgement. Begin to imagine this breath as a soothing and supportive presence, filling your lungs and expanding your body with each in-breath, releasing your tensions and letting you settle with each out-breath. Gently allow your breathing to slow down, maybe counting to 4 and then to 5 on each inhale and exhale […]"

Therapist Script 3.2: Attention as a Spotlight (10 minutes)

It is important to remember that during all these exercises our minds will wander elsewhere – let us remember that it is no tour fault, and that we should simply praise ourselves for noticing this process occurring, and then, with kindness, return to the exercise we are doing.

First off, we will begin by exploring how our attention can shift between bodily sensations.

Begin this exercise by sitting comfortably in your chair with your hands resting gently on your lap. Now bring your attention, on purpose, to your left foot. Notice the feelings in your toes and sole of your foot. Try to be curious without bringing any judgement to your experience. [10 seconds]

Now switch your attention to your right foot. [10 seconds]

Now rub you thumbs over your fingers [10 seconds]

[Things to look out for include: *what happened to the part of the body that we brought our attention to? What happened to the part of the body that we shifted our attention away from?*]

Now, we will explore how our attention can shift between memories.

Once again, we're going to be moving our attention around in our minds on purpose. Sit comfortably for a moment or two, then try to deliberately bring your attention to a memory of a time when you were smiling or laughing. Maybe somebody had told you a good joke or you were at a party; just call that to mind something that was very funny. If nothing immediately comes to mind, try to remember a funny moment from a TV show or movie, just something that made you smile or laugh.

Notice what happened to your facial muscles and your inner feelings.

Okay, now bring your attention to a memory of a time when you had either a slight worry about something or a slight irritation about something. Try to choose a memory that is not too distressing. Really go over in your mind what that was like and try to observe the feeling again.

Notice what happened in your body, to your facial expressions and your feelings.
Now, see if you can shift your attention to something that was pleasant to you, like having a nice meal, going on vacation, watching a programme you enjoy. Give yourself some time to try to engage with these feelings again. Was it easy to focus once again on something positive after having remembered something negative? If you were able to do so, how did it make you feel?

Lastly, we will try to orient our attention towards a situation in which you received or offered compassion.

Once more, find a comfortable seated position and close your eyes if that feels OK for you. Try to consciously put the spotlight on a situation in which you were helpful to someone, or someone was helpful to you. Maybe you received a smile, maybe you were given something that you felt was helpful to you. For example, someone might have held the door for you while you were running to catch the train.
Try to notice what changes occur within you when you focus on the idea of receiving and giving compassion. Notice what bodily sensations, what feelings arise.

The following are some reflection questions and points that can be used for a group discussion:

- What happened when we shifted attention from one part of the body to another?
- We don't have control over where our attention naturally goes, but we do have control over where we want to bring it – attention is like breathing (it is partially voluntary): it normally shifts without us having to think about it, but, when we choose to, we can take control over it so that it can be helpful
- For many people it is harder to focus on the positive thought the second time (after having brought to mind a negative thought) – this is normal: it's our negativity bias. This is not our fault, but simply the way our brains are wired

Therapist Script 3.3: Mindful Breathing (5 minutes)

Begin this practice by finding a comfortable seating position. Place your feet shoulder-width apart, flat on the ground. We wish to find a position that is comfortable, but not so comfortable that we fall asleep. You might like to close your eyes if you feel comfortable doing so, or you may wish to leave them slightly open, finding a spot on the wall or on the ground to focus on throughout the exercise.

Now, gently focus your attention on your breathing. Breathe so that the air enters your diaphragm – just at the bottom of the ribcage. Notice your abdomen rising and falling as you breathe in and out. Just observe your breathing for about 30 seconds.

If you're like most of us, your mind probably wandered away fairly quickly. You may have had thoughts like "How is this supposed to help me?" or "I'm hungry. I can't wait to eat". Or maybe "am I doing this right?"

The idea is just to observe your breathing and begin to notice when your attention drifts off. When you notice that your attention has left your breathing, praise yourself for having noticed it and just gently bring your attention back to your breathing again and again, over and over.

Remember that mind wandering is not your fault. In fact, it's not a fault at all. It is the very act of noticing that minds wander that enables us to develop insight, to cultivate gentle patience, that is at the heart of our practice.

We should try not to judge our thoughts and emotions when they show up; we should try not to push them away or chase them, but rather to notice them as mental events ("Oh, there's another thought") and then come back to the breath. Everything is happening exactly as it is supposed to, this is what minds are designed to do, to produce thoughts and feelings – that is exactly what you are observing now.

You can pause for some more breaths, simply observing these mental events.

Then, when you feel ready, you can start opening your eyes again and coming back to the room.

Did you notice any changes in the sizes of your three systems before and after this practice?

Therapist Script 3.4: Compassionate Labelling (7 minutes)

For this practice, we will use a memory of yours that awakens within you a specific threat-based emotion.

Begin by finding a comfortable posture, with your back well extended and your shoulders open. Once you have found it, you can begin to close your eyes, or if you prefer you can keep them slightly open, your gaze looking downwards.

Take a few moments to connect to your calming breathing, whatever form it prefers to take today.

Remain in open awareness of the sensations that are present in your body right now. Notice all these sensations, just as they are, without cultivating a desire to change them at this time. Take a few breaths to simply be one with the experience of the here and now.

Now, try to think back to a time when you felt anxiety – choose a situation that was not too distressing; it might have been, for example, the beginning of a new journey, such as the one we are on together. Try to recollect the feelings that accompanied that moment – how your body felt, what was going on in your mind, what you wanted to do.

Then, when you feel connected with the sensations involved in this anxiety, try telling yourself in a calm voice "This is my anxiety" and notice how you can observe and label it. "This is me experiencing anxiety" or "This is me in the company of my anxiety". Or simply, with a calm tone of voice, say: "anxiety" or "Hi anxiety". The intention is to notice the existence of these emotional states within us, not to chase them, or try to eliminate them.

Stay in the company of your inner states for a few more moments, noticing what happens when you begin to name them in this way.

If you notice any other emotional states in your inner landscape, try to label them this way too, and notice what happens.

Before concluding, if you feel that your anxiety is manifesting in some specific part of your body, bring one hand there, perhaps while continuing to name what you are feeling, with the intention of welcoming it as best as you can.

Then, bring your hands back to your lap, and gently when you feel up to it open your eyes again.

Therapist Script 3.5: Mindful Compassionate Walking (8 minutes)

Mindful walking is a well-known practice among mindfulness practitioners; if you or your clients are not familiar with this practice, we suggest you refer to any mindfulness manual to get a sense of how it is conducted. The script we offer here integrates elements of compassion into the traditional practice.

Begin the practice by standing up, closing your eyes for a few moments and grounding yourself in the sensations under your feet.

Notice the connection to the earth beneath you, observing the weight of your body as it is distributed on the soles of your feet. Take as much time as you need to find your centre, that point where you feel most stable, strong and solid. Assume an upright posture, your shoulders open and relaxed, your back relaxed. Notice your facial expression... Try experimenting by bringing a slight smile to your lips.

Now take a few moments to connect with your calming breath.

Then, from this grounded open posture, you can open your eyes again and begin to walk into space. If you can, allow the gentle smile to stay with you on your lips and let your gaze rest lightly on your surroundings, so that you can welcome everything that enters your field of vision with a new softness... imagine this is the first time you seeing everything around you.

Continue walking, being very mindful of the way your feet touch the ground, how the weight of your body is distributed as you place one foot in front of the other. Try to notice the rhythm of your steps, what is the pace of your walk.

[If offering this practice in a group setting, you can suggest offering a smile and connecting mindfully through your breathing to the other people who are exploring the practice together with us].

If at any time you notice your mind wandering elsewhere, gently bring it back to your step, right here, right now. Observe how grounding it can be to have a place in your body, a movement you can come back to.

As you continue to travel with your body and gaze, at all that is around you, you may wish to touch your surroundings, to establish a new kind of contact and exchange with them. You might contemplate the people that have built the walls or have painted them... or those who have laid the floor you're walking on... or all the hands that have created the objects that you're touching... or the clothes you're wearing... thank these strangers... contemplate this ongoing interconnection that we are always immersed in... Notice how it feels to be experiencing space through this compassionate, mindful stance.

Then, when you feel ready to finish the practice, you can gently stop, close your eyes once more, take one or two last mindful breaths and then open your eyes and gently transition out of the practice.

[After the practice, you can suggest that people bring this exercise with them into the outside world. If possible, they can make their way outside the building and, at first, walk as they normally would. Then, begin walking as we did during the exercise, practicing awareness and being guided by a compassionate intention. What changes in our experience of the inner and outer world?]

Therapist Script 3.6: Mindful Eating (10 minutes)

This exercise can be done with any piece of food; however, we suggest choosing a food that can be easily picked up in the hands and manipulated (e.g., a raisin, a piece of bread).

Begin this practice by picking up the piece of food and observing it. Try to notice all the different colours that characterise this piece of food, the way the light hits it, any shadows that appear in the creases outer surface of the food.

Then, start to take note of its texture, the way it feels against the skin of your fingers; notice if there are different parts to this food, with different textures. Notice how heavy or light it is.

Then smell it. Maybe close your eyes, so you can focus only on the smell of this piece of food; does it remind you of something? Does smelling it, maybe activate something in your taste buds?

Then, finally, place the piece of food in your mouth; begin to explore its texture with your tongue, then maybe with your teeth; notice how different the food's texture is when sensing it through your fingers compared with your mouth. You can then explore its taste and slowly swallow. Try to explore the sense of swallowing and how it feels to let this piece of food enter your body.

What difference did you notice with your habitual way of eating? Did you notice any differences in the food? Did you notice any differences in yourself as you were eating the food?

You can try experimenting with this way of eating at your next meal and then take some time to reflect on how it could be useful to bring the quality of mindfulness to the act of eating.

Therapist Script 3.7: Mindful Listening (10 minutes)

In this exercise, to be done in pairs, the intention is to practise mindful listening, in a way which is totally present and non-judgemental, curious about what the person in front of us is expressing not only through their words, but also through their tone of voice, facial expressions, posture, etc.

Find apartner and choose who will start talking. In turn, you will need to answer the following question: "What is alive in you right now?" Each person will have 1 minute 30 seconds to speak.

If you are talking, let the words come out freely, without judgement, knowing that the person in front of you is also bringing themselves into this space with total openness and acceptance. If at some point you do not know what to say, you can choose to remain silent or repeat the last thing you just said until nothing else that you wish to share comes up.

If you are listening, try to listen with all the presence you are capable of today. Try to notice how often your mind tends to wander elsewhere while you are listening to your partner, perhaps caught up in some external stimulus, or a thought of your own. Perhaps you might notice that you tend to immediately look for a point of contact with the person in front of you, comparing their experience to yours, or you might notice a desire or impulse to intervene, to interrupt, to suggest something. In this moment, however, all you need to do is openly listen and notice what is going on inside you and come back to listening the person in front of you. Try to listen not only to your partner's words, but also to their body, their energy.

Alternate speaking and listening 3 times in, always for a time of of 1.5 minutes.

At the end of the exercise, share with the other person what you noticed about them as you listened and what you noticed about yourself. How mindfully were you at listening to the person in front of you and how mindfully were you at listening to what dwelt within you while listening to them?

Therapist Script 3.8: Closing Practice (5 minutes)

Use the Closing practice script in Module 2 **(Therapist Script 2.5)** and integrate some references to what was addressed in the module we just finished.

For example:

"[...] And if you notice your mind being particularly distracted at this time, maybe lost in thoughts about the future or the past, recognise that this is not your fault.

Our brains are built exactly for this purpose: mind wandering does not mean we are doing something wrong. Actually, it can be at the heart of our creativity, our problem solving... but at the same time, it reminds us of our human nature, the difficulty of having a tricky brain that sometimes makes it challenging to really be present.

Simply bring your attention back here, to the present moment, and congratulate yourself for being here.

Client Handouts

Client Handout 3.1: Compassionate Weekly Reflection

Let's do a curious, friendly reflection on this past week:

Which part of the self-practice did I do and why?

Which part of the self-practice did I not do

Was this due to any anxieties or blocks regarding the practice or the path? Which ones can you identify?

We extend gratitude, respect, and compassion to resistances: What would make you and your resistances feel safer in going forward on this path?

Client Handout 3.2: Spotlight on My Day: Three Compassion Episodes

To train ourselves to orient our attention deliberately, try to think back to the past week and consciously place the spotlight on three situations in which you were kind to someone or someone was helpful to you.

Keep in mind that these can be very "small" things, like someone smiling at you, holding the door for you, calling a friend in need, carrying the groceries for an old lady at the store...

Try to focus on things you felt were helpful to you, things that made you feel good, or maybe just a bit "less bad".

For each of these situations, try to describe the bodily sensations, feelings, and thoughts that accompanied them.

My First Compassion Episode

What sensations, feeling, and thoughts accompanied or followed this compassion episode?

My Second Compassion Episode

What sensations, feeling, and thoughts accompanied or followed this compassion episode?

My Third Compassion Episode

What sensations, feeling, and thoughts accompanied or followed this compassion episode?

Client Handout 3.4: The Cycle of Mindfulness

Mindfulness is a way of paying attention and knowing that one is paying attention, in a non-judgemental way.

Mindfulness is not trying to push things away, emptying the mind of thoughts or making the mind settled. Once we view mindfulness as an activity with a specific goal, it transforms into a task, which can lead to a state of self-monitoring, as we ask ourselves whether we are doing it correctly, if others are doing it better, and so on.

Mindfulness is a process which unravels moment by moment, where we give direction but don't focus on expectation. It is like sleep: we try to create the conditions for sleep, but if we keep checking it, then we end up with thoughts like "I have to fall asleep if I want to make it through my busy day tomorrow!"

During your next Mindfulness practice, try to notice if your mind keeps returning to something in particular; what is it?

Do you notice a sense of threat?
Do you notice a sense of competition, of striving for a goal?
Do you notice a desire to cultivate calm?

THE CYCLE OF MINDFULNESS

Mindfulness is a practice of noticing and gently returning to the present moment - without trying to block or eliminate thoughts from the mind. Through mindfulness we can give conscious direction to our actions.

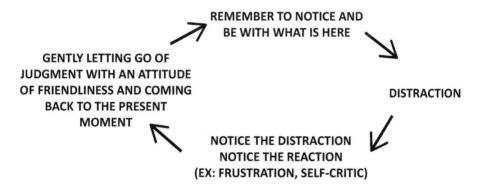

Figure 3.2 The Cycle of Mindfulness.

Take a few moments to write down your reflections:

Remember that mindfulness can be practiced with various dimensions. This applies to both the intention behind why we are practicing (why am I doing it?) and the attitude we cultivate while practicing (how am I doing it?). Try to connect with these two dimensions each time you choose to engage in mindfulness practice.

MOTIVES THAT SUSTAIN MINDFULNESS

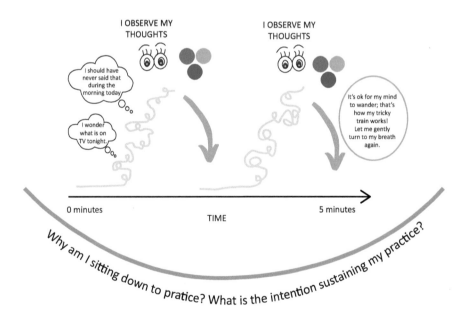

Figure 3.3 Motives That Sustain Mindfulness.

Client Handout 3.5: Fears of Mindfulness

In the box below, write or draw any fears that you feel emerge before, during or after practicing mindfulness. It is OK if you have not pinpointed the reason why these fears arise – try to focus on giving them space and a voice in this handout.

In practicing mindfulness, I noticed....

Client Handout 3.6: Mindful Café

For this practice we invite you to take your mind for a special coffee, where we will cultivate a mindful compassionate look at what we notice in the world around us.

To begin the practice, leave the house and find a place to sit: it can be a table at a coffee shop, or a bench, or maybe on some steps on the curb... choose a place from which you can observe a good flow of people.

Start by paying attention to your posture while you are sitting: what position do your shoulders take? Your arms? Is your heart open or closed? Is your gaze hard, or soft?

Now turn your curious attention to your breathing: feel the air flowing through you, the exchange you have in this moment with the space around you. Feel the air filling your chest and perhaps gently inviting it to soften.

Now, from this state of connection with yourself, bring your gaze straight ahead – everything that enters your field of vision at this moment will become the object of your attention for this exercise.

Keep your gaze straight ahead for the rest of this practice. Notice everything that enters and leaves your field of vision. Maybe there are people, beings, objects, entering and leaving your field of vision. How fast do they do it? How are they moving? Notice what effect these images have on your mind.

Notice what thoughts are activated within you as you look at the people, beings, or objects your gaze encounters; observe what quality these thoughts have. Are they neutral thoughts? Of comparison? Of criticism? Of appreciation? What do you first notice about a person or an object? What caught your attention? What system gets activated?

Gently alternate between observing what appears in your field of vision, and what manifests within you in response to what you see...both the external and internal views are unchosen, but what we can choose is the attitude of openness and curiosity toward both.

Continue practicing in this way for 5–10 minutes. Then, you can end the practice by standing up or, one last time, letting your gaze scan the space around you. Before you go turn to where you were sitting and thank it for being the place, however informal it may seem, where you allowed yourself this deeper awareness of the flow of things. Take a few moments to write what emerged during the practice.

Chapter 4

Module 4

Safety and Safeness & Receiving Compassion from Others

Aims

- To introduce the difference between safety and safeness, highlighting how safety is linked to the threat system and safeness to the soothing system
- To explore what it feels like to experience safety and what is feels like to experience safeness
- To revisit the concept of the three flows of compassion and focus on the first flow: receiving compassion from others
- To examine the concept of a compassionate image and experience what is feels like to receive compassion from another

 Deepen Your Knowledge

In Gilbert, P. & Simos, G. (Eds). (2022). *Compassion Focused Therapy: Clinical Practice and Applications*. Routledge, please refer to:

Chapter 3. The Evolved Functions of Caring Connections as a Basis For Compassion

In Gilbert, P. (2010). *Compassion Focused Therapy: Distinctive Features* (1st ed.). Routledge, please refer to:

Chapter 18. Introducing Imagery
Chapter 19. Creating a Safe Place

DOI: 10.4324/9781003436058-6

Summary of Key Processes

Table 4.1 Module 4: Safety and Safeness, Compassion From Others

Phase		Main Touch Points		Therapist Scripts		Client Handouts
1	Introduction	1a) Compassionate Landing 1b) Revision of personal practice and recap of previous session	☐	Script 4.1: Compassionate Landing	☐	Handout 4.1: Compassionate Weekly Reflection
2	Safety vs Safeness	2a) Distinguishing safety and safeness 2b) Exploring a place of safety 2c) Exploring a place of safeness 2d) Exploring a compassionate place	☐ ☐ ☐	Script 4.2: Your place of safety Script 4.3: Your place of safeness Script 4.4: Bringing others into your place of safeness	☐ ☐ ☐ ☐	Handout 4.2: Safety vs Safeness Handout 4.3: Your place of safety Handout 4.4: Your place of safeness Handout 4.5: Your compassionate place
3	The Three Flows of Compassion	3a) Compassion has three directions	☐	Script 4.5: The three flows of compassion	☐	Handout 4.6: Your three flows of compassion
4	Compassion from Others	4a) The power of imagery 4b) Receiving compassion from others	☐ ☐ ☐	Script 4.6: Compassionate Colour Script 4.7: Compassionate Image Script 4.8: Talking to your Compassionate Image	☐ ☐	Handout 4.7: Getting to know your Compassionate Image Handout 4.8: Writing a letter to your Compassionate Image
5	Wrap-up	5a) Summary of the session and suggestions for personal practice 5b) Closing practice			☐	Handout B: Personal practice diary

Phase 1: Introduction

Main Touch Points

Therapist Script 4.1 – Compassionate Landing
Client Handout 4.1 – Compassionate Weekly Reflection

1a) Compassionate Landing

   Therapist Task

As in previous modules, the compassionate landing always provides the opportunity to transition from daily life to a space of practice, compassionate inquiry, and reflection.

It is an opportunity to remind participants that they are working with the flows of compassion, which will be addressed in this very module. This routine at the beginning of every session is very important and it develops a therapeutic effect over time.

To bridge with the previous module, whose main theme was mindfulness, we shall weave into this landing meditation elements of mindfulness and soothing rhythm breathing.

You may follow the **Therapist Script 4.1** to guide participants through the compassionate landing.

Before the landing, offer a moment for a Three-Circle Check-In.

Three-Circle Check-In

1b) Revision of Personal Practice and Recap of Previous Session

   Therapist Task

Invite participants to use the **Client Handout 4.1** to reflect upon the past week/weeks; then get them into pairs or small groups and invite them to share anything relevant about their past week, including any compassion episodes or any fear, blocks, and resistances (FBRs) they might have experienced.

As always, remind them to notice the change in their tone of voice, facial expression, posture and overall physical sensations when they speak about their compassion episodes – both in themselves and in their partner – so that they can notice possible changes in their physiology when they remember moments of compassion.

Before moving on, the therapist can provide a brief recap of the last session, in which the main points were:

- The nature of attention
- Mindfulness and its applications

This can also be a space to setting the scene for the current module; the main themes that are going to be explored are:

- Safety and Safeness
- The flows of compassion
- The power of imagery
- Receiving Compassion from Others

Phase 2: Safety vs Safeness

The goal of this phase is to explore and clearly distinguish between the states of safety and safeness. This theme will be addressed through brief theoretical introductions and several experiential practices which help participants get in touch with their own felt sense of these different states of their body's physiological systems.

Main Touch Points

Therapist Script 4.2 – Your Place of Safety
Therapist Script 4.3 – Your Place of Safeness
Therapist Script 4.4 – Bringing Others into your Place of Safeness
Client Handout 4.2 – Safety vs Safeness
Client Handout 4.3 – Your Place of Safety
Client Handout 4.4 – Your Place of Safeness
Client Handout 4.5 – Your Compassionate Place

2a) Distinguishing Safety and Safeness

 Therapist Task

Learning to distinguish between safety and safeness is one of the central teachings of Compassion Focused Therapy (CFT).

We can define safety as the absence of threat, or the removal of danger; this concept evokes a sense of avoidance of what is perceived as a threat. On the other hand, safeness is defined by the presence of support; it is a set of positive, deep feelings that facilitate openness and discovery and are not equivalent to an absence of threat, but rather a presence of resources to cope with danger and exposure to threat should they do appear.

When we feel a sense of safeness, we can relax and enjoy our surroundings, take pleasure in the moment and begin to explore and try new things – we allow ourselves to be playful.

  Therapist Tips

It is important at this point to help participants become progressively aware that they are likely living in safety mode most of the time. Imagine a bird on a lawn, searching for food and eating yet constantly scanning and looking for potential threats so that it can fly away very quickly; this image probably describes how many of us feel daily. We too are prone to scanning the environment (both external and internal) to notice any signal of alarm; this is not our fault, but rather the result of our evolved brains and our automatic threat/defence system (the red circle). What distinguishes us from birds, and which makes things even harder for us, is that we are also capable of meta-cognition – we can have thoughts and harsh negative judgements (e.g., you idiot) about our worrying thoughts. These mental loops further intensify the feeling of threat and our search for safety.

The difference between the concept of safety and safeness can be exemplified through a variety of metaphors.

One such metaphor is that of the ocean.

> An example of a situation of threat would be if I wanted to cross a stretch of sea to reach a destination that is very important to me. However, there is a big storm, the sea conditions are terribly rough and the boat is at high risk of being overturned.
>
> A situation of safety would be giving up on my dream, giving up on crossing the stretch of sea and instead going as far away from the sea as possible (avoiding danger) **(safe from)**.
>
> A situation of safeness, involves the feeling of resourcefulness, strength, stability and agency even in the presence of threat – in this metaphor, it might be knowing that I'm not alone on the crossing and I have someone with me to help me make it, or that I know how to handle the boat or I have a life jacket that allows me to keep swimming **(safe to)**.

Another metaphor would be that of rock climbing.

> If we are stuck in safety mode, we will be constantly focusing on threat and trying to stop bad things from happening; this makes good sense, however it will also be stopping us from doing what we wish to do – in this case, climbing up the cliff or boulder. It might mean strapping on our harness to ensure our safety, but without ever getting off the ground.
>
> Safeness on the other hand focuses on creating the conditions to allow us to explore our surroundings and gives us courage to experience things we might fear or worry about. With a feeling of safeness comes the freedom to explore, being open to experience, enabling growth, development, and flourishing. A sense of safeness allows us to go rock climbing knowing and feeling we are secure in our harness.

You can refer participants to **Client Handout 4.2** as you explain these concepts.

As we will demonstrate in the following paragraphs, encouraging the group to come up with their own metaphors for conditions of safety and safeness can also be beneficial; when working with groups on specific issues (for example negative body image) you can prompt them to focus on safety and safeness in that particular domain.

2b) Exploring a Place of Safety

   Therapist Task

The first step in the experiential exploration of safety vs safeness is to accompany participants through the felt sense of safety. We will do so through a guided discovery; remind participants there is no right or wrong way to do this. It is an opportunity we are offering ourselves to explore our nervous system and its states.

Use **Therapist Script 4.2** or some variation of it to guide the visualisation of a place associated with safety. Remember, safety is the avoidance of threat – so this must be a place where threats are as far away as possible.

   Therapist Tips

Be mindful of the fact that this can be a particularly activating exercise for people: some might not be able to even imagine a feeling of safety, as the sense of threat can be internalised. Always validate their experience while, at the same time, trying to keep them curious about the possibility of such a place existing.

With all experiential exercises there is a chance that clients will go deep into the practice and reconnect to painful memories which can be difficult for them. As we go through the practices of safety and safeness, consider that some people might dissociate from the practice because of activating or triggering memories. If working in a group, remind participants of the guidelines of the group as you proceed with the practices.

Once you have completed the visualisation, invite participants to do some self-reflection using the following prompts, which they will also find in their **Client Handout 4.3**.

- *What bodily sensations did you experience when in a space of safety?*
- *What facial expression and what body posture do you associate with safety?*
- *Imagine walking around the room as if you were primed for safety – how would you do so?*
- *What is the configuration of your three circles when in a place of safety?*

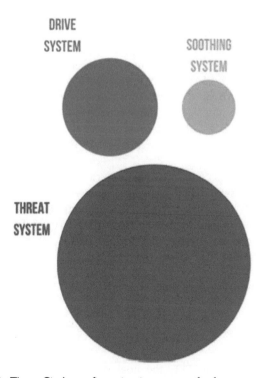

Figure 4.1 Possible Three-Circle configuration in a space of safety

Once they have explored these questions, take a moment to link the state of safety to the three-circle model. Highlight how this state can be associated with a configuration of the three circles that sees an imbalance in favour of the red circle. Have participants discuss why this might be the case. Indeed, even if the threat has been avoided, the mind may continue to anxiously monitor the environment for it; or the concept that safety prevents us from exploring the environment as much as we would like.

2c) Exploring a Place of Safeness

    Therapist Task

Having had the experience of safety, we will now go on to explore the felt sense of safeness.

Remember that safeness does not mean absence/avoidance of threat, but rather the presence of support and resources that can help us in the presence of threat. Again, use a form of guided discovery to help participants tune into what safeness feels and looks like for them. You can use **Therapist Script 4.3** or some variation of it to guide them through this visualisation exercise.

Again, once you have completed the visualisation, invite participants to do some self-reflection around the following questions:

- *What bodily sensations did you experience when in a space of safeness?*
- *What facial expression and what body posture do you associate with safeness?*
- *Imagine walking around the room as if you were primed for safeness – how would you do so?*
- *What do you like to do when you feel safeness?*
- *What is the configuration of your three circles when in a place of safeness?*

Then, link the sense of safeness to the three-circle model. Encourage them to notice how a state of safeness might be associated with a bigger green circle; the red circle might still be active, but now it is regulated by the presence of the green circle as well as a healthy blue circle, since this is a state in which we feel connected, ready to explore and primed for purposeful action.

Invite them to fill out their **Client Handout 4.4**.

2d) Exploring a Compassionate Place

    Therapist Task

As with most processes in CFT, the goal is differentiation and integration. We have distinguished our felt senses of safety and safeness, but they

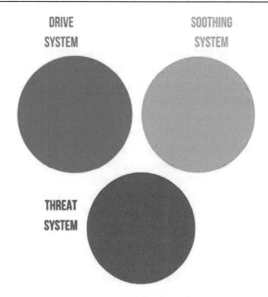

Figure 4.2 Three-Circle configuration in space of safeness

should be now integrated. In fact, while safety and safeness might appear as mutually exclusive states, the truth is we need them both in our lives. We want to have the capacity to protect ourselves, to try to avoid threats as best as possible, but also to go out into the world and explore, with the knowledge that facing some obstacles and difficulties is a natural part of life. We should, therefore, begin to contemplate the possibility that both safety and safeness must have a place and a time in our daily lives.

This integration is what occurs within our compassionate place, with this guided imagery exercise (see **Therapist Scripts 4.3, 4.4**).

After leading participants through the guided meditation, you could offer them some time for self-reflection with the help of the **Client Handout 4.5**. You can then invite them to share their experiences with the group, reminding them that we are not searching for a crystal-clear picture of this place, but rather inquiring into how imagining the existence of such a place makes us feel; one of the reasons for our doing this practice is to stimulate brain pathways and body systems.

Three-Circle Check-In

Optional Practice

A further exploration can be done through the guided meditation of *Bringing Others into your Place of Safeness* (**Therapist Script 4.5**). You can debrief this exercise by asking participants to be curious about why they wanted or why they did not want other people there – what was it about their being there that was irritating or that they wanted to reject?

Try to reflect on how bringing others into the scene might bring thoughts and feelings of being judged; not feeling judged when others are around is difficult and this is partly what makes us anxious to be around people. In the following sections we will understand how we can use the concept of flows of compassion to promote a motivational switch and turn towards compassion when this kind of anxiety might start creeping in. Remind them, however, that experiencing this fear is totally normal and not our fault – it is simply a consequence of having our red circle as the default system.

Finally, try to discuss what qualities people would need to have so that participants could still feel safe if such people were to enter their compassionate place – this discussion will be helpful when doing the work on the Compassionate Image.

 Therapist Tips

In Module 2 we touched upon the importance of distinguishing a red-fuelled drive system from a green-fuelled drive system. You can bring back this concept after the place of safeness and the compassionate place practices, asking participants to reflect on what they imagined themselves doing when they felt safe and free. These insights can be helpful on the path to building a healthy and thriving drive system which is key to living a life that feels authentic and fulfilling.

Phase 3: The Three Flows of Compassion

In this phase we will delve into a central concept of CFT, which is the idea that full compassion moves along three directional flows. Participants will already have indirectly experienced these flows during the practices we have shared up to this point, but it will be important for them to reflect on how they are tightly interwoven and often occur at the same time.

Main Touch Points

 Therapist Script 4.6 – The Three Flows of Compassion
Client Handout 4.6 – Your Three Flows of Compassion

3a) Compassion has three directions

 Therapist Task

Compassion follows three directional flows which co-exist and reciprocally strengthen each other: receiving compassion from others, giving compassion to others and giving ourselves compassion. Each of these flows has its own facilitators and inhibitors. Help participants reflect on what their facilitators and inhibitors might be using the **Client Handout 4.5**. Although one of the flows might be more difficult for us than the others, it is through working on all three together that we can really strengthen the one we feel is weaker.

 Therapist Tips

The issue of compassion fatigue might come up; this is confusion between compassion and empathy. Empathy can be a very helpful skill for us to engage with suffering, but compassion requires engagement and action. Also, there can be times when we feel burnt out or exhausted and in these instances it is most likely because our compassionate efforts are only channelled into one direction, with flow from other directions, such as receiving compassion from others, being almost completely empty. At times of burnout and exhaustion it is useful to ask yourself the following question: How much compassion am I receiving from others and how much compassion am I giving myself?

To help participants become better acquainted with the three flows of compassion and gain awareness of their experience of them, lead the group through the exercise *The Three Flows of Compassion* (**Therapist Script 4.6**). The script offers two different versions of this practice, one which works with nature images, the other which works with colour; feel free to choose the one that feels best for the group you are working with. Feel free to adapt this practice to the specific needs of your group, making sure to maintain the core element of exploring the three flows of compassion within the same exercise.

Phase 4: Compassion from Others

 Therapist Task

The first flow of compassion we begin exploring is receiving compassion from others. In this phase we will start by focusing on our ability to stimulate the brain through imagery and how this can be help with our development of compassion. We will discover how to be open to the helpfulness of others. We will engage in receiving compassion from something abstract through the *Compassionate colour* exercise and then we will build our very own *Compassionate image*.

Main Touch Points

Therapist Script 4.7 – Compassionate Colour
Therapist Script 4.8 – Compassionate Image
Therapist Script 4.8 – Talking to your Compassionate Image
Client Handout 4.7 – Getting to Know your Compassionate Image
Client Handout 4.8 – Writing a Letter to your Compassionate Image

4a) The Power of Imagery

   Therapist Task

The human brain has the capacity to produce images that affect different aspects of our bodies and minds; we use this ability in our everyday lives, often without even realising it!

By way of example, invite the group to imagine being hungry and being faced with a tempting meal; as you focus on this meal, what happens in your body?

The sight of food stimulates an area of the brain that sends messages to our body and, as a result, our mouth begins to salivate, and our stomach begins to produce gastric juices.

Then offer them the following prompts:

> Suppose you are very hungry but there is nothing to eat in the house and, therefore, you close your eyes and imagine a wonderful meal.

> What happens in your body at that point?

> Stop for a moment and really think about what is happening.

Now ask participants to salivate, on demand. They will realise that this is not possible – it's not like lifting an arm. To activate specific chemical and physiological reactions in the body, we must imagine something – imagination is the interface between our will (what we want to feel) and what happens in our body.

The images that we deliberately create in our mind are capable of stimulating the physiological systems responsible for saliva production. The same thing happens if we see or imagine sexual stimuli – the effect they have on our bodies are the same.

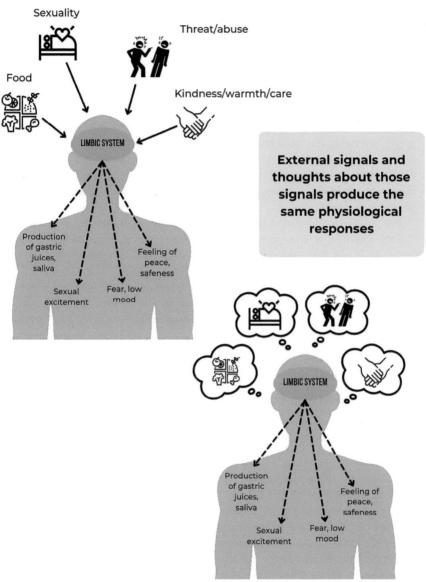

Figure 4.3 External signals and mental images both stimulate physiological systems in our bodies. Source: Adapted from Gilbert, P. (2009). *The Compassionate Mind*. London: Constable & Robinson and Oaklands, CA: New Harbinger.

We can use our ability to create mental images and focus our attention to sti-mulate systems in our bodies that are useful to us, but it is important to remember that how we stimulate our minds always plays out in our bodies too. Deliberately creating an image of safeness and compassion can help build our parasympathetic, rest.-and-digest soothing system by strengthening our vagal tone.

Therapist Tips

Constantly remind the group what is helpful here is not so much the clarity of the images, but rather the act of focusing on a particular theme. We are not trying to create perfect polaroid pictures in the mind, just fleeting impressions. We only need enough details (whichever are "right for us") to create some physical reactions (the same goes for sexual fantasies). Some participants might have greater difficulty in producing mental images. Ask them some questions to evoke fleeting images: "What is a bicycle? What is an elephant? What did you have for breakfast?"

Explain that the only way they can answer these questions is because their mind brings up images for them – they might not be crystal clear images, but good enough to give sense to what they are trying to recall.

It is also important to remember that negative images will always be more intense – this is the nature of the threat system. It's not our fault. It is therefore important to understand the motivation with which we use imagination – not to erase negative images, trying to prevent them from coming back (safety) but rather to increase our capacity to access the positive ones, so as to create balance within us (safeness).

4b) Receiving compassion from others

 Therapist Task

Opening up to receiving compassion from others is not always easy – maybe we do not trust it, we think we do not deserve it, we feel overwhelmed by it or too angry to allow it. However, being open to compassion and allowing it to come in can help our bodies and brains to become acquainted with this flow, so that it no longer activates our threat system, but rather our soothing system.

The first exercise we can try is more abstract in nature and can be useful in those cases in which there are greater FBRs towards receiving compassion from others. This practice involves identifying our *Compassionate Colour* (**Therapist Script 4.7**) and letting it move through our bodies, tuning our minds and bodies into the experience of receiving compassion and its qualities.

Optional Practice

Another way to connect to the compassion we receive from others is to focus on memories of compassionate others from our past, situations in which we have received help and support from someone. You can find a short script for leading this imagery exercise in the optional practices from Module 1, Phase 2: *Compassion from Others.*

The next step invites participants to focus on what a compassionate ideal other would look like to them and how they can relate to this *Compassionate Image.* This is often one of the most transformative practices for people, as it provides them with an image that becomes a guide and point of reference for them with their difficulties. The function of this exercise is to help people understand what are the core qualities that make someone compassionate and how it feels to be on the receiving end of that compassion.

The therapist can decide whether to guide participants through the imagery exercise before (**Therapist Script 4.8**) or after having completed the handout for *Building the Compassionate Image* (**Client Handout 4.7**). Going through the imagery exercise first might be helpful as it allows participants to tap into their inner resources without activating too much thinking, which is needed to write a description of an image.

Invite a group discussion about the compassionate image, inviting participants to share what particularly struck them about their image and the moment of their encounter. This practice can bring up a lot of emotions for some people, so be sure to allow some time to let these land and be welcomed by the energy of the group.

 Therapist Tips

It might not be easy for participants to receive a clear image at first, or they might argue that it is unrealistic to picture such an image or creature. Remind them that this practice works even when we do not have a clear image at all: we are training our minds to stimulate brain and body systems, we are learning how to work with them in an attuned way. So even the intention of creating the image helps stimulate those systems without requiring a clear image at all. It provides a felt sense of it, which is what we need.

The compassionate image is built not to soothe our problems away, but rather to act as a secure base which provides encouragement, understanding and non-judgement in the face of our distress and difficulties. Also remind them that as we repeat the practice, our compassionate image might change and this is completely fine — again, we are not really focusing on the form of this image, but on its qualities. The changing nature of the image is a testament that compassion is something fluid and flexible, which takes the form we need it to take depending on what we are going through at that moment.

 Optional Practice

If you feel there is the space for it, you can further explore the work with the compassionate image by guiding participants through the experience of *Talking to the Compassionate Image* (**Therapist Script 4.8**).

 Optional Practice

You can either ask clients to graphically represent their compassionate image; they can just depict the colours that characterise it and imagine writing a letter to this representation.

We usually suggest the practice of writing a letter to the Compassionate Image (**Client Handout 4.8**).

 Optional Practice

After writing a letter to their compassionate image, you can ask clients to take a chair, place it in front of them, and imagine their compassionate image sitting on that chair; they can then read the letter to the chair. Alternatively, in a group setting, participants can read their letters to each other in pairs.

Phase 5: Wrap-Up

The final phase of the module is a wrap-up of the theme that has been explored. Emphasise how continuing to work on your **personal practice** (whether formal or informal) can help with the development of our compassionate minds.

Main Touch Points

 Client Handout B – Personal Practice Diary

5a) Summary of the session and suggestions for personal practice

 Therapist Task

Take 5–10 minutes to briefly summarise the points that you have gone through in this module. Repetition is important to help fix the main concepts that you wish participants to focus on and take with them into the following modules.

You may want to provide participants with some suggestions for personal practice and self-reflection:

- Complete the **Client Handouts** (you may select when and how to assign handouts to complete – with some groups, it might be more useful to go through the handouts together during sessions rather than as homework, even if that means leaving some handouts out of the programme)
- Choose the homework you would like them to complete (which practice and how often); if you are not sure, listen to the audio track of one of the practices done together (this might be the *Compassionate Place* or the *Compassionate Image*, for example)
- Complete the practice diary in **Client Handout B**

5b) Closing practice

 Therapist Task

Remember to take a moment at the end of the session to acknowledge anything and everything that has come up for participants while exploring the themes offered.

As in previous sessions, invite them to share in one sentence:

- What do I take home from today's session (because I feel it's going to be helpful)?
- What are some key things that I would like to share and tell other people about?

Finally, guide participants through a short closing practice, referring to **Therapist Script 2.5.** from **Module 2** and weaving in some elements from the current session, such as referring to the concept of safeness and receiving compassion from others. Here is an example of how you could do it:

"[...] Allow your breath to land here with you, as you reconnect with the qualities of the compassionate place you created today...and maybe sense once again the presence of your compassionate image here with you...]"

Three-Circle Check-In

Therapist Scripts

Therapist Script 4.1: Compassionate Landing (5 minutes)

(Refer to Therapist Script 2.1 in Chapter 2)

You can add the following elements to link back to the previous module:

Let us welcome our Soothing Rhythm Breathing. breathe in 2, 3, 4 and out 2, 3, 4; and in 2, 3, 4, 5 and out, 2, 3, 4, 5. When we breathe out let it be a gentle, smooth exhale rather than anything forced.

Try to notice how your body responds to your breathing, as if you are linking up with a rhythm within your body that is soothing and calming to you. Feel this not just as your breathing but as an inner rhythm.

And if you notice your mind being particularly distracted at this time, perhaps lost in thoughts about the future or the past, recognise that this is not your fault.

Our brains are built exactly for this purpose: mind wandering does not mean we are doing something wrong. Actually, it can be at the heart of our creativity, of our problem solving... but at the same time, it reminds us of our human nature, the difficulty of having a tricky brain that sometimes makes it challenging to really be present.

Simply bring your attention back here, to the present moment, and congratulate yourself for coming back...

Therapist Script 4.2: Your Place of Safety (5 minutes)

In this practice we are going to explore a place of safety, a place where you feel safe and protected from threats. I will be providing suggestions for what this place might look like, but I encourage you to depict your own place and time if you do not resonate with what I am suggesting.

Begin by taking a comfortable seat on a chair or on the floor. Give yourself a moment to close your eyes, if it feels OK to do so today, and to ground yourself into your seat. Feel your breath, and remember that it is your anchor – you can come back to the present moment any time you want by keeping a connection with the sensations of your breathing.

Now, when you are ready, begin to depict in your mind a place in which you feel you have been able to avoid or escape from threats. You know that threats exist, that they are "out there somewhere", but the place where you are now is protected, shielded, so that you can keep them far way, so that you can avoid them.

You might picture yourself surrounded by a fortified building, or by a luminous circle that creates an impassable barrier from all the threats out there, or perhaps even in a bunker. Try to imagine the protective walls that keep you away from outside threats. How do you imagine this protective barrier? Is it a circle? A bubble? Insurmountable walls? A bunker? Look around you, are there items in this protected space that contribute to your feeling of safety? How big is this space? Are there people with you, or are you alone?

Try to notice how your body feels and moves in this space surrounded by protective boundaries. Notice how your mind feels; what kind of thoughts arise?

Do any thoughts arise at all? What emotions do you feel being inside this space protected from outside threats? What colours do you associate with this space of safety? Are there any sounds?

What do you feel you would like to do or not do in this place of safety? Do you feel you would like to stay here longer or not? Give yourself permission to explore with curiosity and non-judgement any awareness that might emerge while you are here.

Then, very gently, begin to let go of this image and when you feel ready come back to the room and open your eyes.

For the therapist: this imagery exercise can present as anxiety-inducing or oppressive for some patients – remind clients to give themselves permission to interrupt the exercise if they wish, or to regulate the intensity. Safety behaviours are focused on the prevention of harm. Attention is focused on the detection of signals of threat and harm. Therefore, it is possible that patients experience this state of safety as inducing anxiety or threat.

Therapist Script 4.3: Your Place of Safeness (8 minutes)

Let's begin with gently turning our attention to the present moment. Let's engage in our soothing rhythm breathing and create a sense of grounding in the body. Bring a quality of openness and stability to your posture...

Now allow your mind to drift and begin welcoming the image of a place that is ideal for you at this moment. It is exactly as you would like it to be, it is the ideal place to give you a feeling of calm, of security, a welcoming energy... you experience a sense of great freedom in this place...

What do you see around you?

What scent should this place have to really make it yours?

What temperature would you like the air to be? Imagine the sensation of this temperature on your skin.

Also try to imagine the sounds you would like to fill this place to make it really comfortable and welcoming for you. Maybe these are the sounds of nature, like the birds singing, or a babbling brook, or a crackling fire...

In this place you are completely free to do as you please.... How would you like to move through the space? What would you like to do? Perhaps sit somewhere, or lie on the floor or maybe walk or dance... or maybe even fly... or swim and be able to breathe underwater... whatever you feel the desire to do in this moment, you can do so now...

The place itself takes joy in you being here. Imagine this place takes pleasure from your presence here. It is your special place, and somehow it shows how happy it is that you have come to visit and that you are here... How does it show you this? How do you feel receiving this message of welcoming and happiness for your presence? In what part of the body do you feel this sensation?

This is your place which is especially for you. Explore your feelings when you imagine this place is happy about your being there. Even if it is just a fleeting sense of where the image might be, create a facial expression of friendliness and openness as you imagine being welcomed; allow yourself to have a soft smile of pleasure at being there.

As you get ready to step away from this place, remember that it will be accessible to you whenever you need it. This place will always be ready to welcome you and will be happy for you to visit it.

You may want to snap an internal picture that captures the most beautiful moment of this visit to this special place.

Return to your breathing and give yourself permission to pause on this breath for a few moments, noticing its quality, whatever it may be.

Then, when you feel ready, return to the room and gently open your eyes.

Further exploration: your compassionate place (6 minutes)

As you connect more deeply with this image, you begin feeling that this is place is an ancient place, with a lot of wisdom.

This place has seen innumerable storms, it has lived through so many changes, it has welcomed many seasons, sun-filled days and dark nights, storms and sun again... it knows that you also have to face your own storms, your dark nights,... Feel the expanse of wisdom in this place, how much it wishes to transfer these qualities to you...

If you turn around, you can see that somewhere in this space there is the entrance to your place of safety – this wise compassionate place knows that we often need to protect ourselves, to hide and seek refuge in our bunker... but at the same time we feel that out there, this place gives us the strength and the courage to face our own hardships, the wisdom to welcome the constant changes of the seasons in our lives.

For a couple of moments, let us try to connect with this quality of our compassionate place, which sees the wisdom in finding refuge as well as in courageously exploring what lies outside, supported and encouraged by its presence.

Therapist Script 4.5: Bringing Others Into Your Place of Safeness (5 minutes)

In this next exercise, we are going to explore what happens when we either bring people in or take people out of our place of safeness. Now remember, there is no right or wrong way of doing it; this is just a way of exploring our minds a little bit and seeing what happens.

For the moment let's get back into our soothing rhythm breathing, posture, and sense of grounding; then when you are ready, just allow the images (which may just be fleeting sensations) of your safe place to emerge.

If you were alone in your place of safeness, try to imagine what would happen if you allowed other people in there. Would they disturb you? Who do you feel might enter this space without changing the sense of safeness that reigns here? There is no right or wrong, just notice what comes up. As best as you can, try to just stay curious.

If you were already with someone in your safe place, try to imagine how you would feel if that person weren't there... how would this place need to change so that you still feel safe here? Imagine being supported, protected... maybe this place changes so you still feel good here... What do you notice?

Pause and then take reflections.

Therapist Script 4.6: The Three Flows of Compassion (10 minutes)

Let us begin by finding a position we are comfortable in at this time; for this practice, you may choose whether to sit on the floor, perhaps with the support of a cushion, or on a chair. Give yourself some time to find what feels ok with your body.

Once you have found your position, begin to settle and when you feel ready, close your eyes; if closing your eyes does not feel comfortable, feel free at any time to open them, maybe keeping your gaze soft and lowered.

Sink into the feeling of your body being here, become aware of the space you are inhabiting. Observe the way your body subtly moves without you having to do anything, and start to follow the rhythm of your breath, entering and exiting the body; ceating space as the air flows in, creating softness as the air flows out.

The breath we are connecting to reminds us that there is always a present moment that we can come back to; it is a friend that helps ground us right here, right now.

For a moment, allow yourself to contemplate all the ways in which the world had been compassionate towards you, in small and big ways. Allow your mind to connect to all the little things that the world and others have done or are doing to help you. We can start with the chair we are sitting on, or the clothes we are wearing – they are all things that other people crafted for us. Small things, that we take for granted - have been designed and thought about by other minds, which we are connected to. We can also connect to people who today, or this past week, have been nice or kind to us, who have shown some form of appreciation or friendliness. Is there someone that has been helpful, or kind, who has done something for you this week? If no one comes to mind, we can connect to the fact that the air we are breathing is the product of the transformative work of plants – we are breathing the gifts of plants.

Now connect to any moments in which you were helpful or kind to someone this week. It might have been someone who needed help, someone you smiled at. Maybe you can remember someone being grateful to you. Can you bring to mind someone whose day you made just a little bit brighter by smiling at them, sending them a message?

Finally, to close the circle of compassion, think back to any small or big ways in which you took carc of yourself, you listened to your needs. Maybe tuking u shower, taking a walk... or maybe realising that you needed a break or to chat *with someone, and you allowed yourself to do so. How were you caring towards yourself this week?*

Before opening your eyes, if it feels right for you, you can capture this flow of compassion with a hand gesture... you can bring one hand to your heart or to rest on your abdomen and one hand with the palm facing outwards, raised in the air in front of you – imagining that at the same time we are receiving compassion from others, giving compassion to others and giving compassion to yourself all at the same time. You are part of the fabric of compassion.

Say thank you to yourself and to others for this connection, then, gently open your eyes.

Therapist Script 4.7: Compassionate Colour (7 minutes)

Practice soothing rhythm breathing for a while, and when you feel ready, imagine a colour that you associate with compassion or a colour that carries within it a sense of warmth and kindness.

Again, it may just be a fuzzy feeling, but when you feel ready, imagine this colour (or colours) being right in front of you, in whatever shape you prefer... maybe a sphere emanating colourful light... these colours are wise, strong and want to help you right now.

Now try to imagine this colour surrounding you.Feel this colourful light presence surrounding your entire body.

At this point, imagine the colour slowly entering inside your body, through a point near your heart area.

Once the colour has entered your body, try to think of it as having wisdom, strength, and deep commitment and intention to help you. If you like, create a friendly facial expression as you do this exercise.

Try to imagine that the colour wants to help you; imagine that its only intention is to help you and to help the parts of your body that are currently in pain or tension. Try to sense this colour's intention of helpfulness as it moves through your body, down your legs, down your arms, and up your back and into your neck and shoulders, moving towards your jaw, face and head.

Do you notice any part of the body that seems to particularly need to be enveloped in and nourished by this colour? Grant this part all the time it needs to feel the compassionate help of the colour around and within it.

Now imagine your whole body is flooded with this colour or touched by this colour of compassion, imbuing you with its wisdom, courage, and warmth.

Then, gently, open your eyes.

Therapist Script 4.8: Compassionate Image (13 minutes)

First, contact your soothing rhythm breathing and compassionate expression; bring your compassionate place, sounds, sensations, and visual features back to mind. Remind yourself that this is your place and that it feels pleasure that you are here. This may be the place where you wish to create and meet your compassionate image.

In a little while you will receive a visitor, a warm and compassionate presence. Whatever image comes to your mind, keep in mind that it is your own creation and, therefore, it embodies your personal ideal – what you would really like to experience from being loved and the object of caring attention.

However, in this part of the practice, it is important that you try to give your image certain qualities....

- It is a wise creature – it knows that "we all just happened to be here," grappling with brains we didn't design and with early life experiences that shaped us, but that we didn't choose... It understands our lives.... what we have done to defend ourselves...our fears...this creature, at some stage in its evolution, has gone through the same experiences as we have...it knows what we are feeling... It has evolved through these very experiences and truly understands the many battles we face in our lives. It knows that we have all "just found ourselves here", trying to do the best we can with the resources we have. They are never judgemental or critical, they understand your struggles and accepts you exactly as you are.
- They are a strong and courageous creature – they are not overwhelmed by your pain or stress, but deeply desires to stay present and face suffering with you....
- They feel real appreciation for you, cares and cherishes you unconditionally. They show a deep commitment to you – they have a strong desire to help you heal, face and alleviate suffering, and experience joy in your life.

You can imagine your image emerging from the mist in front of you, for example. The image can also walk toward you. What do you see, what does it feel like? Where does it stand? Place yourself at the ideal distance.

Now focus on the idea that your compassionate image is looking at you with an expression of great affection and warmth. Imagine that it has the deepest desire:

- That you are well
- That you are happy
- That you are free from suffering

Now this image would like to tell you something, something that is exactly what you would need to hear at this time in your life. If it has nothing to say to you, that is okay too. Stay with your image until it has given you the feeling that it has conveyed all of its presence to you.

Or maybe you want to say something. The image is there to listen to you completely and deeply, whatever you want to share.

In a little while your compassionate image will be gone, but first it would like to give you something? Perhaps a material object? It places it in your open hands or it simply appears in your hands. What is it? Take a good look at it. Try *to feel its texture, its weight, its shape and observe what feelings it sends back to you.*

Then, thank your compassionate image for the message it brought you today, for the object it left you, or even simply for its presence.

Imagine capturing this encounter in a photograph or a painting, that captures the most helpful moment of your encounter with this creature.

Prepare to say goodbye. Remember that you can re-contact your compassionate image whenever you feel the need, and the creature will always be really happy to meet you, spend time with you and offer you support with whatever you are going through. Slowly let go of your compassionate image, but somehow you feel its presence and energy remain within you. When you feel ready, gently, reopen your eyes.

Therapist Script 4.9: Talking to Your Compassionate Image (7 minutes)

(Begin with Practice 4.8)

Bring your Compassionate Image to mind and then imagine that you can ask its help regarding an unresolved issue.

When you are facing your compassionate image, begin telling them your problem or the situation that you would like to receive help with. How would you speak to your image?

Try to explore with curiosity what your compassionate creature feels and thinks about the issue, whether it openly tells you or not. Spend time in its presence, without expecting an answer but with a genuine desire to receive its support.

The compassionate creature may want to tell you something....something that springs from the depths of their wisdom, strength, and intention to help you.

Or maybe your compassionate image would like to give you an object that captures and communicates its message of presence and help. What object would it be?

Whatever happens or does not happen, try to cultivate the sole intention of openness toward the presence of this creature, whose only intent is to be supportive of you and to ease your burden during this difficult time.

When you feel ready, you can thank the image and say goodbye if you wish to do so, feeling its happiness that you have turned to them for advice... and how much they wish for you to come back for advice any time you wish...

Now you can kindly come back to the awareness of the sensations present in your body in this moment and open your eyes.

Client Handouts

Client Handout 4.1: Compassionate Weekly Reflection

Let's do a curious, friendly reflection on this past week:

Which part of the self-practice did I do and why?

Which part of the self-practice did I not do?

Was this due to any anxieties or blocks regarding the practice or the path? Which ones can you identify?

We extend gratitude, respect, and compassion to the resistances: What would make you and your resistances feel safer in going forward on this path?

Client Handout 4.2: Safety vs Safeness

Safety

Safety is when you are focused on threats and look to stop bad things happening. This makes good sense, but constantly checking if you are in a situation of safety can stop you from doing what you want or need to do.

Figure 4.4 Expression of safety (1).
Source: Image generated by Midjourney 5.1

Figure 4.5 Expression of safety (2).
Source: Image generated by Midjourney 5.1

Safeness

Safeness focuses on creating the conditions to allow us to explore our surroundings and gives us courage to explore things we might fear or worry about. With a feeling of safeness come the freedom to explore, to be open to new experiences, enabling growth, development, and flourishing.

Figure 4.6 Expression of safeness.
Source: Image generated by Midjourney 5.1

Client Handout 4.3: Your Place of Safety

Describe your place of safety; do not worry about grammar, you can just use key words if you prefer!

Draw your place of safety (or elements of it). The drawing does not need to be perfect and sometimes simply colours alone are enough to capture the idea of your place of safety:

What metaphor would you use to describe the sensations you experience when in a state of safety? Or what would you say your experience of safety was like or similar to?

What do your three circles look like when you are in a state of safety or seeking a state of safety?

You might wish to use other mediums to explore your place of safety.

- You can create a vision board (either digital or using a poster) where you can include images from the Internet or magazines, pictures, drawings, or words that evoke a sense of safety.
- Reflect on what smells bring you a sense of safety; try to surround yourself with these smells and notice what sensations and states of mind these smells spark.
- Create a Spotify playlist for your place of safety; if you want, you can share this with the group!

Client Handout 4.4: Your Place of Safeness

Describe your place of safeness:

Draw your place of safeness (or elements of it). The drawing does not need to be perfect and sometimes colours alone are enough to capture the idea of your place of safeness:

What metaphor would you use to describe the sensations you experience when in a state of safeness? Or what would you say your experience of safeness was like or similar to?

What do your three circles look like when you are in a state of safeness?

You might wish to use other mediums to explore your place of safeness.

Client Handout 4.5: Your Compassionate Place

Describe your compassionate place:

Draw your compassionate place (or elements of it): The drawing does not need to be perfect and sometimes colours alone are enough to capture the idea of your place of safeness:

What metaphor would you use to describe the sensations you experience when in your compassionate place? Or what would you say your experience of the compassionate place was like or similar to?

What do your three circles look like when you are in a compassionate space?

You might wish to use other mediums to explore your compassionate place and space:

- You can create a vision board (either digital or using a poster) where you can include images from the internet or magazines, pictures, drawings, or words that evoke a sense of safeness and safety together.
- Reflect on what smells you would want to have in your compassionate place; try to surround yourself with these smells and notice what sensations and states of mind these smells spark.
- Create a Spotify playlist for your compassionate place, a soundtrack you would like to play when you occupy this space; if you want, you can share this with the group.

Client Handout 4.6: Your Three Flows of Compassion

YOUR THREE FLOWS OF COMPASSION

FACILITATORS   INHIBITORS

_____   _____
_____   _____
_____   _____
_____   _____
_____   _____
_____   _____

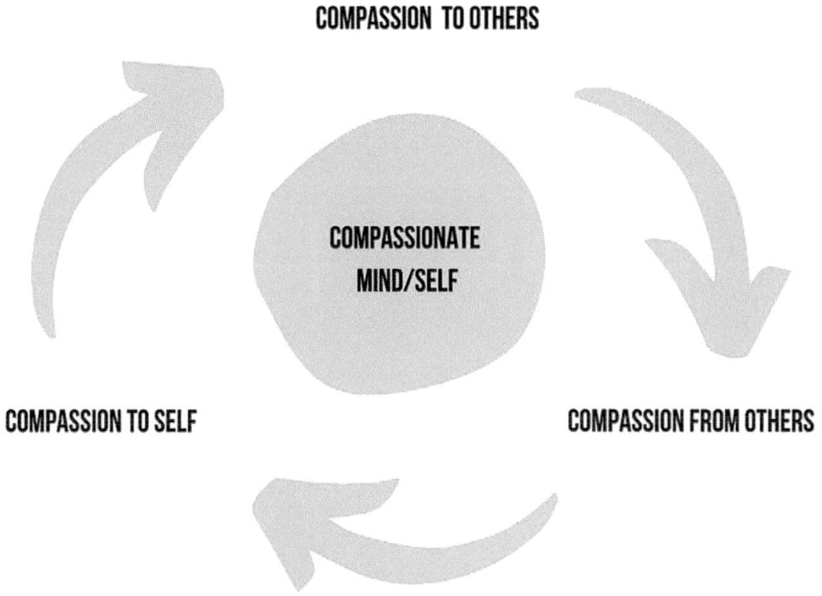

COMPASSION TO OTHERS

COMPASSIONATE
MIND/SELF

COMPASSION TO SELF   COMPASSION FROM OTHERS

FACILITATORS   INHIBITORS   FACILITATORS   INHIBITORS

_____ _____   _____ _____
_____ _____   _____ _____
_____ _____   _____ _____
_____ _____   _____ _____
_____ _____   _____ _____
_____ _____   _____ _____

Figure 4.7 Your three flows of compassion.

© Petrocchi, Kirby and Baldi (2025), *Essentials of Compassion Focused Therapy*, Routledge

Client Handout 4.7: Getting to Know Your Compassionate Image

Try answering these questions, which will help you reflect on what you would really like to receive from a compassionate presence. Remember that this image possesses three very important qualities: the wisdom derived from the knowledge that we are all here, on this Earth, without having chosen our complex brain, place, or family into which we were born; the strength, determination, and courage to cope with our difficulties and suffering; and the deep desire to be supportive and to alleviate our pain and suffering.

How would you like your compassionate image to appear (e.g., human or non- human features, male or female, age – try to reflect on his or her visual image – eye colour, hair length, facial expression). Is he or she standing beside you or in front of you? Remember that you may not get clear images but rather a vague idea, a hint of what you would like this figure to look like – that is perfectly fine.

What sounds would you like to characterise your ideal compassionate image (e.g.: volume and tone of voice)?

What other sensory qualities would you like it to have?

How would you like the compassionate image to interact with you?

How would you like to interact with this compassionate image?

Focus on what you feel is most helpful about the image. Always consider the three core qualities of a compassionate image.

- *Wisdom/insight*
- *Strength/determination*
- *Commitment/dedication*

Client Handout 4.8: Writing a Letter to Your Compassionate Image

Imagine writing a letter to your compassionate image.

You can write it by hand and place it in an envelope, perhaps actually putting it in the mailbox; or you can write it on the computer and use a programme that allows you to receive it as an email in five years (www.futureme.org).

Imagine writing to your compassionate image who sees you through their immense wisdom and non-judgemental gaze, great solidity and the desire to be there for you and with you, especially in the most difficult times.

What would you need to say right now to your compassionate image, knowing that you will not be judged in any way and that it is there with the profound desire to help you, whatever you might be going through (including difficulty with experiencing compassion!)?

What questions would you like to share, knowing that you will receive unconditional acceptance, but not necessarily an answer?

You can begin your letter like this:

Dear compassionate image (or, if you have a name or a nickname, you may go with that).

Thank you for appearing, I have just met you....

Chapter 5

Module 5

The Compassionate Self

DOI: 10.4324/9781003436058-7

Aims

- To introduce the idea of different motives and social mentalities
- To introduce the idea of the Compassionate Self as an evolved social mentality
- To build and train the Compassionate Self
- To learn to use the Compassionate Self through acting skills
- To embody the Compassionate Self in our daily lives

 Deepen Your Knowledge

In Gilbert, P. & Simos, G. (Eds). (2022). *Compassion Focused Therapy: Clinical Practice and Applications*. Routledge, please refer to:

Chapter 8. Compassionate Mind Training: Key Themes

In Gilbert, P. (2010). *Compassion Focused Therapy: Distinctive Features* (1st ed.). Routledge, please refer to:

Chapter 21. Developing the Compassionate Self

Summary of Key Processes

Table 5.1 Module 5: The Compassionate Self

Phase		Main Touch Points	Therapist scripts	Client Handouts
1	Introduction	**1a)** Compassionate landing **1b)** Revision of personal practice and recap of previous session	☐ **Script 5.1**: Compassionate Landing	☐ **Handout 5.1**: Compassionate Weekly Reflection
2	Compassion as a brain-body pattern	**2a)** Motives and social mentalities **2b)** The concept of self	☐ **Script 5.2**: Tapping into our social mentalities ☐ **Script 5.3**: Memory of a Compassionate Self	☐ **Handout 5.2**: Social Mentalities ☐ **Handout 5.3**: Memory of a Compassionate Self
3	Building and training the Compassionate Self	**3a)** The Compassionate Self as a "role"	☐ **Script 5.4**: Embodying the Compassionate Self	☐ **Handout 5.4**: The intent of my Compassionate Self
4	The Compassionate Self in Action	**4a)** The Compassionate Self at work	☐ **Script 5.5**: Compassionate Listening ☐ **Script 5.6**: Compassionate Companions	☐ **Handout 5.5**: Compassionate Listening for the Self
5	Wrap-up	**5a)** Summary of the session and suggestions for personal practice **5b)** Closing practice	☐ **Script 5.7**: A Day as my Compassionate Self	☐ **Handout B**: Personal practice diary

Phase 1: Introduction

Main Touch Points

Therapist Script 5.1 – Compassionate Landing
Client Handout 5.1 – Compassionate Weekly Reflection

1a) Compassionate Landing

  Therapist Task

The last module was in part dedicated to delving into the concept of the three flows of compassion – this landing can be a good time to remind participants that they are already cultivating the three flows of compassion during these very sessions, as they begin to welcome the difficulties of others, are exposed to their supportive presence and learn to offer themselves that same kind of support.

To bridge with the previous module, whose main theme was safety, safeness and receiving compassion, you can use elements of the safe place practice as well as the compassionate image practice to help participants land.

You may follow the **Therapist Script 5.1** to guide participants through the Compassionate Landing.

Three-Circle Check-In

1b) Revision of personal practice and recap of previous session

  Therapist Task

Invite participants to use the **Client Handout 5.1** to reflect upon the past week/weeks; then get them into pairs or small groups and invite them to share (if they would like to do so) anything relevant about their past week, including any practices done or any fears, blocks, and resistances (FBRs) they might have experienced.

Again, remind them to notice the change in their tone of voice, facial expression, posture, and overall physical sensations when they speak of their compassion episodes – both in themselves and in their partner.

Therapist Tips

As you move forward with the sessions, both you (the therapist) and the participants will begin to feel more at ease with each other. Where and when appropriate, you might feel called to share your own reflections and personal experiences with integrating aspects of what is covered in the module (self-disclosure). This is not mandatory nor necessary for the training to work, but in our experience, it does help to create a greater sense of shared humanity (universality) and it is a powerful reminder that we are all facing difficulties. A key component of Compassion Focused Therapy (CFT) is the group context, so letting yourself be an integrated part of the group becomes an instructive experience for the participants. Before any self-disclosure, remember why you are doing it: to be as helpful as possible to the group or client. Remember that sharing one's own moments of difficulty and/or resentment when doing the same practices that we are teaching can be extremely validating for the participants.

Before moving on, the therapist can provide a brief recap of the last session, in which the main points were:

- Safety and safeness
- The flows of compassion
- The power of imagery
- Receiving Compassion from others

This can also be a space to setting the scene for the current module; the main themes that will be explored are:

- Compassion as a brain-body pattern
- Understanding the differences between motives and social mentalities
- Getting to know our Compassionate Self
- Using the Compassionate Self

Phase 2: Compassion as a Brain-Body Pattern

In this phase we aim to introduce participants to the core concepts of motives and social mentalities. Furthermore, we will reflect on the concept of the self, with the realisation that humans have many different potential patterns within them, some which can be chosen voluntarily, others which turn up involuntarily. The Compassionate Self is a motivational state we can choose and which becomes rooted within us with time and practice.

Main Touch Points

Therapist Script 5.2– Tapping into our Social Mentalities
Therapist Script 5.3– Memory of a Compassionate Self
Client Handout 5.2 – Social Mentalities
Client Handout 5.3 – Memory of a Compassionate Self

2a) Motives and social mentalities

 Therapist Background Knowledge

Social Mentality Theory underpins CFT, and within this theoretical framework it is critical to understand what is meant by motives and social mentalities. For more in-depth discussion on the theoretical underpinnings of CFT, please see Chapter 2 in Gilbert & Simos.

Motives are the reasons we think, feel and do things. Motives can be employed in all life tasks. Life tasks can be both non-social and social. The first of these to be addressed are the non-social tasks, i.e., our three basic survival life tasks, which in CFT are represented through the Three-Circle model (see Module 2): 1) harm avoidance; 2) seeking resources necessary for survival and reproduction; and 3) rest and digest.

As humans are a hyper-social species and social processing involves important contextual role relationships and challenges, in CFT we are very focused on social life tasks, which are called social mentalities. CFT distinguishes five main social mentalities (see Figure 5.1 below). What is key in each social mentality is the interplay and co-regulation with others. In fact, these mentalities send and receive information to create role formation and facilitate role synchrony. For example, care seeking and care providing are reciprocal in nature and have co-evolved; one cannot survive without the other. Each social mentality has core fears, which CFT targets in formulations and interventions (e.g., internal and external fears and safety behaviours).

 Therapist Task

Inform your clients that CFT is very focused on motivation, and given humans are a hyper-social species we have deep rooted social motives. The five main social motives are: competing, cooperating, sexual, care seeking and care receiving. These social motives are provided in **Client Handout 5.2**.

Rather than just reading and becoming aware of these social motives, it can be a useful exercise to provide participants with a felt experience of how these motives orient body sensations and how they organise the mind. You may use

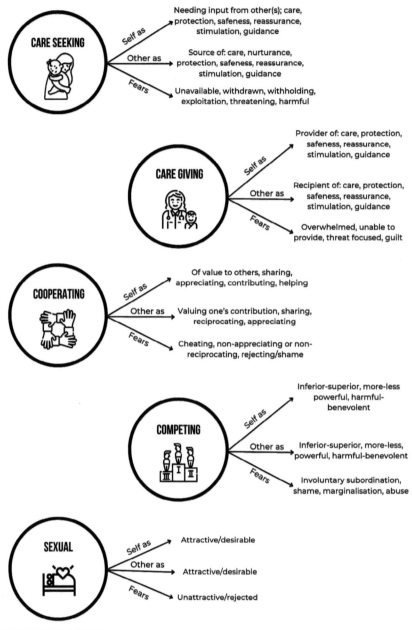

Designed using iages from flaticon.com

Figure 5.1 The social mentalities.
Source: Adapted from Adapted from Gilbert, P. (1992). *The evolution of powerlessness.*
Psychology Press

Therapist Script 5.2 to guide them through a practice that uses imagery to elicit the five social mentalities: competing, cooperating, sexual, care seeking, and care receiving.

After the exercise, offer some space for discussion about what they noticed and experienced – this practice provides a powerful example of motivational shifting. In fact, it can help participants acquire greater awareness of how quickly our bodies and minds can shift between social mentalities. Sometimes, when feature detection occurs below the level of conscious awareness, these shifts can occur in a very subtle way, and we can end up finding ourselves immersed in sensations and emotions we have a hard time cognitively understanding. This is when leaning into our Compassionate Self can be of great help.

The use of metaphors to illustrate these points is sometimes very helpful. Here are two you can use with your clients.

> *If you noticed your boss was struggling with something, really stressed out – what would you do? What mentality would you be in?*
> *Now let's imagine while listening to your boss about their difficulty they say to you that you have been underperforming at work:*
> *What are you thinking and feeling now, what do you want to do – what mentality are you in?*
>
> *Imagine someone you find attractive is trying to order a drink, so you help and get the waiters attention.*
> *What mentality are you in? How are you feeling and thinking?*
> *When they reply, "Thank you so much, I've been waiting so long my boyfriend/girlfriend will be getting annoyed".*
> *What mentality are you in now? How are you feeling/thinking?*

These examples often help clients realise that mentalities can bounce around very quickly.

It is also important to remember that social mentalities can overlap (when a father is playing a game of tennis with his daughter, the competitive mindset overlaps, momentarily, with the caretaking mindset, which is activated at baseline), some are more conscious than others, some are compensations (e.g., competing for status could be because we want affection), and people switch between them. Indeed, the ability to switch between them is a mark of health, for example, a man who can successfully compete in the job market but be a loving father at home, rather than also trying to compete with his children for his wife's affection and time.

How Does Compassion Fit Into All of This?

Compassion acts as an overarching regulator of motives and social mentalities; in fact, it has evolved from the social mentalities themselves, in particular the care giving/care receiving mentalities. As introduced in Module 1, compassion can be defined as *a sensitivity to suffering in the self and others with a commitment to try to alleviate and prevent it*. It differs from caring because it uses new brain competencies, in particular knowing awareness, empathic awareness and knowing intentionality.

As illustrated in the image below, in CFT compassion occurs when we deliberately and intentionally use our new brain competencies to guide our caring social mentalities to address the suffering and needs of others and ourselves.

A lion could never with knowing awareness, empathic awareness and knowing intentionality stop eating baby zebras. It cannot go "you know what, I feel so bad about eating these baby zebras, about their mothers grieving (knowing awareness and empathic awareness), just terrible. I am going to go vegetarian (knowing intentionality)".

Yet, as humans, with our new brains competencies we can make those choices all the time. Given that humans can have a knowing awareness, there are people choosing to dedicate their lives to helping others with knowing awareness and intentionality. And even though we might not feel like helping people, we do, and we actively choose to override emotions at times, or make deliberate choices to help others.

So, compassion is the transformation of basic care giving and care eliciting, and it is crucial in our world.

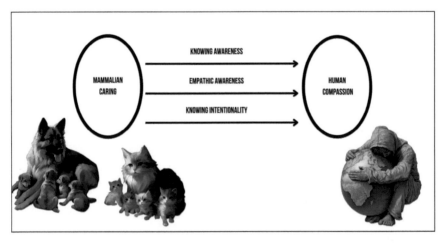

Figure 5.2 Compassion as an evolved social mentality.
Source: Adapted from Gilbert, P. (2018). Living Like Crazy with permission Annwyn House – images generated by Midjourney 5.1

2a) The concept of self

    Therapist Background Knowledge

In this section of the training, we have the opportunity of discussing the multi-layered essence of self-identities – CFT posits that there is no unitary self, but rather that we carry specific identities linked to specific roles, each with their own specific competencies.

Some identities may be chosen voluntarily, others may turn up involuntarily and may be unwanted or unpleasant. For examples, self-identities can be:

- An identity that you have but do not want because of the hurt that comes with it (being part of a gender, or sexual, or racial minority; or perhaps a culturally relevant social stigma, for example being overweight).
- An identity that you seek in relationship to a group that gives you a sense of social connectedness and safeness (being part of a political group).
- An identity you feel you do not have (maybe you have not really thought about it) but that you can work on creating and cultivating (for example, a person may not regard themselves as a competent musician, or golfer but can become one). As we shall see, the compassionate identity is something we can cultivate.

    Therapist Task

A central concept in CFT is the fact that we did not choose some of the identities that we "inhabit" more or less rigidly (refer to Module 1 and the Realities of Life practice). However, given that we are dealing with the brain, which has been choreographed to mold to an identity to fit a certain social niche (family and group), we need to learn how to consciously switch into new self-identities and brain patterns. This is a very crucial narrative at the center of CFT – and one which you will come back to time and time again.

Rather than considering the existence of one true, single self, we are called to adopt the view whereby all of us are a collection of many patterns. You may remind participants of the discussion on brain patterns and emotions in Module 2, and elicit a short discussion by asking: *"Which pattern is the real you?"* There is no "real you," or "real pattern," of course, but the one we nourish and train is the one that we will feel is the strongest.

How many "selves" have you been today? Some "roles" can induce the emergence of specific self-states. These examples may not work for everyone, but they can provide opportunity for reflection.

"Maybe you woke up and prepared breakfast for your children (caring self), then went to work and prepared a presentation that needs to win over your boss (competitive self), then you stopped by your elderly mother's house, who had prepared your favourite cake, to spend some time with her ("attached self"), then, you finally came back home to share dinner with your partner – you are finally alone because the children are at their aunt's house (romantic attachment – sexual). Did you notice any changes? Which is your real self? Does such a thing exist?"

The Compassionate Self is one of the possible identities we can intentionally choose to cultivate. It is a way of orientating ourselves to be caring, to live to be helpful rather than harmful, using brain and body systems that have evolved to allow caring behaviour and stimulating particular brain and body patterns that will be helpful to us and others.

At this point, it can be useful to invite participants to explore the Compassionate Self by activating a compassionate memory, just as was practiced in Module 1.

Invite them to recollect a memory of a time in their life when they noticed someone was struggling and they felt called to help. Invite them not to focus so much on the distress, but rather on their own wish to be helpful. Encourage participants to notice that their desire oriented their thoughts and behaviour in a certain way. You may use the **Therapist Script 5.3** to help you guide this practice.

After the practice, encourage participants to explore the following questions in self-reflection (**Client Handout 5.3**) or in group reflection:

- What were you paying attention to?
- What were you thinking?
- How did that feel in your body?
- How did you want to act?

Therapist Tips

Note that it is rare they will talk about being calm as they recall the memory. Therefore, it's important to highlight the distinction between calmness and the activation of the compassionate motive. Invite them to reflect on how compassion can sometimes translate into sensations of strength and groundedness, and what these may actually feel like in the body. Invite reflection on how compassion can look different in different situations for different people.

Harnessing what emerged from the guided practice and/or discussion, revisit the three key qualities of compassion (you can refer back to **Client Handout 1.2** from Module 1)

- Wisdom (knowledge/understanding/experience)
- Strength (courage/authority/groundedness)
- Commitment (intention to help)

Ask participants to describe how these qualities were present in their memory.

Phase 3: Building and Training the Compassionate Self

This phase is dedicated to the practices that enable us to uncover, train and strengthen our Compassionate Self. As we have seen in the previous phase of this module, although compassion motivation is part of human potential, it can only become a powerful way to deal with difficulties in the world if we train it and grow it. Even though we all have bicep muscles, we actually need to train them so they may grow stronger and serve us better. Not only do we need to facilitate access to the skills that support a compassionate motive (**building phase**), but also repeatedly go through the motions so that we get better at these skills (**training phase**). Drawing on the muscle-building metaphor, we cannot expect to see a muscle grow by just buying a pair of dumbbells and learning the technique for bicep curls – we actually need to show up and repeat that movement, giving ourselves adequate time to rest and recover. There are two key elements to this process: time and application. Time is part of the commitment we are choosing to make, and it allows us to integrate the skills acquired. Moving beyond building and training entails applying the skills in real life, in relationships and everyday situations.

 Therapist Task

2c) Introduce the concept of the Compassion Break

 Therapist Tips

Compassion is about noticing and leaning into our suffering and difficulties: at times, this can become overwhelming. As with any training programme, it is important to allow ourselves to go through phases of programming, some more intense, some less so; training at full capacity all the time is rarely beneficial.

In Buddhism, Compassion (*karuna*), is practiced alongside the other "divine abodes" or 'four immeasurables", which are Loving Kindness also known as Friendly Kindness (*metta*), Sympathetic Joy (*mudita*) and Equanimity (*upekkha*). The idea at the heart of these different practices is that one may complement and balance the other. We can learn from this approach, letting ourselves turn towards other sources of self-soothing that help support and make us feel good.

It is important to encourage participants to listen to and honour their need to take a break from compassion practices. Initiate a group discussion about what activities might be useful to their rest and recovery in this training programme; these might still be meditation practices, just with a different focus (for example rejoicing for other people's joy). Just as our muscles grow during the time they are at rest and have a chance to repair from the micro-tears that occur during weight training, so too do our synapses grow during rest.

Main Touch Points

 Therapist Script 5.4 – Embodying the Compassionate Self
Client Handout 5.4 – The Intent of my Compassionate Self

3a) The Compassionate Self as a role

   Therapist Task

The Compassionate Self is just one of the many identities we can choose to nourish, and it is accompanied by a certain brain-body pattern. There are many ways to activate specific brain-body patterns, some more cognitive in nature, others which ask us to recruit other channels of awareness, such as the body.

Method acting is a technique in which actors are required to focus on some key elements of the characters they must play, adopting their way of thinking, world outlook, postures, general bearing, or tone of voice. If we were to subject an actor to an MRI while they are acting, and ask them to go into an angry, anxious, or joyful state of mind, we could see that they are able to change their brain patterns – so even though they are just acting something, importantly the changes are still happening in their brains. This is important when we think of loops in the brain: even though what we imagine is not there, our brain and bodies are still responding to those images. By the same process, when we activate our Compassionate Self, even though we do not believe we are this Compassionate Self, the brain will enter that pattern as though we were.

Larry Moss, a successor and student of Stella Adler, one of the great teachers associated with Method Acting, said that an actor must know three things about the character to find truth in their performance: objectives, obstacles and intentions. If we translate this concept to CFT, we can think of it this way: *objectives* are the life tasks we must attend to/we wish to attend to in a compassionate way; *obstacles* are FBRs; the *intention* is the act of being helpful and alleviating suffering through something we choose to do or not do.

We can borrow method acting from the theatre to practice generating the main qualities of compassion inside us, even at times when we do not feel particularly compassionate.

Once they have the basic idea of method acting, you can then begin to move towards reflecting on the Compassionate Self. You can invite a self-reflection or a group reflection about the qualities they would like to have if they were at their *compassionate best*: these might be things like patience, tolerance, friendliness, courage, or being a good listener. It is important to remind them to look for qualities that they would really like to have and embody (intrinsic motivation), and not that they "should have" because these aspects are often dictated by family, culture, or religion (extrinsic motivation/ pseudo-compassion).

Now, move into a more experiential practice; you may follow the **Therapist Script 5.4** to guide participants through embodying their Compassionate Self. As always, before and after practices it is helpful to invite them to do a three-circle check-in so that they can have a direct assessment of the effects of a practice.

Three-Circle Check-In

After the practice, allow some time for the group to share their experience. Welcome any struggles that might have occurred during the practice and be sure to remind them that it is normal for this exercise to be difficult at first; after all, this is when our FBRs will be triggered. Highlight that by doing this exercise we are actually already embodying one of the core qualities of compassion: courage.

To help the group reflect on the experience of embodying their Compassionate Self and connect to their intention to train this self-identity, invite them to complete the **Client Handout 5.4**. This can be done either as personal practice, or during the session as a moment of self-reflection, to be followed by sharing in pairs or as a group.

Phase 4: The Compassionate Self in Action

After having experienced what it feels like to enter our Compassionate Self, we begin to understand how to actually apply it and integrate it into our daily lives. This phase provides participants the opportunity to work on life difficulties through the lens of their Compassionate Self. This phase of the module can be thought of as bringing our training outside of the gym and into the outside world.

Main Touch Points

 Therapist Script 5.5 – Compassionate Listening
Therapist Script 5.6 – Compassionate Companions
Client Handout 5.5 – Compassionate Listening for the Self

4a) The Compassionate Self at work

 Therapist Task

We will now begin to put our Compassionate Self to work in real life situations.

The first exercise we will offer the group is about using the Compassionate Self with the difficulties in other people's lives. This experiential exercise it to be done in pairs and requires some space for people to move around the room. Please use the **Therapist Script 5.5**.

Another practice is about seeing another the realities of anothers person's life through the Compassionate Self; follow **Therapist Script 5.6** for this exercise, which is usually done in pairs.

Once they have experienced turning towards someone else through the lens of their Compassionate Self we will guide participants through turning towards themselves in this way; this will be a first experience of compassion for the self, which we will continue to work on in the following modules.

Please invite them to use **Client Handout 5.5** for this practice. Have them fill out the first column of the handout, then guide them through a short induction of the Compassionate Self and lastly have them fill out the second column of the handout.

Remind participants that it is not important whether they feel compassionate – the goal is forming the intention and then getting a sense of the Compassionate Self, as best as possible. Invite participants to explore this with playful curiosity; for example, we can behave compassionately even when we don't feel like it. In debriefing the exercise, remind participants:

- Of the fact they already have an internal wisdom
- That when we put the Compassionate Self to work, it's not weak or self-indulgent, but actually offers wise and powerful insight
- That training is the key

Phase 5: Wrap-Up

Main Touch Points

Therapist Script 5.7 – A Day as my Compassionate Self
Client Handout B – Personal Practice Diary

5a) Summary of the session and suggestions for personal practice

 Therapist Task

Take 5–10 minutes to briefly summarise the points that you have gone through in this module.

You may want to provide participants with some suggestions for personal practice and self-reflection:

- Invite them to use **Client Handout 5.5** on multiple occasions during their week, so as to begin training the flow of compassion towards themselves. Invite them to notice what might be useful to them in those situations.
- Complete the practice diary in **Client Handout B** maybe focusing specifically on how their Compassionate Self helped them engage with others and with themselves that day. They can choose a situation in which to experiment acting their Compassionate Self in their everyday life.

 Optional Practice

Practicing with the Compassionate Self at Home

Ask clients to find an object that can anchor them to their Compassionate Self; sometimes it is useful for them to do practices with a sensory linkage to them. They might do a meditation while holding a semiprecious stone or pebble; maybe there is a smell that gives them a sense of soothing (common options include the smell of lavender or other distinct scents).

Sometimes people like to find postcards with pictures that give them a sense of grounding or calming – this could be a postcard of a mountain or a beautiful scene; anything really that gives them that extra sense of feeling slowed down and grounded. You could invite the group to bring this item with them at the next session too.

Another important thing to highlight is that stepping into their Compassionate Self can be practised in many daily situations. Refer to **Therapist Script 5.7**.

5b) Closing practice

 Therapist Task

Remember to take a moment at the end of the session to acknowledge anything and everything that has come up for participants while exploring the themes offered.

As in previous sessions, invite them to share in one sentence:

- What do I take home from today's session (because I feel it's going to be helpful)?

- What are some key things that I would like to share and tell other people about?

Invite participants to bring their attention to their intention to be helpful to self and others rather than neglectful. On many occasions we will not be able to do so and that is totally ok and human, but it is always possible tune into this intention.

Finally, guide participants through a short closing practice using the **Therapist Script 2.5 in Module 2** and include some references to the Compassionate Self that they connected with during this session.

Here is an example of how you could do it:

"[...] Allow your breath to land here with you...now, from this grounded posture and calming breath, briefly reconnect with the compassionate version of you...feel the wisdom, the strength and courage, determination, and a desire to be helpful that are already here with you. [...]"

Three-Circle Check-In

Therapist Scripts

Therapist Script 5.1: Compassionate Landing (5 minutes)

(Refer to therapist Script 2.1 in Chapter 2)

You can add the following elements to link back to the previous module:

Slowly let your safe place appear in front of your mind's eye. As it appears in front of you, as you move through this space and take in the air, the colours, the smells, remember that this place is happy to have you here, to connect with you and welcome you.

Here, you can once again invite your compassionate image to appear briefly; as it gently enters your safe place, notice its outer features, its appearance, facial expression, and smell. Then begin to get a sense of its inner qualities: its strength, authority, wisdom, stability, and its commitment to help you.

Briefly feel the sensation of being in front of this perfectly compassionate figure, even for just one minute. As you acknowledge its presence, perhaps you wish to ask if there something you need to know today... Curiously listen. Silence is also OK.

Now, gently let your compassionate image fade, and let go of your safe place.

Therapist Script 5.2: Tuning Into Our Social Mentalities (10 minutes)

Try looking at the person next to you or imagining a person sitting close to you.

(If delivering this practice online through a platform such as Zoom, you can ask them to look at the person in the square immediately to the right or to the left, or choose a face from the many that are in the group, and anonymously doing the practice with them.)

We will try to imagine how different scenarios and experience how they modulate our body's responses.

Imagine that this person is a colleague of yours. Your boss tells you that there will be a promotion for whichever one of you can complete a task. You are both highly qualified for the task and you both want the promotion very much; you know the other is very good at it. However, there is only one position, and only one of you will be able to get the promotion. How do you feel about this person, knowing that he/she is competing for your same position? What kind of thoughts do you notice arising? What do you observe about the other person? If you imagine being in the room with that person, what posture would your body take, what sensations would you have in your body? How would you naturally behave towards this person? If this person were to get sick for two weeks, how would you feel? What emotion would you feel? Let this image settle, observe if a memory comes to mind of a time when you actually experienced a similar situation.

Then clear your mental slate, imagine this first image drifting away.

Then, look again at the person by your side or who you imagine to be at your side. This time, your boss tells you that two promotions are available, which will only be awarded to you if you can complete a very difficult task, one that is so difficult that it is impossible for you to complete on your own. Observe the other person and imagine that they also want the promotion and want to collaborate. How do you feel now about the fact that this person is very good? How do you feel about sharing a room with this person who wishes to collaborate with you, who is in your same team, sharing your same goals? What sensations awaken in your body? How does your breathing change? How would you naturally behave towards this person? If this person were to become ill for two weeks, how would you feel? What emotions would you feel? Notice the difference with the previous scenario.

If you do not have much time, the exercise can end here, because the aim of the practice is to help clients perceive the physical changes that occur depending on the motivational state we are in – this has probably already occurred by this time. If you wish, you can continue with the following scenarios...

Now, go back to the person by your side and imagine that you have crossed paths with him/her at a bar and that you are deeply attracted to this person (if you need to change the sexual gender of the person, feel free to do so). Notice how being in the same room as this person lands within you...what physical sensations are awakened? How does your breathing change? What details do you pay attention to?

Again, let go of the image of this person in this form, and allow it to transform.

(This scenario can be complicated in and in-person setting and easier in an online setting where it can be done anonymously – if you are delivering it in-person, try to make it as playful as possible or skip it all together – especially if working with clients who have potentially experienced sexual trauma).

Now being really creative here, imagine that this person beside you was your mother/father. How does this realisation land within you? What sensations come into your body? How would you naturally behave towards them if you were in the same room? If this person knew you were sick, how would they feel? How would they act toward you? What would you like them to do for you? For a few moments, stay in touch with what this image awakens in you, welcoming any feelings, emotions and thoughts that come your way.

Then, one last time, allow your mental slate to clear, making room for a new image. Now recognise that the person who is at your side, was once a child, maybe even imagining what it would be like if they were your child. How does this realisation land within you? What sensations come into your body? How would you naturally behave towards this person if you were in the same room? How would you feel if you knew he/she was sick? Knowing that, what would you want to do?

Stay in touch for a few moments with what this image awakens in you, welcoming any feelings, emotions and thoughts that come your way.

Here are some reflection prompts and questions you can suggest to the client after the practice:

- *Were some mentalities easier to activate than others? Were some more difficult? Did you experience any distress in engaging with some of these mentalities?*
- *Did you feel that one of these mentalities represents you best?*
- *We can switch from one social mentality to another, intentionally*
- *Some emotions/thoughts/physical sensations spontaneously emerge when we decide to activate a certain mentality*

Therapist Script 5.3: Memory of a Compassionate Self (7 minutes)

In this practice we will try to connect to the part of us that has been compassionate before. When we focus on an emotional memory, we are often able to relive the same emotions we experienced at the time we had that experience.

Take a comfortable position, with your back straight, shoulders relaxed, feet rooted to the ground. Resume your soothing breath for a few minutes, giving your breath permission to flow through you, perhaps to slow down a little. Let your attention rest gently on the flow of air coming in and out of your nose.

Try to pause with this breath, allowing your face to soften with it, bringing a slight smile to your lips.

When you feel ready, let your mind naturally float back to a time when you remember feeling compassion for another person or animal. It does not have to be something very intense. It could be a time when you noticed that someone was suffering, maybe about something that you had already experienced in the past... a time when you offered to help a person who was struggling at work, or in their relationships. It could be when you were close to a person who was hurting and you offered your supportive presence. It could be when you gave an uncomfortable piece of advice to a friend, knowing that you were doing so with the intent of easing their pain. Or maybe when you fed an animal or watered a plant, maybe you felt the need to shelter them... Choose a situation where this person or animal was not experiencing too much pain so that this memory does not trigger you excessively.

Try to connect with the moment when you recognised the discomfort of the others person and began to cultivate a specific intention or wish toward this living thing – what did you want for this creature? What did you wish for it? Try to keep that intention in mind. You may not have been able to do anything, but you still felt the wish that that person would no longer suffer, that they would experience well-being

Now you are in that moment again, imagine you are reliving it. How is your body responding, if it at all? Do you notice any changes in your facial expression, posture?

What thoughts are in your mind? (Remember to focus not so much on the other person's pain, but rather on the desire for happiness and alleviation of pain that you feel toward the other person.)

Is there anything you would like to do or say? While remembering all of these elements, begin to notice how it is that they land in you right now, what feelings they bring within your body right now.

Spend a few minutes focusing on the memory. When you are ready, let go of this memory and return to your calming breath for a few moments.

Then, when you feel up to it, you can gently reopen your eyes.

Therapist Script 5.4: Embodying the Compassionate Self (10 minutes)

To begin the practice, find a comfortable position where you can feel fully supported by the surface beneath you. When you feel up to it you can begin to close your eyes, or if you prefer you can keep them half-closed with your gaze downward.

Connect with the soles of your feet rooted in the ground, your pelvis rooted in the chair, and begin to imagine yourself sitting with a dignified posture, your back straight, your shoulders open and soft, your heart spacious.

Begin to connect with your breath, following the flow of air in and out of your nose. Imagine that this breath has a benevolent intention towards you, that it wishes to offer you a sense of nourishment, of calm and grounding. Take a few moments to spend time in the company of this calming breath.

Now, from this grounded posture position and calming breath, try to imagine that you could embody a deeply compassionate version of yourself. What qualities would this version of you have? Try listening to three specific qualities: wisdom, strength and courage, determination, and a desire to be helpful.

Imagine that in this moment you are deeply wise – you are aware that we all ended up with a brain that evolved for us, not by us. We didn't choose it, and it can be chaotic, confusing, deceptive, and painful at times, causing us to get caught up in all sorts of angry and worry loops – which is not our fault. Today you have this wisdom and you understand that other people are experiencing the same difficulty. We are all trying to find happiness and avoid suffering. This wisdom gives us freedom from judgement of ourselves and others. If you find it helpful, you can imagine, with each next breath, that you are inhaling the quality of wisdom and non-judgement, in the form of a colour...and this colour is expanding throughout your body.

Now imagine you are welcoming in this moment your qualities of strength and courage. As you drop more into your body posture, focus on your strong and stable back, like a mountain, and bring attention to this sense of stability and centered strength. Focus on a sense of inner authority. Imagine yourself with calm confidence. Notice how this lands in your body. If you find it helpful, you can imagine, with each next breath, that you are inhaling the quality of strength and courage, in the form of a colour...and this is then blending with the previous colour of wisdom.

Imagine that you now have the desire to be helpful to yourself and to others; to use wisdom when and how you can to be helpful – notice how this lands within you. It doesn't mean that everyone you try to help will actually get better, or be grateful if they notice this desire of yours – accepting this is also part of your commitment. You can imagine with each next breath that you are inhaling this intention and desire to be helpful, in the form of a colour...which blends with the previous ones, maybe creating a unique and vibrant colour that envelops you.

Imagine yourself expanding as if your wisdom is making you bigger, more powerful, in a mature compassionate way. You may even think of yourself as older.

Now, begin to imagine how you would like your Compassionate Self to look: What would your facial expression be? Would you have a neutral expression, or perhaps a slight smile on your lips? What would your posture be? How would you move through space? You can start doing this now. Get up from your chair and walking around the room, just as your Compassionate Self would do.

Maybe your Compassionate Self realises how everything is connected; the objects, your clothes and even the floor you are walking on are all connect to other beings... beings who have created them, or even just assembled them... or maybe the truck drivers who have delivered them where we are... the Compassionate Self could touch the walls and imagine the construction workers who have built them and painted them... maybe a very long time ago... if you feel called to do so, you may send gratitude to all these people who have made it possible for us to use these objects today.

What is in the mind of your Compassionate Self; what are you thinking?

After exploring the space from this perspective, slowly return to your seat, again trying to do so exactly as you imagine this deeply Compassionate Self might do. Once you are seated, close your eyes again and go back inside yourself, back into your body in this moment; take a few minutes to notice what effect it has on you to bring yourself into the world by embodying this Compassionate Self.

Then gently reopen your eyes.

The following are some prompts for reflection and discussion after the practice:

- Which qualities did you find easier to imagine? Which most difficult?
- Some people are helped by the idea of "acting" the part of the Compassionate Self (if I act, I can give myself permission to be anything and everything, even if just for a moment), while for others this might hinder the process. How was it for you?
- When one practices something new for the first time (like a new language), feelings of shame and self-criticism can come up. Did you notice these coming up for you during the practice?

Therapist Script 5.5: Compassionate Listening (10 minutes)

To begin with, invite people to stand up and wander around the room as they adopt their Compassionate Self body posture; invite them to embody the qualities of wisdom, courage, strength and intention to be helpful...

While they are walking around the room as their compassionate best selves, maybe meeting each other's gaze, invite them to think about how they would like to greet others in the room. Reminding them that the person they see in front of them is also here immersed in the flow of life. The others present also have not chosen many things about their life path; they are fighting their own battles... how does it feel looking at these people as travel companions? In seeing these people through the wisdom and shared humanity of compassion, are there any wishes they would like to offer? They can try to whisper them softly to themselves...

Try to help them get a feel of it in the body – how they would hold their back, their heart space, their arms, their shoulders? How they would place their legs and feet?

After having them walk around this way for about three to five minutes (try to get a feel of the pace that best serves your group), ask participants to pair with the person closest to them in the room and sit with chairs facing each other.

Each participant will tell the other about one small life difficulty (nothing too major) for two minutes, while the listener remains silent. Then, the roles are inverted.

Then, debrief the exercise with the whole group, using the following prompts:

- What was it like to sit quietly without being able to talk and just allow time to listen?
- What was it like to have somebody listen to you and not talk but intently listen?

Repeat the exercise asking participants to tune into their Compassionate Self, maybe guiding a short meditation to help them connect with their Compassionate Self again.

Have them repeat the exercise, sharing the same difficulty with the same person, this time while embodying their Compassionate Self. Invite the couple to express gratitude to one another for creating a safe space to share.

Again, debrief the exercise with the whole group, using the following prompts:

- What differences did you notice between doing it two different ways – when you were in your Compassionate Self and when you were not?
- Where could you "use" this exercise in your daily life?

Therapist Script 5.6: Compassionate Companions (13 minutes)

This practice is done in pairs: before starting, decide who is A and who is B.

To begin, both of you should close your eyes. For a few moments, connect to the soothing rhythm of the breath.

Now A can gently open their eyes, while B remains with their eyes closed.

A can open the eyes of their Compassionate Self on B; A can begin to contemplate some things about the creature in front of them. Maybe they don't know this creature, who exactly like us has been in the flow of life, has not decided any of the most important things in their life: the family in which they were born, the sex, the body, the colour of their skin, the kind of difficulties they have encountered. They didn't decide them.

Let's try to look at the arms, the torso, the arms, the face, of this creature who is in the flow of life, just as we are. Let's try to realise how this creature has tried to do its best since it was born, inevitably encountering mistakes, but always trying to navigate this life the best it could.

This creature didn't choose where to be born, but neither did it choose the kind of emotions, thoughts, or feelings to have – it didn't choose its brain, a complex brain that we all find ourselves having and trying to manage.

If we look at the face of this creature before us we can see how this face has had so many moments in which it opened into a smile, into a loving gaze – but as with all of us, this face has also seen tears, moments of doubt, of loneliness. These eyes will have sought relief, moments of peace.

For there is one thing we have in common with this creature before us, however distant and different we may be: this creature is also seeking happiness, it also hopes to be well, to find its peace in this constantly changing world.

We see this creature having had all its experiences of growing up, its sorrows, its friendships... we imagine this creature going on its journey, having countless life experiences, growing old. This creature, exactly like us, will at some point leave existence. Exactly like us, it lives this life without instructions.

A – let's try to imagine what it would be like to make a wish for this Being. The wish might be something like, "Dear fellow traveller, may you have all the compassion you need to go through this. May we both have all the compassion we need to deal with this. May you see, embrace, and honour your uniqueness. May you remember that you are not alone in this journey, which we did not choose.

Try to look at this creature's face and see if there is any special wish we would like to make, just for this creature – maybe there is something that struck us, inspired us about its face, its hands, its life. You may mentally repeat or whisper these wishes, sending them to the creature in front of you.

The person who has their eyes closed (B) listens to what is happening inside of them as they know that the other person is repeating these wishes, these wishes that are coming from someone who may be a complete stranger.

A can write the wish they created for this creature (on a piece of paper or through chat if in an online setting).

Now B can open their eyes and read it, perhaps thanking the person in front of them. If they wish, A can read their wish to the person.

Stay a few moments connecting through the gaze and notice what emerges within. Repeat, this time switching roles.

Therapist Tips

This can be a very intense practice for clients – it is useful to give some extra time at the end for the pair to have some moments for intimate debriefing.

Therapist Script 5.7: A Day as Your Compassionate Self (8 minutes)

(Connect with your Compassionate Self through a brief induction)

Imagine your Compassionate Self waking up in the morning... be playful in this exploration; what would be the first words you would tell yourself as your Compassionate Self? What are the first things you would do? How would you walk around your home? How would you leave your house or apartment and walk into the outside world?

As you enter your workplace, how would you do so?

Try to continue this movie in whatever way you like, until you arrive at the end of your day; how would your Compassionate Self feel at the end of the day?

Now try to choose a situation in the future that you perceive as a bit difficult... it might be an interaction with someone difficult for you or a meeting at work...

Observe from the outside how your Compassionate Self would act...

Then try to embody the Compassionate Self as you imagine being in that scene; this Self remembers that all people are somehow living a life that they did not fully choose... they are living with brains that they did not choose... this Self knows that in the end, all we and other people want is to be happy and to not suffer; this wish is always connecting us as human beings. Tapping into the wisdom of the Compassionate Self, does anything change about the future situation that awaits you?

Therapist Tips

This practice can activate a form of self-criticism or sense of constraint in the client ("I'll never be able to behave this way" or "Now that I know how my Compassionate Self would behave, I have to act that way!"); in reality, this is simply an exercise that helps us discover new colours in our palette – we will be able to use them, not because we "have to" be compassionate, but rather because we wish to be helpful to ourselves in that situation.

Optional Practice

Try to recollect a moment during your day in which you felt connected in a compassionate way to someone or something; it might have been a friend, a plant, or maybe after reading the news, you felt the desire that the suffering of that person could be alleviated.

We were not necessarily able to do something, but we felt the desire and expressed the wish that the suffering wasn't there... this is a compassionate intention.

You can then wonder what the obstacles were in doing something: for example, having the thought that whatever you were able to do would not be enough, that it would be useless, or that you don't have enough energy for yourself so you cannot help others...

Even as you contemplate the possible obstacles to action, try to focus as best as you can on **the intention that you expressed, that the suffering may be alleviated in some way.**

Intention will always be the initial driving force of compassion, to which we can connect to often during our day.

Client Handouts

Client Handout 5.1: Compassionate Weekly Reflection

Let's do a curious friendly reflection on this past week:

Which part of the self-practice did I do and why?

Which part of the self-practice did I not do?

Was this due to any anxieties or blocks regarding the practice or the path? Which ones can you identify?

We extend gratitude, respect, and compassion to the resistances: What would make you and your resistances feel safer in going forward on this path?

Client Handout 5.2: Social Mentalities

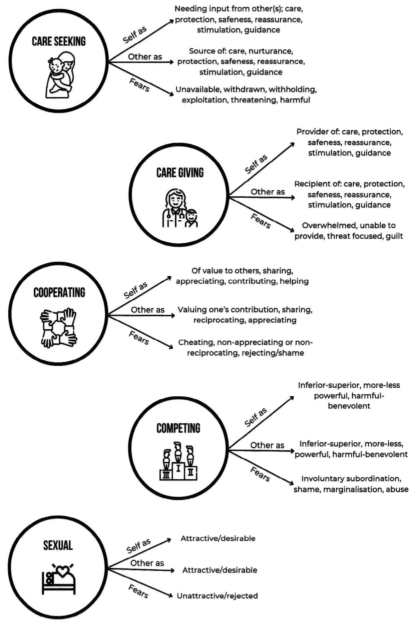

Designed using iages from flaticon.com

Figure 5.3 The social mentalities.
Source: Adapted from Adapted from Gilbert, P. (1992). *The evolution of powerlessness.* Psychology Press

© Petrocchi, Kirby and Baldi (2025), *Essentials of Compassion Focused Therapy*, Routledge

Client Handout 5.3: Memory of a Compassionate Self

Bring to mind a memory of a time in your life when you noticed someone was struggling and you felt called to help. Try not to focus so much on the distress, but rather on your own wish to be helpful. Notice the way your desire oriented your thoughts and behaviour.

Briefly describe the memory:

What were you paying attention to?

What were you thinking?

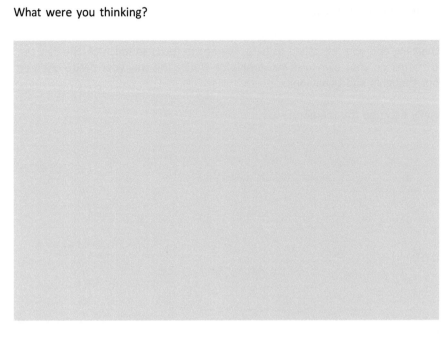

How did that feel in your body?

How did you want to act?

Client Handout 5.4: The Intention of My Compassionate Self

Why do I want to develop my Compassionate Self? How do I want it to help me?

What qualities do I already possess that belong to the Compassionate Self? What other qualities do I need to develop?

What will help me as I cultivate my Compassionate Self more and more in my life?

What obstacles might I encounter within me and outside of me?

How will I try to accept and overcome these obstacles?

Client Handout 5.5: Compassionate Listening for the Self

Think about a difficult situation, but nothing too major. As best as you can, write some thoughts and beliefs that your usual self would have (these are usually short affirmations that we have in our mind in those situations. For example: 'I can't handle situations like this, I get too emotional,' or something similar).

Then, let's change role: activate your Compassionate Self (remember to close your eyes, connect with soothing rhythm breathing and a compassionate posture), and for each affirmation of the usual self, explore how the Compassionate Self would think, act, and desire.

Example of a difficult situation: The difficult situation is that I feel guilty about going out with my friends and leaving my partner at home, even if they encourage me to go out.

The difficult situation is:

Table 5.2 Patterns of My Usual Self and My Compassionate Self

My "usual self" thinks:	My "Compassionate Self" thinks:
Jodie is annoyed at me and disappointed	*Jodie has already shown they were honest with me in the past, if they feel something is wrong, they will tell me, they are assertive*
My "usual self" does:	My "Compassionate Self" does:
I stall and ask them a thousand times if they are REALLY ok with me going out	*I tell them I am grateful to be with someone who encourages me in this way and to have such a transparent relationship*
My "usual self" wants (intention):	My "Compassionate Self" wants (intention):
To be 100% sure that they never feel annoyed by something I do	*For me to go out and spend a nice evening with my friends and remember that Jodie is happy about me being happy*
How do I feel now (as my usual self):	How do I feel now (as my Compassionate Self):
Fear, I feel as if there was an alarm going off inside me	*I feel more relaxed, like I am not doing anything wrong*

Chapter 6

Module 6

The Multiple Selves

Aims

- To introduce the concept of multiple selves, with a particular focus on threat-based emotions (angry self, anxious self and sad self)
- To explore how each of these multiple selves come with specific thoughts, bodily states, action impulses, memories and ways of settling
- To understand and experience the relationship between the multiple selves
- To recruit the compassionate self to build insight, understanding, and integration of our multiple selves
- To work with chairs and the multiple selves

 Deepen Your Knowledge

In Gilbert, P. & Simos, G. (Eds). (2022). *Compassion Focused Therapy: Clinical Practice and Applications*. Routledge, please refer to:

Chapter 6. Compassionate Mind Training: Key Themes
Chapter 9. Meeting the Challenges of a Multi-Mind and the Role of Grieving

DOI: 10.4324/9781003436058-8

Summary of Key Processes

Table 6.1 Module 6: Multiple Selves

Phase		Main Touch Points	Therapist Scripts	Client Handouts
1	Introduction	**1a)** Compassionate landing **1b)** Revision of personal practice and recap of the previous session	☐ **Script 6.1:** Compassionate Landing	☐ **Handout 6.1:** Compassionate Weekly Reflection
2	Discovering multiplicity	**2a)** Introducing the idea of multiple emotions, interpretations, and motives		☐ **Handout 6.2:** Components of an emotion ☐ **Handout 6.3:** What emotions were present?
3	Multiple selves	**3a)** Getting to know the multiple selves **3b)** Relationship between the multiple selves **3c)** Compassionate Beliefs about Emotions	☐ **Script 6.2:** The Multiple Selves ☐ **Script 6.3:** Relationship between the multiple selves	☐ **Handout 6.4:** The Multiple Selves ☐ **Handout 6.5:** Compassionate Beliefs about Emotions
4	Compassionate-self Integration	**4a)** Perspective of the Compassionate Self **4b)** Working with chairs and the multiple selves	☐ **Script 6.4:** Compassionate Self Integration ☐ **Script 6.5:** Multiple selves chair practice	
5	Wrap-up	**5a)** Summary of the session and suggestions for personal practice **5b)** Closing practice		☐ **Handout B:** Personal practice diary

Phase 1: Introduction

Main Touch Points

Therapist Script 6.1 – Compassionate Landing
Client Handout 6.1 – Compassionate Weekly Reflection

1a) Compassionate Landing

   Therapist Task

To welcome the group, guide them through a Compassionate Landing (**Therapist Script 6.1**). Since the last module was spent strengthening the Compassionate Self, the landing will evoke the qualities of the compassionate self and invite participants to adopt their compassionate posture and tune into their soothing rhythm breathing as they transition from their daily lives into the session.

Three-Circle Check-In

1b) Revision of personal practice and recap of previous session

   Therapist Task

Invite participants to use the **Client Handout 6.1** to reflect upon the past week/ weeks; then divide them into pairs or small groups and invite them to share anything relevant about their past week, including any moments where they experienced episodes of compassion, as well as any fears, blocks, and resistances they might have experienced.

Did they try the practice of the Compassionate Self? Did they try to embody the Compassionate Self as they went about their daily tasks? Did they notice any differences when embodying their Compassionate Self? What difficulties/resistances did they encounter? The therapist should pay attention to any comments about the feeling of the Compassionate Self "feeling like a fake" or "it's not my real self" – it can be useful to remind clients that it is just like choosing to learn a new language. At first, we have to think about it and thinking about it will feel artificial and cumbersome, but through repetition it will start to feel more authentic.

Before moving on, the therapist can provide a brief recap of the last session, in which the main points were:

- Compassion as a social mentality
- Building and training the Compassionate Self
- Putting the Compassionate Self to work

This can also be a space to set the scene for the current module; the main themes that are going to be explored are:

- The multiplicity of our emotional experience
- Our multiple selves as mind and body patterns
- How the compassionate self can help integrate our multiple selves

Phase 2: Discovering Multiplicity

The goal of this phase is to introduce the concept of multiplicity and the idea of working with multiple parts and patterns of the self. We will help clients move away from the idea of a "real" self as a fixed identity, while promoting the idea of a complex pattern of changing mental states. In particular, we will discover how our brains can take many different patterns relating to anger, anxiety, sadness, joy and so on. We want the group to understand that we are all made up of different parts and potential patterns that can feel and want different things, can think in different ways, often at the same time. For a more in-depth analysis of multiplicity, please refer to Chapter 9 of the book *CFT – Clinical Practice and Applications*.

Main Touch Points

Client Handout 6.2 – Components of an Emotion
Client Handout 6.3 – What Emotions were Present?

2a) Introducing the idea of multiple emotions, interpretations and motives

 Therapist Background Knowledge

In many life situations, it is common for multiple emotions to be triggered by the same event. Developing awareness of these different emotions and the motives underpinning them, can help greatly in both understanding our own needs and with regulating our emotions and the behavioural impulses that are involved.

We can think of our emotional experiences as a pattern comprising a number of important components: an attentional part, a thinking part, a bodily aspect, a behavioural impulse, memories associated with the emotion, and ways that the emotional experience can be settled. Therefore it is important to differentiate the emotions we experience so we can understand the varied patterns of our emotions.

Making this distinction is important as it allows us to better understand if the difficulties experienced with a specific emotion relate to a particular component of that emotion. For example, one person might have difficulty with anger because it elicits specific traumatic memories, rather than for fear of the bodily activation it entails.

   Therapist Task

You can have clients think about one emotion that they are more familiar with, and then complete **Client Handout 6.2** to familiarise themselves with the different components of that emotion.

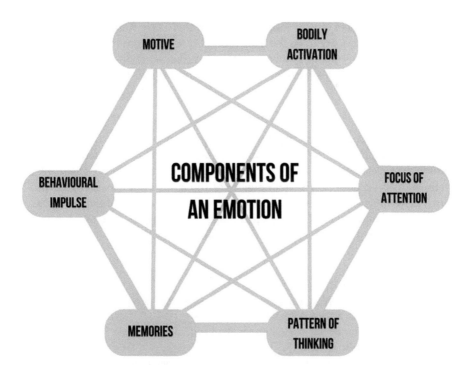

Figure 6.1 Components of an Emotion.

To begin to work with different emotions that can arise simultaneously we invite participants to bring to mind an argument that they recently had with someone they care about. Invite them to recollect a memory which is not too activating, but just enough to give them an indication of how different feelings and emotions can arise within us. Give them a moment to call this memory to mind.

Then, have the group break into pairs and invite them to share with each other about the argument they reflected on. Verbal recounting can help them better focus the emotions that were lived and experienced at the time of the argument. After doing so, ask them to use **Client Handout 6.3** to note down which emotions where present during the argument.

Invite the group to come back together and offer the opportunity to discuss the emotions that emerged, providing the following prompts:

- *Which emotion usually comes first? Which one(s) follow?*
- *Which is the emotion do you prefer/which emotion do you not like (and try to avoid)? Why?*
- *In your opinion, why did we have different emotions? What causes this multiplicity?*

As people begin to explore the many different emotions that can arise as well as their different nuances, try to highlight the fact that each emotion has its own desire and motivation. Try to tie the exploration of the emotions to the three-circle model; begin to show that each circle contains certain emotions. Emotions are a signal that a certain desire, wish, need or motive is being met or unmet.

Phase 3: Multiple Selves

The goal of this phase is to take the group through a guided discovery of their multiplicity, understanding that evolution creates integrated patterns that include many elements at once. For example, when we are in an angry mind state, we will experience a certain quality of thoughts, body, physiological patterns, behaviours, and specific memories. Through the Multiple Selves set practice, Compassion Focused Therapy (CFT) helps people understand, differentiate, tolerate, and integrate their patterns of activation.

Main Touch Points

Therapist Script 6.2 – The Multiple Selves
Therapist Script 6.3 – Relationship between the Multiple Selves
Client Handout 6.4 – The Multiple Selves
Client Handout 6.5 – Compassionate Beliefs about Emotions

3a) Getting to know the Multiple Selves

 Therapist Background Knowledge

The Multiple Selves guided exercise is an important CFT set piece. It is based on the premise that each of our emotions represents a different "self". This means we all have an angry self, an anxious self, and a sad self. The exercise mainly focuses on these three emotions, also known as "The Big Three", since they are the ones that usually create greater difficulties within the red circle. However, the principle can be applied to all emotions. This means we also have a joyful self, a shamed self, a guilty self, a disgusted self and so on.

Just like in the previous exercise, the Multiple Selves exercise begins with the recollection of an argument the individual had with somebody they care about; at this point, we can ask them to talk about the different emotions as if they were an outside observer.

For each emotion, the main points we will be exploring are:

- Motives associated with the emotion – what it wants, its desires or needs
- Thoughts – what it thinks
- Body posture and movements – what happens in its body
- Action tendencies – what it wants to do
- Memories – which memories it carries
- Settle – how it settles

A key point in this exercise is to give space and validate each self; we are not trying to divide the scene between "good selves" and "bad selves" but rather trying to better understand the multiplicity that inhabits us and that sometimes makes navigating life so tricky. In fact, many of our emotions can be in conflict; this is partly due to the fact that our modern brain is capable of anticipating the consequences of a particular action. Emotional conflict, where one emotion suppresses the other, can sometimes lead to dissociation; hence helping people very gently explore and tolerate emotions and recognise their simultaneous existence can be helpful.

The multiple selves exercise has three main parts:

- In the first part, we explore one single self at a time; this is done both through imagery, embodiment and then written self-reflection
- In the second part, we explore the ways in which the different selves relate to each other
- In the third part, we invoke the Compassionate Self to help with the process of integration of the multiple selves

Therapist Task

We typically begin with exploring the angry self, because it tends to be the most activating emotion in terms of energy. The exercise is conducted through the combination of a guided imagery meditation and written self-reflection following the prompts which can be found in **Client Handout 6.4**. In individual therapy it can also be combined with chairwork, which is frequently used in CFT (for more about this, you can refer to Chapter 17 of *CFT – Clinical Practice and Applications*). We suggest guiding the group through the meditation and then inviting them to open their eyes and take a moment to write down any insights they might have received in their client handout.

The same process is then repeated then with anxiety and sadness, shaking off each emotion (e.g., standing up, taking a breath, and moving about) before moving onto the next. We do not ask participants to dwell at length on their difficult memory, for this is not an exercise focusing on emotion exposure (although it will inevitably occur to some extent), but rather to touch upon it only to the extend needed to promote insight and differentiation of our emotional states.

3b) Relationship between the multiple selves

Therapist Task

The second phase of this exercise focuses on the relationships between our multiple selves. In fact, the difficulty of emotional conflicts can be navigated by investigating the motives that sustain our emotions and how they relate to each other. This phase can provide powerful insights into the ways in which emotions may try to suppress each other or strengthen particular beliefs. Normalising the conflict which often occurs between emotions can be very beneficial for participants. You can use **Therapist Script 6.3** to guide this part of the exploration.

   OPTIONAL PRACTICE

3c) Compassionate beliefs about emotions

Therapist Task

You might not have time for this, but it can be a useful exercise to deepen understanding of our typical beliefs about emotions and how the Compassionate Self might view an emotion. Be sure to make clear this is supplemental material and that if clients do decide to do this exercise, it is important for them to properly engage with their compassionate orientation. Ask clients to complete **Client Handout 6.5** in pairs or groups of three people, then come back and share as a group. It is possible that the therapist needs to guide the client's compassionate self in formulating their own adaptive belief in this exercise. Also, keep in mind that multiple adaptive beliefs are possible. As an alternative, you can invite clients to complete the handout as a form of self-reflection in their own time.

Phase 4: Compassionate Self Integration

The goal of this phase is to see how the Compassionate Self enables us to see the functions of each emotion, promoting their integration. In this phase, we shift out of the threat and harm avoidance protection system (red-circle dominated) into the caring motivation system; this means we form an intention and bring wisdom, strength, and commitment to understand our difficult emotions.

Main Touch Points

Therapist Script 6.4 – Compassionate Self Integration
Therapist Script 6.5 – Multiple Selves Chair Practice
Client Handout 6.6 – The Multiple Selves

4a) Perspective of the Compassionate Self

  Therapist Background Knowledge

The final step of this exercise is to shift into our Compassionate Self to help with regulating the complexities and conflicts between the multiple selves. Compared to the other multiple selves, the Compassionate Self belongs to a different motivational system, presents different pattern of psychophysiological activation, and most importantly has a capacity for mentalization. We then use this capacity to engage with the angry, anxious, and sad self, so that the Compassionate Self may become a truly secure base and safe haven to work with our threat emotions. The compassionate mind state promotes the abilities of self-soothing and self-reassurance, which aids in tolerating, integrating and transforming our difficult emotional states.

  Therapist Task

We then invite them to explore once again their memory of an argument, this time from the perspective of the Compassionate Self. Remember to highlight the intention of the Compassionate Self, which is to be helpful, not harmful in this situation, to deepen our understanding of the argument, to promote dialogue and integration.

An important development of this practice, which can be delivered at this stage or at a later stage, is about exploring one of the emotions that is particularly difficult for the participants. After leading a Compassionate Self induction, you can invite them to imagine seeing the difficult self in front of them, trying to understand what is driving this self, what are its fears, and deep needs. This enables the group to gain insight into how to validate and work with this part of the self.

4b) Working with chairs and the multiple selves

  Therapist Background Knowledge

Chairwork is a powerful, experiential method that involves using chairs, modifying their positioning, and inviting clients to move between them for specific therapeutic objectives. In CFT, chairwork can be used to apply the compassionate self and mind state to situations involving the multiple selves, facilitating the externalisation of the inner dialogue and promoting perspective-taking. In this way, during a single session of chairwork, clients are able to experience the different flows of compassion, both offering and receiving help and support in a difficult situation. Furthermore, chairwork provides an opportunity to interweave elements of embodiment into the self-reflective process, bringing oneself into different states of mind through changing body posture, pace and tone of voice, facial expression, gestures and movement. Therefore, these sessions operate at the intersection between a cognitive and a physical understanding of one's multiplicity.

  Therapist Task

Chairwork is usually used in a one-on-one setting but it can also be adapted to working in groups. In individual settings you can use different chairs for each self, arranging them in a semi-circle or in a line based on the space you are working with and the distances you (and the client) believe would be most appropriate. Invite the client to choose where they feel more comfortable, positioning the selves in relation to themselves – would they like the chair closest to them be the seat of the angry, sad, or anxious self? Feel free to play around in a collaborative way with the positioning of the chairs, taking into account that your therapist chair will always provide a safe haven for the client, who should not feel alone in the process of exploring the multiplicity of the self.

In group settings, chairwork can be adapted by using one single chair, shifting positions in the same chair – it has been shown that this very small shift still does provide the opportunity for a change of perspective and, therefore, creates an insightful experience. Furthermore, moving positions in a single chair provides an experience that is often less shameful for people, so it can help them ease into this immersive practice.

For the multiple selves, an ideal setting in a group would be for each person to have two chairs: one chair will be used to explore the three positions of the multiple selves (by slightly shifting to the right, to centre, or to the left while sitting on the chair) and the other chair will be used for the compassionate self. As always, feel free to find alternative ways to deliver this practice based on the needs and characteristics of the group you are leading.

Although the selves we are working with are all parts of us, when working with one specific self, we want to avoid leakage from the others. While in individual settings it can be easier for the therapist to regulate this and bring the client's focus back to the self they are working on at that moment, preventing leakage in group settings requires slightly different strategies. For example, you could prepare name tags (angry self, anxious self, sad self, compassionate self) and invite participants to change name tags when changing positions and perspective.

You may use **Therapist Script 6.5** for some guidance for the multiple selves chair practice.

Therapist Tips

For clients who have never done any chairwork, this experience may leave a feeling of slight confusion and at times dissociation – validate this, and reassure them that it is normal to have this feeling when we explore this method. Try to have at least 10–15 minutes before the end of the session to guide the person through a soothing practice such as soothing rhythm breathing, soothing touch, or compassionate place.

Phase 5: Wrap-Up

The final phase of the module is a wrap-up of the theme that has been explored. Emphasise how continuing to work on one's **personal practice** (whether formal or informal) can help with the development of our compassionate minds.

Main Touch Points

Therapist Script 6.6 – Closing Practice
Client Handout B – Personal Practice Diary

5a) Summary of the session and suggestions for personal practice

  Therapist Task

Take 5–10 minutes to briefly summarise the points that you have gone through in this module.

You may want to provide participants with some suggestions for personal practice and self-reflection:

- Invite them to use **Client Handout B,** suggesting they focus on one compassionate activity per day, maybe focusing specifically on how their Compassionate Self helped them engage with others and with some of their selves that showed up that day
- Invite them to use the guided audio meditation for the Compassionate Self practice at least twice during the week, so that they may continue to connect with this part of themselves

5b) Closing practice

  Therapist Task

Remember to take a moment at the end of the session to acknowledge anything and everything that has come up for participants while exploring the themes presented.

As in previous sessions, invite them to share in one sentence:

- *What do I take home from today's session (because I feel it's going to be helpful)?*

- *What are some key things that I would like to share and tell other people about?*

Finally, guide participants through a short closing practice using **Therapist Script 2.5** and perhaps add a sentence or two that links to the work done during this session. It could be something like, *"Let us thank once again all the parts of ourselves that opened up to us today"* or, *"Connect with the Compassionate Self one last time, feeling its strength, courage, wisdom and desire to help the multiple selves that show up in our lives"*.

Three-Circle Check-In

Therapist Scripts

Therapist Script 6.1: Compassionate Landing (5 minutes)

(Refer to Therapist Script 2.1 in Chapter 2)

You can add the following elements to link back to the previous module:

Now, try to reconnect with what we developed together last week...and in this moment, on this chair, with each breath, let us connect with and embody our Compassionate Self.

Now, in this moment, with each breath, you connect more and more with wisdom, strength, courage and the intent to help of this self..., perhaps you could recall situations during this past week in which you felt you embodied these qualities.

Then, try to capture an internal picture of your compassionate self and how you feel when embodying it – bring it with you throughout the session.

Therapist Script 6.2: Multiple Selves

 Therapist Tips

This exercise is typically done with **Client Handout 6.4**.

It can either be done by alternating guided meditation with written self-reflection (as demonstrated here) for each self we are working with, or by delivering the entire guided meditation and then allowing time for self-reflection at the end.

Another choice to be made is whether people become the part they are working with using acting techniques and embodied positions, speaking as if they were the part itself, or adopting the position of an observer reflecting on the experience. For example, saying to someone *"When you feel angry, where is that in your body?"* is different from saying, *"Stepping into your angry self – what do you feel right now?"*. When using chairwork, we typically use the latter perspective – that is, embodying and inhabiting the emotional self we are engaged with. However, when we do group work for the first time in the process of guided discovery, we may prefer to take the observer position. In this script, we provide brief examples of the embodied perspective, but mostly use the observer perspective.

It is important in CFT to distinguish between attention that is focused externally on the outside world or the minds of others, in contrast to internally on one's own mind. Ideally, you are mostly looking at externally focused emotions, particularly in the case of anger. If the person switches to internal anger and in particular, self-criticism, then guide them away from that, let them know we will be listening to that part at a later stage. Switching from externally to internally directed anger is usually a sign of fear of anger.

We will provide many questions which can be used to explore each self in depth, however feel free to pick only some of the questions from the lists, maybe those you feel would work best with your clients.

When working with the different selves, try to avoid leakage, which is when a different self turns up while working with a particular other self. For example, when working with the angry self, the person might experience the anxious or the sad self instead – when this happens, remind the person that we will be talking to that self at a later stage and bring them once again back to focusing on the emotion at hand.

Throughout the script, you will find some more **Therapist Tips** in yellow boxes to help you conduct this complex set piece exercise.

In this practice, we will be exploring different emotions and mental states, learning more about them and how to work with them. We will be focusing, in particular, on three threat-based emotions, anger, anxiety, and sadness, and understanding how our compassionate self can help us with them. We will be using both guided discovery and written self-reflection to tune into our emotional experience, so please keep your Handout 6.3 close to you.

To begin the practice, gently close your eyes and find a comfortable position in your chair. We will be using our bodies during this practice, so let us take a couple of breaths to get grounded in our position, feeling our feet firmly rooted into the floor, our buttocks stable on our chair, our back fully supported by the back of the chair.

Now, try to recall an argument you had with someone you cared about – try to choose a memory that is not too triggering for you or that could stir up very intense feelings in you. As you recall the memory of the argument, take some time to picture where you were, who you were with... remember what was said, how it was said and what you were feeling, thinking and wanting to do and say.

Angry Self (5 minutes)

We will start with our angry self.

Now, imagine you are sitting in a theatre; this is your inner theatre, you are the stage director here. This is where you will meet the theatrical company that acts out the episodes from our lives so skilfully.

The first emotion to make its way on stage is your angry self. Imagine it stepping onto the stage, observe how it appears, how it moves, what its facial expression is (if it has a face). Is it speaking? If so, what is its tone of voice? Now, let's just take a couple of moments to imagine being this angry self – How would you move? What do you feel in your body? Try to stay with these sensations for a while, really connecting to the felt experience of this angry self.

Then, coming back to your position as a spectator in this theatre, let us explore how the angry self was involved in this argument.

Motives:

- *What triggered the angry self?*
- *What is the function of anger in this situation?*
- *What harmful thing is anger worried about?*
- *What do you think this angry self is trying to protect you from?*
- *How would you feel if you didn't have this angry self in your theater company?*

If observing the angry self from an embodied perspective, you may wish to use the following questions:

- *What triggered you, angry self?*
- *What do you want? What outcome would satisfy your needs?*
- *What harmful thing are you worried about? What are you trying to prevent?*
- *What are you defending [name] from?*
- *What do you feel would happen if you weren't able to express yourself?*

Thoughts:

- *What does this angry self think about the situation? What are the thoughts going through its mind?*

Embodied perspective:

- *What are you thinking about that situation, angry self?*
- *What is frustrating you?*
- *What is getting in the way of your needs being satisfied?*

Body reaction

- *What do you feel in the body in this moment?*

 Therapist Tips

You can use a few Socratic questions and try to elicit the first thoughts of the angry self. Encourage the angry self to be uncensored – some people may use "bad" language, and that is totally fine. Clients can have these thoughts but are frightened to verbalise them. Validate the fact that the angry self does not always think nice things or say things in nice ways because it is not designed to.

Behaviour

- *What does the angry self want to do?*
- *If the angry self was in complete control and didn't really care about the consequences, what would it do?*
- *Does the angry self have any fantasies of what you might do even though in your heart you know you would never actually act on that?*

Embodied perspective:

- *If you were free of constraints, what would you do?*
- *If you were not worried of the outcome, what is the course of action that you'd like to take?*

 Therapist Tips

As an option, you can ask people to think about the reasons we don't act on our anger or you can talk to them about it. When clients share their fantasies it can be very normalising and de-shaming – and the therapist can throw in some of their own as well to the de-catastrophise aggressive fantasises.

We also want to help clients recognise that there are different types of anger. There is anger which is trying to make the other person change their behaviour, such as to listen more, be more helpful; we might call this assertive anger or even power anger. There is also what we call vengeful anger, where the focus is on getting one's own back and hurting the other person. The type of anger is linked to motivation; vengeful anger has the motive to retaliate and cause harm.

Memories

- *Do any memories come to mind when you think of your angry self?*
- *What are the memories you associate with feeling angry that are particularly important or powerful for you?*
- *How far do they go back in time? Childhood?*

 Therapist Tips

Help participants gain some insight into the fact that every emotion has a history; very few emotions are newly experienced. Some people have much more intense anger or fear of anger responses than others because of their history; for others it may not be easily triggered or it may be more intense or last longer.

Settling

- *How do you usually settle or regulate your angry self?*
- *What do they need to settle down?*
- *How do you think your angry self feels when it is being settled in this way?*

At this point, invite clients to open their eyes, take their handout and take a few minutes to complete the box related to their angry self, using the insights they received during the guided exploration. You could have a mini group discussion here, but make sure to be mindful of time.

When finished, you can ask clients to take a moment to reset, maybe stand up, shake their arms, and imagine just letting go of the angry self.

Now, close your eyes again and thank the angry self for coming on the stage today, for opening up to us in a genuine manner. If possible, imagine your angry self pleased about having been seen.

Anxious Self (5 minutes)

You will now go through the same process, in exactly the same way as you did for anger, this time inviting the anxious self onto the stage, exploring aspects of its physical appearance, looking at the different dimensions of motives, thoughts, actions, memories, and settling/coping/regulating processes. Invite the group to once again recollect once again their memory of an argument and to focus on the part of themselves that was feeling anxious, concerned about the argument.

After visualising the anxious part stepping onto the stage, take a minute or so to embody the anxious self; invite participants to recognise that the body is automatically preparing for action in defence. Help them recognise that their heart rate can go up automatically and they may find themselves trembling – they might even feel sick if it is a major conflict.

You may use some or all of the following questions for exploration; as always, feel free to continue the exploration from an observer or an embodied perspective.

Motives

- *What triggered your anxious self?*
- *What is the anxious self concerned with?*
- *What harmful thing is the anxious self worried about and therefore moti-vated to try to prevent?*
- *What is the purpose and point of the anxious self?*
- *What is the anxious self trying to protect you from?*
- *What do you feel would happen if you did not have your anxious self?*

Thoughts

- *What does your anxious self actually think about that situation?*
- *Does your anxious self experience any frightening thoughts and fantasies?*
- *Do you find these thoughts and images come back to your anxious self even after the argument is over?*

Therapist Tips

Clarify internally versus externally focused anxiety. External anxiety is the anxiety they have towards another person – that the other person will lose interest in them or become aggressive. They may feel unable to trust the other person to like them or maintain the relationship if they show anger or assertiveness. Distinguish this from anxiety for themselves – that they may do or say things that are inappropriate. They may even be anxious that they are not able to be assertive.

Behaviour

- *What does the anxious self want to do?*
- *If this part of you was completely in control, how would it want you to act?*

Therapist Tips

There are different types of behaviour relating to anxiety in the context of an argument, and these can be reflected in the actions we see our anxious self playing out.

One is submissiveness and appeasing, trying to cover one's anxiety in an effort to keep the lid on any tension and conflict – however, this can lead to resentment. We can see that when people are in less powerful positions they can be appeasing and submissive to the more powerful person in order to keep the more powerful person's anger under control. Issues of submissiveness and self-blame/criticism are very important in CFT, and this can help people think about submissiveness and self-blame as a safety strategy.

A second type of behaviour is trying to escape and get away – sometimes just walking out or cutting off the interaction.

A third response is a type of freezing – where our mind gets blocked, we become immobile and we cannot really think of what to say. We can also start feeling self-conscious or even ashamed; we can worry about coming over as silly or not being valued because we do not say things clearly.

Another response is distraction where we try to avoid feeling the anxiety too deeply.

Memories

- *What memories come to mind when you are in contact with your anxious self?*
- *What are the memories you associate with feeling anxious? Are there any that are particularly powerful or important for you? How far do they go back in time? To childhood?*

Settling

- *How do you settle your anxious self?*
- *What would soothe your anxious self?*
- *What strategies do you use to regulate your anxious self?*
- *How does your anxious self feel about you using these strategies?*

At this point, invite participants to open their eyes, take out their handout and give them a few minutes to complete the box related to their anxious self, using the insights they received during the guided exploration. You could have a mini group discussion here, but make sure to be mindful of time. When finished, you can ask the person/group to take a moment to reset, maybe stand up, shake their arms, and imagine just letting go of the anxious self.

Now, close your eyes again and thank the anxious self for coming on the stage today, for opening up to us in a genuine manner. If possible, imagine your anxious self pleased about having been seen. Let's ask it to find a place on the stage – where would it like to sit? Does it take position close to or far away from the angry self? Notice where it decides to go.

Sad Self (5 minutes)

Once again, we repeat the same process with the sad self.

The therapist must be clear that sadness is about a sense of loss, and it must not be confused with depression, which is not so much about loss but a sense of defeat, being blocked, helpless and lost sometimes. Some clients may go straight into a kind of anhedonic depression, where they talk about feeling lost, empty, hopeless. Help them recognise that they are bypassing sadness.

Repeat the same process of inviting the sad self onto the stage, exploring its appearance and embodying it for a minute or so, really tapping into the felt experience of the sad self.

After recalling the memory of the argument through the eyes of the sad self, proceed with the following questions:

Motives

- *What triggered your sad self?*
- *What does your sad self want? What does it need?*

- *What harmful thing is the sad self worried about and therefore motivated to try to prevent?*
- *What is the point of the sad self, its function?*
- *What is the sad self trying to defend us from?*

Thoughts

- *What does your sad self actually think?*
- *Do any distressing/sad thoughts or fantasies come to your sad self's mind?*
- *Do you find these thoughts and images come back even after the argument/event is over?*

Behaviour

What does the sad self want to do?
If your sad self was completely in control, what would it do?
Does the sad self have any fantasies?

 Therapist Tips

Generally, there are three types of behaviour we might see. We might want to cry or have a the feeling of our heart sinking. We might withdraw into ourselves and shutdown. We can feel kind of "frozen and switched off". Another is feeling lost and going blank – not out of anxiety but just feeling lost and confused. Another is distraction, where we try to avoid feeling the emotion too deeply.

Memories

- *What memories does your sad self recollect?*
- *What are the memories that you associate with your sad self? Are there any particularly important or powerful ones for you?*
- *How far do they go back in time? To childhood?*

Settling

- *What would help the sad self calm down?*
- *What helps you to settle or regulate your sad self?*
- *How does your sad self feel about the way you try to regulate it?*

At this point, invite participants to open their eyes, take their handout and take a few minutes to complete the box related to their sad self, using the insights they received during the guided exploration. You could have a mini group dis-cussion here, but make sure to be mindful of time.

Now, close your eyes again and thank the anxious self for coming on the stage today, for opening up to us in a genuine manner. If possible, imagine your sad self pleased about having been seen. Let's ask it to find a place on the stage – where does it choose to go, considering the positions of the angry self and the anxious self? Notice with curiosity where it chooses to settle.

Therapist Tips

Sadness might require a bit more in-depth discussion due to it very complex nature. As mentioned at the beginning, it is important to distinguish between sadness and depression, so it may be worthwhile to exploring this link with the group.

Another useful discussion to have with your clients is about why sadness is a danger-ous emotion. This is particularly important if you are working with aggressive males. The reason is that when we cry, we cannot see, we cannot breathe very well, and our muscles tend to lose their ability to contract. We encourage you to have a discussion with clients about why sadness is important, what it would be like for human beings if we never felt sad about anything, if we were not able to cry. Sadness exists because we value things.

At the end of the focus part of this exercise ask the participants to reflect. Given what we have just been through what did/do you notice? Encourage their own "noticing" and guided discovery about the multiple selves and how they all have their own ways of thinking, feeling, action tendencies and also importantly, memories.

Therapist Script 6.3: Relationship Between the Multiple Selves (5 minutes)

Many of our motives and emotions can be in conflict, particularly within our modern human brain. This is partly because we are able to anticipate the con-sequences of any particular action. It is not our fault that we may experience tricky relationships between our multiple selves.

Now that we have seen the different aspects, parts, and patterns of our multi-ple selves, let us see how they relate to each other. Invite all the selves to step onto the stage once again so that they are free to interact with one another. Notice how the angry self positions itself in relation to the other two selves.

- *What does your angry self think about your anxious self?*
- *If you step for a brief moment into your angry self, what are you thinking about the anxious self?*

- *Do you like the anxious self?*
- *To what extent would you like to control the anxious self?*
- *Is there any particular aspect of the anxious self that you don't like?*
- *What would you like to do with the anxious self?*

Ask the same questions, but this time about the angry-self/sad-self relationship. Now let us focus on the anxious self.

- *Does the anxious self feel frightened of the angry self?*
- *Is it afraid of a particular aspect of the angry self?*
- *What would the anxious self like to do with the angry self?*
- *What is the anxious self's greatest concern about the angry self?*

Now let us turn the spotlight on the sad self:

- *What do you think the sad self feels about the anxious self and the angry self?*

Therapist Tips

Each of the questions we suggest could activate deep thought processes and open up discussions that are likely to take up a lot of the session's time or become "too cognitive". Remember that these are only questions are only meant to activate a curious and non-judgemental relationship with our various selves – many clients can have deep insights just by seeing their selves in front of them. Trust your clinical intuition and your ability to "feel the group" to decide how many questions to ask, so that there is sufficient exploration but at the same time the "felt sense" of the visualisation practice is not interrupted.

Therapist Script 6.4: Compassionate Self Integration (10 minutes)

Therapist Tips

This exercise is typically done with **Client Handout 6.4**.

We suggest that the Compassionate Self be explored through an embodied perspective, so all questions will be addressed in the first person.

Let us close our eyes again and return to the theatre where we met our angry self, anxious self and sad self; take your seat, make yourself comfortable, with your shoulders back, your spine straight, your chest soft and open. Try to create a friendly facial expression by bringing a light smile to your lips.

Now let us turn our attention to our breathing, connecting to our soothing rhythm breathing. Notice the sensation of the mind slowing down, the body slowing down, as we are getting more grounded and stable in the body.

Slowly but deliberately begin to embody your compassionate self and its core qualities; let your wisdom emerge, the deep knowing that we all just happen to find ourselves here as part of the flow of life, with tricky brains – none of us chose to be here; we didn't choose the genes we inherited from our parents, we didn't design the brains we have and that give rise to all kinds of emotions from our threat system, such as anger, anxiety and sadness. Nor did we choose the environments that we grew up in, that shaped us for good and perhaps not so good.

As your compassionate self, you are also very strong and brave, and you are committed to engaging with the suffering of the flow of life and being helpful, supportive towards others and towards ourselves.

Now, as your compassionate self, bring back to mind the argument once again. Begin contemplating these questions.

Motives

- *What do you wish in this situation? What is your desire regarding this difficulty?*

Thoughts

- *What do you think about this argument?*
- *What thoughts come to mind when you take up this compassionate position?*

Therapist Tips

Sometimes people begin with a slight invalidation or justification – such as, the argument is not important or "it's not my fault". Again the focus is on the "I". However, what you're guiding them towards is the idea that the Compassionate Self will have a different perspective which will usually (in this case) involve empathetic bridging and mentalising – this may be something that you will need to guide and train – using Socratic questions that are focused on mentalising. You could, for example, suggest *"I wonder, from this compassionate part of you if you have any thoughts about what might be happening in the mind of the other person; what might be motivating or causing them to act in the way that they are?"*

Body State

- *Where in your body do you most feel compassion?*
- *What is your facial expression like?*
- *What is your tone of voice like?*

Behaviour and Actions

- *What does the compassionate self want to do?*
- *If this part of you was in complete control, what would you do?*

Memories

- *Thinking back to when you or others have acted compassionately, what memories come to mind?*
- *How did you find that helpful?*

Growth

- *What would help you to cultivate your compassionate self?*
  At this point you may wish to take a pause and invite participants to complete the box for their compassionate self in **Client Handout 6.4**.
- *Now, as your compassionate self, imagine standing up from your seat and walking onto the stage yourself.*
- *Looking through the eyes and mind of your compassionate self, turn your gaze towards your angry self; see the angry self in front of you, observe its facial expression, tone of voice.*
- *As the compassionate self, what are your thoughts about the angry self?*
- *What has triggered the angry self?*
- *What is the angry self really worried about? What is it defending?*
- *Can you see the distress behind your angry self?*
- *How might you try to help the angry self?*
- *What would you like to do for your angry self?*

If it is difficult for you to imagine doing or saying something to help your angry self, imagine sending a flow of compassion towards the angry self with each exhale. Imagine that this flow of compassion, communicating the desire to help, enveloping or being absorbed by the angry self. Stay with this image until you feel it ok for you. Notice if there are any changes in the angry self when is has finally absorbed all the compassion it needs.

Next, turn towards your anxious self. Again, see it in front of you, observe its facial expression, tone of voice.

- *What do you think about the anxious self?*

- *What has triggered the anxious self?*
- *What is the anxious self really worried about? What is it defending?*
- *Can you see the distress behind your anxious self?*
- *How might you try to help the anxious self?*
- *What would you like to do for your anxious self?*

If it is difficult for you to imagine doing or saying something to help your anxious self, imagine sending a flow of compassion towards the anxious self with each exhale. Imagine this flow of compassion, communicating the desire to help, enveloping or being absorbed by the anxious self. Stay with this image until you feel it ok for you. Notice if there are any changes in the anxious self when is has finally absorbed all the compassion it needs.

Finally, turn towards your sad self, seeing its facial expression, body posture, tone of voice; notice what the sad self is thinking and how it is behaving.

- *What are you thinking about your sad self?*
- *What has triggered the sad self?*
- *What is the sad self really worried about? What is it defending?*
- *Can you see the distress behind your sad self?*
- *How might you try and help your sad self?*
- *What would you like to do for your sad self?*

If it is difficult for you to imagine doing or saying something to help your sad self, imagine sending a flow of compassion towards the sad self with each exhale. Imagine that this flow of compassion, communicating the desire to help, enveloping or being absorbed by the sad self. Stay with this image until you feel it ok for you. Notice if there are any changes in the sad self when is has finally absorbed all the compassion it needs.

Now, thank all these parts, all these selves, for making themselves seen and heard on this stage today. As your compassionate self, send them wishes of wellbeing.

- *May you all feel heard.*
- *May you all feel seen.*
- *May your needs be met.*
- *May you all feel accepted.*
- *Observe how they respond when receiving these wishes.*
- *Does anything change about their facial expression, tone of voice, body posture, movement?*
- *Imagine closing this scene however you feel right for you – this is the beginning of a new relationship between all these parts and there will be many other moments in which they will be able to come together. If you feel like it, imagine taking a picture (maybe a selfie or even painting a portrait) of the most*

memorable moment of this encounter. What word or message would you insert as a caption to this image?

- *Then, gently let go of this scene, come back to your breath and when you feel ready, open your eyes again.*

Table 6.2 Multiple Selves – Worked Example

ANGRY SELF (transgression)	ANXIOUS SELF (danger)
Motives: to be heard, I want change, I want them to do what I want and now, to listen to me. Get my own back, make them pay, make them feel guilty	*Motives:* safety, control, certainty, support, make this stop, get away
Thoughts: idiot, you think I'm not important, you're an asshole, I told you, I am right, you are wrong, I'll get you for this	*Thoughts:* it's too much, they don't really care for me, don't like me, they are going to leave, something bad is going to happen to this relationship
Body: tight shoulders, burning stomach, hot skin, tight jaw, neck, chest, fists, tingling hands	*Body:* churning stomach, sore throat, heavy chest, wobbly legs, shaky
Actions: shout and swear, punch, smash, hit, punish, scream, threaten, throw things, slam doors, storm out; agree and fight later	*Actions:* hide, escape, run, get away, never come back, stop it, submissive apology, submit to make it all okay
Memories: history of anger experience back in childhood of not been heard or been dismissed or being hurt	*Memories:* emotional memories going back to childhood – unpredictable no control
Settle: going outside, drinking, cutting, fighting breathing, practicing, exercise, eating, shouting, ranting to a friend	*Settle:* eat, smoke, drink, watch TV, clean, eat ice cream, take drugs

SAD SELF (loss)	COMPASSIONATE SELF
Motives: caring, comfort, to be understood again -wanted, wants (re)connection, repairing loss	**Motives:** connection, peace, find a resolution that is helpful for everybody, acceptance of what is, not carelessly or purposely causing harm but equally not allowing it
Thoughts: you are hurting me, I'm lonely, I am alone	**Thoughts:** it's alright, sadly arguments are part of life and common to all living things; I wonder what the other is thinking/feeling
Body: angry tears, eyes, throat, heart, muscles collapse and lose tone, weak body, collapsing inward, weakening muscle frame	**Body:** heart, grounded, rooted, settled, effort to slow the breath
Actions: hide, curl up, make oneself small, step into a hole, sleep, seek support, seek comfort	**Actions:** take a step back, open up, embrace the other person, have a conversation about what is causing the problem, be patient, work it out, talk about it, listen
Memories: sad memories throughout the lifespan	**Memories:** remembering times when things worked out, times when you've been helpful
Settle: grieve, distract, avoid	**Grow:** be fully present for a friend in difficulty, cheering oneself on before a difficult feat

Therapist Script 6.5: Multiple Selves Chair Practice (15 minutes)

Before starting this practice, find three additional chairs to work with and arrange them in the space available to you; these three chairs will be hosting the angry self, the anxious self and the sad self. Before starting, invite the client to choose where they wish each self to sit down. Alternatively, if you are working in a limited space, do not have chairs available to you, or are working in a group setting, you can use the "shifting position" method, inviting the participants to shift in their chair as they embody and explore the perspective of each different self. If working in a group setting, people will answer the questions asked through an internal process; if working in an individual setting, the practice will be more dialogical in nature.

To begin this practice, close your eyes and just take a couple of moments to become aware of your body sitting on this chair, your natural posture, getting a feel of the space you are inhabiting, allowing the breath to settle.

Keeping your eyes closed, bring back to mind the memory of the difficult situation you have been exploring in the previous exercises. Take some moments to let this memory form an image, feelings and sensations in your body, thoughts in your mind.

[If working in an individual setting, the client can recount this memory out loud]

Certainly, many parts of you were involved in this situation, each feeling their own feelings, thinking their own thoughts, maybe pushing you to take different actions. We will try to invite each of these parts to tell their own version of this situation.

Let us start by embodying the angry self; please take the seat of the angry self. [The client is invited to move into the chair of the angry self]. *You are now the angry self – thank you angry self for being here. What do you think about this situation that happened? Try to feel your position in this chair, allow yourself to be exactly as you are. How does it feel to be in this body? What are you feeling right now? Are there any sensations in particular that emerge? What would you need right now? What do you think would feel good for you? Thank you for having shared your perspective and telling us how you are feeling.*

Now, take the seat of the sad self. [The client is invited to move into the chair of the sad self]. *You are now your sad self. Thank you for being here with us. We would like to know what do you think about this situation? What do you feel in your body? Do you feel free to move as you would like to move? What are you afraid of if you were to give yourself unconditional permission to be yourself? What do you think would really help you to feel better? What would you need? Thank you for having shared your perspective and telling us how you are feeling.*

Now, take the seat of the anxious self. [The client is invited to move into the chair of the anxious self]. *You are now your anxious self. Thank you for being here with us. What are you thinking about this situation? How would you say this? What are you feeling in your body right now? Do you feel free to be yourself? If not, are there any of the other selves sitting here with us that make it hard for you to be yourself? What would you need to feel heard? To feel better? What would you need from others? Thank you for having shared your perspective and telling us how you are feeling.*

[Invite the client back to their chair]

How do you feel about this encounter? What are you feeling right now?

Now, let us ask our Compassionate Self to help us with this situation.

Begin by rooting yourself in your soothing rhythm breathing. Now, begin to create your compassionate posture – what kind of facial expression, position of the arms, legs, back and shoulders would help you embody your compassionate self? With your next breaths, imagine you are breathing in the quality of wisdom, the quality of courage, the quality strength. Each time you breathe in, you feel your body becoming wiser, more stable; you begin to feel the desire to help these parts to feel welcome here.

When you are ready, open your eyes. You are now your Compassionate Self.

Thank you for being here with us. What do you think about this situation? What do you think about all these parts that emerged? Which part would you like to speak with? Which self do you think most needs your support, your wisdom, your courage?

Look towards the chair where that self is sitting. What would you like to tell that self? What do you feel that part would need to hear from you? If you could enter the very vulnerable heart of this part, what would it like to hear from you?

Now, move into the chair of that self. [The client moves in the chair of the chosen self].

How does it feel receiving this gaze, these words, this support from the Compassionate Self? What do you feel like right now? Do you like receiving these words? What feels most helpful? Is there anything else you would like to ask your Compassionate Self? To say to your Compassionate Self? Try doing so right now.

How does that feel? How do you feel?

[These steps can be replicated for each self].

Now, move back into the chair of the Compassionate Self. [The client moves into the chair of the Compassionate Self.]

Is there any last thing you would like to tell your multiple selves?

Find your sense of groundedness again in your body and breathing, close your eyes, and settle into your soothing rhythm breathing.

If you feel like it, try exploring if there is any movement of your hands or the arms that you would like to do that represents the connection between all these parts (maybe opening the arms, and if it feels ok, imagining containing them as best as we can with this gesture). Or you can notice what comes up when ima-gining that your multiple selves hold hands now.

Then, when you feel ready, come back to the room.

Client Handouts

Client Handout 6.1: Compassionate Weekly Reflection

Let's do a curious friendly reflection on this past week:

Which part of the self-practice did I do and why?

Which part of the self-practice did I not do?

Was this due to any anxieties or block regarding the practice or the path? Which ones can you identify?

We extend gratitude, respect, and compassion to the resistances: What would make you and your resistances feel safer in going forward on this path?

Client Handout 6.2: Components of an Emotion

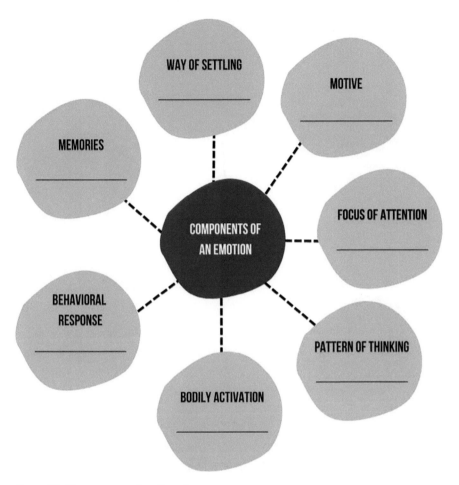

Figure 6.2 Components of an Emotion.

Client Handout 6.3: What Emotions Were Present?

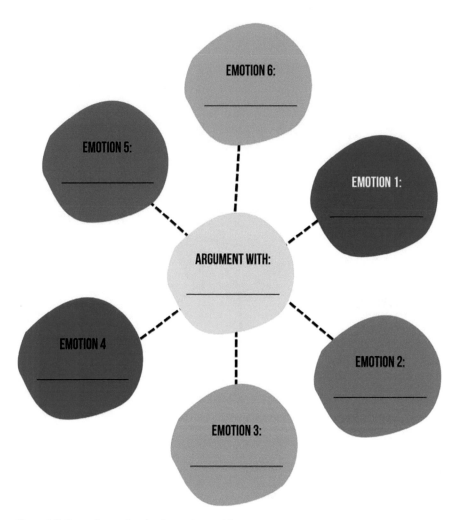

Figure 6.3 Several emotional selves triggered by an argument.

Client Handout 6.4: The Multiple Selves

Table 6.3 Multiple Selves

ANGRY SELF (transgression)	ANXIOUS SELF (danger)
Motives:	Motives:
Thoughts:	Thoughts:
Body:	Body:
Actions:	Actions:
Memories:	Memories:
Settle:	Settle:

SAD SELF (loss)	COMPASSIONATE SELF
Motives:	*Motives:*
Thoughts:	*Thoughts*:
Body:	*Body*:
Actions:	*Actions*:
Memories:	*Memories*:
Settle:	*Growth:*

Client Handout 6.5: Compassionate Beliefs About Emotions

This exercise is to be carried out after having embodied the compassionate self. Keep in mind that for each usual belief, there are multiple possible adaptive alternative beliefs

Table 6.4 Usual Self and Compassionate Self Beliefs About Emotions

USUAL BELIEFS ABOUT EMOTIONS	COMPASSIONATES SELF'S BELIEFS ABOUT EMOTIONS
Certain strong emotions are dangerous and easily get out of hand.	*Example: strong emotions are scary, especially if I have not given myself permission to feel them often... but they are not dangerous... my body can contain them and manage them...*
Other people don't feel strong emotions the way I do.	
My emotions are inappropriate.	
If you love someone, you shouldn't have times when you are angry or even want to leave them.	
If other people love you, they should not be selfish, thoughtless, or feel, at times, that they want to leave you.	

USUAL BELIEFS ABOUT EMOTIONS	COMPASSIONATES SELF'S BELIEFS ABOUT EMOTIONS
You shouldn't have mixed emotions because you should know your own mind.	
If people knew what I feel, they would not like me.	
I don't like myself because of my feelings.	
I just want to get rid of these feelings.	

Chapter 7

Module 7

Self-Criticism

Aims

- To understand the process and functions of self-monitoring
- To explore the origin, forms, and functions of self-criticism
- To identify self-criticism as an attempt to resolve the mismatches between the ideal and the actual self
- To recognise the process of self-attacking in contexts of fear of failure
- To use the Compassionate Self to work with the Self-Critic and the Criticised Self
- To distinguish compassionate improvement from shame-based self-criticism

 Deepen Your Knowledge

In Gilbert, P. & Simos, G. (Eds). (2022). *Compassion Focused Therapy: Clinical Practice and Applications.* Routledge, please refer to:

    Chapter 1. Setting the Scene
    Chapter 5. Internal Shame and Self-Disconnection: From Hostile Self-Criticism to Compassionate Improvement and Guidance

In Gilbert, P. (2010). *Compassion Focused Therapy: Distinctive Features* (1st ed.). Routledge, please refer to:

    Chapter 11: Self-Criticism

DOI: 10.4324/9781003436058-9

Summary of Key Processes

Table 7.1 Module 7: Self-Criticism

Phase		Main Touch Points		Therapist Scripts		Client Handouts
1	Introduction	**1a)** Compassionate Landing **1b)** Revision of personal practice and recap of previous session	☐	**Script 7.1:** Compassionate Landing	☐	**Handout 7.1:** Compassionate Weekly Reflection
2	Self-monitoring	**2a)** Process and functions of self-monitoring				
3	Self-criticism	**3a)** Triggers and forms of self-criticism **3b)** Origins of self-criticism **3b)** Functions and effects of self-criticism	☐ ☐	**Script 7.2:** Origins of self-criticism **Script 7.3:** Functional analysis the Self-critic	☐ ☐	**Handout 7.2:** Possible functions of the Self-Critic **Handout 7.3:** Functional analysis of the Self-Critic
4	Compassionate-Self Integration	**4a)** Differentiating between compassionate improvement and shame-based self-criticism **4b)** Meeting the Self-Critic from the Compassionate Self perspective **4c)** Working with the Criticised Self **4d)** Chairwork and the Self-Critic	☐ ☐ ☐ ☐	**Script 7.4:** Functional analysis of the Compassionate Self **Script 7.5:** The Compassionate Self meets the Self-Critic **Script 7.6:** The Compassionate Self meets the Criticised Self **Script 7.7:** Chairwork and the Self-Critic	☐ ☐ ☐ ☐ ☐	**Handout 7.4:** Functional analysis of the Compassionate Self **Handout 7.5:** Self-criticism vs. compassionate improvement **Handout 7.6:** Writing a letter to my Self-Critic **Handout 7.7:** Representing the Self-Critic and the Criticised Self **Handout 7.8:** Getting to know the Self-Critic through touch
5	Wrap-up	**5a)** Summary of the session and suggestions for personal practice **5b)** Closing practice			☐	**Handout B:** Personal practice diary

Phase I: Introduction

Main Touch Points

Therapist Script 7.1 – Compassionate Landing
Client Handout 7.1 – Compassionate Weekly Reflection

1a) Compassionate Landing

   Therapist Task

To welcome the group, guide them through a Compassionate Landing session (**Therapist Script 7.1**).

   In the previous module we focused on our multiplicity, getting to know our multiple selves, their conflicts and how to harness the wisdom of our Compassionate Self to welcome and integrate them. We will try to link with this concept during the Compassionate Landing practice in this module, witnessing and inviting all the selves that are alive in us today to accompany us during the session.

Three-Circle Check-In

   Therapist Tips

As a therapist it is very important to cultivate your own Compassionate Self practice to lead the group through this work from a place of groundedness, safety, and safeness. Before beginning the sessions, try to always take a moment (this can just be a couple of minutes) to create a compassionate posture, engage in soothing rhythm breathing, connecting to your compassionate intention. Throughout the sessions, be mindful of creating your own inner state of safeness and groundedness repeatedly. After the session is completed it can also be useful to connect with your Compassionate Self to help with bringing the session to a close, allowing self-reflection, and to help re-orient yourself before moving on to your next activities. We can sometimes refer to this as the "therapist warm-up and warm-down".

1b) Revision of personal practice and recap of previous session

 Therapist Task

Invite participants to use the **Client Handout 7.1** to reflect upon the past week/weeks; then get them into pairs or small groups and invite them to share (if they feel like doing so) anything relevant about their past week, including any compassion episodes or any FBRs they might have experienced.

Did they continue with their practice of the Compassionate Self? Were they more aware of their multiple selves? Did they try to embody their Compassionate Self to work with the multiple selves in daily situations? What difficulties did they encounter?

Focus on group processes, try to be validating and positively rewarding of changed behaviours while at the same time not alienating those who are struggling. At the same time, if you focus (only) on struggles, you will be educating your group to pay attention to difficulties and not to benefits (feeding negativity bias). Validate their concerns and try to get to know more.

Before moving on, the therapist can provide a brief recap of the last session, in which the main points were:

- The multiplicity of our emotional experience
- Our multiple selves as mind and body patterns
- How the Compassionate Self can help integrate our multiple selves

This can also be a space to setting the scene for the current module; the main themes that are going to be explored are:

- Our capacity for self-monitoring
- The origins and forms of self-criticism
- The functions and effects of self-criticism
- How to work with our self-criticism using a compassionate approach
- Distinguishing between compassionate improvement and shame-based self-criticism

 Therapist Tips

Be aware that the practices we will introduce in this module can bring forth intense emotions for some people. We wish to shed light on the detrimental impact that the self-to-self relationship has on our psychophysiological conditions but also on the achievement of our goals. Be sure to take plenty of time for group processing and to create space to voice clients' struggles, promoting a deeper understanding of the emotional experiences of group members.

Phase 2: Self-Monitoring

The goal of this phase is to make people aware of our mechanisms of self-monitoring and how important they are for self-regulation and social adaptation. We also try to understand what the purpose of our self-monitoring is. We make a distinction between self-monitoring and self-attacking.

2a) Process and functions of self-monitoring

 Therapist Background Knowledge

We constantly monitor, consciously and unconsciously, what is happening both inside and outside of us. The self-monitoring process is vital for our self-regulation and adaptation. In fact, all motivational systems set up attentional monitoring processes, all algorithms have self-monitoring processes built in them; so, for example, a central heating system will monitor and then respond to changes in temperature. In its simple form, self-monitoring is just noting variations in a particular variable or process.

The brain is no different, except that the self-monitoring can be done in very complex ways; brains are also monitoring systems. For example, we can get into a car and monitor our behaviour in terms of steering, changing gears, breaking, driving in traffic, and constantly change our behaviour moment by moment.

Some other ways we constantly monitor are:

- Am I feeling pain or not?
- Do I feel tired or energized?
- Am I achieving my goals or not?
- Are these thoughts and feelings tolerable or are they overwhelming; helpful or unhelpful?
- Am I doing well or badly?

We can monitor and make judgements on all sorts of things, from memories to feeling states, sometimes simultaneously. For example, participants may be monitoring what is happening in group therapy, how they think therapy is going, how they think they are being perceived by other people, whether other people are doing better than them. This is the way our brains are wired.

In our self-monitoring, we compare thoughts, behaviours, and emotions to some internal standard or ideal. How the ideal self is formed depends on a whole range of factors, many linked to the experiences we had growing up (so again, vastly "not our fault").

When our self-monitoring notices a mismatch between the ideal and the observed self, this can set in motion a host of different self-correcting mechanisms: one of which is self-criticism. And self-criticism can become very hostile and attacking.

To explore the concept of self-monitoring, you can ask the clients if they are monitoring anything about themselves right now – maybe something that has to do with the way they sit, they talk or the way they entered the room at the beginning of the session.

Therapist Tips

Try to keep this phase rather short and use it as a brief introduction to the main topic of this module, which is self-criticism.

Phase 3: Self-Criticism

The aim of this phase is to discover the different forms and functions of self-criticism; in particular, we wish to distinguish between self-improving self-criticism and self-hating self-criticism. Through guided practices we will explore the origins of our self-critic and carry out a functional analysis of self-criticism.

For further information about the theory of self-criticism, please refer to Section I, Chapter 5 of the book *CFT – Clinical Practice and Applications*.

Main Touch Points

Therapist Script 7.2 – Origins of Self-Criticism
Therapist Script 7.3 – Functional Analysis of the Self-Critic
Client Handout 7.2 – Possible Functions of Self-Criticism
Client Handout 7.3 – Functional Analysis of my Self-Critic

3a) Triggers and forms of self-criticism

 Therapist Background Knowledge

Self-criticism is a form of self-monitoring that is layered with a specific emotional texture. In particular, it is a threat-monitoring process.

It often stems from the so called "disappointment gap," which is the space that separates our ideal self from our actual self.

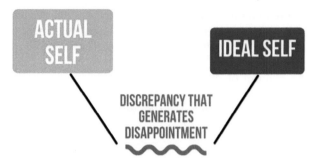

Figure 7.1 Discrepancy between the Actual Self and the Ideal Self

Self-criticism is the way we often deal with this gap, in particular the frustration emerging from the disappointment gap.

The core threat that is linked to self-criticism is about social rejection, isolation, and abandonment. If we consider this from an evolutionary perspective, the greatest archetypal fear for humans is rejection and isolation (e.g., hence the phrase "a lone monkey is a dead monkey"). The surface fear (which is consciously available) of failing or making mistakes, is linked to a deeper, evolved basic fear of not being wanted, rejected, and excluded. In addition, we must always think of how the evolved basic threat of rejection might have been sensitised during childhood or subsequent trauma (history of criticism, bullying, rejection, abuse, competitive social culture).

Children who are bullied can become very self-critical; they can become disappointed with themselves because they feel if they didn't have certain traits, look a certain way, or were more talented, they would be free of being bullied. So, they are sensitised to having a yearning to be "better than they are" in order to avoid being bullied and rejected. From an evolutionary point of view, this form of self-criticism is designed to maintain subordinate submissive status.

Self-criticism can manifest in many different forms.

1   Some individuals become self-critical because they feel they could and should do better in order to achieve their potential
2   Other individuals can have a chronic sense of inferiority and inadequacy; they feel they should do better because they have to make up for their inadequacies, and have a more chronic self-critical style of internal dialogue. These people often compare themselves with others, are perfectionistic and worried about making mistakes, or feeling ashamed of their flaws being revealed
3   Then, there are those people who are more self-hating and self-loathing. These individuals do not self-criticise just out of frustration or as a style of trying to improve themselves and prevent mistakes, but rather because they do not like themselves even hate themselves or aspects of themselves – rather than wanting to improve things, they want to get rid of

"parts'"of themselves. They can have a chronic sense of self-disgust, marked by an internal dialogue of this kind: "I hate myself when I feel like this; I hate myself when I look like this"

In all these cases, the therapeutic task will be to go beyond self-criticism and get into the evolved threat and unprocessed anger, fear, and commonly intense inner loneliness and grief; we need to help clients be clear about what they are trying to reach safety from.

   Therapist Task

As a first exercise to elicit discussion about self-criticism and the disappointment gap, invite participants to reflect upon their ideal self. We all have images that come to mind of what we are aiming for and what we would like to be, or how we would hope to be. And what happens when we do not meet that ideal, for example, when we have a moment of failure? What kind of fears emerge at the idea of never reaching that ideal? How do we view and treat ourselves then?

These questions begin to uncover the fears that lie beneath our self-criticism. In Compassion Focused Therapy, we are always thinking about what the basic fear is, about what the thing that the person would be most frightened of happening is if they were not to reach their goal. During the group discussion, as a way to begin to trace the process that links self-criticism to some form of basic fear (which will be done in more depth at a later stage), the therapist may incorporate the downward arrow technique for questions, commonly used in Cognitive Behavioural Therapy (You are afraid of not getting the top grade. What would happen if you didn't? What would that mean for you? ...)

3b) Origins of Self-Criticism

   Therapist Task

At this point, it is important to investigate about the origins of self-criticism. While we might not want to delve too deeply into some very painful memories, it can be useful to just get a feel and a sense of how our Self-Critic was born and its functions during our development. Take the group through a guided discovery following **Therapist Script 7.2**.

Therapist Tips

When working with the Self-Critic, it is very useful to bring awareness to the fact that people have not chosen their criticism: if they could have chosen how parents, or others at school behaved towards them, would they have chosen for them to act that way? What would they have chosen? Generally, people will report that they would have chosen to be cared for, over being criticised. The same thing goes for our inner critic. Point to the fact that they have this internal compassionate wisdom that will orient them towards what is helpful, not harmful. Our inner voice has a lot of compassionate wisdom and courage, and it will guide us if we let it do so.

3c) Functions and effects of Self-Criticism

    Therapist Task

Just like there are different possible origins and forms of self-criticism, there are also different possible functions.

For example, we know that children who grow up with very powerful and frightening parents can learn to self-blame for conflicts with their parents; they can be submissive – and be focused on self-monitoring their own behaviour. Self-blaming is a safety strategy that is often used by our brain when we are confronted with other people who seem more powerful than us. We see this also in certain religions a lot too. Freud called this anger turned inwards, and with a slight change of emphasis, it can be seen as a safety strategy to avoid injury or rejection from powerful others.

> *When ancient populations encountered a disappointment regarding their expectations – for example a crop season being destroyed by a storm – their human brain would immediately translate this fact into the message "someone is angry with me". The disappointment gap would light up their rank-based inner dialogue, bringing them to adopt coping strategies to try to reduce that gap. One such example would be making sacrifices to the Gods so they might cease to be angry at them.*

Another metaphor is:

> *Imagine finding yourself in a cage with a sleeping tiger. If you make any sounds, the tiger will wake up and eat you. In that moment, you're probably going to be monitoring yourself accurately, because you don't want to*

make any mistakes. If you do make a sound, you'll probably tell yourself "Ah, that was so stupid of me!". You would probably never even think of blaming the tiger. However, if someone else arrived on the scene, they would be wondering why you were in a cage in the first place, not why you made a noise.

To explore your clients' evaluation of their self-criticism we can start by asking:

- *Imagine we could take away your self-criticism, so that you would never get angry with yourself or beat yourself up in the future – What would your greatest fear be?*
- *What would you worry about if you could not be self-critical any more?*

Typical fears of letting go of self-criticism are becoming lazy, arrogant, not learning from one's mistakes, not developing, not seeing one's flaws. We must acknowledge that these goals are totally fine, there is nothing wrong with the goals themselves – it is how we react when those fears arise that causes problems.

You can invite clients to use **Client Handout 7.2** to read about more the functions of self-criticism and write down their own.

To further explore the functions of self-criticism, we use the guided experiential exercise called *Functional Analysis of the Self-Critic* (**Therapist Script 7.3**). The idea here is to have an emotional felt experience of the harmfulness of shame-based self-criticism, and to become aware of its consequences on our physiology and mental patterns.

You may use the following prompts for discussion:

- This self-critical part, does it really have your best interest at heart?
- Does it rejoice in your well-being?
- When you are in its presence, do you feel it is bringing you closer to your purpose?

Phase 4: Compassionate Self Integration

The goal of this phase is to understand how the Compassionate Self can help us address our disappointment and translate the self-critic into a form of compassionate improvement. Furthermore, we will also work with the Criticised Self, whose needs and emotions have long been invalidated by the Self-Critic.

Main Touch Points

> **Therapist Script 7.4** – Functional Analysis of the Compassionate Self
> **Therapist Script 7.5** – The Compassionate Self meets the Self-Critic
> **Therapist Script 7.6** – The Compassionate Self meets the Criticised Self

Therapist Script 7.7 – Chairwork and the Self-.Critic
Client Handout 7.4 – Functional Analysis of the Compassionate Self
Client Handout 7.5 – Self-Criticism vs. Compassionate Improvement
Client Handout 7.6 – Writing a Letter to my Self-Critic
Client Handout 7.7 – Representing the Self-Critic and the Criticised Self
Client Handout 7.8 – Getting to Know the Self-Critic through Touch

4a) Differentiating between compassionate improvement and shame-based self-criticism

 Therapist Task

As previously discussed, the gap we perceive between our current self and our ideal self creates disappointment, which we often deal with through harsh and sometimes even hostile self-criticism. This, however, is not the only option we have. Those fears that emerge when we think of what might happen if we were to let go of our Self-Critic, such as becoming lazy, arrogant, or hurtful can be addressed through the lens of our Compassionate Self. How might the Compassionate Self help us with those fears, in a way that is more helpful than the strategies of the Self-Critic?

In order to access compassionate improvement, we must first connect to the Compassionate Self. You may do so by guiding clients through the *Compassionate Self Functional Analysis* which can be done either as an imagery or a written exercise, or as a combination of both (**Therapist Script 7.4**).

There are two very different ways of relating with ourselves that can help us reach the same goals, but with very different processes and by-products: self-criticism and compassionate improvement. To introduce this concept, you can use the example of the two schools.

> *Imagine you have a child you love and you have a choice of two schools to send your child to. At one of these schools, as you walk through the gates you see a group of teachers that look remarkably like your Self-Critic (take examples from the group's own self-critic functional analyses exercise). They say they will ensure your child learns because if your child makes mistakes or is lazy or arrogant in some way, they will be critical and harsh, express anger and contempt, they will ensure strong discipline and the fear of authority through punishment.*
>
> *So, you thank that school very much and then you walk to the other school. Here you find teachers who are concerned with your child's well-being. These teachers are very similar to your compassionate image. Try imagining what they would look like, their voice tone, posture. They want*

to help your child feel safe and encourage them to learn and be enthusiastic about their abilities; when they make mistakes, the teachers will support them so that they may learn from them, feel open to seeking help and are keen to learn to be better.

Which school would you choose for your child?

How would two people growing up in the two schools differ?

Which school would you send yourself to?

This example often gets people to smile and at the same time proves to be very insightful; it provides them with a concrete example of what a great impact our inner dialogue can have on us and our development.

What are the characteristics of our shame-based self-criticism? What are the characteristics of our compassionate improvement?

You can choose to let this be an opportunity for group discussion or a moment of psychoeducation.

 Optional Practice

You may invite participants to complete **Client Handout 7.5** to begin reflecting on the difference between shame-based self-criticism and compassionate improvement. Highlight the way both may be trying to help us achieve a certain goal, but they do so with a very different emotional texture and therefore have very different effects on our psychophysiology. Invite them to transform their self-critical remarks into compassionate improvement remarks.

Table 7.2 Shame-based Self-Criticism versus Compassionate Improvement

Shame based self-criticism	Compassionate improvement
• *Desire to punish and condemn* • *Backward looking* • *Linked to disappointment* • *Focusing on deficits errors* • *Emotions are anger, frustration anxiety, contempt*	• *Desire to improve, to be the best version of myself* • *Forward looking* • *Linked to building on the positives and developing abilities* • *Validation of setbacks and encouragement*
Consider a critical teacher with a child who is struggling	*Consider a compassionate teacher with a child who is struggling*

4b) Meeting the Self-Critic from the Compassionate Self perspective

 Therapist Task

The next step in working with the Self-Critic is all about using the wisdom and courage of the Compassionate Self to approach this difficult part of our being and try to find a helpful dialogue with it. The Compassionate Self helps us to see the fear and hurt behind criticism and offers us the support needed to actually face them, instead of avoiding through self-reprimand.

 Therapist Tips

As a therapist, you must be aware that sometimes people might identify their inner critical voice with the voice of someone else in their lives; in this case, the Compassionate Self will probably need to work alongside the angry self, validating its need for assertiveness.

Lead the group through the imagery practice (using **Therapist Script 7.5**), then come back and allow some time for group discussion.

 Optional Practices

As an additional exercise for self-reflection to be done either during the session or as homework, you can suggest the idea of writing a letter to their Self-Critic (**Client Handout 7.6**), from the Compassionate Self. Individuals may refer to a specific event in which the Self-Critic was triggered.

Another exercise you can suggest participants try out at home to unveil further characteristics of their Self-Critic is using touch. Ask them to find an object at home that reminds them of their Self-Critic, that they believe represents this part of them. Invite them to use **Client Handout 7.8** to complete this exercise.

4c) Working with the Criticized Self

 Therapist Task

Whenever self-criticism comes into play, we must be aware that there are at least two parts at play: 1) the Self-Critic and 2) the Criticised Self. In addition to these, our multiple selves might also appear, strengthening or creating resistance towards the other two. Activating the Compassionate Self can be helpful to transform the words of the Self-Critic and providing support and alleviate the suffering of the Criticised Self.

You may use **Therapist Script 7.5** to guide the participants through this practice. Please be mindful that this can be a profound experience for some people, since it might unlock grief about what kind of support and care they would have liked to receive but were never provided.

 ### Optional practice

Another way to explore the interwoven tapestry of the threads that connect the Self-Critic, Criticised Self, and the Compassionate Self is through creative expression. You can ask clients to draw their Self-Critic and Criticised Self before and after receiving compassionate care, support, and wisdom from the Compassionate Self, observing what changes in the way in which they are perceived. Please refer to **Client Handout 7.7**.

 ### Optional Practice

4d) Chairwork and the Self-Critic

 Therapist Task

Chairwork can be a powerful method to use when working with different selves. It can be applied to receive further insights into the experience of both the Self-Critic and the Criticised Self, and call upon the Compassionate Self to help validate these parts and meet their needs. This practice (optional) can be used both in group and individual settings, although you may need to make some adjustments (please refer to Module 6) in order for it to work in a group setting. Use **Therapist Script 7.7** to guide this practice.

Phase 5: Wrap-Up

The final phase of the module is a wrap-up of the theme that has been explored. Emphasise how continuing to work on our **personal practice** (whether formal or informal) can help with the development of our compassionate minds.

Main Touch Points

 Client Handout B – Personal Practice Diary

5a) Summary of the session and suggestions for personal practice

   Therapist Task

Take 5–10 minutes to briefly summarise the points that you have gone through in this module.

You may want to provide participants with some suggestions for personal practice and self-reflection:

- Invite them to use **Client Handout 7.8** suggesting they try to focus on one compassionate activity per day, maybe focusing specifically on how their Compassionate Self helped them engage with others and with themselves that day
- Invite them to follow the guided audio meditation for the Compassionate Self meets the Self-Critic or the Criticised Self at least once during the week, so that they may continue to connect with these parts of themselves

5b) Closing practice

   Therapist Task

Remember to take a moment at the end of the session to acknowledge anything and everything that has come up for participants while exploring the themes introduced.

As in previous sessions, invite them to share in one sentence:

What do I take home from today's session (because I feel it's going to be helpful)?
What are some key things that I would like to share and tell other people about?

Invite participants to bring their attention to their intention to be helpful to themselves and others rather than neglectful.

Finally, guide participants through a short closing practice using **Therapist Script 2.5** and perhaps you could add a sentence or two that links back to the work done during the session. It could be something like: *"Briefly acknowledge yourself for simply being here; with all your doubts, all your resistances, and all your difficulties, but also with the courage and the willingness to meet one of your most difficult selves today,"* or *"Recognise the courage and wisdom it has taken to meet your Self-Critic today and cultivate gratitude for this opportunity you've granted yourself"*. Remember that it is *only the first of many encounters with this self, and that each time it shows up, it will be an opportunity for you to extend a helpful intention to this self, which is so connected to the deep fears all of us have as human beings, which we did not choose ourselves..."*

Three-Circle Check-In

Therapist Scripts

Therapist Script 7.1: Compassionate Landing (5 minutes)

(Refer to Therapist Script 2.1 in Chapter 2)

You can add the following elements to connect to the previous module.

From your compassionate stance, try to curiously observe which selves feel alive in you now. Perhaps you can hear signs of your angry or anxious self, or your happy self...

As you become more aware of what is alive inside you today, welcome whatever arises. If it is helpful to you, you can whisper to yourself, "You are all welcome" ...and as you feel a self appear, repeat, "You are welcome"...notice what happens if you keep repeating this "welcome mantra" with each feeling that comes up. Imagine that through your breath, you are creating a spacious temple in your body, where each self can find its place.

Remember your wishes to learn to be helpful to yourself, to support others on their journey and to be open to the helpfulness of others.

Therapist Script 7.2: Origins of Self-Criticism (10 minutes)

To begin this guided meditation, find a comfortable position; allow your body to assume the posture it feels most comfortable in this moment. Remember that the aim of this practice is not to create perfect images, or to have specific sensations, but to observe whatever arises and is useful for us. There is no way to get this practice wrong. Feel free to open your eyes in any moment if you feel the need to do so.

Try to really feel all the points of contact on your body with the surface beneath you, to allow your shoulders to soften, creating space in your chest and stretching your back. Then, gently, you can begin to close your eyes or, if you prefer, you can keep them slightly open with your gaze downward.

Try to imagine going back in time to the moment when, as a child, you started to think that you were not doing well... maybe it was in elementary school, junior high... it may have been a time when you experienced a sense of shame, or perhaps guilt... or when you had other unpleasant feelings and emotions that caused you to want to make yourself small, to want to hide, to feel "not enough" or "too much".

If you don't remember the exact moment, try creating a mental image of yourself as a child affected by your self-criticism. Try looking at yourself from the outside: what kind of expression does this child have? What kind of posture do they tend to assume? What is going on around this child? What would this child like to do?

Also, perhaps try asking this child directly: what are you afraid of? What fear are you feeling right now? What needs do you have? What needs do you feel are not being met?

Now, try to imagine how self-criticism tries to protect this child. Try to ask yourself if self-criticism is truly succeeding in protecting them...how does it make this child feel? Now imagine that this child, in their daily activities like going to school or playing, is always accompanied by this self-critical voice.

Try to observe what you see: is this critical voice helping the child?

Now imagine that you can time travel, imagine this child growing up and becoming a teenager, in middle school and then in high school. Imagine observing yourself, at this age, from the outside. What is this teenager feeling? What are they afraid of? What needs are not being met? Is their self-criticism still present? Has it changed? How does it make this teenager feel? Is this critical voice helping them?

Would this teenager be afraid of letting go of their self-criticism?

Take a few moments to contemplate these questions and simply notice what arises without forcing anything, while your mind stays on the image of this teenager.

Imagine that you can travel further forward in time, and you see this teenager grow up… as best as you can, observe yourself in the different phases of your life… looking from the outside… how is this person? What are they afraid of? What are they ashamed of? What do they suffer for? Is the Self-Critic still there? How does it make them feel? is this critical voice helping them?

Now land exactly here and now, where you are today.

Try to observe yourself from the outside; as best as you can, observe your face… what are you afraid of? What needs do you feel are going unheard in your life? Is the self-criticism still there? How does it act towards this person today? Does it still have the same voice? Do you feel it is helping this person in front of you?

How does it make you feel? What is it stopping you from doing? What would you wish for this person you see in front of you today?

Take a few moments to contemplate these questions and welcome all that emerges – thoughts, emotions, sensations. Imagine yourself returning to your body now, embodying your Compassionate Self and being able to observe and allow whatever you are feeling.

Then, you can return to your breathing again and ground yourself for a few minutes in your calming breath. When you feel ready, you can open your eyes again.

Therapist Script 7.3: Functional Analysis of Self-Criticism (10 minutes)

Therapist Tips

This exercise is typically done with **Client Handout 7.3**. It can either be done by alternating guided meditation with written self-reflection or by delivering the entire guided meditation and then allowing time for self-reflection at the end.

To begin this practice, find a comfortable position in your chair, sitting upright, feet flat on the ground, and then focus on finding your natural breathing rhythm for a couple of minutes.

Now, bring to mind a situation, recent or from your past, where your Self-Critic was particularly active – nothing too major to begin with, just a typical situation that results in you being self-critical, frustrated, annoyed and disappointed with yourself.

Now that you are in touch with this memory and can sense it, imagine this self-critical part of you appearing on the scene. Imagine it takes a form of its own. What sort of shapes, colours, textures belong to this image? You might receive a clear image, or you might just have a sense of something.

Observe if your Self-Critic moves; if it moves at all, what position does it take in space?

Then, begin inquiring into what the Self-Critic is actually saying – What words does it use towards you? What does it think about you?

As you are looking at your self-critical part and hearing it saying all these things, what emotions do you believe it is feeling? What does it actually feel about you?

Now, try to turn towards the sense of action – what do you think your Self-Critic wants to do to you or with you? What actions might it like to act out?

Turn back to yourself right now – how are you feeling? What are you feeling about yourself right now?

Now, you can begin to let go of this image, take a couple of conscious breaths, and then open your eyes and return to the room.

The therapist may use the following prompts for discussion:

- This self-critical part, does it really have your best interest at heart?
- Does it rejoice in your well-being?
- When you are in its presence, do you feel it is bringing you closer to your purpose?

Therapist Script 7.4: Functional Analysis of the Compassionate Self (10 minutes)

Therapist Tips

This exercise is typically done with **Client Handout 7.4**.

It can either be done by alternating guided meditation with written self-reflection or by delivering the entire guided meditation and then allowing time for self-reflection at the end.

To begin this practice, find a comfortable position in your chair, sitting upright, feet flat on the ground, and then focus on finding your natural breathing rhythm for a couple of minutes.

Bring to mind once again the same situation that we previously worked on.

Now that you in touch with this memory and can sense it, imagine your Compassionate Self appearing on the scene. Imagine it takes a form of its own. What sort of shapes, colours, textures belong to this image? You might receive a clear image, or you might just have a sense of something.

Observe if your Compassionate Self moves, if it moves at all, what position does it take in space? How do its qualities of strength, courage, wisdom, and its deep desire to help manifest through its presence?

Then, begin inquiring into what the Compassionate Self is actually saying – Is it speaking to you? What does it think about you?

As you are looking at your Compassionate Self and hearing it saying all these things, how do you think it feels towards you?

What makes you think it is feeling a certain emotion?

Now, try to turn towards the sense of action – is there anything that your Compassionate Self would like to do for you? Anything it wishes for you?

Turn back to yourself right now – how are you feeling right now? What are you feeling about yourself in this moment, after having been in the validating presence of your Compassionate Self?

Now, you can begin to let go of this image, take a couple of conscious breaths and then open your eyes and return to the room.

The therapist may use the following prompts for discussion:

- Does your Compassionate Self really have your best interests at heart?
- Does it rejoice in your well-being?
- When you are in its presence, do you feel it is bringing you closer to your purpose?

Therapist Script 7.4: The Compassionate Script Meets the Self-Critic (7 minutes)

To begin the practice, find your comfortable position and close your eyes (or keep them half-closed if you prefer).

First, try to contact your Compassionate Self, assuming an upright and open position, your back strong, your heart open, your feet rooted to the ground, perhaps a slight smile appearing on your lips; allow your breath to slow down, becoming friendly and calming.

Take a few moments to allow the sensations of your Compassionate Self to land in your body.

Now, imagine that your Self-Critic appears right in front of you right now, and begins to talk and move as it usually does – you observe it, maintaining your compassionate posture, embodying your Compassionate Self. Now, as you observe your Self-Critic doing their critical actions, try to notice if you can see beyond the criticism and grasp what is driving them to speak and act in this way.

Through the wise and courageous eyes of the Compassionate Self, can you see any fears? They could be fears of inferiority or rejection – of not being wanted. You might also consider the hurts that has prompted this fear – disappointments or what other people have said.

Imagine being able to connect with the sadness or pain, the fear of solitude that underlies this criticism. Imagine that your Compassionate Self is curious about the needs and fears of this self-critical part of your being.

While maintaining this compassionate posture, try making a compassionate wish: "may the deeper causes of this desire of yours to criticise me – to say and feel those things about me – cease, and may you find peace".

What compassionate message would you like to leave with your Self-Critic? Embodying your Compassionate Self, try your Self-Critic these questions:

What would you like to hear and how would you like to hear it? What would you need to feel at peace?

If you feel like words are too hard to express, simply imagine using your out-breath to send your Self-Critic a flow of compassion, a wish for peace and support – this flow is exactly what its needs in this moment to feel safer, seen...try to imagine your Self-Critic absorbing all the compassion it needs. How would it appear if it absorbed all the compassion it needed? How do you see it change?

Continue to imagine this exchange of compassion until it feels nurtured.

If you feel called to do so, create an image that captures this encounter – imagine taking a photo or drawing a portrait. Is there a word that you feel captures this moment?

Therapist Script 7.5: The Compassionate Self Meets the Criticised Self (7 minutes)

In this practice we will see what happens when we bring compassionate attention to the criticised self. This can be quite moving so, as with all our practices, feel free to go at your own pace.

First, let us get into our Compassionate Self, and feel its intention to be helpful; you may find connection with it through your posture, your gaze, your smile, your thoughts, a memory or an image. Find whatever anchors you to your Compassionate Self and try to get a felt sense of it, to embody it.

Now, try to recollect a situation in which your Self-Critic made itself heard. Now, imagine being able to see the part of you that feels hurt by the criticism. See if you can get a sense of that part of you. What does it look like? What is its facial expression? What posture does it assume? What does it want to do? What is it thinking? What is it feeling hurt about?

If you feel you are being drawn into the deep and intense emotions felt by your criticised self, try to return as best as you can to your compassionate body awareness, grounding yourself in your soothing rhythm breathing.

Imagine now that you are able to take hold of this hurt part of you with compassion, wisdom, and strength.

How would you like this part of you to know that you support it, that you understand its suffering, that you simply wish to be there for it?

What kind of support – maybe touch, maybe words, maybe just a presence – would your Criticised Self like to receive from your Compassionate Self?

Take a couple of moments to allow this encounter to happen and observe if there are any changes in the Criticised Self. How does it feel to receive this kind of support? How does it feel to be seen through these eyes?

If you feel like words are difficult to express, simply imagine using your out-breath to send your Criticised Self a flow of compassion, a wish for peace and support – this flow is exactly what its needs in this moment to feel safer, seen, enveloped by compassion... try to imagine the Criticised Self absorbing all the compassion it needs. How would this part appear if it absorbed all the compassion it needed? How do you see it change?

Continue to imagine this exchange of compassion until it feels nurtured.

If you feel called to do so, create an image that captures this encounter – imagine taking photo or drawing a portrait. Is there a word that you feel captures this moment?

Now, gently let go the image of the Criticised Self, let go the image of this situation and, gently return to your body right here. Try to focus once again on the sense of the body slowing down, the mind slowing down. Connect once again to your compassionate posture, sensing your intuitive wisdom.

Therapist Script 7.6: Chair Work and the Self-Critic (10 minutes)

Before starting this practice, find two additional chairs to work with and arrange them in the space available to you; these three chairs will accomodate the Self-Critic and the Criticised Self. Before starting, invite the client to choose where they wish each self to sit down.

Alternatively, if you are working in a limited space, do not have chairs available to you, or are working in a group setting, you can use the "shifting position" method, inviting the participants to shift in their chair as they embody and explore the perspective of each different self. If working in a group setting, people will answer the questions asked through an internal process; if working in an individual setting, the practice will be more dialogical in nature.

To begin this practice, close your eyes and just take a couple of moments to become aware of your body sitting on this chair, your natural posture, getting a feel of the space you are inhabiting, allowing your breathing to settle.

Keeping your eyes closed, call back to mind the memory of a situation in which your Self-Critic made its appearance. Take some moments to let this memory form an image, feelings and sensations in your body, thoughts in your mind.

[If working in an individual setting, the client can recount this memory out loud.]

Certainly, many parts of you were involved in this situation, each feeling their own feelings, thinking their own thoughts, perhaps pushing you to take different actions. We will try to invite two of these parts, your Self-Critic and your Criticised Self, to offer us their perspectives on this situation.

Let us start by embodying the Self-Critic; please take the seat of the Self-Critic. [Client is invited to move into the chair of the Self-Critic]. *You are now the Self-Critic — thank you Self-Critic for being here. What do you think about this situation that happened? What do you feel in your body? Why do you think you acted the way you did? What are you afraid would happen had you not intervened in this situation? What do you think would really help you to feel better? What would you need?*

Turing towards the Criticised Self, what do you think about this part? What do you feel towards this part? What would you like to say to it? How would you say it? Say it now.

[The client moves into the chair of the Criticised Self.]

How does it feel receiving this gaze, these words, these judgements from the Self-Critic? How are you feeling in the body right now? What are your thoughts? What do you think of yourself? How would you like to sit right now? How would you like to reply?

You can give the client the chance to have a back-and-forth discussion between the Self-Critic and the Criticised Self, so that all the emotions linked to this inner dialogue are elicited.

[The client returns to their initial chair.]

How do you feel about this encounter? What are you feeling right now?
Now, let us ask our Compassionate Self to help us with this situation.
The therapist guides the client through a Compassionate Self activation in the chair.

Let us get into our Compassionate Self, and its intention to be helpful; you may find connection with it through your posture, your gaze, your smile, your thoughts, a memory, or an image. Find whatever anchors you to your Compassionate Self and try to get a felt sense of it, to embody it.

When you are ready, open your eyes. You are now your Compassionate Self.

Thank you for being here with us. What do you think about this situation?

Now, look towards the chair where the Self-Critic is sitting. From the point of view of the Compassionate Self, what would you like to tell the Self-Critic? What do you feel that part would need to hear from you? If you could enter the very vulnerable heart of this part, what would it like to hear from you? Say it.

Now, move into the chair of the Self-Critic. [The client moves in the chair of the Self-Critic].

How does it feel to receive this gaze, these words, this support from the Compassionate Self? What do you feel like right now? Do you like receiving these words? What feels most helpful? Is there anything else you would like to ask your Compassionate Self? To say to your Compassionate Self? Try doing so right now.

Now, move back into the chair of the Compassionate Self. [The client moves into the chair of the Compassionate Self, and embodies it once again – if appropriate, the client can say what they just felt.]

Now, look towards the chair where the Criticised Self is sitting. What would you like to tell the Criticised Self? What do you feel that part would need to hear from you? If you could enter the very vulnerable heart of this part, what would it like to hear from you, that would really be helpful?

Now, move into the chair of the Criticised Self. [The client moves in the chair of the Criticised Self.]

How does it feel receiving this gaze, these words, this support from the Compassionate Self? How do you feel right now? Do you like receiving these words? What feels most helpful? Is there anything else you would like to ask your Compassionate Self? To say to your Compassionate Self? Try doing so right now. How does that feel? How do you feel?

[The client returns to their Compassionate Self seat.] *Is there something that the Compassionate Self would like to say?*

Is there any last thing you would like to tell your critical and criticised selves?

Is there a gesture that you feel you would like to do to capture the encounter with these parts? Imagine taking a photo of this moment – what would it look like? What word or message best describes this image?

Reconnet to your body and breathing, close your eyes, and settle into your soothing rhythm breathing.

Then, when you feel ready, come back to the room.

Client Handouts

Client Handout 7.1: Compassionate Weekly Reflection

Let's do a curious friendly reflection on this past week:

Which part of the self-practice did I do and why?

Which part of the self-practice did I not do?

Was this due to any anxieties or blocks regarding the practice or the path? Which ones can you identify?

We extend gratitude, respect, and compassion to the resistances: What would make you and your resistances feel safer in going forward on this path?

Client Handout 7.2: Possible Functions of the Self-Critic

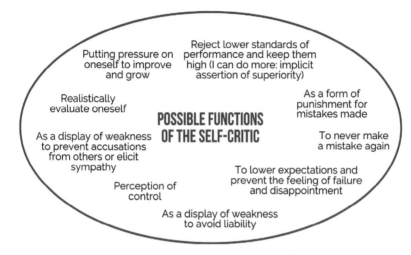

Figure 7.2 Possible functions of the Self-Critic.

Which of these resonate most with you?
Which ones do you recognise yourself in the most?
Why? In what specific situations do you notice them?

Client Handout 7.3: Functional Analysis of My Self-Critic

Its greatest fears are:

How it appears:

What it tells me:

What emotions it feels towards me:

What it wants to do to me or with me:

Now, what do I feel and think about myself?

Client Handout 7.4: Functional Analysis of My Compassionate Self

How it appears:

What it tells me:

What emotions it feels towards me:

What it wishes for me:

Now, what do I feel and think about myself?

Client Handout 7.5: Self-Criticism vs Compassionate Improvement

Table 7.3

Self-Criticism	Compassionate Improvement
Focused on the desire to condemn and punish	Focused on the desire to improve
Focused on punishing past mistakes	Focused on growth and expansion
Often focused on the past	Often focused on the future
Criticism roused by anger, frustration, contempt, disappointment	Criticism roused by encouragement, support, and kindness
Focused on shortcomings and fear of exposure	Builds on the positives (e.g., remembering what you did well in the past and considering things to learn from)
Focused on global sense of self (if I make a mistake, I extend it to my entire sense of self)	Focused on specific attributes and qualities of the self (if I make a mistake, I put things in perspective)
Focused on the fear of failure	Focused on success and hope for success
Increases the likelihood of avoidance and abandonment	Increases the likelihood of engagement
Like a criticising and judgemental teacher towards a struggling child	Like a compassionate teacher towards a struggling child
In the face of mistakes and wrongdoings:	*In the face of mistakes and wrongdoings:*
Shame, avoidance, fear	Guilt, involvement
"heartbreak," mood deflection	regret, remorse
Aggression	Repair

Think about some of the most frequent remarks your Self-Critic makes; how might you transform these into Compassionate encouragements?

Table 7.4

Self-Critical Remark	Compassionate Encouragement
Example: you're lazy! You're not as reliable as everyone thinks... you're an impostor!	*Example: I know that not observing the deadlines is scary for you... that's why the Self-Critic is so restless. But you are very tired these days and it is important that you respect yourself at this time. It is ok not to be perfect – nobody is. Remember all the times you've completed your projects and duties. People can count on you. You can count on you.*

Client Handout 7.6: Writing a Letter to My Self-Critic

Try writing a letter to your Self-Critic from your Compassionate Self.

If you want, you can refer to a specific event in which your Self-Critic was triggered.

Remember that what is important is to cultivate the intention to be helpful, to speak to the suffering and pain of the Self-Critic. There is no right or wrong way to write this letter.

Before writing, close your eyes and give yourself time to activate your compassionate self, starting with your breathing, posture, facial expression, and then connect with the wise and courageous intention to be helpful.

From this position, recall the image of self-criticism in front of you.

When you feel ready, you can begin writing your letter to your Self-Critic using these prompts, if you like:

Dear Critical [your name]....

I've just met your and I started to realise that the fear you stem from is what drives your behaviour...

Now I see that what you are afraid of is...

It is understandable that you have been feeling this way. In fact, you came at a time in ....'s life when they felt .... And you acted this way with .... because you wanted that.........(or you wanted to prevent that...).

I would like you to know that I now see what your intention was more clearly ...

However now...... (describe the consequences of self-criticism that you are facing... how you may be blocked... what you are forced to do or not do because of your self-criticism)

And what I wish for.... is ....

I would like you to know that you are safe with me, that now I wish for you to....

Final message/wish

Signature

Client Handout 7.7: Representing the Self-Critic and Criticised Self

We have many channels through which we can connect to our different selves: one of these is through creative expression with colours and shapes.

Represent your Self-Critic and your Criticised Self through colours and shapes: it might be an abstract representation or a figure drawing:

Table 7.5 Representing the Criticised Self

Criticised Self

Table 7.6 Representing the Self-Critic

Self-Critic

Now connect to your Compassionate Self through one of the practices you have learned; spend some minutes feeling its courageous wisdom and desire to be of help to both those parts. If you imagine that both these parts, both the Self-Critic and the Criticised Self, were to absorb all the compassion they needed, how would they transform? Would you add different colours? Would they change shape?

Draw them below:

Table 7.7

Criticised Self

Table 7.8

Self-Critic

Client Handout 7.8: Getting to Know the Self-Critic Through Touch

Try walking around the house or outside (you can do this by following the Mindful Walk – Practice 5.6 in your booklet).

During this walk, find a rough, angular object that can represent your self-criticism. Take a few moments to run your hands over it, touching its pro-truding, perhaps even a little sharp, edges. Observe all the nuances, creases, corners; try to close your eyes and perceive it only through touch – What feelings does it evoke in you?

Then, still holding it in your hand, try to hold it tightly, as if you wanted to suffocate it, or destroy or hide it – What feelings does it evoke in you?

Soften your grip, and embodying your Compassionate Self, imagine now that you can gently caress it – What feelings does it evoke in you?

You can write down the insights that emerged from this short experiential practice.

Chapter 8

Module 8

Shame and Guilt

Aims

- To explain how evolution has designed us to be social from the first days of our lives and the fact that the threat, drive and soothing systems are regulated through social relationships
- To recognise that shame, humiliation, and guilt are all threat emotions related to the experience of the self as a social agent
- To understand the difference between shame and guilt
- To explore how tuning into the Compassionate Self can help "heal shame" and, when appropriate, shift into a reparation-oriented experience of guilt

 Deepen Your Knowledge

In Gilbert, P. & Simos, G. (Eds). (2022). *Compassion Focused Therapy: Clinical Practice and Applications*. Routledge, please refer to:

Chapter 4. Shame, Humiliation, Guilt, and Social Status: The Distress and Harms of Social Disconnection

DOI: 10.4324/9781003436058-10

Summary of Key Processes

Table 8.1 Module 8: Shame and Guilt

Phase		Main Touch Points	Therapist Scripts	Client Handouts
1	Introduction	**1a)** Compassionate landing **1b)** Revision of personal practice and recap of previous session	☐ **Script 8.1**: Compassionate Landing	☐ **Handout 8.1**: Compassionate Weekly Reflection
2	Introducing shame	**2a)** Nature of shame **2b)** Distinction between internal shame, external shame and humiliation **2c)** Internal shame and the undesired self	☐ **Script 8.2**: Meeting the undesired self	☐ **Handout 8.2**: Exploring shame ☐ **Handout 8.3**: Undesired, Actual and Ideal Self
3	Differences between shame and guilt	**3a)** Guilt **3b)** Differences between shame, humiliation and guilt	☐ **Script 8.3**: Shifting from shame to guilt	☐ **Handout 8.4**: Distinguishing self-conscious emotions
4	Healing the wounds of shame	**4a)** Beginning the journey to heal the wounds of shame	☐ **Script 8.4**: Unravelling shame in the body ☐ **Script 8.5**: Compassionate imagery with rescripting ☐ **Script 8.6**: Reconnecting	☐ **Handout 8.5**: Compassionate imagery with rescripting
5	Wrap-up	**5a)** Summary of the session and suggestions for personal practice **5b)** Closing practice		**Handout B**: Personal Practice Diary

Phase I: Introduction

Main Touch Points

Therapist Script 8.1 – Compassionate Landing
Client Handout 8.1 – Compassionate Weekly Reflection

1a) Compassionate Landing

 Therapist Task

To welcome the group, guide them through a Compassionate Landing (**Therapist Script 8.1**).

Three-Circle Check-In

In the previous module, we raised the spotlight on one of the parts of ourselves, our self-critic. It was probably an intense experience for many participants, one which forced them to face one of the most difficult and vulnerable parts of their multiplicity. During the landing, try to briefly touch upon the presence of the self-critic in the present moment and in the past week(s). Invite them to bring the same mindful welcoming they cultivate for their breath, their physical sensations and their thoughts, and extend it toward their self-critic.

1b) Revision of personal practice and recap of previous session

 Therapist Task

Invite participants to use **Client Handout 8.1** to reflect upon the past week/ weeks; then get them into pairs or small groups and invite them to share (if they would like to do so) anything relevant about their past week, including any compassion episodes or fears, blocks, and resistances (FBRs) they might have experienced.

Did they continue with their practice of the Compassionate Self? Were they more aware of their self-critic? Did they try to embody their Compassionate Self to work with the self-critic in daily situations? Were they able to see the fears underlying their self-critic in that moment? What difficulties did they encounter?

Focus on being validating and positively rewarding of any changes in behaviours, and if in a group settings be mindful not to alienate those who might be struggling.

Before moving on, the therapist can provide a brief recap of the last session, in which the main points were:

- Our capacity for self-monitoring
- The origins and forms of self-criticism
- The functions and effects of self-criticism
- How to work with our self-criticism using a compassionate approach
- Distinguishing between compassionate self-improvement and shame-based self-criticism

This can also be a space to set the scene for the current module; the main themes that are going to be explored are:

- The nature of shame
- The distinction between internal and external shame, and humiliation
- Meeting the undesired ("shadow") self
- The differences between shame and guilt
- How to heal shame using the Compassionate Self

Phase 2: Introducing Shame

In this phase we shall introduce the concept of shame. We will try to get a better understanding of what the evolutionary background of shame is, focusing on the way it is linked to the competitive social rank system. We will delve into the bodily experience associated with shame through experiential guided exercises and understand what emotions it can be associated with. Working with memories and embodiment will also help in exploring which behavioural reactions are triggered by the shame response. An important distinction is made between internal and external shame, leading us to explore the undesired self (or shadow self) and its role in the way we relate to ourselves.

Main Touch Points

Therapist Script 8.2 – Meeting the undesired self
Client Handout 8.2 – Exploring shame
Client Handout 8.3 – Undesired, Actual and Ideal Self

2a) The nature of shame

 Therapist Task

In the previous module, as we explored self-criticism, we shed light on the process of self-monitoring, which we often engage in, harbouring negative judgement and feelings towards ourselves. When we learn to be compassionately self-improving, this helps us to orient our attention to what is not working with the intention of being of support and promoting helpful change (of perspective or of a situation).

To initiate a discussion on shame, it is important that we create a link with its defensive function. We can invite the group to reflect on this: if we think of a wildlife documentary in which animals are fighting each other over a resource, what happens if one individual feels weaker and more vulnerable than another? What kind of behaviours do they manifest toward the stronger individual? What we usually see is some kind of submissive behaviour (flight). However, other individuals might react by engaging in a fight.

We can observe these same reactions in human beings; when we are socially frightened and threatened, our body can go into a defensive state (flight), one accompanied by anxiety and submissive tendencies, or it can go into a state of fight, accompanied by aggressive, attacking tendencies.

To continue the discussion among the group about these different responses to social threats, invite them to reflect on how differently they might respond when they feel inferior and weaker, compared to when they feel secure and powerful. Also, invite them to reflect on the dynamics in childhood and why as children we tend to adopt a submissive defence rather than an aggressive defence when faced with criticism.

You might want to introduce an example:

> Imagine Sally, a young child whose mother and father are quite critical and aggressive towards her and perhaps often blame her for things. For example, they might say: "You've dirtied your shirt again?! You do this every time— you'll drive me crazy trying to keep up with all this laundry!!".
>
> Sally is actually quite frightened of her parents and how her behaviour might influence them. How do you think she will behave when she thinks they are getting angry with her? Would she learn to be submissive and feel ashamed? Would she attack or be aggressive towards her parents? How do you think that might affect her later in life?
>
> It is highly probable that Sally will learn to blame herself and try to be submissive in order to protect the self – she will be quite vulnerable to the fear of being criticised and rejected. We can also imagine that Sally might be quite frightened of her anger because that could produce a scary counter-attack from a the parent. From this perspective, it all makes sense.

Therapist Tips

If members of the group say, "If it were me, I'd hit them back or yell at them or get aggressive" be sure to validate that intuitive wisdom, by agreeing with them, about how much sense that would make.

However, we should also extend the discussion by saying, that although we might push the boundaries (which can be a very good thing at times), typically the alpha figure will end up in the dominant position once again, and may now attack more or be harder/stronger, etc. In these cycles, the child is learning that their source of safety is also a source of threat – linking back to the metaphor of being in the cage with a tiger that we illustrated in the previous module.

You could also offer additional examples that the group can work through together, inquiring into how they would respond to each of these situations:

- You have some stomach problems, and while you are walking around a store you burp
- You work hard for an exam but you fail it
- You ask someone out on a date but they turn you down, saying they don't find you attractive at all
- You go for a job interview; when they tell you didn't get it, they also say they did not think you were up to the job and had not prepared very well

 Therapist Background Knowledge

The emotions we feel when we are exposed to social threats are called self-conscious emotions and are linked to our feelings about ourselves, in particular our selves as relational entities. Self-conscious emotions can be positive as well as negative; for example pride is linked to the feeling that other people admire you or like you; it only become harmful when we begin to depend on the approval of others, when our wellbeing is linked exclusively to what others say or think of us.

 Therapist Task

The two main self-conscious emotions we will be focusing on in this module are shame and guilt.

Shame is typically related to a global sense of the self. When we feel shame about our weight for example, we do not think, "Oh no, I'm not as thin as I'd like to be", rather we have a deep sense of being fat or out of control. If we feel ashamed about our appearance for some reason, twe don't think "I'm not as attractive as I'd like to be", we probably have a deep sense of being ugly or unattractive. Shame is, therefore, linked with a negative self-identity.

As social beings, we are all very concerned about what other people think about us; this is common and important, as we need the help and support of others (e.g., care, relationships). To tap into this wisdom, try guiding a brief exercise.

Invite the group to bring to mind a memory of shame, and imagine what would happen if we asked them to reveal that shameful memory to you or the group. We will not actually do so, but let us just imagine that we are going to do this.

Therapist Tips

This exercise can be led in different ways. You might deliver it as more of an experiential practice, inviting the group to close their eyes, attune to their inner sensations and mentally respond to the questions before opening their eyes and then writing them in their handout. You might also choose to deliver it as a reflection practice, simply inviting them to reflect on how they would respond, and then to write their responses in their handout.

The main questions to raise are:

- What feelings and physical sensations would you be experiencing?
- What would other people think and do?
- What would you think and do?
- How would you try to cope with the situation?

After leading the exercise, invite them to use **Client Handout 8.2** as written self-reflection.

 Therapist Background Knowledge

The aim of this exercise is to help participants realise that 1) there is no one particular emotion associated with shame, but rather that it is a complex, multi-dimensional emotional experience which triggers many of our multiple selves; and that 2) there is nothing inherently wrong with feeling shame, it is part of being human. What we do have to address is the possible negative consequences and coping strategies that we adopt when entering a state of shame.

From an evolutionary perspective, shame originally emerged to prevent distancing from others. Link this back to the exercise they just did and highlight whether they were feeling close or distant from the others who were perceived as judgemental – chances are, they were feeling distant. The paradoxical nature of shame is that it brings us to experience the very thing it evolved to protect us from – disconnection from others, isolation (for many, shame generates the desire to hide/sink/flee and therefore disconnect).

As with all emotions, shame is a bodily experience. When people respond critically and negatively to us, or even when we just feel like they might, or when we respond critically and negatively to ourselves, our bodies have a physiological response to social threat.

We will see how to approach shame through a Compassionate Self perspective using a variety of practices later on in this module.

2b) The Distinction between external shame, internal shame, and humiliation

   Therapist Task

Guide clients through the following exploration:

Humans are very sensitive to how they exist in the minds of others and are highly oriented to eliciting validation and approval, becoming very defensive if they don't get it or experience the opposite, such as disapproval or outright criticism. Individuals are therefore constantly monitoring the minds of others for how they exist in the mind of the other.

Imagine that you are on a bus, you bought the ticket but when the ticket controller arrives you cannot find it... how do you feel?

In external shame, the monitoring attention system is in the mind of the other. The key fear is having a sense that you exist in the mind of others as a negative or inferior. This is the type of shame that emerges when we ask "What would other people think and do?" when imagining we have to reveal something we are ashamed of about ourselves. In external shame, our attention is on what the other is thinking and feeling, and what they might want to do to us (for example reject, avoid, attack).

Importantly, external shame can manifest in response to situations of exclusion, in which there is no active rejection, merely that others have been inattentive to our needs; this can lead the person to feel "forgettable" or "invisible". These kinds of situations lead to a feeling of not being good enough to deserve attention, not feeling wanted, or not being chosen. External shame can also manifest in situations in which the individual is seen, but through a negative lens. This involves the feeling of not being understood by the other. It can entail verbal abuse (name calling, scornful labelling), where the self is defined by others in some way. This leads to a feeling of deep isolation, of being different, not deserving of belonging.

It is important to highlight that the desire to be well-regarded in the minds of others is not narcissistic but is an evolved human need. We are constantly

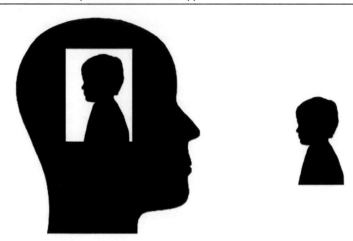

Figure 8.1 External Shame Is About Existing Negatively in the Minds of Others.

concerned about what other people think about us. If you are in a group set-ting, you can invite the group to reflect on this by asking what it is that helps them talk openly in the group.

- What helps them to share, and, by contrast, what blocks them from talking about things and keeping them secret?
- To what extent do their fears stop them from talking and sharing?
- How often have they had ideas in their minds they are unable to express?

In internal shame, the monitoring attention system is focused inwards, on our-selves, on what we think and feel about ourselves. In this case the threat is internal, and the key fear is that of revealing ourselves as truly negative or inferior. It is what emerges when we ask the question "What do you think about yourself" in a situa-tion in which we feel shame. As we will discuss, internal shame is closely linked with self-criticism, although we might experience self-criticism for our behaviour without moving necessarily into shame. The primary emotions associated with internal shame are ones of anxiety, disgust, and a "heart-sinking" sensation.

There is also another emotion that we can experience when people criticise or treat us badly, when we feel others are shaming us. Suppose someone put you down unfairly; what emotion might arise in you?

This feeling is called humiliation. When we experience humiliation and the anger of humiliation our attention is on the mind of the other person, however our feelings are not ones of anxiety or wanting to appease, submit, or hide away (as in external shame) but rather a desire to attack. We might have thoughts of the kind "How dare they? What gives them the right to do this? They are being unreasonable! I'm going to get my own back on them!"

Figure 8.2 Internal Shame is about Internalising Other People.

At this point, we can ask them to think of a recent episode in their life that they associate with shame, and reflect on these questions:

- Was there internal shame?
- Was there external shame?
- Was it about not being seen?
- Was is about being bullied?
- Was it both?
- Was it humiliation?

   Therapist Tips

Remind people that even talking about shame can be shameful for them, and be sure to validate their experience. Opening up about these topics requires our compassionate courage as it exposes our most vulnerable parts to others – try to use the idea of shared humanity to create a soft landing space for these insights and experiences to come to rest on.

2c) Internal shame and the undesired self

    Therapist Task

Internal shame is when we internalise the negative judgements of others, which generates and feeds our self-critic. For example, a child who is called "stupid" or "bad" by their parents will start re-telling this narrative internally.

To further deepen our awareness of how shame came into our existence, you can lead the *Origins of Self Criticism* (**Therapist Script 7.2**) practice, focusing on shame instead of self-criticism. This guided exercise will help people dive deeper into what sensations, thoughts and feelings are associated with shame.

    Therapist Tips

This practice helps people attune to the basic fears that underlie their shame and understand how these fears have given rise to coping mechanisms and views of the self that might have been harmful during their lives.

The compassionate gaze helps us to see the unaware, vulnerable child, who simply tried to do their best in a threatening situation, and to forgive them for whatever unhelpful coping strategy they might have resorted to: it was never their fault, they never chose the body they were born into, the family they were born into, nor the brain they received. After the exercise, be sure to allow time for group discussion.

Internal shame is strongly linked to what we can call the undesired self: the part of us that if formed from the combination of all those traits and characteristics that we, through the judgement of others and society at large, begin to believe are wrong, shameful, or to be avoided at all costs. Internal shame emerges when we feel we are getting close to the undesired self and further away from the actual self; thus, existence becomes a struggle, a constant tension between the undesired self and the ideal self.

We can begin working on the undesired self by inviting people to reflect on the characteristics they would attribute to each of these three selves. Before asking them to fill out **Client Handout 8.4** you can go through the most common general traits of these three selves as shown in the image below.

"Letting go, is letting be" says Pema Chödrön, a famous Buddhist monk and teacher. We believe this is the approach to adopt with our own undesired self. While many of us tend to run away from the undesired self, its impending presence just seems to get bigger and more threatening in our lives. What we are trying to encourage through the Compassionate Self approach is to embrace all our parts, to have compassionate encounters even with those selves are most threatening to us.

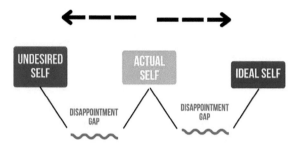

Figure 8.3 Discrepancies Among the Actual, Ideal and Undesired Self.
Source: Adapted from Gilbert, P. & Simos, G. (Eds). (2022). *Compassion Focused Therapy: Clinical Practice and Applications*

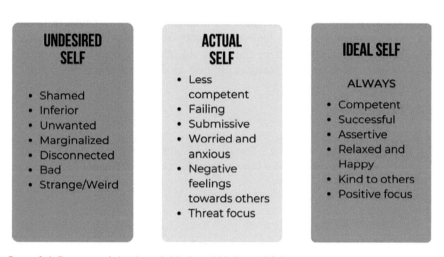

Figure 8.4 Features of the Actual, Ideal, and Undesired Selves.
Source: Adapted from Gilbert, P. & Simos, G. (Eds). (2022). *Compassion Focused Therapy: Clinical Practice and Applications*

 Optional Practice

Just as we did with the self-critic, we want to meet our undesired self through compassionate practice. As an **optional practice**, we suggest a guided imagery exercise (**Therapist Script 8.2**) to visualise the undesired self, notice our own reactions to it, and then embody our Compassionate Self to meet it with a gentle gaze and a desire to be helpful, not harmful towards it.

Therapist Tips

In addition to this practice and to the self-reflection handout, you may choose to invite participants to explore their undesired self though other expressive mediums, such as paint or clay; giving a form to our undesired self, being able to touch it, could be incredibly powerful in lessening our sense of threat for its presence and instead starting to embrace it.

Phase 3: Differences Between Shame and Guilt

In this phase of the module, we will introduce another emotion which is often confused with shame: guilt. We explain the evolutionary origins of guilt, its nature as a moral emotion, and what feelings, thoughts, and sensations it is associated with. The focus is then shifted onto identifying the differences between shame and guilt, and understanding what practices can help us shift from one to the other.

Main Touch Points

Therapist Script 8.3 – Shifting from Shame to Guilt
Client Handout 8.4 – Distinguishing Self-Conscious Emotions

3a) Guilt

Therapist Task

Guilt is a self-conscious emotion related to our caring motivation. Guilt often manifests when our intention is to be helpful and not harmful but we end up being harmful. Guilt is often accompanied by a sense of sadness, sorrow and remorse for what we have done. We do not attack ourselves, we do not focus on what others might think of us, but rather tune into a sense of responsibility. Healthy guilt requires us to attune to empathy and is built on a desire to repair; guilt is therefore crucial for our ability to be compassionate.

3b) Differences between shame and guilt

Therapist Background Knowledge

While shame and guilt can sometimes blend together, it is important to learn to distinguish between these two self-conscious emotions. One common, albeit simplistic difference is that shame is experienced as, "I am wrong", while guilt is experienced as "I did something wrong".

In Compassion Focused Therapy (CFT), an evolutionary-based psycho-social approach, the main difference we highlight regards the motivational systems: guilt is linked to the caring system, while shame is linked to the rank system. This has repercussions in terms of the behavioural response that follows these emotions: while shame can trigger a hiding response or an attacking (self-defensive) response, guilt usually triggers a reparative response. They also differ in terms of the focus: the self for shame, the other for guilt.

If there are things we have done that are harmful, when we stop shaming ourselves, we are much more able to feel a sense of responsibility and the sadness of guilt. Being able to tolerate that sadness without attacking ourselves is very helpful to learn. What we want to promote in CFT is a shift from self-critical shaming to repairing guilt.

  Therapist Task

To help clients better understand the difference between shame and guilt, you can provide an example:

> *Imagine that two people, we will call them Tom and Harry, have an affair with two other people, and they are found out. Tom feels shame because he automatically thinks, "oh, people will not like me now and my wife will be angry and not love me" – so he is focusing on what the world thinks about him – external shame. He might also feel bad about himself, "I'm a bad person to have done this". This is internal shame. Everything is focused on himself – it's all about "me, me, me".*

Table 8.2 Differences Between Shame and Guilt

SHAME *Rank mentality*	GUILT *Caring Mentality*
Attention is on damage to self and reputation (inward)	**Attention** is on hurt caused to the other (outward)
Feelings: anxiety, paralysis, confusion, emptiness, self-directed anger	**Feelings**: sorrow, sadness, and remorse
Thoughts focused on negative judgements of the "whole self"	**Thoughts** focused on the others, sympathy and empathy. Focus on behaviour – what one did
Behaviours focused on submissive appeasement, escape, apologetic denial, self-harm, attack back	**Behaviours** focused on genuine apologies, reparation, making amends

> *Harry on the other hand does not focus on himself but on the harm that he has done, with a great sense of remorse and sorrow for the upset that he has caused, and the genuine wish to try to repair or make amends or support the person he has hurt. His attention is not on himself but on the harm he has done. This is called guilt.*

Guilt is very important for us because when we open up to guilt, we are opening up to recognising how we can hurt people, often unintentionally, and we take responsibility, own up to it, and turn our focus to putting things right if we can. In CFT our intention is always to try to address suffering and certainly not cause it. So, if we are the cause of the suffering, we need to see what we can do to make amends. The problem of self-focused shame is one will only feel bad about oneself and that is not the best way to motivate a person to improve and grow.

Another example you can offer the group is the following (this is provided in **Client Handout 8.3**):

Table 8.3 Differences Between External Shame, Internal Shame, Humiliation, and Guilt

Situation: you are driving home and suddenly a dog runs out in front of you and is clipped by your car. No serious damage is done, but it leaves you shaken.

These are the feelings and thoughts that would go with the various self-conscious emotions:

External shame	Internal shame	Humiliation	Guilt
Your main emotion here will be anxiety Your attention will be on what other people who may have witnessed this (or the dog owner) will be thinking and whether they will blame you for not being careful.	Your main emotion here will be anxiety, but also possibly lowering of mood slightly. Here your attention will be on yourself, possibly blaming yourself for not being careful enough.	Here your emotion is primarily one of anger. You might think: "why don't people keep their dogs tied up – they are so irresponsible! I hope this bloody dog hasn't damaged my car!"	Here your focus is on your behaviour, not a global sense of self in any way and your emotions will be primarily ones of sadness and possibly remorse because this was unintentional.
You might have a sense of being exposed in some way. So, your attention and thinking are focused on the mind of others; about what they are feeling and thinking about you.	Maybe you noticed you were on automatic pilot while you were driving thinking about something else, as we often do. So, your attention is internal, thinking you should have been more careful in some way. You might also have thoughts that it's typical of you and perhaps you are not careful enough a person.	Or you might think that other people do not realize it was not your fault and might blame you unfairly. Your attention is on other people's behavior, on blaming them, and feeling angry with others for one reason or another.	You really did not want to cause pain to an animal. Your attention will be on the dog and concern for the dog and checking that it is okay. You are not particularly worried what others might be thinking about you and you're not putting yourself down in any way. Nor are you feeling angry with dog owners – you see it as just an unfortunate accident.

To begin distinguishing between these different possible emotional reactions, invite them to fill out **Client Handout 8.4**. You could also come up with other examples based on the group or person you are working with. Ask them to only fill out the four columns regarding the self-conscious emotions; the part about the Compassionate Self will be addressed at a later stage.

Discuss as a group the answers to the several examples and ask them what response they would prefer and would be most helpful.

Phase 4: Healing the Wounds of Shame

After addressing shame, humiliation, and guilt, we move on to compassionate integration. We will explore the ways in which the qualities of compassion – courage in particular – can help us in healing the wounds of shame. In fact, the intensity of shame reduces when we being to accept our vulnerabilities as human beings and reach out to reconnect to others. We move away from the rank-based motivational system into the caring motivational system, which activates a different brain-body pattern within us.

Main Touch Points

Therapist Script 8.4 – Unravelling Shame in the Body
Therapist Script 8.5 – Compassionate Imagery with Rescripting
Therapist Script 8.6 – Reconnecting
Client Handout 8.5 – Compassionate Imagery with Rescripting

4a) Beginning the journey to heal the wounds of shame

 Therapist Task

When we work with the intention of beginning to heal the wounds of shame, we need to address the main fears, blocks and resistances to working with this emotion.

You can invite an individual or group discussion about the following questions:

- *What would be the most frightening thing if you were to soften down around feelings of shame or inferiority?*
- *Without thinking too much about what your shame is about, what might be frightening or overwhelming about letting go, giving up your feelings of shame?*
- *Do these fears of giving up shame remind you of any part of yourself?*

The idea here is to help people realise that often, but not always, our FBRs linked to shame are about our self-critic. The other fear that can come up is to be overwhelmed or frightened of engaging with shameful memories. It is crucial to remind the people that we can work in small incremental steps when facing difficult emotions. Normalise and highlight the fact that the work should be challenging, not overwhelming, so we can take it in small, manageable "chunks".

We can do a similar process with guilt, which is often enmeshed with shame.

- *Would you be afraid of giving up your sense of guilt?*

4b) Practices for healing the wounds of shame

   Therapist Task

As with all emotions, shame also has body-based manifestations. Working with shame requires us to explore how this emotion wants us to move our bodies and how we can use the body itself to move out of shame.

The guided exploration *Unravelling shame in the body* (**Therapist Script 8.4**) helps clients experience first-hand how powerful the compassionate posture can be to switch between emotional states. It allows us to explore how shame is communicated through the body, what posture it encourages us to adopt, how it invites us to take a place in the room.

After guiding the practice, initiate a group discussion about what they noticed when shifting from one posture to another. How did their bodily sensations change? How did their internal tone of voice change? How did it feel to transition between one state and another?

After having worked on one component of shame – the body – we can begin to explore the cognitive and emotional aspects. We will do this through an exercise using imagery with rescripting (**Therapist Script 8.5**). By rescripting ideas, you enable people to bring back a memory and think about what they would like to have happened at the time, how they would have liked to receive compassionate support. This can be thought of in terms of classical conditioning, where we bring back the memory while trying to stimulate the physiological systems of compassion (vagus nerve).

After the compassionate rescripting exercise, encourage participants to take some time for self-reflection; this can be free writing on the experience they have just had or guided self-reflection by using **Client Handout 8.5**.

To close this part of the module, guide the group through the *Reconnecting* practice (**Therapist Script 8.6**). Shame is an emotion which makes us feel disconnected, separate from others – with this practice we try to reconnect to the group and to our common human experiences of shame and compassion.

Phase 5: Wrap-Up

The final phase of the module is a wrap-up of the theme that has been explored. Emphasise how continuing to work on one's **personal practice** (whether formal or informal) can help with the development of our compassionate minds.

Main Touch Points

Client Handout B – Personal Practice Diary

5a) Summary of the session and suggestions for personal practice

    Therapist Task

Take 5–10 minutes to briefly summarise the points that you have gone through in this module.

You may want to provide participants with some suggestions for personal practice and self-reflection:

- Invite them to use **Client Handout B,** suggesting they trying to focus on one compassionate activity per day, perhaps focusing specifically on how their Compassionate Self helped them engage with others and with themselves on that day
- Invite them to follow the guided audio meditation for unravelling shame in the body at least once during the week, so that they may continue to connect with their shame with an attitude of compassion

5b) Closing practice

    Therapist Task

Remember to take a moment at the end of the session to acknowledge anything and everything that has come up for participants while exploring the themes presented.

As in previous sessions, invite them to share in one sentence:

- What do I take home from today's session (because I feel it's going to be helpful)?
- What are some key things that I would like to share and tell other people about?

Invite participants to bring their attention to their intention to be helpful to self and others rather than neglectful. Remind them that on many occasions we will not be able to do so, and that is totally OK and human; remind them that what is truly important is to tune into this intention.

Finally, guide participants through a short closing practice using **Therapist Script 2.5** and adding perhaps with the addition of a couple of sentences that link back to the work done during the session. This could be something like: *"We have begun to look at our multiple selves, who have felt ashamed for so long, with compassion... all those parts that have wanted to hide in the shadows – we have begun to understand the fear that moves them; if you feel OK with it, thank them for being here with us today, maybe let them know that, whenever they are ready, we will be here to meet them again"*, or *"Contemplate how many people experiencing shame are on this Earth right now – all those beings who are afraid to show themselves – may they one day feel ready to manifest just as they are, led by the true desire to connect with others"*.

Three-Circle Check-In

Therapist Scripts

Therapist Script 8.1: Compassionate Landing (5 minutes)

(Refer to therapist Script 2.1 in Chapter 2.)

You can add the following elements to connect to the previous module:

From your compassionate stance, try to curiously observe if the self-critic has joined you here today.

Perhaps you feel its presence through words...or bodily sensations....

Perhaps you feel that, after last encounter, something has slightly changed in your relationship with self-criticism ... perhaps now it is easier for you to remember its story ... the fear it comes from...

Imagine letting your self-critic know that it can rest today, that you will be taking things from here on. How does it feel even just to contemplate this option?

Therapist Script 8.2: Meeting the Undesired Self (10 minutes)

In this practice we will explore what happens when we bring compassionate attention toward our undesired self. This is the part of us that includes all the characteristics that we believe are wrong, shameful, or that we feel should be hidden from others. Remember to take this practice at your own pace and do not hesitate to take a breather should you feel you are getting too triggered.

Also, remember to keep a curious and explorative attitude, respect whatever comes up, including your resistances. It's not important that you do this practice "well" but that you remain open and curious towards whatever you observe.

When you feel ready, you can start closing your eyes if that feels OK for you today, and take some moments to settle your posture, making any adjustments needed.

As best as you can, imagine inviting your undesired or shadow self, with the intention of getting to know them better – this creature embodies all those traits and characteristics that you are afraid you might one day have, things that you feel would make you a bad person, someone to be kept at a distance, a weirdo, someone to be marginalised. Let this image slowly form in front of you, maybe appearing from out a thick fog.

What does your shadow self look like? How does it materialise in front of you? It might have defined contours, or you might just have a felt sense of its presence. What is it wearing? How does it move in space? Imagine it stops at a distance from you that you feel comfortable with. Do you feel you would like it close to you or far away?

What do you feel when standing in front of your undesired self? Are there any fears coming up? Anger? Sadness? Simply notice what emotions arise in the presence of this part of us that we always keep at bay and hidden.

Now, let us get into our Compassionate Self; in the presence of your shadow self, begin creating your compassionate posture. Sit upright, your back straight but not rigid, your heart soft and open, your shoulders in line with your hips. From this dignified posture, start to deepen and slow down your breathing, getting a sense of grounding in your body. Connect with your intention to be helpful.

Try as best as you can to connect to your non-judgemental inner wisdom – deep down you know that we all just find ourselves here, with this mind that can be very tricky and that we did not choose, trying to find happiness. Sense the strength that your body can hold, and tune into the shared wish to try as best as we can to be helpful, not harmful.

Now, try looking at your undesired self through your compassionate eyes.

You, as your Compassionate Self, know that this undesired self is deeply human, too – their undesired qualities are things that can be found in many beings. And perhaps many beings try to hide them. Maybe the undesired self too is also afraid – afraid of being isolated, of being ignored, of being abandoned.

Imagine being able to hold the fear and hurt of the undesired self with compassion, wisdom and strength. Imagine sending an intention to help this creature-what would it need?

What kind of help – maybe touch, maybe words, maybe just a presence – would your undesired self like to receive from your Compassionate Self?

Imagine being able to offer this kind of support. If you are not ready for it, you can just focus on the wish to offer help and presence. You can also just imagine that with each out breath, you are sending your undesired self a flow of compassion – something that your undesired self really needs right now to feel safe.

Take a couple of moments to allow this encounter to happen and observe if there are any changes in the undesired self. How does it feel to receive this kind of help? How does it feel to be seen through these eyes?

Now imagine ending this compassionate meeting with the undesired self in whatever way feels best and most helpful to you right now… if you want, you can imagine taking a picture of the most significant moment of this encounter. What do you feel in your body right now after having had this encounter?

Remember your commitment to bring your wisdom and understanding to this part of you. Sense the people around you, with all their undesired selves, who are on the same journey as you and offer them your support.

Then, when you feel ready, you can open your eyes and come back to the room.

 Optional Practice

Being Guided by the Compassionate Connection with the Undesired Self

Imagine a past scenario in which you felt ashamed, you felt small in the presence of someone, or embarrassed by the idea of expressing who you really *were, or scared by the idea of showing the parts of you that you fear others won't like.*

Begin to imagine the qualities of strength, deep wisdom, and the desire for connection and compassion. Imagine feeling your undesired self next to you, invite them to stay by your side and, if you feel it is OK, create some sort of contact with them – so that you can be together to face whatever you may encounter.

Feel the connection with the undesired self, the compassion with which you gazed at them, and maybe even the gratitude that this creature feels toward you as it receives this compassion – allow all of this to help you feel stronger, more grounded, and more willing to show yourself to the world exactly as you are, knowing that others also have hidden parts of themselves that they are always fighting.

Without expecting any reaction in particular, try asking yourself how your sensations change? If you knew you had access to a compassionate connection, a real alliance with your undesired self, if you knew they felt safe with you, how would you feel different? What would you do differently, say differently?

If you have a future scenario that you know may cause some kind of anxiety or embarrassment, for example going to a party where you are afraid of feeling ashamed, try to think what it would be like to go to that party hand in hand with your undesired self (instead of fighting it), feeling like you are linked by a compassionate alliance? How do you think things would be different if this part of you felt seen and protected?

Therapist Script 8.3: Shifting from Shame to Guilt (8 minutes)

Begin to recall a small event, nothing too major, in which you felt ashamed for something you did to someone, someone you know suffered because of you and maybe to whom you were never able to say sorry, or with whom you never tried to reconnect.

Try to go back to the scene: what happened? what you said or did that hurt the other? how did the other person react and how did you realise that the other person was suffering because of the thing you did.

Try to reconnect, inside you, with the emotions and feelings that emerge. Connect to that part of yourself that felt at fault for how you made the other person feel – so much at fault that it was only able to avoid or run away from the pain it had caused. As they begin to emerge, try to name them by whispering their names... where do you feel these emotions in the body? What would your body like to do when you connect to that episode?

Now imagine that with your next in-breath, you breathe in the deep quality of wisdom and non-judgement... of courage... and the desire to alleviate suffering when possible... Maybe you can adjust your posture to make "space" for your Compassionate Self...and connect with the courageous intention to see the suffering and try to be helpful.

Within the wisdom that you breathe in is the certainty that because of the way our brains are wired, we will all sooner or later be captured by emotions, desires, prejudices, and impulses that often do not allow us to see the effects we have on others… and all of us, unfortunately, have been hurt by others in a continuous cycle that we did not choose…

As you breathe in, connect to the quality of courage, and open your heart to seeing what you did to the other person, the hurt you have generated, but also to the suffering that this generates within you… breathe in and breathe out… let your body and your heart make space for this painful realisation… what you did or did not do has caused suffering in someone… I too, just like everyone else, am in this never-ending cycle of suffering that is caused and received…

Hold this compassionate stance, this wisdom, the knowledge that we constantly hurt each other, whether consciously or unconsciously, and that we nurture a deep desire to alleviate this suffering whenever possible… how would you like to address the other person who is suffering? What would you like to say or do?

If you were standing in front of the other person as your Compassionate Self, what would you like to say to them?

When you feel ready, you can open your eyes and come back to the room.

 Optional Practice

The Compassionate Self can help us write a letter to the person we have hurt. It does not necessarily have to be mailed, but we are curious to know what this compassionate part would write to the other person.

Therapist Script 8.4: Unravelling Shame in the Body (10 minutes)

In this practice the body will support us in shifting from shame to compassion.

You may choose to do this practice standing or sitting.

Once you have chosen your posture, begin by closing your eyes or, if you prefer, just soften your gaze. Take a few minutes to connect with your breathing, making it progressively more conscious, slowing its pace and prolonging the exhalation.

Now, begin bringing to mind a situation in which you felt ashamed; it may be a memory related to your childhood, perhaps a time when you felt there was something deeply wrong with you; or it may be a more recent memory, perhaps a situation you experienced recently in which you felt like you wanted to make yourself small, to hide, when you felt "not enough" or "too much". If no memory comes to you, you could imagine a scenario in which, right now, all the people you know found out something about you that you would never want them to know, a secret that only you or a few select people know.

Begin to get in touch with that feeling of shame and of wanting to make yourself small; ask your body how it feels in this situation. What posture would you like to take? Maybe it wants to roll up, make itself smaller, almost invisible, close in on itself, hide. Give your body a chance to take this posture. Perhaps you bow your head, your shoulders close in on themselves, your breath becomes shallower, maybe your legs bend and your arms close around your legs. You may want to come down to floor level – feel free to do this if this is what your body is asking you to do.

Keep this position for a few moments and notice what thoughts come over you at this time. What are your thoughts about yourself? To which part of you do these thoughts belong? If they are thoughts of self-criticism, how do they make you feel? How do they land in the body?

Now, keep these thoughts in your mind, perhaps mentally repeating them, and imagine yourself turning into a fern in the morning. Feel the dew drops weighing down your leaves and slowly let the warmth of compassion reach your surface. Draw energy and courage from this warmth, and just like a fern leaf, begin to unwind your posture; allow your spine to slowly relax, one vertebra at a time. Continue mentally repeating your thoughts of shame in this unwinding process. But at the same time you feel that you are breathing into your body the qualities of compassion: courage, wisdom, the desire to be helpful.

Finally find a position that embodies the qualities of courage, strength, solidity, and openness. You are embodying your compassionate posture: the wise opening, the solidity, the courage to create space for whatever feels threatened in us. Let the same thoughts as before come... try to welcome them within this solid, open body space.

Now try to notice how those same thoughts of shame resonate within you – are they still alive in you? Do they resonate as before? Has their volume changed? Has the way they land in the body changed? Have they perhaps transformed into new thoughts?

Take a few moments to explore this new state, observing how you feel. Imagine yourself surrounded by many other ferns that, like you, are choosing to unfold in the sunlight, are choosing to open up with the wisdom, courage, and solidity of compassion, to reconnect, and heal the wounds of shame.

Then, very gently, begin to return to the room and open your eyes again when you feel ready.

Therapist Script 8.5: Compassionate Imagery with Rescripting (15 minutes)

 Therapist Tips

In this exercise we are working with shame memories; these can sometimes be linked to intense traumatic experiences, such as abuse or violence.

If working in an individual setting, you can take adequate measures to work with the memory (for example asking the patient to stop before the abuse took place and letting the Compassionate Self enter the scene before the event takes place).

If working in group settings, you should highlight that we do not want to recollect a memory that is too intense for us in order to avoid excessive dysregulation (re-traumatisation).

To begin this practice, call to mind a memory of a recent event when you felt ashamed. Let this unpleasant memory come back to you.

What was happening? What were you feeling? What were you thinking about yourself? What were you feeling in your body?

Now, begin letting go of this memory and allow your mind to wander back in time, recollecting a past event, maybe in your early life, when you were a child... or the memory of an event in which you felt like a child ...maybe small, unwanted, invisible, maybe humiliated...

What is about to happen? Or what has just happened? If a memory of abuse emerges, it is crucial that the memory is stopped before the abuse takes place.

Concentrate your attention on that child who is feeling ashamed: go back to the sensations that the child was experiencing. What do you see? What sounds can you hear? Which smells can you recognise? Who is with you? How old are you? What are you wearing? What do you feel in that moment?

Now, exit this memory for a moment. Settle your breathing, taking long and slow exhales, welcoming a feeling of expansion in your chest as you inhale. Feel grounded in your posture, letting your spine become long and your heart soft. Connect to your Compassionate Self – that part of you that is profoundly wise, that knows very well how hard it is to be alive in this world, and how we never chose many of the most painful experiences that we have lived through; this part is also very strong, courageous, able to face difficulties, to protect and take care of that child... It is a part that is motivated by the deep desire to be helpful and alleviate suffering with courage and wisdom...

Now, embody your Compassionate Self... change your posture, change your facial expression, change your breathing rhythm and feel deep in your skin the desire to do something for that suffering, for that child who is facing this difficult situation and is feeling so exposed, vulnerable, and full of shame.

Imagine entering the scene of your past memory as your Compassionate Self. Look at this child through the eyes of the Compassionate Self, who is strong, very wise and wants help... you can see the child clearly... what emotions is the child feeling in this moment? You can really see the fear in their eyes. What are their fears? What are their needs?

You can deeply feel your groundedness, your strength, your wisdom and from this perspective you understand that that child is simply experiencing human needs, and that for no reason does this child deserve to suffer in this way and feel this shame... No child deserves this... that child simply has human needs, there is nothing wrong with them... but the child doesn't know this...

Now, from your grounded wise stance, from your desire to be helpful, you are able to see how normal all those emotions are, and you can see clearly that everything that is happening is not the child's fault, how innocent he/she is and how much he/she just needs to be heard, protected, helped, validated...

From this perspective, taking in all your strength, wisdom and desire to help, start interacting with the child exactly as they would like you to, exactly as they need you to... do something that the child genuinely needs right now... what do you do to show this little one how much you care about them, how much you wish to take care of them, to protect them...

As you do this, notice that the child really does feel how solid and reliable you are, how much you wish to help them and finally starts feeling protected... heard... in some way you can see that they finally feel safe with you...

If there are any other people in the scene: *Now, if you feel it is appropriate for the memory you received, using the strength and wisdom of the Compassionate Self, you can turn toward the other person or people involved in the scene, if they are present, who were causing the child to suffer.*

From this position of deep wisdom, you can see in some way what is behind those people... what they are carrying inside them... what kind of suffering is causing them to act this way...

From its position of deep wisdom and strength, the Compassionate Self speaks to the person that is causing the suffering... or does something so that the child feels better.

At this point, the person (or people) that were causing the suffering become smaller and, if it is appropriate, feels a sense of deep guilt and regret... regardless, they can no longer do what they were doing to the child...

As the Compassionate Self, you turn towards the child once again and ask them if there is something else they wish you would do to alleviate their shame... whatever it may be, do it.

Then, just for now, come back to the eyes of the child and see the Compassionate Self as it enters the scene, does what it has chosen to – try to notice how you feel receiving this kind of support, protection and validation. If there is anything else that you would like the Compassionate Self to do for you, to make you feel better, imagine it understanding, validating and unconditionally welcoming your needs. Let this feeling of safeness sink into your body.

Then gently let go of the images and come back to your body in the present moment. Take some breaths to reconnect with your feelings after having explored this memory. When you feel ready, you can open your eyes and come back to the room.

Therapist Script 8.6: Reconnecting (8 minutes)

We begin this practice by closing our eyes and feeling how we are sitting in our chair right now.

Let us find our compassionate posture with our back straight, shoulders in line with our hips, and with our diaphragm open. Now let us begin to slow down our breathing, and with each slower, deeper breath, we try to mentally repeat, in a friendly tone: "mind slowing down" and then "body slowing down" slowly, following the inhalation and exhalation, gradually noticing a sense of grounding. Slowly, feel a sense of stillness, but also a sense of mental presence growing within you. Notice yourself becoming more grounded and stable – with the same majesty as a mountain.

Let your awareness expand to include your entire body. Begin to embrace the wholeness of your being – of your presence. Include the sensations of your head and torso, arms and hands, legs, and feet.

Feel your body sitting here in this room. Try to stay with this experience for a few breaths.

Now allow the awareness to expand to include your environment.First feel the air around you. For a few breaths feel the air as it touches your body.

Notice how the air touches, in the same way, everyone in the building, on the street, in the city, and everyone who is meditating in this group at this moment.

Now, remember that we are all human beings. None of us chose to be born, and we all have a brain and bodies that we did not choose. Like all the millions and billions of human beings outside this room, we all have experiences of shame, discomfort, anger, and anxiety.

Let us contemplate that we all have experiences or fantasies that we would not want to share with others. Shame is one of life's shared challenges that we all face. We all have vulnerabilities, weaknesses and flaws. We all make mistakes. And we all struggle with aspects of our personalities at times. We are all part of this stream of life. But, at the same time, we are here, together, wanting to face this deeply isolating emotion with the strength, wisdom and commitment of the Compassionate Self.

Just being here, as we are, is a sign that we are beginning to face this emotion with a willingness to heal our wounds. Experience the connection with the group and all other human beings for a few breaths.

With each breath out, you can whisper to yourself the wish: "may I make space for this painful emotion with courage and wisdom, and a desire to be supportive... may I remember that it is not my fault if I have a brain I did not choose, which has desires, thoughts and emotions that are at times so painful... may I remember that I am not alone on this path".

With each breath out, imagine sending this compassionate wish to others, too ... those in this group and those outside of this group, who in this same moment, are also suffering because of shame... "may you make space for this painful emotion with courage and wisdom and desire to be supportive of it...

may you remember that it is not your fault if you have a brain you did not choose, which has desires, thoughts, and emotions that are so painful... may you remember that you are not alone on this path".

Try to listen to the way this wish for yourself and for others lands within you... and try to connect to the fact that while you are sending others this wish, at the same time, you are receiving these wishes from others... notice what physical sensations this brings.

Then, very gently, when you feel ready, you can open your eyes again and return to the room.

Client Handouts

Client Handout 8.1: Compassionate Weekly Reflection

Let's do a curious, friendly reflection on this past week:

Which part of the self-practice did I do and why?

Which part of the self-practice did I not do?

Was this due to any anxieties or blocks regarding the practice or the path? Which ones can you identify?

We extend gratitude, respect, and compassion to resistances: What would make you and your resistances feel safer in going forward on this path?

Client Handout 8.2: Exploring Shame

What feelings arose in me when I thought I might have to reveal something I am ashamed of?

What was happening in my body as I thought I might have to reveal something I am ashamed of?

What would other people think and how would they now act toward me as a result?

What do I think about myself and how do I act as a result?

How am I going to cope with this situation?

How have these fears of shame influenced my life?

Client Handout 8.3: Distinguishing Self-Conscious Emotions

Example:

Table 8.4 Differences Between External Shame, Internal Shame, Humiliation, and Guilt

Situation: you are driving home and suddenly a dog runs out in front of you and is clipped by your car. No serious damage is done, but it leaves you shaken.

These are the feelings and thoughts that would go with the various self-conscious emotions:

External shame	Internal shame	Humiliation	Guilt
Your main emotion here will be anxiety. Your attention will be on what other people who may have witnessed this (or the dog owner) will be thinking and whether they will blame you for not being careful. You might have a sense of being exposed in some way. So, your attention and thinking are focused on the mind of others; about what they are feeling and thinking about you.	Your main emotion here will be anxiety, but also possibly lowering of mood slightly. Here your attention will be on yourself, possibly blaming yourself for not being careful enough. Maybe you noticed you were on automatic pilot while you were driving thinking about something else, as we often do. So, your attention is internal, thinking you should have been more careful in some way. You might also have thoughts that it's typical of you and perhaps you are not careful enough a person.	Here your emotion is primarily one of anger. You might think: "why don't people keep their dogs tied up – they are so irresponsible! I hope this bloody dog hasn't damaged my car!" Or you might think that other people do not realize it was not your fault and might blame you unfairly. Your attention is on other people's behavior, on blaming them, and feeling angry with others for one reason or another.	Here your focus is on your behaviour, not a global sense of self in any way and your emotions will be primarily ones of sadness and possibly remorse because this was unintentional. You really did not want to cause pain to an animal. Your attention will be on the dog and concern for the dog and checking that it is okay. You are not particularly worried what others might be thinking about you and you're not putting yourself down in any way. Nor are you feeling angry with dog owners – you see it as just an unfortunate accident.

Scenario A.

Table 8.5

Situation: you forget your friend's birthday and they call you to remind you.			
These are the feelings and thoughts, and maybe behaviours that would go with your various self-conscious emotions:			
External shame	**Internal shame**	**Humiliation**	**Guilt**
How would your Compassionate Self help you?			

Scenario B.

Table 8.6

Situation: you lose your temper with your children and you are rushing around shouting at them.			
These are the feelings and thoughts and maybe behaviours that would go with your various self-conscious emotions:			
External shame	**Internal shame**	**Humiliation**	**Guilt**
How would your Compassionate Self help you?			

Scenario C.

Table 8.7

Situation: because life has been difficult you get into drugs and that causes pain to people around you.

These are the feelings and thoughts and maybe behaviours that would go with different self-conscious emotions:

External shame	Internal shame	Humiliation	Guilt

How would your Compassionate Self help you?

Scenario D.

Table 8.8

Situation: think of a personal situation where you somehow behaved 'wrongly' towards someone.			
These are the feelings and thoughts, and maybe behaviours that would go with your various self-conscious emotions:			
External shame	**Internal shame**	**Humiliation**	**Guilt**
How would your Compassionate Self help you?			

Client Handout 8.4: Undesired, Actual, and Ideal Self

Here are some commonly reported characteristics of the Undesired, Actual, and Ideal Self.

Figure 8.5 Undesired, Actual, and Ideal Self.

Reflect on the characteristics that you would attribute to your own Undesired, Actual and Ideal Self and write them down below:

My Undesired Self

My Actual Self

My Ideal Self

Client Handout 8.5: Compassionate Imagery with Rescripting

What were the strongest beliefs (about the self and/or the world) of the child who experienced shame?

What did the Compassionate Self do, say or express that was most helpful for this child?

When in the company of the Compassionate Self, what does that child think of themselves? What do they feel?

Use this space to write down any other thoughts or reflections you might have, things you would like to remember, think about or put into practice in your work or daily life.

Chapter 9

Module 9

Deepening Compassion for the Self

Aims

- To deepen compassion for the self through experiential practices, and by switching between mind/body states
- To explore the usefulness of compassionate letter writing
- To guide compassionate mirror work
- To build a compassionate relationship with our bodies through a compassion-focused body scan
- To plan compassionate behaviours
- To acquire practical techniques to step into a compassionate mind state that is helpful to oneself

 Deepen Your Knowledge

In Gilbert, P. & Simos, G. (Eds). (2022). *Compassion Focused Therapy: Clinical Practice and Applications*. Routledge, please refer to:

Chapter 8. Compassionate Mind Training: Key Themes

DOI: 10.4324/9781003436058-11

Summary of Key Processes

Table 9.1 Module 9: Deepening Compassion for the Self

Phase		Main Touch Points	Therapist Scripts	Client Handouts
1	Introduction	**1a)** Compassionate landing **1b)** Revision of personal practice and recap of previous session	□ **Script 9.1:** Compassionate Landing	□ **Handout 9.1:** Compassionate Weekly Reflection
2	Compassion for the self	**2a)** Compassionate letter writing **2b)** Compassionate mirror work **2c)** Self-compassion in video **2d)** Compassionate flashcards	□ **Script 9.2:** Compassionate letter writing □ **Script 9.3:** Compassion at the mirror	□ **Handout 9.2:** Compassionate letter writing □ **Handout 9.3:** Compassion at the mirror □ **Handout 9.4:** Self-compassion in video
3	Compassion for the body	**3a)** Compassion-focused body scan	□ **Script 9.4:** Compassion-focused body scan	□ **Handout 9.5:** Compassionate letter to the body □ **Handout 9.6:** FBRs in the body
4	Nurturing a healthy blue circle	**4a)** Compassion in action **4b)** Compassion in different areas of life **4c)** Compassionate switch **4d)** Planning compassionate behaviours		□ **Handout 9.7:** Compassion pie chart □ **Handout 9.8:** Acts of compassion and kindness
5	Wrap-up	**5a)** Summary of the session and suggestions for personal practice **5b)** Closing practice		□ **Handout B:** Personal Practice Diary

Phase I: Introduction

Main Touch Points

Therapist Script 9.1 – Compassionate Landing
Client Handout 9.1 – Compassionate Weekly Reflection

1a) Compassionate Landing

   Therapist Task

To welcome the group, guide them through a Compassionate Landing (**Therapist Script 9.1**).

The last couple of modules have been focused on exploring the most difficult and painful parts of ourselves in order to understand the intersections between self-criticism, shame, and guilt. This module will provide us with some powerful practices to strengthen and deepen compassion for the self. During the landing, we lightly touch upon their experience of self-criticism and shame, and initiate the movement of self-compassion.

Three-Circle Check-In

1b) Revision of personal practice and recap of previous session

   Therapist Task

Invite participants to use **Client Handout 9.1** to reflect upon the past week/ weeks; then get them into pairs or small groups and invite them to share (if they feel they would like to) anything relevant about their past week, including any compassion episodes or any fears, blocks, and resistances (FBRs) they might have experienced.

Did they continue with their practice of the Compassionate Self? Were they more aware of their self-critic or of moments when they were feeling shame? Was it internal or external shame? Did they try to embody their Compassionate Self to reassure their fears? What difficulties did they encounter?

Before moving on, the therapist can provide a brief recap of the previous session, in which the main points were:

- The nature of shame
- The distinction between internal and external shame, and humiliation
- Meeting the undesired self
- The differences between shame and guilt
- How to heal shame through the Compassionate Self

This can also be a space to setting the scene for the current module; the main themes that are going to be explored are:

- Why it is important to develop compassion for the self
- Practices to develop the flow of self-compassion
- Practicing self-compassion for the body
- Using compassion to nurture a healthy drive system

Phase 2: Compassion for the Self

In this phase we will work on integration. While in previous modules we developed compassion for the parts of ourselves, through working with the multiple selves, the self-critic, shame, and guilt, in this module we wish to address the self we are experiencing in this very moment. The practices we will introduce are designed to help participants contact their self and experience the many ways in which we can be self-compassionate.

Main Touch Points

→ **Therapist Script 9.2** – Compassionate Letter Writing
→ **Therapist Script 9.3** – Compassion at the Mirror
→ **Client Handout 9.2** – Compassionate Letter Writing
→ **Client Handout 9.3** – Compassion at the Mirror
→ **Client Handout 9.4** – Self-compassionate Videos

2a) Compassionate letter writing

 Therapist Background Knowledge

Letter writing is something that human beings have been doing since the beginning of time. There is something profoundly intimate about having the chance to pour one's thoughts and feelings onto paper (or, these days, a keyboard). Writing allows us to contact to our innermost being and put these insights and experiences into words.

Letter writing can be used as a powerful therapeutic tool to explore things that have been left unsaid or unexpressed and that need space and time to be processed. It can also be used with a compassionate intention, to help people engage with their problems, with a focus on the deep motivation to be helpful, supportive, and encouraging.

 Therapist Task

Compassionate letter writing can be done as an individual exercise, where people bring to mind a difficulty in their life or aspect of themselves they want to express compassion to. The person writes a letter about that issue from their compassionate self and then slowly reads it back to themselves, with a compassionate posture and tone of voice .

In a group format, the exercise can also be done in pairs; having another witness (paired partner) the experience for the client of reading their letter to themselves and then having the paired partner read the letter back to them can provide a safe container in which to explore the feeling of being seen and heard and receiving compassion.

Before starting the compassionate letter exercise, guide people through a brief Compassionate Self induction, to help them attune to their inner qualities of compassion.

It is important to remind people what the intention of this exercise is. We are not necessarily turning to this letter for solutions to our problems, but rather to help us deal with our pain with a sense of deep understanding, warmth, grounded presence, and unconditional support, and a helpful intention.

There are also some other ways that you can be creative with this process. For example, you could invite people to imagine writing the letter while in their compassionate place, creating a sense of self while residing in this calm, safe, and connected place.

You could also ask them to imagine their compassionate image with them, or even that the compassionate image is dictating the letter as they write it.

You can use **Therapist Script 9.2** for guidance in leading this exercise and ask participants to use **Client Handout 9.2**, which offers some useful writing prompts.

 Therapist Tips

Ask your clients how it felt when they heard the letter being read. Was it validating, supportive, reassuring, and encouraging? If not, let the clients know that they can always change what the Compassionate Self says in the letter. Sometimes hearing the words aloud provides a different experience to writing them. And the client has the opportunity to re-shape and change what has been written. There is no final draft. Over time, what the Compassionate Self provides and expresses in the letter may change in terms of emphasis and what is expressed, particularly as the client becomes more skilful at connecting with what they need from their Compassionate Self.

2b) Compassionate mirror work

 Therapist Background Knowledge

The mirror has been considered a powerful therapeutic tool if guided by a compassionate intention. Using a mirror can be a way of externalising the "object" of our compassion (the self), making practices involving repetition of self-compassionate affirmations even more powerful. It seems that using a mirror enhances our experience of compassion for the self, because it increases the number of signals that we are able to process (not only the voice, but also facial features and expressions). Using the mirror also helps to create a little bit of distance between us and the person we are offering compassion to (which is still the self), increasing the sense of shared humanity (universality) and decreasing blame and judgement.

 Therapist Task

For this practice, participants will need a mirror; the practice can also be done using a phone camera or computer/laptop camera, however, it will be less powerful since the person will not be able to look into their own eyes.

 Therapist Tips

Be sure to remind participants that it is normal to encounter strong FBRs during this practice. Always try to see FBRs through a compassionate lens, just like we have been doing during the course of this training, as a reminder of our human nature. Also, remind participants that just like any other practice, using a mirror for self-compassion becomes a little less difficult the more we do it. Invite them to establish a regular practise with the mirror in order to start seeing the benefits and promoting a more compassionate inner dialogue.

Follow **Therapist Script 9.3** to guide the practice, then offer some time for self-reflection using **Client Handout 9.3**.

Three-Circle Check-In

2c) Self-compassion in video

 Therapist Background Knowledge

This exercise is inspired by a psychotherapeutic approach called Self-Mirroring Therapy to promote the use of mirror neurons in a therapeutic setting.

Self-mirroring consists in filming oneself while recalling a difficult or emotionally intense event and then looking back at the video, leveraging those mechanisms of empathic resonance towards the self that are mediated by mirror neurons, which we commonly use to connect with others. This helps the person connect to their emotional experience through their non-verbal communication, their tone of voice, their posture, and facial expressions, rather than relying solely on their introspective abilities. This facilitates the activation of the compassionate motivation towards themselves; in fact, when we look at ourselves, we can use the same circuits as when we give compassion to others.

Moreover, this principle can be used twice: the person can record themselves while speaking about a difficult experience, then rewatch the video and record themselves while rewatching the video. Thus, they will be able to observe not only how they act and communicate while speaking about something difficult, but also how they react to seeing themselves in an emotionally charged moment. When we see ourselves as being compassionate in the face of a challenge, this increases our chance of re-activating that motivation towards the self in the future.

 Therapist Task

We suggest you have the group do this exercise in pairs, so they can take turns using their two phones to record both phases of the exercise. If in an individual setting, this can be done between therapist and client. However, if you are delivering this manual over zoom, this particular exercise does not lend itself very well to this medium.

Begin with one person speaking into the camera and recalling a stressful or distressing experience they have had (either recent or past). Then, set up a second phone and record them while the watch the first video.

Invite the person to embody their Compassionate Self as they watch the first video; invite them to look at this person speaking to them with a compassionate gaze, trying to connect to their lived experience, to their fears, to their deeply human nature.

Finally, invite the person to look at the video of themselves while they were rewatching the first video.

After having completed the exercise, you can invite them to explore the following prompts, either individually (using **Client Handout 9.4**), in pairs, or in a group setting.

Provide some time for group discussion at the end.

2d) Compassionate flashcards

 Therapist Background Knowledge

As already discussed, compassion has two parts that coexist, one more focused on being open to and sensitive towards challenging or unwanted emotions, thoughts, sensations, and situations, the other which is more focused on "doing", on alleviating suffering and distress.

In this exercise, we will focus on finding ways to use both expressions of compassion to be helpful and not harmful towards ourselves. This exercise can be done individually, in pairs, or in a group setting.

 Therapist Task

Invite each person or the group to think about some difficult situations they have had to face or are facing right now (as usual, remind them not to choose something too overwhelming – at the same time, validate their inner wisdom if they feel like they would like to work on something particularly disturbing for them).

Then, invite them to enter their Compassionate Self (you could even offer a brief meditation here to connect with compassionate qualities), and to focus on the desire to be helpful. Keeping this desire in their heart, ask them to think about ways to apply the "being open to" and the "doing" parts of compassion to this situation, with the intention of alleviating their suffering.

- If done individually, the person will first think about the "being open to" and then the "doing" statements, affirmations, or actions
- If done in pairs, invite them to first tell each other about the difficult situation; then both will write the "being open to" and "doing" compassionate suggestions for their own and for the other person's difficult situation
- If done in a group setting, choose one difficult situation to focus on; then divide the group into two groups and ask one part of the group to focus on

the "being open to" and the other on the "doing". You can write their suggestions on a whiteboard so that they can all benefit from the suggestions offered. You can then change the situation they work with, and swap groups (those who first focused on the "being open to" will now focus on the "doing" and vice versa).

The main idea of this exercise is to help people generate alternative, compassionate coping thoughts and actions, leveraging the ideas of the bigger group. It is important to always loop back to the theme of shared humanity (universality), as they share their difficulties and compassionate suggestions and maybe realise that some of things that others do to cope might be helpful for them, too.

Finally, collect all the compassionate suggestions and compile them into two sets of flashcards: one set of flashcards will contain all the "being open to" suggestions, the other will contain all the "doing" suggestions. You can either send participants the list of collected suggestions and ask them to make flashcards out of them, or you can prepare the flashcards yourself and send them to the participants to print for themselves.

Participants can then use these flashcards as tools when they find themselves in a situation of difficulty and are unsure how to be of support to themselves; they will be able to pick a card from each deck and see if the suggestions resonate and feel helpful in that specific situation.

Phase 3: Compassion for the Body

In this phase we connect to the unchosen nature of our body and practise extending compassion and gratitude towards it.

Main Touch Points

Therapist Script 9.4 – Compassion Focused Body Scan
Client Handout 9.5 – Compassionate Letter to the Body
Client Handout 9.6 – FBRs in the Body

3a) Compassion focused Body Scan

 Therapist Background Knowledge

The compassion-focused body scan allows us to reconnect with all parts of the body and have a compassionate check-in with them. Many parts of the body are often cut off from our awareness – or maybe by focusing our attention on them, we might switch on the threat system. Activating a compassionate intention allows us to extend to these parts the calming effect of vagal toning (green system) to these parts, thereby allowing us to perceive a deeper integration with the complexity of our body.

   Therapist Task

After guiding the practice (**Therapist Script 9.4**), encourage a moment of self-reflection on what they have felt. You can also ask participants to write a compassionate letter specifically to their body (**Client Handout 9.5**).

Invite a discussion around any fears, blocks or resisteances that clients may have experienced when expressing compassion to the body. You can ask them to take a moment, maybe even with their eyes closed, to recollect where they might have felt these FBRs in the body – were there any areas of the body tensing up, contracting, getting hot, tingly, or losing all sensations at the thought of extending compassion towards their body?

As an optional practice, you can use a creative exercise to work on FBRs in the body. Ask clients to draw on a silhouette of the body (**Client Handout 9.6**) where they felt the FBRs manifesting in their body. They may use colours, different textures, or different types of lines to represent how these FBRs felt in the body – if they had a particular shape, size; if there were many or just one. After completing the drawing, guide them through a brief Compassionate Self induction (using breath, posture, facial expression of the face, touch – any of the modalities that we explored in the previous modules). Then, ask them to come back to their drawing, and now add to it anything that they feel would be of support to those FBRs; what colour, shape, or texture would make those FBRs feel seen and supported? How would they represent their compassionate intention to welcome those FBRs and soothe them? Remind them there is not right or wrong way to do this; let it be an intuitive experiment.

Once they have completed the drawing, ask them to close their eyes and observe what they feel in the body – Has anything changed?

Phase 4: Nurturing a Healthy Blue Circle

In this phase, we will build upon a concept that we have already mentioned in Module 2, when we first introduced the three-circle model of emotion regulation: building a healthy drive system. Our drive system is responsible for our seeking behaviour and it can provide great pleasure and satisfaction when it is balanced by our other two systems. We will see how building a healthy blue circle can occur through practicing compassion.

Main Touch Points

Client Handout 9.7 – Compassion Pie Chart
Client Handout 9.8 – Acts of Compassion and Kindness

4a) Compassion in action

Therapist Background Knowledge

Much research has been done on the positive effects of random acts of kindness on our mental health and overall wellbeing. Working on our behaviour can be useful when it is done with intention and purpose. We have seen that entering "doing mode" (our blue circle) can indeed be driven by threat – although this is sometimes necessary, if repeated over time, it often leads to states of overdrive and burnout. What we wish to do instead is to learn how to let compassionate wisdom guide us in our actions.

Therapist Task

At this point of our compassionate training, you will have noticed how embodying and connecting with our Compassionate Self naturally leads us to choose some behaviours over others (e.g., friendly connecting).
    Are there any specific behaviours that you have noticed increased since starting this training?
    Allow time for discussion.

4b) Compassion in different areas of life

Therapist Task

At this point, we can start investigating how compassion plays out in different areas of life. Just as some of us might recognise one of the flows of compassion to be stronger that the others, we might also realise that some areas of our lives are more influenced by compassion than others.
    We will use a pie chart with eight slices representing the eight different areas of life. Ask participants to fill out three different pie charts: one to reflect our compassion levels before starting the compassionate training, one to reflect our compassion levels at the present moment, and the third to reflect what we would like our compassion levels to be in the future.

Therapist Tips

Note that compassion levels are probably different for the different areas of life; highlight the fact that there may be areas of life where we more easily express compassion, while others might require more time for compassion to blossom. Ask participants to keep in mind the three flows of compassion when filling out their pie chart.

Use **Client Handout 9.7** for this exercise.

4c) Compassionate switch

Therapist Background Knowledge

Each day brings with it occasions for meeting with different degrees of suffering, both our own and that of others. If we cannot access our compassionate motivation, these occasions often turn into situations of avoidance, frustration and/or distress. Neuroscience studies tell us that empathy towards pain can lead to fatigue (empathic distress fatigue) if the empathic process is not led by a compassionate motivation. Naturally our threat system tends to avoid and dissociate from the suffering we witness or experience; this natural tendency to dissociate from suffering might also end up also separating us from the possibility to connect and engage with others and with a sense of shared humanity (universality).

Practicing compassion through random acts during our day can help strengthen our compassionate motivation and allow us to live life in more engaged and present manner, which also improves our own wellbeing. Indeed, studies tell us that activating our compassionate motivation, for example through small or big acts of volunteering guided by compassion, is a form of training of our parasympathetic nervous system: HRV (an index of longevity) increases and, along with it, our immune system strengthens.

Therapist Task

You can offer participants the following exercise to try:

> The next time you are walking along the street, notice if there is any manifestation of suffering around you or maybe in yourself; it might be someone walking with crutches, someone who has a sad expression, a homeless person on the sidewalk... As you witness this suffering, try to orient yourself towards it rather than away from it.

> *Acknowledge the suffering with wisdom and non-judgement: "This person is suffering," or notice that you are suffering in this moment.*
>
> *Feel how your body reacts or contracts in response to that suffering – maybe it tries to avoid it, or to find some form of distraction, or maybe you become aware of some parts tensing up in fear of what they can see.*
>
> *Connect to your Compassionate Self: create a slight smile, open your shoulders wide and expand your posture, focusing on the heart space and imagining that it opens and becomes warm and tender – connect to the wisdom of: "It's not your fault if there is so much suffering in the world as humans we all found ourselves in this flow of life, no one chose to be here" – it is no one's fault if our first instinct is to avoid, distract ourselves, or try to flee this suffering that we are all afraid of.*
>
> *Connect to the courage, strength, and the intention to open up to that suffering even if just by a little bit, to welcome it into your area of awareness and feel the emotions that it awakens.*
>
> *Connect to the authentic wish that the suffering may be reduced, or that whoever is experiencing it may have the strength to do so to the best of their capacity. Send compassionate wishes to the person in front of you (or to yourself, if you are the one suffering): may you have all the courage to face this suffering; may you remember that you are not alone in all this, may you have all the compassion that you need to face this moment.*
>
> *If we are unable to say anything, let's imagine a flow of compassion that, with each exhale, reaches the person and envelops them, while also enveloping you in the process of sending compassion to this person.*

It is important to highlight that a random act of compassion does not necessarily translate into an observable action (for example, we are not always in a position to give time or money to someone that needs it, even if we would like to). It is precisely this "not being able to do" that inhibits the connection with a compassionate wish for many people. Compassion always starts with a wish, a direction we are giving to our spirit and thoughts – that motivational switch is always accessible.

4d) Planning compassionate behaviours

   Therapist Task

When training ourselves to orient spontaneously towards compassion, being more deliberate in the first phases of our training can be helpful. This can mean planning the random acts of compassion we wish to offer or receive during the day (remember there are three flows of compassion; it is through training all three that we are able to give more compassion to the self).

Again, a random act of compassion can be something very small, such as offering to help someone get on the bus, holding the elevator door for them or accepting your partner's offer to drop you off at work when you are running late. Or allowing yourself to take a walk to decompress after an intense work meeting.

The idea here is to notice how these random acts of compassion influence each other: are you more open to further acts of compassion once you have practised or received one?

Also try to notice how they influence your emotional tone during the day: Do you feel more or less triggered? Do you feel more or less connected? Do you feel more or less lonely?

For some inspiration regarding acts of compassion and kindness that can be practised during the week, refer to **Client Handout 9.8**. You can also invite clients to come up with their own list and then share it among themselves, if you are working in a group setting.

Phase 5: Wrap-Up

The final phase in this module is a wrap-up of the theme that has been explored. Emphasise how continuing to work on one's **personal practice** (whether formal or informal) can help with the development of our compassionate minds.

Main Touch Points

> **Therapist Script 9.5** – Closing Practice
> **Client Handout B** – Personal Practice Diary

5a) Summary of the session and suggestions for personal practice

 Therapist Task

Take 5–10 minutes to briefly summarise the points that you have gone through in this module.

You may want to provide participants with some suggestions for personal practice and self-reflection:

- Invite them to use **Client Handout 9.8**, specifically focusing on acts of compassion and kindness
- Invite them to follow one of the guided audio meditations in this module, so that they may continue to connect with the idea of strengthening the flow of compassion towards the self

5b) Closing practice

    Therapist Task

Remember to take a moment at the end of the session to acknowledge anything and everything that has come up for participants while exploring the themes offered.

As in previous sessions, invite them to share in one sentence:

What do I take home from today's session (because I feel it's going to be helpful)?

What are some key things that I would like to share and tell other people about?

Invite participants to bring their attention to their intention to be helpful to the self and others rather than neglectful. What is truly important is to tune into this intention.

Finally, guide participants through a short closing practice using **Therapist Script 2.5** and adding maybe a couple of sentences that link back to the work done during the session. This could be something like:

"We have begun to look at the possibility of extending compassion to ourselves...we are discovering that we can connect to the qualities of wisdom and courage to help the different selves that might be experiencing suffering in this moment...

...may we remember that this possibility exists...and that, if it is still difficult to imagine being fully compassionate to ourselves, we can begin setting our intention...may I begin to give myself the compassion I need this week...".

Therapist Scripts

Therapist Script 9.1: Compassionate Landing (5 minutes)

(Refer to Therapist Script 2.1 in Chapter 2.)

You can add the following elements to connect to the previous module:

Holding the compassionate intention to be of support to ourselves and to others in moments of difficulty, let your mind wander to any moments of shame you might have experienced during the week.

Give yourself permission to welcome whatever emerges. Imagine that with each in-breath you are welcoming your profoundly human experience of shame, with each out-breath you are sending warmth to the part of you that is simply afraid and needs connection.

Remind your self-critic that it is welcome to join us in this meditation today, that your compassionate self will be taking things from here on.

Therapist Script 9.2: Compassionate Letter Writing (10 minutes)

Before beginning this practice, take a few moments to reconnect to the Compassionate self. You may wish to guide the group through a brief Compassionate Self meditation, either choosing from one of the scripts in previous modules or finding your own way to bring them back to their compassionate qualities.

It is important to remember that the aim is not to write a "nice letter" or one that is grammatically correct, but rather to give oneself the time and space to find the words that really make us feel good, seen, understood, and enveloped by the gaze of compassion. To connect with the intention to find the right words and grant ourselves permission to change them when we find others that resonate more... this is what this exercise is truly about.

Think back to something you usually criticise yourself for or of which you feel ashamed about. It could be something that has happened or maybe a characteristic of yourself that you don't like. Let any negative sensations and feelings arise as you focus on this.

Now close your eyes and gently connect with your breathing, trying to engage in your soothing rhythm breathing. When you feel that your body and mind have slowed down, step into your Compassionate Self and its courageous, wise, solid intention to help, and begin writing a letter to yourself, explaining this event that you are criticising yourself about and/or that has made you suffer.

Inhale the qualities of wisdom and non-judgement, courage, and strength, and focus on the heartfelt desire to help the person receiving this letter, the wish that this person will be happy and feel supported and understood through all the difficulties that they are facing.

From this perspective, begin writing a letter starting with:

"Dear [your name] ... "

This letter does not need to have a set structure, but it may have these elements:

- **Sensitivity, sympathy and empathy for the pain and suffering involved**
  What do we notice about ourselves in this moment? What makes us realise we are not feeling good? What makes us realise we are criticising ourselves? If we were to look at ourselves from the outside, what would we notice?
  "I can understand that you are feeling sad right now... I can see that you're very tired, and would probably just need someone to offer comfort... I feel how confused you are and maybe you feel alone in this confusion, and I imagine that you would maybe like to have some form of guide, someone that understands you..."

- **Validation**
  Why is what I am feeling understandable? Based on your story, on your past experiences, based on the current circumstances that you are living at this time, based on the very human needs that none of us chose for themselves...
  "It makes total sense that you are feeling this way... you're going through a lot right now... I understand why you are having these kinds of thoughts... throughout your life you have often experienced this... you have often had to make it on your own..."

- **Connecting to the realities of life – Not our fault**
  "It's not your fault that we all have this tricky brain"
  "It's not your fault that..."
  "All human beings have experienced some form of what you are going through right now...."

- **Compassionate wishes**
  What would we like to say to ourselves when in difficulty? What would really be helpful? What words would make us genuinely say: "Thank you for having written them in this letter... thank you so much... this is extremely helpful..."
  "I just want to let you know that I am here for you; you can count on me whatever happens from here on; I just wish for you to feel better and that you may find a sense of solace from this... if you need support, I am here to help..."

Allow for 5–10 minutes of writing. Some groups might need more, so be sure to provide the time needed – it is important not to rush this process.

Once they have finished writing their letters, they can either read them back to themselves, privately, or they can go into a pair reading.

A and B will take turns in reading their letters to one another.

Invite A to read their letter to B. Invite both to embody their compassionate self as they are reading and listening. Have them set an intention before they start to read: How would you read this letter if you really wanted them to feel it? What tone of voice would you use? What speed would you use? How many pauses would you take?

After the reading, B can act as a mirror for what they heard. For example, they might highlight the warmth they felt A was trying to convey, the understanding they provided, the friendly tone of voice that they used.

Then, have B read A's letter back to them, using all the energy and presence of their compassionate self.

Invite them to reverse roles. So now B will be reading B's letter to A. Then A will provide mirroring, and then read B's letter to B.

Encourage the two to discuss:

- *What was it like writing a letter from your Compassionate Self?*
- *What was it like listening as a Compassionate Self to somebody's compassionate letter?*
- *What was it like reading another person's compassionate letter back to them?*
- *What was it like hearing your own compassionate words and wisdom being read to you?*

You can then invite a group discussion of the process.

Therapist Tips

Letters can be written throughout the entire therapeutic process as an additional way to trace improvements in the client's capacity for self-mentalisation and self-soothing. Together with the client, you may compare letters from the beginning of the therapeutic rapport to the end, and discuss any changes observed. This can also be done in a group setting.

You may ask the client to record themselves while reading the compassionate letter out loud to themselves and connect with the intention to listen to the recording during the week or in times of need.

Therapist Script 9.3: Compassion at the Mirror (8 minutes)

Begin this practice with a few minutes of soothing rhythm breathing to cultivate a sense of grounding and presence in your body.

Now, from this posture, pick up the mirror and start by looking at your eyes (limit the field of observation) – what do you notice? Who do you see in these eyes? Begin to contemplate of how many images and places these eyes have seen...how many wonders and how many unpleasant scenarios.

Now begin to widen your field of vision, trying to look at your face the way you naturally would; try to notice any comments or thoughts that emerge.

Maybe you notice the most common forms of resistance coming up: for example, focusing on appearance – noticing wrinkles, adjusting hair, makeup; distracting oneself (avoiding one's gaze), laughing – this can indicate self-deprecation, boredom, embarrassment, shame...

Simply notice these resistances, welcome them... they are part of a natural process... remember that we can do this practice with them, not against them...

Take a few moments to bring your compassionate posture back into your body.

Begin to contemplate that you have the same eyes as the child who was afraid and began to criticise themselves many, many years ago. What do you notice in those eyes today? Are they expressing any emotion? Are they trying to communicate any suffering, hurt or pain in this moment?

For a few seconds just stay with whatever comes up if you look into these eyes, as if they belonged to someone you care about...just try to listen to what they are saying....

Now, try talking to yourself as if your Compassionate Self or the person most familiar with you were looking at you. If it feels helpful, imagine talking to that child who still needs to hear something that could really support and soothe them.

What would this child like to hear? Try whispering it as you look at these eyes. Try to hear what words resonate, what message feels most grounded... imagine what words you could say that would bring a smile to that person in the mirror... maybe you would say "Thank you...that's just what I needed to hear..."

Remember that however imperfect, what you see in front of you is something that will never manifest in this form again; for better or worse, you are looking at something profoundly unique. While you look into these eyes, this face, contemplate that this person never even chose to be here... this being just wishes to be happy and not suffer, just like everyone else on this planet...

And just like everyone else finds themselves here in the flow of life... and just like everyone else, is trying to navigate this flow to the best of their abilities... but maybe they are confused, afraid or often feel emotions that really upset them...

Remember to keep coming back to the intention to convey a sense of affection, courage, acceptance, and the intention to be helpful to this person.

What would they need to hear right now, in this very moment? If you look at this person in the eyes, which words would they really need to hear? Which words would really reach their heart? Which words would really allow them to feel supported, seen, not judged?

When you notice any resistance arising, try closing your eyes slightly, breathing and refocusing. Remember that all resistances, are parts of us and that they need our patience, repetition, understanding and compassion just as much as any other part of us...

Try whispering phrases of welcoming and presence with the intention of getting them across –as if you were to whisper them to your best friend who is suffering.

The purpose is not to feel something special; it is to spend time with our-selves, to create a welcoming and accepting space for the resistances that emerge by doing this practice.

Here some suggestions:

- *I forgive you for not being perfect*
- *I'm willing to forgive you for not being perfect*
- *Forgive me for not taking care of you until today... I intend to do so from here onwards*
- *I am here for you, and I always will be*
- *I accept you exactly as you are and I am here to help you*
- *What can I do to make you feel better?*
- *Thank you for all that you've done for me and with me*

If words are too difficult, try to simply continue looking at your eyes and face with a slight smile that conveys an intention to help the person you see in the mirror.

When you feel ready, you can end the practice.

Therapist Script 9.4: Compassion-Focused Body Scan (15 minutes)

In this meditation we will simply choose to listen to our body and try to connect with the deep nature of what we call our body. We may have criticised this body, we may have picked it apart, but we may not yet have realised some of the deep realities that speak of its story and its nature, and which may help us meet our body with greater respect.

Like all meditations, we are not here to reach some particular state or to achieve some specific feeling, we are simply choosing to spend some time with our body, with the intention of observing its unchosen nature, with non-judge-ment, courage, and a wish for the suffering parts to feel better.

As we close our eyes, we can start sinking into the feelings and sensations that come from the various parts of our body; recognise that this ability to feel is part of the wonderous nature of our body.

For example, we do not have an inanimate shell that produces no sensation (like a crab or a snail does); we have skin, and on this skin, we have special sensors that were made for us, but not by us. So, we recognise that even just closing our eyes and entering into this complex inner landscape is already a profound act of respect and curiosity toward this body that we have been given. This is already a meditation in itself.

We will now start listening and looking deeper into this body of ours, as if we were gazing at the ever-changing sky. Sometimes there is lightning, sometimes there are clouds, sometimes there are stars.

As we observe all that moves and changes within us, maybe with a little wonder, we start connecting with the wisdom that we are observing something that we did not make, that was somehow shaped for us by nature. Yet today we do have the chance to make a choice. We can choose to look at our body with eyes of deep curiosity, awareness, respect of the uniqueness of this organism that we are observing. And the uniqueness of the various processes that take place in it. Just as if we were sitting and observing the ever-changing sky.

Let us first bring our attention to our feet. Feel from within our feet, feeling our capacity to feel our feet. Simply choosing to listen to sensations that are present here is a deep declaration of alliance with our body. Observe if and how our body naturally reacts to this decision of ours to listen to it from within, even though we may not know what to do with these sensations. You can try whispering with a friendly tone of voice: "I am here for you, I want to look at you, and right now I am not going to change you. I simply wish to look at you with the highest level of respect I am capable of today".

We start to realise that we did not choose the shape of our feet, we did not choose the colour of our feet. And as we contemplate the unchosen nature of this part of us, we also realise all the ways they have served us. They are here for us. So, we are in a position to perhaps say thank you to this part of the body that has been selected by nature over millions of years. If we now say something to this part of our body, perhaps expressing our thanks, imagine this part being happy for being seen and greeted.

Let us now move our attention upwards, as we are trying to observe with respect and curiosity the ancient history of our legs, the deep complexity of our knees, the muscles of our thighs, their natural ability to carry us around. We do not only understand their utility, but also their history. These legs may have been fins once. Maybe we can thank the ancient nature of these legs, we can wonder if there is anything we can do for these legs. And perhaps there is something that we want to say to these legs, something that they are asking of us. If we say something to this part of the body, maybe giving thanks, let us imagine this part of the body feeling happy about being seen and greeted.

And again, letting our attention gently drift towards the pelvis, looking at this part of the body that contains organs that might have been a source of difficult emotions such as shame at times. And yet there is also a powerful nature to this part of our body. The profound power to make us experience pleasure and to be a source of life. Try to feel the deep meaning of this gift, of this part of the body and its potential.

Let us thank all the organs that find their seat in our pelvis, breathing our gratitude into it. Thank you. If we now say something to this part of the body, perhaps expressing our thanks, let us imagine this part of the body feeling happy about being seen and greeted.

Let us then move towards all the organs housed in our torso: our intestines, our liver, stomach, our pancreas, kidneys, our lungs, our heart. We think of all the animals that have these very same organs. For all of them and for us, these organs are life-transforming and function silently, without asking us for anything in return. For a few moments let us open ourselves to offering gratitude to this part of our body. Observe how these organs feel when they receive our grati-tude; maybe they are able to relax just a little bit more. As we breathe in and out of our abdomen, our chest and our back, feel the intention to keep con-nected to these parts of our body – knowing that they will be ready and willing to reconnect with us.

Let us nourish the connection with all these body parts that we may have hurt or mistreated. If we now say something to this part of the body, maybe giving thanks, let us imagine this part of the body feeling happy about being seen and greeted.

Let's move from the chest to the shoulders, arms and hands. As we tune into the sensations in our hands, imagine for a moment what might be the sensa-tions of the hands of a monkey, of the paws of a kitten, of the claws of an eagle – feel this mysterious and wonderous connection to other living beings. We are all intimately connected, all share the same ancestors. If we now say something to this part of the body, maybe giving thanks, let us imagine this part of the body feeling happy about being seen and greeted.

Let this feeling of reconnection extend to all your body parts, our hands could come to touch our heart if we feel like it, as a signal of this intention to be in communion with of all parts. Maybe we could visualise thin, glowing threads beginning to float throughout our body, connecting the various parts. Feel our neck, our hair, all the small muscles of our face as they light up and connect with all others parts of the body.

As we turn towards our face, perhaps a slight friendly smile starts to form. We contemplate the deeply social nature of this part of the body, the way that we humans have achieved the ability to convey emotions in such a refined and powerful way. We think of a child's smile, a child's tears. Or the smile of our best friend. And we remember that, even this part of our body, this face, was not chosen by us. These features were not chosen by us, but are the result of all those who have come before us; the final stretch on the path that has been traced by all the many ancestors that have come before us. If we now say something to this part of the body, perhaps expressing our thanks, let us ima-gine this part of the body feeling happy about being seen and greeted.

Finally, we greet our brain. This brain that is so wonderfully complex and that often gets stuck, but that has this profound, incredibly unique ability to perceive itself, to understand itself. In this instant this brain of ours is contemplating itself. We contemplate with wonder this ability to be aware of ourselves in this body, in this life, in this precise space in time. If we now say something to this part of the body, maybe giving thanks, let us imagine this part of the body feeling happy about being seen and greeted.

Now try to look at this body from the outside; observe all these threads of light, connecting the distant parts of the body. Are there some parts that have been left out? Imagine being able to extend this network to all parts of the body, from the outside and from the inside. Feel for a few moments the magic of this powerful integration of the entire body.

And now we expand this connection by going outside of the body. We begin to perceive all the other bodies, perhaps the people in this building, the people in this group. And we realise that even their bodies were not chosen and are the result of a long path of evolution. We greet and honour them as well.

Many of those bodies, many of those people are helping others in the world... all these bodies can choose to bring compassion to this world... let us send a wish to these living bodies... a signal of respect for their capacity to bring compassionate acts into the world. And as we continue breathing, we also connect to other living creatures on this earth, the animals, plants, fungi, algae, and microorganisms. Imagine the entire planet breathing along with you. Inhaling and exhaling through space and time, reconnecting to our common nature. And we feel that our body can see itself for what it always was and always will be: a molecule in an immense living organism, breathing in unison.

As you continue to feel your entire body breathing as one with the Earth, which is supporting it, gently come back to the awareness of your seat and when you feel ready, you can open your eyes and come back to the room.

Client Handouts

Client Handout 9.1: Compassionate Weekly Reflection

Let's do a curious friendly reflection on this past week:

Which part of the self-practice did I do and why?

Which part of the self-practice did I not do?

Was this due to any anxieties or block regarding the practice or the path? Which ones can you identify?

We extend gratitude, respect, and compassion to resistances: What would make you and your resistances feel safer in going forward on this path?

Client Handout 9.2: Compassionate Letter

This practice will help you refocus your thoughts and feelings on being supportive, helpful and caring toward yourself.

 **COMPASSIONATE LETTER WRITING**

SENSITIVITY, SYMPATHY AND EMPATHY FOR THE PAIN AND SUFFERING

"I can understand that you are feeling sad right now... I can see that you're very tired, and would probably just need someone to offer comfort... I feel how confused you are and maybe you feel alone in this confusion, and I imagine that you would maybe like to have some form of guidance, someone that understands you..."

VALIDATION

"It makes total sense that you are feeling this way... you're going through a lot right now... I understand why you are having this kind of thoughts... throughout your life you have often experienced this... you have often had to make it on your own..."

CONNECTING TO THE REALITIES OF LIFE

- *"It is not your fault if we all have this tricky brain"*
"It is not your fault if..."
"all human beings have experienced some form of what you are going through right now...."

COMPASSIONATE WISHES

"I just want to let you know that I am here for you; you can count on me whatever happens from here on; I just wish for you to feel better and that you may find a sense of solace from this... if you need support, I am here to help..."

Figure 9.1 Compassionate Letter Writing.

To start your letter, try to attune to your Compassionate Self – that part of you that has the deep desire to be helpful, not harmful, to be supportive and caring. Think about that part of you as the type of self you would like to be – think about the qualities you would like your compassionate self to have; it does not matter if you do not really feel this way yet, what really matters here is that we are setting an intention, a heartfelt desire and commitment.

If it helps, you can take inspiration from the four points described above.

Dear......................................

Client Handout 9.3: Compassion at the Mirror

Draw the outline of your mirror below.

Try writing into the mirror anything that you noticed during the practice, any words or phrases that you felt helpful, reassuring and caring.

Feel free to return to this handout and add any positive and compassionate affirmations that you find helpful when you repeat the mirror practice.

Client Handout 9.4: Self-Compassion in Video

After viewing the two recordings of yourself, answer the following prompts:

What did you notice after watching the first video? What struck you? What emotions did you notice come up for you?

What were you thinking and feeling toward yourself as you told the story in the first video? Was there any moment in the video that made you experience desire to help that person (yourself)? If yes, what would you have wanted to tell them?

What did you notice while watching the second video? What struck you the most?

Did you notice any expressions of compassion in the second video? If yes, which ones?

Client Handout 9.5: Compassionate Letter to the Body

After completing the compassion-focused body scan, try writing a letter to your body.

As always, you begin by connecting with your soothing rhythm breathing… and with your intention to write something that might be in any way helpful for your body with this issue. Perhaps you would like to express the compassion and gratitude you may have felt during the practice or that you wish to cultivate towards your body. Or whatever else you would like to say to your body that comes from the wise, courageous part of you, which is set on being helpful. You may choose to focus on a specific body part if you feel called to do so. Here are some ideas to get you started:

> *Dear body,*
> *I've just completed a long meditation where I tried to get in touch with your ancient origins….*
> *The thing that struck me the most is ….*
> *The thing that I really want to thank you for is …*
> *What I realised today is that….*
> *I am sorry that in the past……*
> *But today, I want you to know that …*
> *Final closing wish*

Client Handout 9.6: FBRs in the Body

Use the space below to draw an outline of your body and then represent the areas where you felt your FBRs manifesting in the body. You may use colours, different textures, different types of lines to represent how these FBRs felt in your body – if they had a particular shape, size, if there were many of them or just one...

Client Handout 9.7: Compassion Pie Chart

How much compassion do you feel is present in the different areas of your life? Are there differences between how this was before, how it is now, and how you would like it to be?

For each pie chart, fill in the slots starting from the centre of the figure, based on how much compassion you were able to bring to that area of your life. By compassion we mean the ability to act sensitively and wisely toward things that were wrong, and to show the courage to create a positive change. Do you notice any repeating patterns?

Compassion in the Past

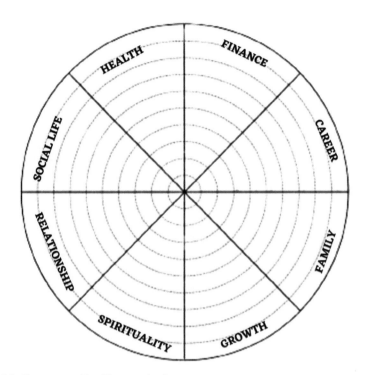

Figure 9.2 Compassion Pie Chart in the Past.

Notes

Compassion in the Present

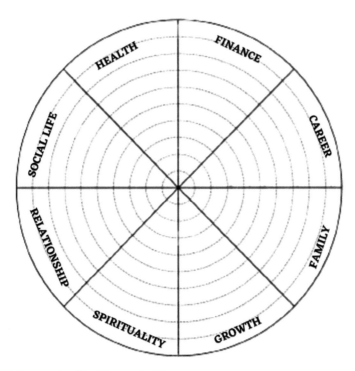

Figure 9.3 Compassion Pie Chart in the Present.

Notes

Compassion in the Future

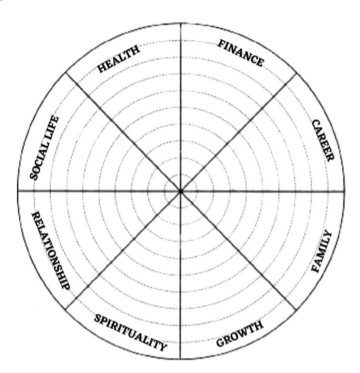

Notes

Client Handout 9.8: Acts of Compassion and Kindness

Below you will find a list of acts of compassion and kindness that you can explore during your week; feel free to add any other acts that come to mind or that you spontaneously find yourself doing in your day.

- *Listen attentively to someone's problems or concerns without judgement.*
- *Offer a genuine smile and kind words to brighten someone's day.*
- *Hold the door open for someone or help them with their bags.*
- *Donate to a charitable organisation or volunteer your time for a good cause.*
- *Offer emotional support to a friend or family member going through a difficult time.*
- *Pay for someone's meal or coffee anonymously.*
- *Write heartfelt letters or send thoughtful gifts to people in need of encouragement.*
- *Engage in random acts of kindness, such as leaving positive notes in public places.*
- *Offer assistance to an elderly person or someone with a physical disability.*
- *Engage in active listening and show empathy when someone shares their experiences or feelings.*
- *Forgive someone who has wronged you and let go of grudges.*
- *Help strangers with directions or offer assistance when they seem lost or confused.*
- *Support and uplift someone who is experiencing self-doubt or low self-esteem.*
- *Rescue or adopt a pet from a shelter.*
- *Volunteer at a local community centre, hospital, or nursing home.*
- *Offer to babysit for a single parent or a family in need.*
- *Share your knowledge or skills with others by offering free lessons or tutoring.*
- *Help someone find employment by offering advice, making connections, or reviewing their resume.*
- *Donate blood or participate in organ donation programmes.*
- *Encourage and support someone's dreams or goals.*
- *Offer a shoulder to cry on and provide comfort to someone in distress.*
- *Support local businesses by shopping at independently owned stores or restaurants.*
- *Share your expertise or professional knowledge with others who can benefit from it.*
- *Extend a helping hand to someone struggling with household chores or tasks.*
- *Advocate for the rights and well-being of marginalised or disadvantaged individuals or communities.*
- *Organise or participate in a community clean-up or environmental conservation initiative.*
- *Foster or provide temporary shelter for animals in need.*

- *Offer to drive someone to appointments or run errands for those who are unable to do so themselves.*
- *Mentor a young person or offer guidance to someone seeking career advice.*
- *Educate yourself about social issues and engage in meaningful conversations to promote understanding and empathy.*
- *Practice self-care by setting aside dedicated time for activities that bring you joy and relaxation.*
- *Prioritise your physical health by engaging in regular exercise, eating nourishing meals, and getting enough rest.*
- *Set boundaries and learn to say no when you need to, honouring your own needs and limitations.*
- *Engage in activities that promote self-reflection and self-discovery, such as journaling or meditation.*
- *Treat yourself with kindness and understanding when you make mistakes or face challenges.*
- *Celebrate your accomplishments, no matter how small, and acknowledge your progress.*
- *Nurture your passions and hobbies, dedicating time to pursue activities that bring you fulfilment.*
- *Surround yourself with positive and supportive people who uplift and encourage you.*
- *Take breaks when you need them and allow yourself to rest without guilt.*
- *Practice self-compassionate self-talk, replacing self-criticism with words of encouragement and self-acceptance.*
- *Engage in activities that promote mental well-being, such as practicing mindfulness or seeking therapy if needed.*
- *Release perfectionism and embrace self-acceptance, understanding that you are worthy and deserving of love and compassion.*
- *Forgive yourself for past mistakes or regrets, allowing yourself to heal and move forward.*
- *Engage in activities that inspire creativity and self-expression, such as painting, writing, or playing an instrument.*
- *Treat yourself to small indulgences or acts of self-pampering, such as taking a bubble bath or enjoying a favourite treat.*

Chapter 10

Module 10

Compassionate Assertiveness

Aims

- To understand what assertiveness is, why it would be helpful in improving the relationship with others and with the self and how a compassionate motivation can support the process
- To recognise the ways in which we communicate with each other and the defensive origin of some forms of complex communication that we get stuck in
- To learn how to say no and set healthy boundaries that derive from the compassionate intention to be helpful to ourselves, the relationship, and the other person
- To learn what the FBRs to showing appreciation could be and how switching to a compassionate motivation can help us to show appreciation

 Deepen Your Knowledge

In Gilbert, P. & Simos, G. (Eds). (2022). *Compassion Focused Therapy: Clinical Practice and Applications*. Routledge, please refer to:

    Chapter 8. Compassionate Mind Training: Key Themes
    Chapter 24. Compassionate Assertiveness With Voice

In Gilbert, P. (2010). *Compassion Focused Therapy: Distinctive Features*.

    Chapter 7. Affiliation, Warmth and Affection. See, in particular, the section on Validation

DOI: 10.4324/9781003436058-12

Summary of Key Processes

Table 10.1 Module 10: Compassionate Assertiveness

Phase		Main Touch Points	Therapist Scripts	Client Handouts
1	Introduction	**1a)** Compassionate landing **1b)** Revision of personal practice and recap of the previous session	□ **Script 10.1:** Compassionate Landing	□ **Handout 10.1:** Compassionate weekly reflection
2	Introduction to Compassionate Assertiveness	**2a)** Compassionate Assertiveness and its expressions **2b)** Fears, Blocks and Resistances to assertiveness **2c)** Identifying our needs and embodying assertiveness	□ **Script 10.2:** Approaching FBRs to assertiveness	□ **Handout 10.2:** Different styles of communication □ **Handout 10.3:** Expressions of assertiveness □ **Handout 10.4:** List of needs □ **Handout 10.5:** The process of assertiveness □ **Handout 10.6:** Embodying Assertiveness □ **Handout 10.7:** Assertiveness is not the outcome
3	Compassionate Assertiveness in action	**3a)** Asking for what we need **3b)** Responding to criticism		□ **Handout 10.8:** Asking for what we need
4	Expressing and receiving appreciation	**4a)** Fears, Blocks and Resistances to receiving appreciation **4b)** Fears, Blocks and Resistances to expressing appreciation **4b)** Ways of expressing appreciation	□ **Script 10.3:** Receiving appreciation	
5	Wrap-up	**5a)** Summary of the session and suggestions for personal practice **5b)** Closing practice		**Handout B:** Personal practice diary

Phase 1: Introduction

Main Touch Points

 Therapist Script 10.1 – Compassionate Landing
Client Handout 10.1 – Compassionate Weekly Reflection

1a) Compassionate Landing

   Therapist Task

The Compassionate Landing is a moment to guide participants into a space for reflection and practice, welcoming themselves as they arrive in the space, noticing any sensations, emotions, and thoughts that they might be carrying with them from the day.

By this point of the training, participants will have learned to expect this moment: you can discuss with them what it feels like to have this opportunity to once again tune into their experience. What is their relationship to these small ritualistic "check-ins"? Has their inner dialogue changed since starting to practise the Compassionate Landings? Have they started to notice anything new?

As always, connect participants to their compassionate motivation and intentions:

- To work on ways to be helpful to oneself
- To support others as best as possible on their journey
- To be open to the helpfulness of others

Before practicing the landing, you could guide them through a short 'three circle check-in'.

Three-Circle Check-In

You may use **Therapist Script 10.1** to guide participants through the compassionate landing.

If you have time, provide some space for intentionally moving toward any fears, blocks, and resistances (FBRs) that might have arisen during the week, using the prompts from **Client Handout 10.1**. At this point in the training, participants might notice changes in their FBRs or in the way they approach them – encourage discussion among the group or in smaller groups.

- *Have any FBRs dissolved since the beginning of the training?*
- *Have any new FBRs arisen?*
- *Has anything changed in the way they perceive and relate to their FBRs?*

1b) Revision of personal practice and recap of the previous session

 Therapist Task

This is a moment to allow the experiences that happened during the week to be shared. Participants may want to reference to their personal practice diary or just share reflections they may have had during the past week on the topics explored together.

Sharing can occur either in the large group or in small groups (this last option is particularly advisable for online trainings).

The therapist can provide a brief recap of the last session, in which the main points were:

- Why it is important to develop the flow of compassion for the self
- Practices to develop the flow of self-compassion
- Practicing self-compassion for the body
- Using compassion to nurture a healthy drive system

This can also be a space to set the scene for the current module; the main themes that are going to be explored are:

- What compassionate assertiveness is
- How we can train compassionate assertiveness
- How to make requests, respond to criticism and affirm our needs in an assertive way
- How to express appreciation

Phase 2: Introduction to Compassionate Assertiveness

In this phase we will introduce the concept of compassionate assertiveness, understanding how it evolved and what its core expressions are. We will also bring awareness to the FBRs that might be hindering us from bringing compassionate assertiveness in our own lives.

Main Touch Points

> **Therapist Script 10.2** – Approaching FBRs to Assertiveness
> **Client Handout 10.2** – Different Styles of Communication

Client Handout 10.3 – Expressions of Assertiveness
Client Handout 10.4 – List of Needs
Client Handout 10.5 – The Process of Assertiveness
Client Handout 10.6 – Embodying Assertiveness
Client Handout 10.7 – Assertiveness is not in the Outcome

2a) Compassionate assertiveness and its expressions

    Therapist Background Knowledge

When speaking of assertiveness, one often thinks about conflict; however, the ability to deal with conflict is only one aspect of assertiveness. The concept of assertiveness also encompasses the way we put forward our ideas, the way we argue in support of our views or values, whether we are open to praise from others or not, if and how we take responsibility, if we claim our and others' rights to be treated with equality and respect.

We can think of it as a communication style, one that enables us to voice our feelings, thoughts, beliefs, and opinions without violating the rights of others. There are, of course, also other communication styles, such as aggressive, passive, and passive-aggressive.

Assertiveness is distinct from these other communication styles because it is grounded in a different motive. While aggressive, passive or passive-aggressive communication styles emerge from a competitive, rank-based social mentality, assertiveness very much stems from a **compassionate motive**.

Three very important skills that pertain to human social intelligence were crucial in allowing for the evolution from a competitive-driven communication style, to a compassionate assertive one. These are the same skills that we have already recognised to be fundamental in shifting from a mammalian caring motive to human compassion.

These three skills are:

- **Knowing awareness**: we are aware that there is a conflict, and we are able to think about the nature of the conflict, and at the same time we remember how normal and "not our fault" is to have conflicting needs, both on an intrapersonal and interpersonal level.
- **Empathic awareness**: insight into why we are feeling what we are feeling and needing, as well as what the other person might be feeling and needing, combined with an empathic understanding of our impact on them.
- **Knowing intentionality**: knowingly, mindfully, and empathically, choosing to try to be helpful not harmful, and to try and find a compromise or mutually beneficial possibilities.

COMMUNICATION STYLES

Human
intelligence skills

KNOWING AWARENESS →

EMPATHIC AWARENESS →

KNOWING INTENTIONALITY →

ASSERTIVE

Respects both own
needs and needs
of others.

COMPASSIONATE MOTIVE

AGGRESSIVE

Violation of others' rights.
Needs of self, at the cost of
disregarding others' needs.

PASSIVE - AGGRESSIVE

Aggressive, in an indrect way.

PASSIVE

Violation of one's own rights.
Needs of other before needs of self.

**RANK-BASED
COMPETITIVE MOTIVE**

Figure 10.1 Social Motives and Communication Styles.

These three skills are fundamental in allowing us to bring a compassionate motive to communication and conflict-resolution, and therefore, moving out of rank-based competition and into assertiveness. Without **knowing awareness**, we might have some insight that we are facing a conflict because we feel angry or anxious, but we do not really have any insight into the dynamic of the conflict itself. Without **empathic awareness**, we are unable to get 'behind the scenes' of the argument or situation and understand why we are feeling the way we are feeling and why the other person might be feeling the way they are feeling; we do not think about the impact of our behaviour on others. Without **knowing intentionality**, we might have a hard time orienting towards our compassionate motivation and simply desire to end the conflict and come out of it as a winner.

We can bring a compassionate motive to our interactions in order to guide our efforts towards being respectful and mutually supportive, as well as taking on a role of authority and responsibility to resolve conflict or manage a situation in a way that we feel is aligned with what matters for us. The following is example of an assertive action: a doctor receives a call about an injured person who needs urgent help, and the doctor pushes people out of the way in a very crowded space to get to the injured person. Holding back because the doctor did not want to be seen as rude would be passive and submissive and not helpful in that context. So, choosing to be compassionately assertive implies focusing on the:

- **Why** (intention): because I want to be sensitive, validating, helpful and more in line with what is important for me, I want to be more authentic in relationships, I want to feel seen and safe in relationships and ultimately have better relationships.
- **How** (attitude): giving direction to the different elements of communication, such as posture (favouring compassionate body grounding over rank-based or overly defensive positions), tone of voice, facial expression, gestures, as well as the verbal content and formulation of my communication (validating one's own needs and those of the other).

Therefore, to be compassionately assertive we need to bring online all the qualities of compassion. In fact, compassionate assertiveness should not be seen as a mere "efficient communication style" (drive system) or as a way to "defend oneself from pressing requests" (threat system), but as a way to train the three flows of compassion.

  Therapist Task

To elicit a discussion on the ways of tackling conflicts, you might ask the client or group to come up with interpersonal conflicts they have had or moments where they were not able to express their needs, and if in a group setting, you could invite one of them to share their example so that you can work on it as a group.

Regarding this interpersonal conflict, invite them to explore what mentality they were in at that moment.

- *Were you in your competitive mentality of winning, losing, aggressing, submission or other fears?*
- *In what ways did you find this mentality to be helpful or harmful?*
- *What might have happened if you stepped into your compassionate mind? Would you have thought of the problem in a different way?*
- *What resistances to and fears about accessing the compassionate mind might arise in that moment?*
- *How would the compassionate qualities of courage and wisdom have helped you in that situation?*

To further explore the difference between the several communication styles, you can offer participants an exercise that entails coming up with aggressive, passive, passive-aggressive, and assertive responses to different scenarios (**Client Handout 10.2**).

This exercise can be delivered in several ways. People can of course do the exercise individually, going through each scenario and writing down their different responses for each style of communication. If working with a group, you can ask participants to work in small groups; each small group will go through all the scenarios provided and come up with responses for each communication style, collectively. Once they have finished, you can have a discussion with the group at large and highlight any patterns that might have emerged. Finally, a third way to offer this exercise is to split the big group into three smaller groups: for each scenario, one group will be tasked with coming up with a passive response, the second group will come up with an aggressive response, the third group will come up with an assertive response; be sure to change roles for each scenario, so that each group has an opportunity to work on all three communication styles.

To link the discussion about communication styles with the Compassion Focused Therapy (CFT) model, encourage the group to reflect on how each style is connected to the threat, drive, or soothing system.

 Therapist Tips

The therapist could highlight how helpful and functional it was to not be assertive at some point of the clients' life. You could even encourage clients to thank their non-assertive self, which in some way helped them in overcoming threat-laden situations in their lives. One of the critical aspects of CFT is to reiterate the concept of "it's not your fault" which has a de-shaming effect on the client. You could potentially ask clients at what point in their lives it made sense for them not to be assertive. The usefulness of non-assertiveness is particularly evident in some cultural contexts – it is, therefore, very important to be culturally sensitive when delivering this module.

Having validated people's intuitive wisdom around assertiveness, you can then move on to explaining the different expressions of assertiveness; you can do this interactively, asking the group for to come up with examples for each of these expressions (**Client Handout 10.3**). Consider assertiveness as a journey, a process. Be sure to highlight that these expressions are just a direction we can use to orient our thoughts, actions and communications, not checkboxes that must be ticked off in order to truly consider ourselves assertive.

Adopting compassionate assertiveness is a form of training of the three qualities of compassion.

- **Wisdom:** I recognise that I did not choose my needs (and others did not choose theirs), I did not choose the environment that made it hard for me to recognise and express my needs (this was actually advantageous at times – I could not afford to lose relationships).
- **Courage and strength**: even if it can generate anxiety at times, I'm willing to develop the courage and strength to be more mindful of myself and others and make my relationships more authentic, even if this might mean changing (or potentially even losing) these relationships.
- **Intention to be helpful:** I am doing all this to alleviate the suffering that comes from invalidating myself and from being in an inauthentic relationship, to improve the relationship with myself and others. I am not doing this to manipulate others.

2b) Fears, blocks and resistances to assertiveness

   Therapist Background Knowledge

As we introduce the concept of assertiveness and begin to delve deeper into its expressions, it is rather common for FBRs to emerge. Some people might be afraid of asserting their needs: if they have always put others' needs before their own to be accepted and seen, they might fear that not doing so will lead them to isolation. This is where we must highlight the element of courage of compassion, which will sustain this process. Other people might experience a resistance – they are focused on their own self-advantage and see no point in looking at others 'needs when all they want is to achieve their own goal.

FBRs to assertiveness can also emerge as a fear of "not getting it right", of not being well-versed enough in the skills of assertiveness. This is where equanimity, a fundamental ingredient of mindfulness and compassion, becomes useful. In fact, not being assertive can easily make us feel self-critical (*Why am I so weak?*)

Moreover, compassionate assertiveness is about wisdom: recognising the unchosen nature of some of our difficulties and conflicts and accepting that some situations go beyond our control to fix things. Once we feel safe enough to validate our human imperfections and limits, it becomes easier for us to activate our mentalising abilities and express our needs, while respecting those of others. In fact, when speaking of needs, one of the most common experiences reported by clients is that of being ashamed; if we acknowledge that we have needs that we have not chosen, if we validate them, the assertive journey becomes more accessible.

Acknowledge that facing FBRs to assertiveness can sometimes uncover grief in the face of conflicts that do not end in a positive resolution. Shifting towards compassionate courage in these cases can sustain clients in processing potential shifts in their relationships.

 Therapist Task

To begin a discussion around the FBRs to assertiveness, consider the expressions of assertiveness (**Client Handout 10.3**) and ask participants to underline the elements they struggle with the most. Invite them to have an open minded and curious approach to these FBRs, maybe considering what lies behind them and how our Compassionate Self can help us to embrace them. Whenever we work with FBRs in CFT, the idea is never to "attack" or "destroy" them, but rather to become aware of them and validate them (welcome them) as a natural part of being human and finding ways of working with them rather than against them.

 Therapist Tips

When working on assertive communication, clients could end up in a competitive motivation by trying to "get it right". If you notice this happening, you could kindly and playfully try pointing it out to them. Highlight that no one communicates perfectly in an assertive way and that finding this style of communication and interaction is the journey itself rather than the destination. Just like compassion, it requires practice and patient re-orienting.

Becoming angry at ourselves, criticising ourselves for not having been perfectly assertive can indeed shift us out of that compassionate motivation. Stress the importance of the motive that lies behind our communication and have them become mindful of those motivational shifts that easily occur when we compare what is happening to what we think we should have done or said.

Another crucial point to be made, which is responsible for many FBRs, it the issue of viewing conflicts as something bad or catastrophic. Compassion is not about avoiding conflicts but rather about approaching them with wisdom and the desire to find what may be helpful in accepting/approaching and hopefully resolving them; as therapists, we should stress that it is perfectly normal for our needs to be conflicting at times, making it tricky to know which one to prioritise. What matters most is if and how we try to find ways to be sensitive to and respect our needs and the needs of others.

To explore this theme of conflicts, you can lead clients through a brief exercise using visualisation (**Therapist Script 10.2**). As always, we suggest you provide some time for self-reflection and/or group discussion at the end of this practice.

2c) Identifying our needs and embodying assertiveness

    Therapist Background Knowledge

With the previous exercise, or simply while talking about assertiveness, two issues might have come up:

- Some clients may realise that they have hard time not only expressing their needs, but even just identifying them
- Some clients may realise that, although they want to be assertive, they have no idea how to do so

    Therapist Task

Regarding needs, it can be useful to spend some time reflecting together about what kinds of needs human beings have. We encourage you as a therapist to choose how to do so, based on the specific group you are working with:

- For example, you could refer to Maslow's hierarchical model when explaining the different levels of needs that we as human beings have.
- You could also refer back to the three-circle model (explored in depth in Module 2), reminding participants of the three basic functions that all living beings need to deal with: protection from threat, seeking resources, and resting. On top of these, human beings also have social and relational needs, as well as needs of the self.
- A very practical and handy tool that can be given to clients is the list of universal needs as specified by Non-Violent Communication, an approach to communication which evolved from person-centred therapy and was developed by clinical psychologist Marshall Rosenberg between the 1960s

and 1970s. Clients can use this as a reference point when entering the first step of assertiveness: recognising.

- It could potentially be useful to share with clients the List of Universal Human Rights published by the UN (freely available online) – having a document that officially lists our rights and therefore our needs, can be very validating for people.

To address needs, you can invite clients to work with a specific argument they have had in the past, perhaps the one used during the *Approaching FBRs to Assertiveness* (**Therapist Script 10.2**) practice, and ask them to recognise what their needs were and what the needs of the person they were arguing with might have been, using the list of needs (**Client Handout 10.4**).

 Therapist Tips

At times, pinpointing our needs might feel impossible: be sure to remind clients that this is normal. Even once we acquire the tools to help us become more aware of how many different needs exist in the human experience, identifying what needs are active in us at a specific time is not easy.

In addition, the fact that we are not able to identify a specific need, can actually be revelatory of the presence of one particular need: the need that you need more time, safety, and safeness to identify what your needs are or may be in a specific situation or circumstance. This is not just word play, but a very honest and compassionate view of the human experience.

Find a way to explain to clients that **the fact we do not know what our needs are, still expresses a need: the need for more time, safety, and safeness in order for us to understand what our needs are.**

It is very hard to identify our needs if we feel threatened (the person I love will humiliate me or will get angry if I express what I need – lack of safety) or if we do not have people in our life who are reassuring, who guide us in self-exploration and validate what we express (lack of safeness).

If your clients are really struggling to identify their needs, you can offer the following short practices to facilitate a shift of perspective, which could, in turn, promote insight into their needs:

- *Take a minute to close your eyes and look at yourself from the outside. Try asking yourself: "What does this person need?"*
- *Imagine being able to speak to your future self (a week, month or year from now): what would they suggest your needs are in this present moment?*

- *Imagine being able to speak from the perspective of your Compassionate Self, maybe through a letter. What would they suggest your needs are in this present moment?*
- *Imagine being able to speak to your ideal compassionate other (a friend, a family member or even your compassionate image): what would they suggest your needs are in this present moment?*

Being compassionately assertive is a process that requires our compassionate embodiment. This is why the first part of the practice *Approaching FBRs to Assertiveness* (**Therapist Script 10.2**) is dedicated to connecting with the Compassionate Self through the body. Compassionate embodiment creates the safe grounding in which we can then confidently move through the four steps of assertiveness: 1) Recognise; 2) Allow; 3) Validate; and 4) Express (both our needs and our FBRs to assertiveness). These steps can be remembered easily using the acronym CRAVE, which stands for "Compassionate Recognising, Allowing, Validating, and Expressing).

The process of assertiveness (**Client Handout 10.5**) is relational, meaning that it involves us going through the four steps, but also trying to do this with the person we have in front of us (or for one of the parts of ourselves, if we are facing an intrapersonal dynamic). Compassionate embodiment can be thought of as the "motivational" soil needed to sow the seeds of assertiveness; without it, it is extremely difficult to welcome and connect to our needs and those of others. Without compassionate intention, setting and embodiment, assertiveness could become nothing more than a way of practicing our communication

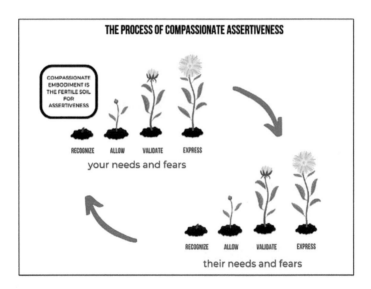

Figure 10.2 The Process of Compassionate Assertiveness.

skills. In our most significant relationships, choosing to be compassionately assertive of our needs always implies a kind of dance with the other person and their needs. Just like the three flows of compassion, assertiveness also has flows: I can be validating and assertive of my needs, help the other person to be validating and assertive of theirs, and open up to the other's effort to recognise the validity of my own needs. In this way, compassionate assertiveness becomes much more than a mere communication style to "defend myself from excessive requests" (threat system) or "express my needs efficiently" (drive system); it transforms into a means to grow in relationships and make them more authentic and safe (soothing system).

 Therapist Tips

It is important for you as a therapist to acknowledge that assertiveness is **context dependent**: it can take different forms based on what the external circumstances are. Unfortunately, there are many situations in which being overtly assertive might not be safe; this is the experience of many minority groups. Nevertheless, this however does not mean that we cannot take a compassionately assertive stance. It does however entail being attuned to our needs and internally validating them, even when this seems impossible to do because of the world we are living in. Sometimes 'masking' or 'hiding' is not a question of not being compassionate to our needs, but rather recognising the importance of survival; be sure to legitimise this strategy and help clients see how much sense it can make in specific situations.

Moreover, in less significant or occasional relationships (a stranger who wants to skip the line while at the store), we might not have a chance to know and validate their needs, and we might not have the intention to improve the relationship, therefore compassionate assertiveness will manifest as the ability to CRAVE (Compassionate Recognising, Allowing, Validating, and Expressing) our needs.

Compassionate wisdom can help clients deal with the following reality check. In nature, having the perfect conditions for a seed to flourish, does not always mean we will be able to reap a good harvest. The same applies to the process of assertiveness; creating the fertile ground for assertive communication and committing to the steps of recognising, allowing, validating, and expressing, will not always result in a positive outcome. This is why it is so crucial to remind clients that assertiveness is not about the outcome, but about the process.

To illustrate this point, it can be useful to go through two possible scenarios together: one in which an assertive communication results in conflict resolution (illustrated in the Vignette A below), another in which the same assertive communication results in rupture (illustrated in Vignette B below). Both of these are examples of assertiveness. Refer clients to **Client Handout 10.7.**

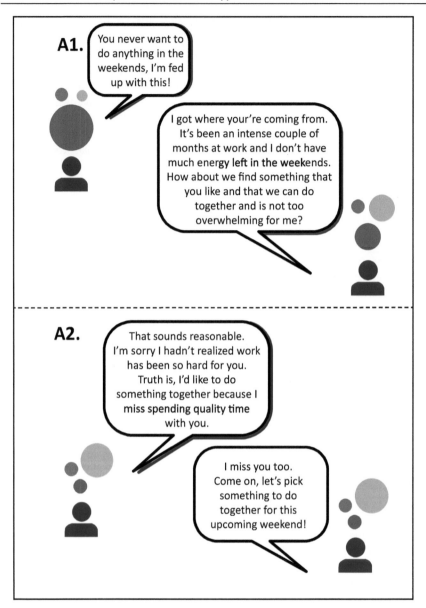

Figure 10.3 Assertive Communication can Result in Conflict Resolution.

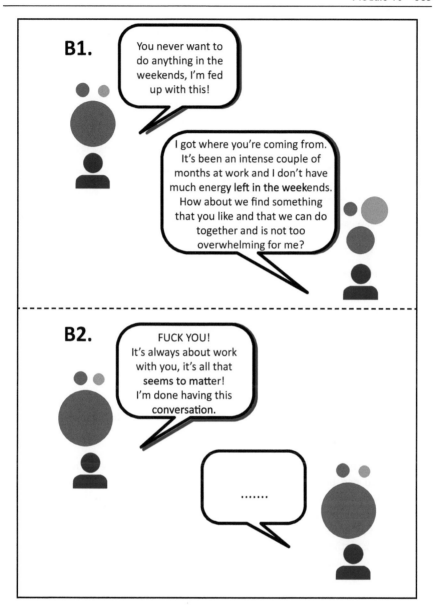

Figure 10.4 Assertive Communication can Result in Rupture.

RECOGNIZING ASSERTIVE COMMUNICATION

VOICE

- Calm
- Steady
- Even
- Sincere
- Audible
- Reassuring
- Certain
- Varied pitch and tone
- Interesting and interested
- Positive

BODY LANGUAGE

- Open body language
- Strong back, soft front
- Relaxed and comfortable
- Making eye contact (if feels comfortable for self)
- Planted/grounded
- Head up
- At the other person's level
- Calm, open gestures
- Soft smile

- Shall we
- What do you think
- I need
- My thoughts are
- I feel that
- Thank you
- What is your opinion of
- I'm not sure I agree with...
- In my opinion...

WORDS

- Can I have a moment to think about that?
- Can we take a pause and come back to this later?
- What do you need
- Thank you for your idea

Figure 10.5 Elements of Assertive Communication.

Discuss what strategies explored in the previous module (Deepening Compassion for the Self) might be helpful when facing rupture or fearing rupture in our relationships.

Regarding the language of compassionate assertiveness (the "how" of assertiveness), you can begin with the points listed in the image below (also **Client Handout 10.6**) and then invite the group to come up with any additional elements they mightassociate with an assertive communication. Invite them to think about someone they know, or someone they have seen, whom they would describe as assertive: how do they move? How do they speak? What kind of words do they choose? What kind of thoughts and emotions do they have? What intentions do they have?

 Optional Practice

Another creative way to explore the language of assertiveness is to encourage clients to go through magazines and online resources in search for examples of assertiveness in text, but also images and pictures; this can be done at home or during the session (if you are able to provide them with printed material). They can then make a collage poster bringing together all the examples of assertiveness they collect, and use it as inspiration when intentionally practicing their own compassionate assertiveness.

Phase 3: Compassionate Assertiveness in Action

In this phase we will go through some exercises to put compassionate assertiveness into action. We will use role playing and exercises in pairs and small groups to explore and practise how we can be compassionately assertive in specific situations. This will provide an opportunity to discuss any difficulties that might arise.

Main Touch Points

 Client Handout 10.8 – Asking for What we Need

3a) Asking for what we need

 Therapist Task

Begin this exercise by discussing with the group or with the client a typical situation in which they have a hard time saying "No" and expressing their needs. Ask them what blocks and resistances might come up and how shame might impair their capacity to connect with their feelings and needs, and their ability to express them. As always, it is important to do so through a compassionate lens, so be sure to highlight that our communication style is not our fault: we learned it in our environment and it was probably the style that "seemed to work best" at the time. At the same time, we can now practise this language and become more adept at speaking it (it becomes our responsibility).

To explore how compassionate assertiveness can help us in saying no and asking for what we need, do the following exercise, which should be done in pairs.

Pair Exercise (A & B)

Ask A and B to identify a situation where someone makes a request that we would normally avoid saying "No" to, where we would feel unable to ask for what we need. This could be a specific person or a recent situation where we have been asked to do something and we said "Yes", when in fact we wanted to say No and express our needs. We can proceed with this exercise in two different ways: Option A or Option B.

OPTION A: Ask A and B to take a moment to embody their Compassionate Self (through posture, facial expression, breathing pattern and intention) and from that position have them go through some self-reflections (**Client Handout 10.8**):

- *What are my feelings in this situation?*
- *What are my needs in this situation?*
- *What are the feelings and needs that led the other person to make the request?*
- *What are my fears about saying "No"?*
- *What would help me to say "No" more assertively?*

Therapist Tips

If clients are struggling with identifying their feelings in a situation, you can invite them to embody their Compassionate Self and look at both themselves and the other person from the outside.

OPTION B: Ask them to write down what possible reactions to "NO" might be for the following:

- The anxious self
- The angry self
- The sad self
- The shameful self
- Other selves?
- The Compassionate Self?

This can also be discussed with the group.

After the self-reflection exercise, invite the pair to do a short role play:

- A briefly tells B the situation
- A embodies their Compassionate Self
- B makes the request to A; A responds from their Compassionate Self position by saying "No" and expressing their needs
- Whenever A feels they are shifting to a passive, aggressive or passive-aggressive communication style, they can slowly and intentionally return to their Compassionate Self
- B provides feedback to A; this can be done by focusing on the following points:

  a   Focus on what the person did well and validate those efforts
  b   Ask, would there would be anything they would like to do differently next time (this prompts self-regulation)
  c   Provide encouragement for next time

Be sure to switch roles so both people can practise being compassionately assertive.

After the role playing, allow some time for group discussion:

- *Did the Compassionate Self help? If so, how?*
- *Were there any struggles, or FBRs?*
- *How can we intend to work with them?*
- *What would be the possible benefits of expressing our needs and feelings this way?*
- *You can try to visualise yourself 5 years from now, and in the meantime you have been using this kind of compassionate communication style – how would you feel? How would your relationships change? Would they benefit?*

3b) Responding to criticism

    Therapist Task

Receiving criticism is something that easily brings us into threat mode. To begin this section focusing on how to assertively respond to criticism, take a moment to go through the many different forms that criticism can take and how these are communicated:

Table 10.2

TYPE OF CRITICISM	CAN BE EXPRESSED AS...
Silent criticism	Rolling the eyes, tapping fingers impatiently, a stern gaze
Hidden criticism	*"Black clothes look good on you – they're so slimming".*
Nasty criticism	*"You are so stupid!"*
Explicit criticism	*"I don't like you!"*

Individuals can begin to reflect on the ways they react to criticisms by thinking about their multiple selves.

OPTION A: close your eyes and do some self-reflection (embody your Compassionate Self and look at the situation from outside)

- *What are my feelings in this situation?*
- *What are my needs in this situation?*
- *What are the feelings and needs that led the other person to make the request?*
- *What are my fears about saying "No"?*
- *What would help me to say "No" more assertively?*

OPTION B. Ask them to write down what he possible reactions to criticism might be for the following:

- The anxious self
- The angry self
- The sad self
- The shameful self
- The Compassionate Self

This can also be discussed with the group.
Then, prepare them for a pair exercise.

Pair Exercise (A & B)

A will briefly tell B about an episode in which they felt criticised and were not able to respond in an assertive way (it could also be a recurring episode).
    Then, begin the role play:

- A embodies their Compassionate Self
- B acts as the criticiser and A's Compassionate Self responds
- A tries to return to their Compassionate Self whenever they feel they are shifting into a passive, aggressive, or passive-aggressive communication style
- B provide feedback to A

Reverse the roles.

After the role play, allow some time for group discussion:

- *Did the Compassionate Self help? If so, how?*
- *Were there any struggles, or FBRs?*
- *How can we intend to work with them?*
- *What would be the possible benefits of responding to criticism in this way?*
- *You can try to visualise yourself five years from, and in the meantime you have been using this kind of compassionate communication style – how would you feel? How would your relationships change? Would they benefit?*

Phase 4: Receiving and Expressing Appreciation

In this phase we will provide an experiential practice to notice resistances and struggles that emerge when expressing and receiving appreciation to and from others.

Main Touch Points

Therapist Script 10.3 – Receiving Appreciation

4a) Fears, Blocks and Resistances to receiving appreciation

Therapist Background Knowledge

As stated at the beginning of this module, assertiveness is not only about conflict resolution but especially about connecting with our needs and the needs of others. This kind of connection is required not only when facing a difficult conversation, but also when faced with a potentially pleasant conversation such as one in which we give and receive appreciation.

Often, receiving compliments can stimulate our rank-motive in several ways and activate emotional reactions connected to the threat system. For example, if we are very self-critical, it is hard to reconcile other people's positive views of us with our own negative views of ourselves. We might be afraid that if the other person were to closely scrutinise me, they would likely realise just how flawed I am, they would surely change their mind about me, and these thoughts then activate our loss-aversion response.

Many of us clumsily react to compliments as an unconscious act of self-preservation. People may divert praise as a way of shielding from future failure, manipulation, disappointment, or rejection from others. Unfortunately, this unconscious self-defence frequently deprives us of interpersonal connection. It prevents us from accepting the gratitude and kind words of others.

Therapist Task

It can be useful to have a brief discussion with the group (or with the client) to explore what the fears linked to receiving appreciation might be. This exploration can begin by asking them to close their eyes and going back to a moment in which someone complimented or appreciated us. What did we experience? Were there any emotions belonging to our threat system? Does anything change if the compliment is about us, in our entirety? Or does it involve something we did? Does anything change if the appreciation is coming from someone we know and whose intention we are able to connect to?

Here are some possible FBRs to receiving appreciations:

- In my culture/religion it is a sign of vanity to "gloat" over a compliment, and I will be punished

- People who have given me compliments in the past have then manipulated me
- In the past, when I received compliments, others around me belittled me, made fun of me/isolated me
- Fear of envy from others

At this point, it is important to help people focus on the possible intention from which the compliment arises. It is helpful to reflect on the fact that appreciation is about the giver, not you (the receiver). When someone says they loved something about us, what motivation moves the person? What needs of the person were met because of what you did or manifested (consciously or unconsciously)?

You can do the *Receiving appreciation* (**Therapist Script 10.3**) practice to help people connect to the motive that lies behind a compliment, which might, in turn, help them to address their FBRs to receiving appreciation.

4b) Fears, Blocks and Resistances to expressing appreciation

   Therapist Background Knowledge

Just as there can be FBRs to receiving appreciation, there can also be FBRs to expressing appreciation. There can be various types of resistances, which may be connected, once again, to the possible activation of a submissive-rank response or the unpredictability of the reaction. If I criticise myself, complimenting someone may sharpen my self-criticism even more, and thus, may be connected to a feeling of envy. I may be highlighting what I perceive to be someone's superiority and consequently my inferiority. We could talk about "submissive" compliment giving. Or, because I don't feel comfortable giving compliments, as they have been misunderstood in the past. And again, because I myself feel uncomfortable receiving compliments, I am afraid of inducing the same discomfort in the other person. Again, unfortunately, this unconscious self-protection robs us of human connection.

   Therapist Task

Once again, it can be useful to have a brief discussion with the group and explore what the fears connected to expressing appreciation could be. This exploration can begin by asking people to close their eyes and go back to a moment when they expressed appreciation to someone or complimented them. What did we experience? Did we experience any emotions linked to our threat system? What were we afraid of? Does anything change if the compliment is about the person in their entirety? Or is it about something that the person did? Does anything change if the compliment is directed at someone we know and whom we know will be able to connect to our real intention?

Just as we did for receiving appreciation, it is important to help people understand what it might be like to give a compliment or express appreciation from our compassionate selves. In fact, once again, a compliment is about the giver, not the receiver. Activating the Compassionate Self can help us give compliments that stem from a true sense of appreciation of what the person has done and what has positively impacted us. Giving compliments from the Compassionate Self can become a way of revealing oneself, and as a result, a way of fostering the courage to increase one's sense of vulnerability, which is aimed at increasing one's connection with the other person. Activating the Compassionate Self can also facilitate awareness of how much the other person might be positively affected by our appreciation, if only they could understand the compassionate intention from which it springs. Again, we try to facilitate the switch from giving and receiving compliments as determined by the rank motivation system, to giving and receiving compliments driven by a compassionate motivation.

Before offering this compassionate assertiveness exercise, ask clients to express if and how they feel uneasy when offering appreciation.

Before starting the role play, highlight that this exercise could activate a lot of resistance in us; remind them that turning towards our Compassionate Self can help us in this process.

Pair Exercise (A & B)

Ask both people to take some time to embody and connect to their Compassionate Self. Then, ask A to express what they appreciate about B, in a friendly tone and with a compassionate facial expression. Invite them to notice how it feels to offer and receive appreciation. Then, reverse the roles.

After the role play, provide some space for a group discussion:

- *Did you notice any resistances coming up?*
- *Did being in your Compassionate Self help with both giving and receiving appreciation? How?*
- *What did you feel when you were expressing appreciation towards the other person?*
- *If this seems too hard right now, can you connect to the part of you that would like to learn to accept appreciation?*

Highlight the fact that compliments/expressions of appreciation from others can "conflict" with what our self-critical part thinks and feels about us. We can consider accepting compliments as a kind of "exposure" to positive feelings. Our Compassionate Self might be helpful when trying to stay open and accept when others say something positive about us; realising how difficult this can be for all of us can support us in this training.

Phase 5: Wrap-Up

Main Touch Points

Client Handout B – Personal Practice Diary

5a) Summary of the session and suggestions for personal practice

 Therapist Task

Take 5–10 minutes to briefly summarise the points that you have gone through in this module.

You may want to provide participants with some suggestions for personal practice and self-reflection:

- Read through the client handouts
- Practise at home, trying to apply what you have learned during this module to situations in your daily-life
- Complete the practice diary in **Client Handout B** trying to focus on one compassionate activity per day

5b) Closing practice

 Therapist Task

It is important to always take a moment at the end of the session to acknowledge anything and everything that has come up for participants while exploring the themes introduced.

Try focus their attention by inviting them to share in one sentence:

What do I take home from today's session (because I feel it's going to be helpful)?

Finally, guide participants through a short closing practice using **Therapist Script 2.5** and perhaps you could add a couple of sentences that link to the work done during this session. Something like *"Let us remember the unchosen nature of our needs and those of others – let us connect as best as we can with the compassionate courage to express them, respecting our resistances but also honouring the desire to have better relationships with* *ourselves and others. Let our heartfelt intention for connection guide us in practicing compassionate assertiveness".*

Three-Circle Check-In

Therapist Scripts

Therapist Script 10.1: Compassionate Landing (5 minutes)

(Refer to Therapist Script 2.1 in Chapter 2.)

You can add the following elements to connect to the previous module:

Now try to do a brief scan of your body, with the sole intention of observing with curiosity what is present in this moment. If you like, imagine you are greeting each part of the body as you encounter it. You could try welcoming your feet, bringing a soft smile to your lips while doing so and imagining they are smiling back at you, happy to be recognised and acknowledged. Repeat this process with your legs, your abdomen, your back, your chest, your shoulders, your arms, and any other part of the body that you feel would like to be seen today.

Then try looking at yourself from the outside, as if you were sitting right in front of yourself, and try observing how that makes you feel. From this perspective, you can see that this being, just like all others living being on this earth, simply wishes to be well and to find peace and connection.

Therapist Script 10.2: Approaching FBRs to Assertiveness (10 minutes)

As we begin this brief exercise, close your eyes (if it feels right for you at this moment) and take some time to settle into your posture, breathing and present-moment awareness.

[Briefly lead clients through embodying their Compassionate Self; to do so, remember to use posture, breathing, facial expression, tone of voice, touch, and the intention to be helpful].

Now bring to mind an argument that you might have had recently or in the past; be mindful to choose an argument that is not too activating for you, so that you are able to sit with it for the length of this exercise.

Observe this scene from the outside, noticing both people involved; from this perspective, do you have a feel of the way they were carrying their body? Can you perceive what the sensations they might have been experiencing in their body?

Now turn towards the other person: can you imagine what might be the needs of this creature? What needs are they trying to satisfy in this moment? What fears lie behind their words, their expression, their bodily posture?

Notice what changes within you as you contemplate that this person, just like any other living creature, has very human needs.

Now, turn towards yourself: can you recognise what your needs were at the time of the argument? What needs were you trying to satisfy in that moment? What fears were lying behind your words, your facial expression? What fears were you carrying within your body?

Notice what changes within you as you contemplate that you, just like any other living creature, have very human needs.

Now imagine you are able to expand your awareness, almost as if it were a circle becoming wider, encompassing both the needs of this person and your own, both the fears of this person and your own. Remember that it is not your fault when these situations occur: our personal needs are sometimes in conflict with those of others. It is not our fault, but we wish to maintain this relationship and therefore, if possible, make the relationship a broader and more compassionate container of the needs of both.

From this perspective, what words would you use to express your needs and at the same time recognise theirs? What words would you use to express what you are afraid of and to recognise that they too might be afraid of something?

It is OK if these words do not come easily, or if it takes a while for them to manifest; remember that what counts here is your desire and effort to take a compassionately assertive stance.

As you do so, observe if any resistances or fears come up. There could be fear of not being liked by the other person, of distancing the other person, of ending up alone. There could be some part of you convinced you are not worthy of having your needs respected. If any fears or resistances come up, observe if there is a narrative about them: do you feel they should not be here? Do you feel they are making you any less assertive?

Let these fears also remind you of your human nature. As you embody the wisdom of your Compassionate Self, remember that everyone has experienced these fears and doubts at some point and as you embody the courage of your Compassionate Self, remember that even with these fears you can practise being assertive with a compassionate intention.

Then, gently come back to the scene once again, observing these two people along with their needs and their fears of assertiveness, and imagine wishing that for them that they find a peaceful resolution. Even if you do not know what that may be.

Now let go of this image, come back to your body, and gently open your eyes.

Therapist Script 10.3: Receiving Appreciation (5 minutes)

Close your eyes and go back to a moment in the past when someone complimented you [it might the same that they worked with in the previous exercise].

Embody your Compassionate Self (breath, posture, and facial expression, then connect to the intention to be receptive to the help that comes from others and open to what we could give others, consciously or unconsciously, in doing so).

From the perspective of the Compassionate Self, look at the person complimenting you. If you welcome their appreciation from your compassionate wisdom, can you perceive what intention motivates it? What need in that person might have been met and that they are making you aware of with this "compliment"?

From this perspective we can respond with the intention to maintain a connection – it can be a simple thank you… "I am glad that that need of yours has been met… thank you for giving me feedback on the helpfulness of my behaviours".

Is there more that the Compassionate Self would like to say? In short, a compliment from someone can be a way to understand what about us was helpful, and to have more clarity with respect to their needs.

Client Handouts

Client Handout 10.1: Compassionate Weekly Reflection

Let's do a curious, friendly reflection on this past week:

Which part of the self-practice did I do and why?

Which part of the self-practice did I not do?

Was this due to any anxieties or blocks regarding the practice or the path? Which ones can you identify?

We extend gratitude, respect, and compassion to resistances: What would make you and your resistances feel safer in going forward on this path?

Client Handout 10.2: Different Styles of Communications

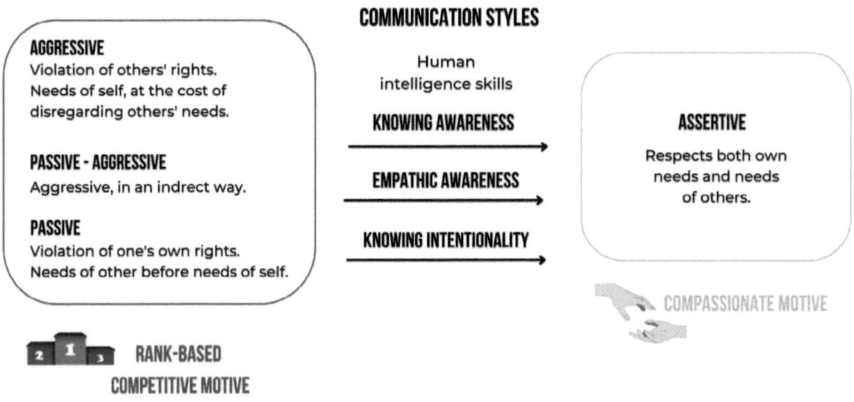

COMMUNICATION STYLES

AGGRESSIVE
Violation of others' rights.
Needs of self, at the cost of
disregarding others' needs.

PASSIVE - AGGRESSIVE
Aggressive, in an indrect way.

PASSIVE
Violation of one's own rights.
Needs of other before needs of self.

Human
intelligence skills

KNOWING AWARENESS

EMPATHIC AWARENESS

KNOWING INTENTIONALITY

ASSERTIVE
Respects both own
needs and needs
of others.

COMPASSIONATE MOTIVE

RANK-BASED
COMPETITIVE MOTIVE

Figure 10.6 Social Mentalities and Different Communication Styles.

For each of the following scenarios, come up with an aggressive, a passive and an assertive response.

Table 10.3

Scenario	
You have bought an item from a shop which is faulty and needs to be returned. The shop assistant is questioning whether they can take it back.	
Passive response	
Aggressive response	
Passive-Aggressive response	
Assertive response	

Table 10.4

Scenario	
You are feeling a bit lonely and you want to ask a friend to go out with you for a drink.	
Passive response	
Aggressive response	
Passive-Aggressive response	
Assertive response	

Table 10.5

Scenario	
You are in a meeting and people are concentrating on one possible solution, but you have thought of a new way that could be used to solve the problem.	
Passive response	
Aggressive response	
Passive-Aggressive response	
Assertive response	

Table 10.6

Scenario	
You are having a conflict with a partner or someone you are very close to.	
Passive response	
Aggressive response	
Passive Aggressive Response	
Assertive response	

Client Handout 10.3: Expressions of Assertiveness

EXPRESSIONS OF ASSERTIVENESS

Confidence in being clear about how we feel and being committed to be helpful and supportive of others

Ability to express dissatisfaction, concern, upsets, including the ability to stand up for one's rights, to say "No" to the requests of others and delimit one's boundaries

Being genuinely empathic to ourselves and others to understand the roots of our conflicts.

Being open to the helpfulness of others.

Taking the lead in praising others and acknowledging their helpfulness. Expressing appreciation and gratitude without feeling undermined.

Initiating an opinion or positive choice and being prepared for others to disagree without feeling attacked or undermined; the acceptance of difference.

Recognizing that what hurts might be our interpretations of what has been said rather than what has actually been said.

Acknowledging and admitting one's limitations or mistakes without feeling personally undermined. Being assertive gives us confidence to be human.

Trying to understand our own minds and the minds of others.

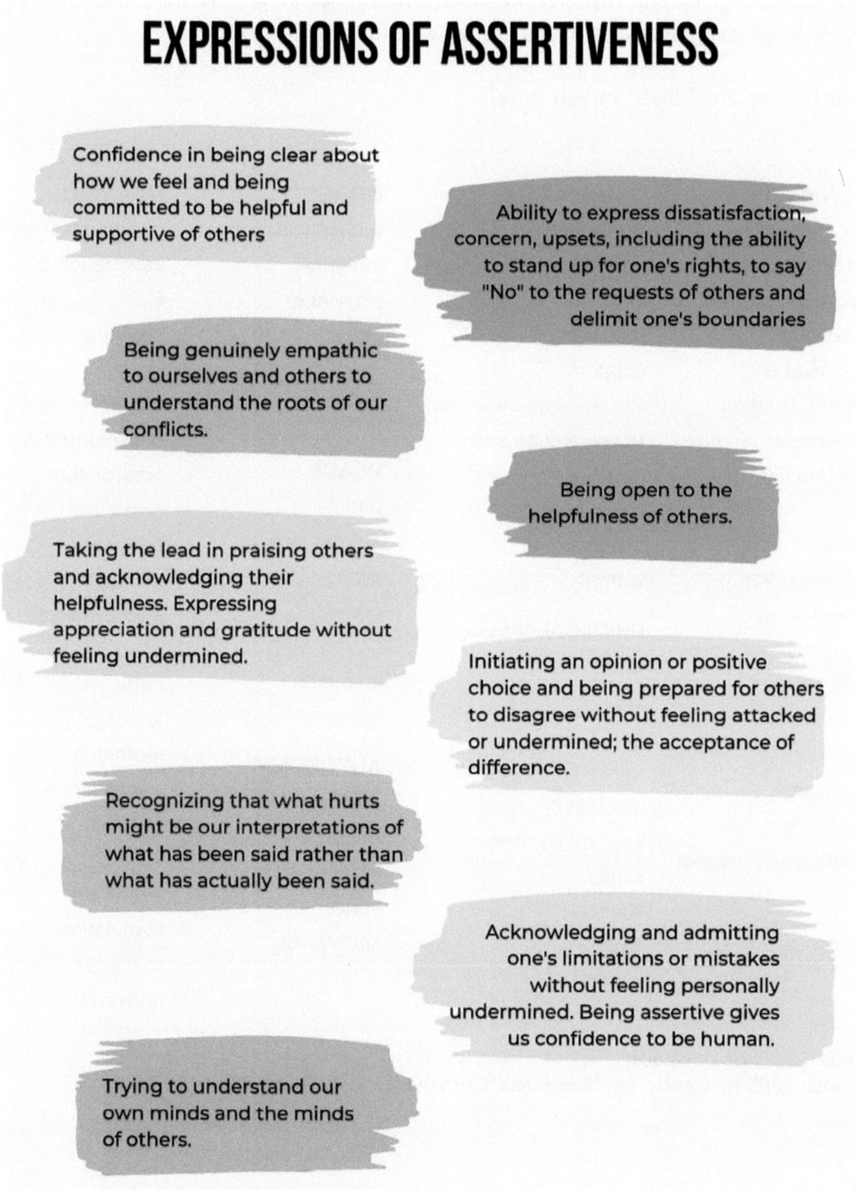

Figure 10.7 Expressions of Assertiveness.

Client Handout 10.4: List of Needs

This is a list of needs, used by the model of Nonviolent Communication model (www.cnvc.org/training/resource/needs-inventory). Although it is not exhaustive, it can help us recognise what needs are active in us at a certain time.

Which ones are "alive" in you now?

CONNECTION

acceptance
affection
appreciation
belonging
cooperation
communication
closeness
community
companionship
compassion
consideration
consistency
empathy
inclusion
intimacy
love
mutuality
nurturing
respect/self-respect

CONNECTION continued

safety
security
stability
support
to know and be known
to see and be seen
to understand and be understood
trust
warmth

PHYSICAL WELL-BEING

air
food
movement/exercise
rest/sleep
sexual expression
safety
shelter
touch
water

HONESTY

authenticity
integrity
presence

PLAY

joy
humor

PEACE

beauty
communion
ease
equality
harmony
inspiration
order

AUTONOMY

choice
freedom
independence
space
spontaneity

MEANING

awareness
celebration of life
challenge
clarity
competence
consciousness
contribution
creativity
discovery
efficacy
effectiveness
growth
hope
learning
mourning
participation
purpose
self-expression
stimulation
to matter
understanding

Figure 10.8 List of Needs.
Source: 2005 by Center for Nonviolent Communication

Client Handout 10.5: The Process of Assertiveness

In our most significant relationships, choosing to be compassionately assertive of our needs always implies a kind of dance with the other person and their needs. Just as in the three flows of compassion, assertiveness also has flows: I can be validating and assertive of my needs, help the other person to be validating and assertive of theirs, and open up to the other's effort to recognise the validity of my own needs. In this way, compassionate assertiveness becomes much more than a mere communication style to "defend myself from excessive requests" (threat system) or "express my needs efficiently" (drive system); it transforms into a means to grow in relationships and make them more authentic and safe (soothing system).

Think back to an argument you recently had.

Try to go through the four steps of the process of assertiveness for both yourself and the other person. Write down the words that you feel would help you for each step.

Remember to first practise embodying your Compassionate Self.

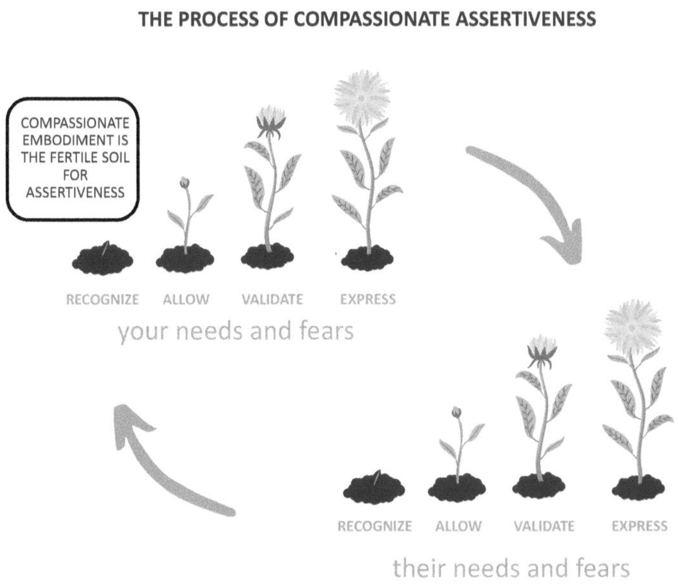

THE PROCESS OF COMPASSIONATE ASSERTIVENESS

Figure 10.9 The Process of Compassionate Assertiveness.

Table 10.7

RECOGNISE

Your needs and fears

The needs and fears of the other

Table 10.8

ALLOW

Your needs and fears

The needs and fears of the other person

Table 10.9

VALIDATE

Your needs and fears

The needs and fears of the other person

Table 10.10

EXPRESS

Your needs and fears

The needs and fears of the other person

Client Handout 10.6: Recognising Assertive Communication

Described below are some "hows," i.e., some ways through which compassionate assertiveness can express itself. What characteristics do you feel you have? What characteristics do you feel would help you grow in your assertiveness? In compassionate assertiveness, it is also important to remember "why" we want to learn to express our needs: not to override others, or to "be better," but to help ourselves (become more validating of our needs), create more authenticity in our relationship, and ultimately help the other person as well (if nothing else, to help them to know us better).

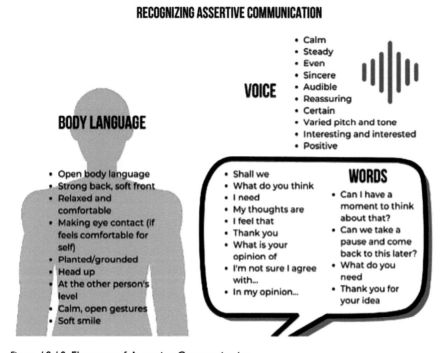

Figure 10.10 Elements of Assertive Communication.

What other elements would you add?

Body language

Voice

Words

Client Handout 10.7: Assertiveness is Not the Outcome

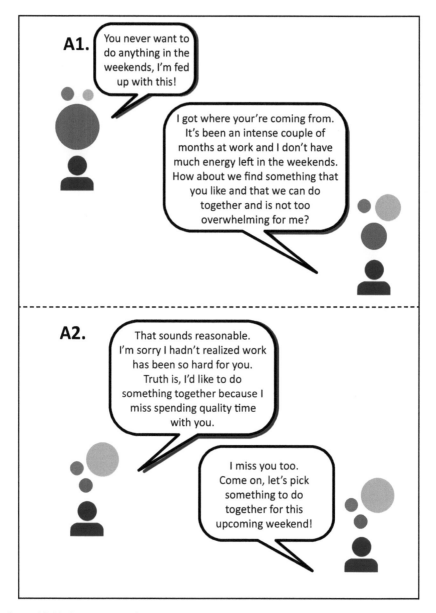

Figure 10.11 Assertiveness Resulting in Resolution.

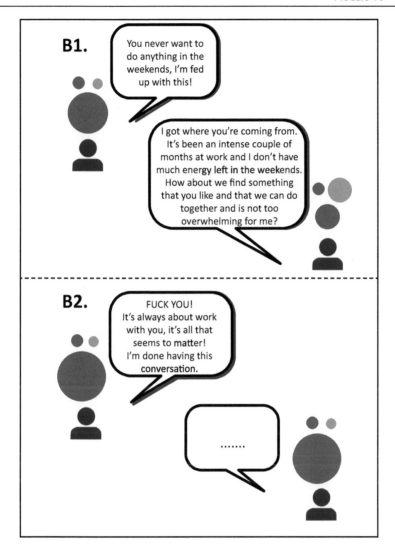

Figure 10.12 Assertiveness Resulting in Rupture.

Have you ever found yourself in a situation similar to B2? You can describe it here if you wish:

How did you feel? What did you do?

Now, start activating your Compassionate Self by connecting to your soothing rhythm breathing, your friendly facial expression, your gentle touch, and grounded and open posture.

Focus on the motivation of the Compassionate Self: to be understanding, validating, respectful, and helpful to ourselves, while listening and trying to meet the needs of others.

Remember, it is not our fault if it is hard for us to express our needs in an assertive way and if conflicts arise – the difficulty in finding compromises between our needs is part of human nature.

At the same time, we nurture the intention to learn and cooperate while doing so, because we want to improve our relationship with ourselves and others (by making it more authentic for example).

How might your Compassionate Self have helped you face that moment of rupture? What would have felt supportive and helpful?

OPTION 1: if it is helpful, you can imagine observing your Compassionate Self from the outside interacting with the other person

OPTION 2: if it is helpful, you can imagine having your compassionate being by your side, offering you support in this interaction. How would you respond, if you knew you had this being by your side, if you felt all the safeness that they provide?

Client Handout 10.8: Asking for What we Need

Think about a situation when you would normally avoid asking for what you need (maybe a specific person or a recent situation where you have been asked to do something and you said "Yes" – but in fact you wanted to say "No" and express your needs).

Activate your Compassionate-Self by connecting to your soothing rhythm breathing, your friendly facial expression, your gentle touch, and grounded and open posture.

Focus on the motivation of the Compassionate Self: to be understanding, respectful, and helpful to ourselves, while listening and trying to meet the needs of others. Remember, it is not our fault it if is hard for us to express our needs assertively – but, at the same, time we have the intention to learn to do so because we want to improve our relationship with the other person (even, simply, by shaping it to be more authentic).

Bringing this moment to mind where you were not assertive from your Compassionate Self's perspective (if it is helpful, observe yourself from the outside through the eyes and intention of your Compassionate Self):

What are my feelings in this situation?

What are my real needs in this situation?

- *Why would it be helpful for me to express my needs in this situation? What benefits would it bring to me (and potentially to the relationship?)*
- *What are my FBRs that emerge?*
- *From my Compassionate Self perspective, what would I like to say? What would I like to do?*

Chapter 11

Module 11

Forgiveness

Aims

- To approach hurt with compassion
- To introduce the concept and process of forgiveness and the flows of forgiveness
- To explore the several misconceptions of forgiveness
- To understand how a compassionate motivation can sustain the process of forgiveness
- To uncover our FBRs to forgiveness
- To understand and experience forgiveness through the lens of the multiple selves
- To cultivate intrapersonal and interpersonal forgiveness

 Deepen Your Knowledge

In Gilbert, P. & Simos, G. (Ed.). (2022). *Compassion focused therapy: clinical practice and applications*. Routledge, please refer to:

Chapter 4. Shame, Humiliation, Guilt, and Social Status: The Distress and Harms of Social Disconnection

In Woodyatt, L., Worthington, Jr., E., Wenzel, M., Griffin, B. (Ed). (2017). *Handbook of the Psychology of Self-Forgiveness*. Springer, Cham.

Chapter 3, by Gilbert & P., Woodyatt. An Evolutionary Approach to Shame-Based Self-Criticism, Self-Forgiveness, and Compassion.

DOI: 10.4324/9781003436058-13

Summary of Key Processes

Table 11.1 Module 11: Forgiveness

Phase		Main Touch Points	Therapist Scripts	Client Handouts
1	Introduction	**1a)** Compassionate landing **1b)** Revision of personal practice and recap of previous session	☐ **Script 11.1:** Compassionate Landing	☐ **Handout 11.1:** Compassionate weekly reflection
2	What is forgiveness?	**2a)** Approaching hurt with compassion **2b)** What forgiveness is and is not **2c)** Why practise forgiveness	☐ **Script 11.2:** Flows of hurt ☐ **Script 11.3:** Memory of forgiveness	☐ **Handout 11.2:** My hurt ladder ☐ **Handout 11.3:** What forgiveness is and is not ☐ **Handout 11.4:** Flows of hurt ☐ **Handout 11.5:** Why practise forgiveness
3	Interpersonal forgiveness	**3a)** Stories of forgiveness **3b)** Uncovering FBRs to forgiveness **3c)** Practicing forgiveness	☐ **Script 11.4:** Compassionate Forgiveness	☐ **Handout 11.6:** Stories of forgiveness ☐ **Handout 11.7:** My FBRs to forgiveness ☐ **Handout 11.8:** Compassionate Forgiveness letter
4	Self-forgiveness	**4a)** Deepening self-empathy **4b)** Forgiveness and multiple selves	☐ Script 11.5: Deepening self-empathy	☐ **Handout 11.9:** Self-forgiveness and multiple selves ☐ **Handout 11.10:** Self-forgiveness letter ☐ **Handout 11.11:** Flows of forgiveness
5	Wrap-up	**5a)** Summary of the session and suggestions for personal practice **5b)** Closing practice		☐ **Handout B:** Personal practice diary

Phase 1: Introduction

Main Touch Points

Therapist Script 11.1 – Compassionate Landing
Client Handout 11.1 – Compassionate Weekly Reflection

1a) Compassionate Landing

    Therapist Task

To welcome the group, guide them through a Compassionate Landing (**Therapist Script 11.1**).

As we approach the end of this 12-module manual of Compassion Focused Therapy (CFT), we are ready to face the most complex processes of our human experience, which we can now face with the wisdom and the courage of our Compassionate Self. This module will be focusing on the practice and process of forgiveness.

During the landing, we begin to open our awareness to the possibility of choice, intention and willingness, which are central concepts when speaking about forgiveness. We also lightly touch upon the importance of patience and time – Are we giving ourselves the space of safety and safeness required to let our emotions settle and transform?

Before practicing the landing, you could guide them through a short three-circle check-in.

Three-Circle Check-In

1b) Revision of Personal Practice and Recap of Previous Session

    Therapist Task

Invite participants to use **Client Handout 11.1** to reflect upon the past week/weeks; then get them into pairs or small groups and invite them to share (if they would like to do so) anything relevant about their past week, including any compassion episodes or any fears, blocks, and resistances (FBRs) they might have experienced.

- Did they try practicing compassionate assertiveness in their everyday life?
- What did they notice when practicing compassionate assertiveness?
- How did it influence their relationship with others?
- How did it influence their relationship with themselves?
- Did the Compassionate Self help them be more assertive?
- Did they encounter any FBRs when wanting to be assertive?

Before moving on, the therapist can provide a brief recap of the last session, in which the main points were:

- What compassionate assertiveness is
- How we can train compassionate assertiveness
- How to make requests, respond to criticism, and affirm our needs in an assertive way
- How to express appreciation

This can also be a space to set the scene for the current module; the main themes that are going to be explored are:

- What forgiveness is and is not
- How a compassionate motivation can sustain the process of forgiveness
- FBRs to forgiveness
- Flows of forgiveness

Phase 2: What is Forgiveness?

In this phase of the module we will focus on the nature of forgiveness and why compassion can help us open up to the first stage of this process: acknowledging the reality of hurt, both the hurt we receive from ourselves and from others, and the hurt that we cause others, while also recognising how deeply ingrained in the human experiences it is. We will reflect on what forgiveness is and is not, and try to understand why it might be useful to engage in the process of forgiveness.

Main Touch Points

Therapist Script 11.2 – Flows of Hurt
Therapist Script 11.3 – Memories of Forgiveness
Client Handout 11.2 – My Hurt Ladder
Client Handout 11.3 – What Forgiveness Is and Is Not
Client Handout 11.4 – Flows of Hurt
Client Handout 11.5 – Why Practice Forgiveness

2a) Approaching Hurt with Compassion

 Therapist Background Knowledge

Forgiveness is something that is deeply interwoven into the fabric of social life. We will dive deeper into what forgiveness is and is not, but it is important to state that from a CFT perspective, forgiveness is about recognising that we have been hurt and choosing not to hurt back, or when we have hurt someone, we deliberately choose, as best as possible, to repair instead of spiralling into shame and avoidance. This means that compassionate forgiveness entails getting closer to the very human domain of hurt.

In fact, the path towards forgiveness begins with this first compassionate reality check: we all hurt each other, with some varying degree of consciousness. As we will see, hurt can go from simply ignoring, and therefore, not meeting reciprocal needs, to a wider catalogue of human exploitation: rape, pillage, extortion, murder, infidelity, kidnap, assault, and even identity theft. The second reality check concerns the common adaptive response to the threat: revenge and retribution, which in our minds can take the wholly intra-psychic form of resentment, avoidance desire, or chronic retaliatory motivation. In many species, punishment frequently provides benefits by modifying the future behaviour of the transgressor, teaching the transgressor to engage in behaviours that are more beneficial, or at least less costly, to the punisher. Thus, the human motivation for revenge emerges not as a disease, but as an adaptation which likely functioned to deter exploitation (at least in the ancestral environment).

However, even if there may be benefits to revenge in an ancestral context, revenge often entails secondary costs. Revenge can activate detrimental feedback loops of counter-retaliation and might also terminate long-standing and potentially productive relationships. Moreover, the emergence of the more advanced capabilities of the human mind, can trap our minds in a loop of resentment and desire for revenge. My mind can "keep in the present time" hurts that were inflicted on me years, if not decades ago, by someone who may now be far away (or even dead) and that can certainly not be changed in any way by my brooding resentment (a process captured by Marianne Williamson's famous phrase: *Unforgiveness is like drinking poison yourself and waiting for the other person to die*).

I can feel "hurt" by abstract entities created entirely by my new brain (adverse fate, unjust society, corrupt politics, and even God) and the consequent desire for vengeance toward these entities will only envelope itself. My capacity for self-reflexivity can make me feel hurt by parts of myself (my jealousy and aggression are driving me away from the person I love), or even by earlier versions of myself (my alcoholic past is now generating chronic health problems for me), making the process of desire for retribution and revenge entirely intra-psychic.

From a CFT perspective, forgiveness is a shift in interpersonal or intra-personal motivation, marked by a reduced retaliatory intention, decreased avoidant sentiment, and/or increased goodwill toward the transgressor. The ultimate purpose of this motivational shift is to regulate the chronic state of activation of the threat system that occurs when we do not forgive, and, when it is possible and wise to do so, to secure a continued, benefit-pro-ducing interaction with the transgressor (both in real life and when it is simply in our minds).

Forgiveness, then, is a complex process generated by the delicate compro-mise between the part of us that desires revenge and punishment and the part of us that desires well-being and peace in the present moment, and potentially the continuation of an important relationship. It is, however, a process that we all enact on a regular basis. Indeed, when speaking of hurt, our brains will probably turn to the biggest examples of hurt we have received or have imparted in our lives, bringing us immediately into a threat state. However, in our exploration of hurt and forgiveness, we would like to start at the very bottom of an imaginary hurt ladder, because it helps us realise that we are all naturally capable of continuous acts of forgiveness.

Therapist Task

In our daily lives, there are many occasions in which we are accidently hurt, or we accidently hurt others, and in these instances, we forgive or are forgiven by others. Think about the person who bumped into your shoulder this morning while you were on the train during your daily commute, the colleague who replied to your email two days after the due date, or your little child spilling their breakfast juice all over your clean pants. These small incidents – often accidents – occur on a daily basis, and we tend to be open and quick to for-giveness. We might not even think of those as conscious acts of forgiveness. Yet in those moments, we are choosing not to be defensive, aggressive, or reactive; for example, we choose not to push the person on the train who bumped into our shoulder, not to make our colleague wait for our feedback three days instead of two for our feedback, and not to spill our latte on our child's favourite dress. All these examples are probably things we would place at the bottom of our hurt ladder.

Have the group come up with their own examples of situations they would place at the bottom of their hurt ladder (**Client Handout 11.2**); invite them to come up with examples of both situations in which they have been hurt and in which they have hurt others. These will probably all be situations in which the hurt was unintentional, nonetheless, you should highlight that the hurt ladder is something totally personal: something that I place at the bottom of my hurt ladder, the person next to me might find very hurtful and would place further up their hurt ladder. Also, be sure that the hurt ladder is contextual: something might hurt when it comes from a specific person, or when it occurs in a specific context, but not when coming from a stranger or when occurring in a different context. Highlight the fact that for low-intensity hurt, many of us spontaneously find it easier to forgive (we can refer to our internal wisdom) and understand the usefulness of not entering a tit-for-tat dynamic. *Which benefits did they find in forgiving? Did they regret doing so?*

Then, ask them to imagine they are moving up the hurt ladder – What would they place around the centre of their hurt ladder? This is probably some kind of hurt that they have received or imparted, that took some time to recover from, but that they were still able to forgive. It might be our partner forgetting a special occasion, a friend lying to us about something, or our child breaking a crystal vase while playing football in the house even after we told them not to. Let them reflect upon the fact that as we move further up along the hurt ladder, it becomes a little harder to forgive. *Which benefits did they find in forgiving? Did they regret doing so?*

Finally, arrive at the top of the hurt ladder. Invite clients, if they are willing, to write down what they would place at the top of the hurt ladder, whether it is something that has happened or something that could happen. Allow time and space for this. You can provide some prompts for guidance:

- *Did they ever think about wanting to forgive?*
- *If they have, why?*
- *What might be the benefits of forgiving?*
- *What makes it harder to forgive, as we step up the hurt ladder?*

Therapist Tips

For the hurt ladder, emphasise to the clients that this is simply a draft of their hurt ladder. In this first version, they might like to create their hurt ladder by focusing on hurts that they are more comfortable approaching for this module. In later versions of their hurt ladder, they may wish to include more painful or intense hurts, which come with greater feelings of shame or rage, for example traumas like abuse (physical, emotional, sexual) or neglect. In addition, at this stage, we are only connecting with hurts – there is no requirement to forgive these hurts at this moment. Indeed, the therapist may like to suggest in the first instance of creating a hurt ladder that clients only consider hurts they feel like they are capable of forgiving.

Invite people to think about what their three circles look like when they are at the bottom of the ladder. How do the three circles shift when we move up the ladder? Make sure to highlight that our red circle tends to become increasingly bigger and our green circle (especially in terms of safeness and connection) tends to become smaller. This is expected, common, and not our fault. In moments of hurt, we are simply trying to self-protect.

As the hurt ladder shows, forgiveness becomes harder as the intensity of the hurt is heightened. As the famous author C. S. Lewis says, "Everyone thinks forgiveness is a lovely idea until he has something to forgive".

Compassion, therefore, invites us to open up to a very important universal truth: human beings hurt each other and themselves (this is not our fault). However, it is our responsibility to notice the automatic reaction of our threat system. This reality of life can be rather difficult for some people to face and will require some time for compassionate reflection.

To help the group gently approach the hurt that being a human being entails, guide them through a brief reality check meditation (you can follow **Therapist Script 11.2**). Be sure to highlight the fact that just like compassion and forgiveness, harm also moves according to three flows: there is harm we receive from others, harm we cause others, and harm we cause ourselves. Of course, the factor of intentionality must also be taken into account, for causing harm with intention involves processes that are quite different from those that occur when harm is done unintentionally. This is also a moment to allow time for reflections on occasions when we were able to spontaneously forgive and how we benefited from following our inner wisdom.

After the meditation, ask clients to self-reflect on the three flows of hurt, maybe by writing down some examples in **Client Handout 11.4**. These will be useful in later stages of the process of forgiveness.

2b) Understanding What Forgiveness Is and Is Not

 Therapist Background Knowledge

Addressing a theme as intense and vulnerable as forgiveness requires all the qualities of compassion: wisdom, courage, and the ultimate commitment to be helpful to ourselves and others. Forgiveness is a multilayered concept that requires our time and patience to be explored and contemplated, without the rush of deadlines or the "right times" for it to manifest. Forgiveness does not follow set agreements, it does not translate into forgetting or in preventing further hurt.

We must at this point recognise that as much as we long for freedom sometimes, remaining within the confines of a known hurt can provide a sense safety, despite the fact that it tends to limit our access to safeness at times (if I don't forgive, I might lose a connection with someone that I actually love and want to keep in my life).

Compassion connects us to a shared humanity that underlies all hurtful experiences and encourages us to shift from the focus of harm to the possibility of helpfulness.

Some of the competencies of compassion that can be useful when engaging with forgiveness are:

- **Attention sensitivity:** the ability to pay attention to the nature and extent of suffering and the source of our or other people's distress
- **Sympathy:** being emotionally moved by the distress we notice
- **Distress tolerance:** being able to engage with the pain, hurt, and angers others have caused us, guilt-based remorse, and sadness
- **Empathy:** the ability to resonate emotionally with our experience and those of others; recognising and anticipating the possible consequences of our behaviour and the impact we have on others
- **Non-judgement:** the ability to be accepting of our experience and those of others, without condemning and shutting down; we are refraining from making judgements about an emotional experience, not a behaviour

 Therapist Task

Before working on forgiveness through experiential exercises, we wish to begin by discussing what forgiveness is and is not; having a shared vocabulary can help when facing a concept that can evoke very strong emotions in people based on their lived experiences.

Invite the group or the client you are working with to state what forgiveness means to them; you could use the ideas that come up as starting points for a discussion. Then, list what forgiveness is and is not; clients can follow along with **Client Handout 11.2**.

Forgiveness **is**:

- A deliberate, personal intentional choice to release feelings of anger, resentment and vengeance and experience a greater sense of freedom
- An opportunity we offer ourselves
- A process
- Emotionally challenging, as it brings us to contact feelings of loss and grief
- Done for ourselves, not for others

Forgiveness **is not**:

- An outcome
- Condoning or approving a harmful behaviour
- Forgetting
- Reconciliation with another person (it could be safer to maintain distance, or the other person might not be alive any more)
- An invitation for friendship

- Something we do for others (either because others expect us to forgive or because we do not like to be seen as people who still hold grudges)
- Passive

As previously stated, forgiveness comes down to acknowledging that someone (including ourselves) has hurt us, recognising the nature of suffering as part of human life, perceiving the spontaneity and automaticity of a reaction to the hurt resulting from the red system (avoidance or revenge) and choosing not to hurt the other person back or not to ruminate on what happened.

2c) Why Practise Forgiveness (setting the compassionate intention)

 Therapist Background Knowledge

Considering why we would want to practise forgiveness is key in this process. As stated above, forgiveness in CFT is viewed as a choice we offer ourselves and springs from having courageously contemplated and embraced, to the best of our ability, the realities of life connected to the normality of hurt, and from having decided to do whatever we can to alleviate the consequences of hurt, to prevent it, and not to perpetuate it.

Indeed, something that we must stress when exploring this theme is volition and agency – some people might consider forgiveness as something passive, as "giving in". On the contrary, forgiveness is actively choosing to keep our minds and hearts open to the possibility of processing and releasing feelings of anger; it is going against the very human tendency for vengeance (stemming from our threat system) and choosing to step into a compassionate motivation.

If time allows, this could be a good time to have a group discussion about what the potential benefits of forgiveness are, considering the practices and insights shared up to this point. Remind clients that in order to actively and intentionally engage in an action, we must remind ourselves why we are doing it. Why might we want to expose ourselves to our hurt ladder, starting from the first rungs and then going upwards?

 Therapist Task

To help clients explore their 'whys' for forgiveness, it can be useful to lead them through a guided meditation focusing on memories of forgiveness; the rationale here is that by remembering how being forgiven or having forgiven felt, and what its consequences were on their well-being and on their relationships, it will be a little easier for them to open up to the idea of forgiveness and to reconnect to their "why". You can use **Therapist Script 11.3** for this meditation.

After the meditation, you can offer some time for written self-reflection (**Client Handout 11.5**), focusing on why they would want to open up to forgiveness (both giving and receiving). Highlight that just like compassion and hurt, forgiveness also moves along three flows: there is forgiveness we give to others, forgiveness we receive from others, and forgiveness we receive from others. This self-reflection gives them the opportunity to sit with the idea both through writing (identifying the benefits of forgiveness) and through drawing (how I feel when holding onto resentment vs. how I feel when opening up to forgiveness).

 Therapist Tips

As you go deeper into the discussion on forgiveness, offer mindful guidance for exploring the theme. If you are working with an individual who has had severe and intense hurts, for example experiences of traumatic relationships, gently invite the client to focus on hurts that might be more approachable in the first instance. If working with a group, invite them to work with things they feel open to addressing without them being excessively activating for them.

Phase 3: Interpersonal Forgiveness

In this phase our focus is on forgiveness that we can give and receive from others. By exploring our own stories of forgiveness, and the stories of other people's forgiveness, we will also begin to uncover what our potential fears, blocks, and resistances to forgiveness might be.

Main Touch Points

 Therapist Script 11.4 – Compassionate Forgiveness
Client Handout 11.6 – Stories of Forgiveness
Client Handout 11.7 – My FBRs to Forgiveness
Client Handout 11.8 – Compassionate Forgiveness Letter

3a) Stories of Forgiveness

 Therapist Background Knowledge

Turning towards stories can be helpful in connecting to the human capacity for forgiveness. What we are looking for here are not necessarily examples of extraordinary acts of forgiveness (such as parents forgiving the murderers of their children), but rather examples of small acts of forgiveness that we might feel are closer to our daily experience and more accessible to us. If you have some examples from your own life or from literature that you feel would be appropriate here, feel free to share with your client or with the group.

 Therapist Task

Emphasise with clients the contextual nature of forgiveness — the fact that there are several elements involved in the forgiveness process. Some of these elements involve the amount of information we are provided about a situation; sometimes we are not initially willing to forgive someone because of our limited perspective on the story. As we collect more information, our capacity to view the situation from the other person's point of view (theory of mind) and empathise are heightened.

To highlight this point, you can use the vignette exercise in **Client Handout 11.6** and invite clients to go through it on their own or discuss it with the larger group. Feel free to also provide additional vignettes that you feel are best suited to the individual or group you are working with.

These brief vignettes highlight how there are many different nuances to forgiveness; invite reflection on how these different elements of forgiveness influence our willingness to forgive. Of course, the combinations of these elements are endless, making it really difficult to have just a single rule for how and when to forgive. It is important, therefore, that the therapist highlight how personal and context-dependent this is, and unfortunately there is no "easy fix" approach.

Some of the elements that could facilitate or hinder the process of forgiveness are:

- Severity of hurt
- Intentionality
- The person (how close they are, whether you like them or not)
- Time
- Empathy (which means understanding the other's point of view, not necessarily agreeing with it)
- Self-identity (whether you've always seen yourself as "an angry person" or a "forgiving person" for example)
- The expectations and reactions of others around us

Whatever the combination of these elements may be, the process of forgiveness will be made easier by engaging with our Compassionate Self. For easier hurts, the idea that there was no intentionality can suffice to open up to forgiveness. For more intense hurts, it might not be sufficient. In these cases, compassion can help us to face the nature of human suffering.

3b) Uncovering FBRs to forgiveness

 Therapist Background Knowledge

By this point, clients may well have realised that even though we might want to practise forgiveness, we might not always be able to do so as expected.

Making the decision to forgive is different from feeling emotional forgiveness; we might rationally recognise that not holding onto hurt and not wanting to hurt the other back is positive for our wellbeing, yet still experience intense feelings of anger, bitterness and resentment, and this could generate further shame and self-criticism.

In each module we have emphasised the importance of addressing FBRs to compassion, and these also exist for forgiveness. The thought of forgiveness, the meditation on memories of forgiveness, might have awoken FBRs, whether in the mind, the body, or both; it is important to recognise, validate, and welcome them right way. FBRs can often arise due to misunderstandings of what forgiveness is, therefore, coming back to the definition of forgiveness is important.

When we engage with forgiveness, we are building insight into its process, we are not telling people whether they should forgive or not. Compassionate wisdom will guide this process, and it allows us to know and see the different selves that are active in us and that can often come into conflict when we confront the hurt that we have generated or that someone has inflicted on us. Acknowledge that FBRs to forgiveness can appear in relation to any of the flows of forgiveness.

 Therapist Task

It might be useful at this point to engage in some self-reflection with the client or clients, or even a group discussion around FBRs to forgiveness.

These are some exploratory questions that can be used as prompts:

- *Do you recognise any FBRs coming up for you around forgiveness?*
- *If so, how do you recognise them? How do they show up for you?*
- *What fears might come up when opening up to forgiveness?*
- *What fears might come up when you think of releasing the desire for revenge?*
- *What do you think could help ease those fears?*

3c) Practicing forgiveness

 Therapist Task

Practicing forgiveness through meditation and letter writing can be a powerful way to engage with the process. It can help us become aware and notice how it feels to open up even just to the idea of forgiving. This process can then translate into a greater willingness to open-up to forgiveness in their daily lives.

Guide clients through the meditation practice *Compassionate Forgiveness* (**Therapist Script 11.4**), which combines meditation and letter writing in a two-step process of 1) opening up to forgiveness of someone they like and are willing to forgive, and then 2) someone they do not like. Connecting with the Compassionate Self before engaging in letter writing helps us to see the situation with wisdom, cultivate courage in facing the hurt that was done, and the desire to help ourself and the other to be free from suffering.

This practice can be done individually, by imagining the person we are extending forgiveness to sitting in an empty chair and reading the letter aloud to them. Alternatively, it can be done in pairs, where the two people take turns reading the forgiveness letter to the other, as if the other were the person who caused the hurt.

After the practice, provide some time for debriefing, discussing if and how it might have helped clients feel how the other person might react to forgiveness. Invite them to notice if, and how, their feelings towards the person who caused them hurt, as well as towards themselves, have changed. We are all in the flow of life, where we inevitably get hurt, and we might hurt others; being able to recognise that we might possibly find ourselves in both positions helps us to diminish the sense of "aloneness" that often arises when we are hurt, and when we are not able to forgive. Highlight the fact that this is a practice that we do in the first place to help ourselves – we try to forgive others as a sign of compassion towards the self.

Phase 4: Self-Forgiveness

In this phase of the module, we will work specifically with the flow of self-forgiveness, understanding what qualities are needed to work on this process, and how we can strengthen them. We will provide some practical exercises to start us off on the journey toward self-forgiveness.

Main Touch Points

Therapist Script 11.5 – Deepening Self-Empathy
Client Handout 11.9 – Self-forgiveness and Multiple Selves
Client Handout 11.10 – Self-forgiveness Letter
Client Handout 11.11 – Flows of Forgiveness

3a) Deepening Self-Empathy

 Therapist Background Knowledge

One of the competencies involved in self-forgiveness is self-empathy. Empathy is a complex ability: we can define it as "the capacity to recognise, share, and understand another person's perspective and feelings, and why they might be feeling that way". However, this definition does not take into account another important element, i.e. the intention that moves and guides the empathic process. In fact, it is possible to activate my empathic abilities without the intention to alleviate the suffering that I encounter, or without the courage and strength to do so. Being empathic without being supported by a compassionate intention can sometimes lead to greater distress.

Furthermore, our complex human mind has the gift (or curse) of self-reflection, so we can use the skill of empathy towards ourselves. Self-empathy is about understanding that we contain multiple selves and relating to those selves as we would with other human beings – with compassionate inquiry towards their motives, needs, and emotions.

 Therapist Task

Guide clients through the brief Deepening Self-Empathy practice (**Therapist Script 11.5**), which encourages them to take an external perspective on an interpersonal argument they were involved in, observing how they reacted, through an empathic and compassionate approach. After the practice, you might want to allow time for personal self-reflection or group discussion on how observing ourselves from the outside and through the eyes of the other might help us to cultivate self-empathy in our daily lives.

4b) Self-Forgiveness and Multiple Selves

 Therapist Background Knowledge

Self-empathy is one of the processes needed for self-forgiveness; it helps us remember our intention before we acted, and the needs that were underlying the hurtful action. Self-empathy can assist us in unlocking forgiveness for the self, which is sometimes what is blocking us from forgiving others. Often, when we do not forgive others and do not accept forgiveness from others, it can be because we are not able to forgive ourselves.

Difficulty in forgiving the self can be linked to many factors. We might have a deep-seated belief that forgiveness is for the weak, and being self-forgiving would mean slacking off or letting ourselves "off the hook" too easily, and so we would never be able to accomplish anything worthwhile. Another reason holding us back from self-forgiveness might be the realisation that opening up to it would inevitably mean recognising and really feeling the hurt we feel.

Compassion is the motivational force that allows us to feel sufficiently strong and courageous to face difficult emotions and realities of life, and consequently welcome self-forgiveness; it is the motivational shift needed for healing to occur. We need compassion to sustain the sadness, anger, and grief that are often connected to the hurt that we inflicted upon ourselves and help us move toward self-forgiveness.

Cultivating self-forgiveness not only requires us to release negative emotions towards the self, but also to cultivate positive ones and accept responsibility for what we have done. It implies a shift from shame to restorative guilt (see Module 8).

   Therapist Task

To practise self-forgiveness, we suggest offering people some time for a written self-reflection, using the multiple-selves approach to get perspective on a situation that they might have a hard time forgiving themselves for (**Client Handout 11.9**). As the client brings to mind each self (angry, anxious, sad), they might want to embody it, or just focus on what they were feeling, thinking, and wanted to do.

The handout also provides some questions to help facilitate the process of self-forgiveness: 1) recognise what was happening; 2) understand how each of your multiple-selves was feeling and what its needs were; 3) cultivate compassion towards the multiple-selves; and 4) let go of the resentment and welcome new freedom and connection. Following the exercise (which can also be conducted as a meditation if you feel this would be better suited to the people you are working with), invite clients to write a self-forgiveness letter (**Client Handout 11.10**).

To close this section on self-forgiveness, focus on the idea of flows of forgiveness. Just like we explored the flows of hurt, we now acknowledge the fact that forgiveness can follow three directions: forgiveness from others, forgiveness to others and forgiveness to the self. You can suggest filling out the flows of forgiveness handout (**Client Handout 11.11**), which helps clients recollect the forgiveness they have experienced in their lives, as well as examples or situations of forgiveness that could potentially await them.

Phase 5: Wrap-Up

The final phase of the module is a wrap-up of the theme that has been explored. Emphasise how continuing to work on one's **personal practice** (whether formal or informal) can help with the development of our compassionate minds.

Main Touch Points

Therapist Script 11.7 – Closing Practice
Client Handout B – Personal Practice Diary

5a) Summary of the Session and Suggestions for Personal Practice

Therapist Task

Take 5–10 minutes to briefly summarise the points that you have gone through in this module.

You may want to provide participants with some suggestions for personal practice and self-reflection:

- Read through the client handouts
- Practise at home, trying to apply what they learned during this module to situations in their daily life
- Complete the practice diary in **Client Handout B**, trying to focus on one compassionate activity per day, reflecting on how this could sustain their practice of forgiveness

5b) Closing Practice

Therapist Task

It is important to always take a moment at the end of the session to acknowledge anything and everything that has come up for participants while exploring the themes covered.

Try to focus their attention by inviting them to share in one sentence:

What do I take home from today's session (because I feel it's going to be helpful)?

Finally, guide participants through a short closing practice using the **Therapist Script 2.5** and perhaps adding a couple of sentences that link back to the work done during the session. This could be something like: *"...as best as we can, " Let's connect to the wisdom and the courage of compassion... today we have begun to look at the possibility of initiating the process of forgiveness...may we remember our deep intention to heal the wounds that we still carry in our hearts...*

...may we remember that the possibility of forgiveness exists...and that, even if it is difficult to imagine being able to forgive, we can begin by setting our intention......".

Three-Circle Check-In

Therapist Scripts

Therapist Script 11.1: Compassionate Landing (5 minutes)

(Refer to therapist Script 2.1 in Chapter 2.)

You can add the following elements to link back to the previous module and prepare for the present module:

Now, try looking at yourself from the outside, as if you were sitting right in front of yourself, and try observing how that makes you feel. From this perspective, you can see the needs of this being, the needs that they did not choose and that are very often difficult to express…. perhaps you can see their fears, connected to losing the people around them, perhaps they show themselves to you in all their authenticity….

Today, however, you might be able to see in them the choice to connect more often to their needs with courage and wisdom…to be able to show more assertiveness in relationships, so that they can become more authentic…

Perhaps you can thank this being for this journey of exploration and learning that they have decided to embark on.

Therapist Script 11.2: Flows of Hurt (8 minutes)

To begin this practice, let us get comfortable in our chairs, feet flat on the floor, sitting straight, shoulders back, and chest open, and if it feels ok for you, gently close our eyes, or if you prefer just direct your gaze downwards.

Now, let's start to slow down our breathing a little. Just settle our mind and body. Start listening to the sensation of air flowing into your nose and air flowing out of your nose…notice how they merge into one another, breath after breath. As you inhale, follow the air as it comes into the nose and expands the lungs, as you exhale, follow the air as it leaves your chest and body and goes back out into the space around you. If it feels ok, you can begin slowing down your breathing now, in order to connect with your soothing rhythm breathing.

As we continue breathing in and out, let us embody the qualities of compassion: let us breathe in wisdom, courage, and the desire to be helpful, not harmful.

Connect to the wisdom that we did not choose to be born, to arrive on this planet, in a certain place, at a certain time, within a certain family….and there are many other experiences we did not choose. We did not choose many of the difficulties we have encountered throughout our lives. We did not choose having to face harm and hurt. Can you remember as a little child having chosen for life to hurt? Harm, suffering, and hurt are intrinsically woven into the fabric of life. Just like you, so many people, in one way or another, consciously or unconsciously, have been hurt. Just like you, so many people in some way or another, voluntarily or involuntarily, have hurt others. Just like you, so many people in some way or another, voluntarily or involuntarily, might have hurt themselves in some way.

Without forcing anything, allow any images of times these three flows of hurt have manifested in your life to come to you.

How does it feel to imagine these flows of hurt? Does anything change in the body? Does anything change in your breathing? How do you feel to realise that it is no one's fault that human beings have this predisposition? Do you feel closer to or more distant from others? As you connect to the image of these flows, notice if any resistances come up. If perhaps you feel the need to build up walls to protect yourself from this hurt. As best as you can, simply observe whatever arises in you.

As we continue on to breathe in and out, let us embody the qualities of compassion: let us breathe in the wisdom that we have not chosen the nature of our existence, that all of us voluntarily or involuntarily hurt and are hurt... we cannot change this nature... but we can focus on the courage and desire to be helpful, not harmful, on the intention to repair and accept reparation if and when life offers us the chance to do so.

Then, when you feel ready, gently place your palms face down on your lap and then open your eyes.

Therapist Script 11.3: Memories of Forgiveness (10 minutes)

To begin this practice, let us get comfortable in our chairs, feet flat on the floor, sitting up straight, with shoulders back, and chest open, and if it feels ok for you, gently close your eyes, or if you prefer just direct your gaze downwards.

Start connecting with your breath, giving yourself some time to settle into your own soothing rhythm breathing.

Now let your mind freely go back in time... it can be any time in your life... and find a memory of a time in which you forgave someone. Let your mind settle on a memory that is not too intense for you, just the right amount to be able to work with it right now. As you begin recollecting this memory, try not to go into the hurt of what was done, but focus rather on the experience of forgiveness itself.

If nothing comes to mind, try to connect to a moment in which you were forgiven for something.

How was the forgiveness offered? How was the forgiveness received? What made you realise that you had forgiven or that the other had forgiven you? If there was an exchange of words, what words were chosen? How did your body feel before being forgiven or forgiving? What happened after forgiveness occurred? Did you notice any changes?

If you notice any unpleasant sensations arising, allow them to remain here; try working with your breath or your touch to welcome them, without necessarily changing them. It is ok for forgiveness to bring up unpleasant sensations, even when this forgiveness ended up being a positive choice for our well-being.

Now...what happened after forgiveness was given or received? How did it change your view of the person? How did it impact your relationship?

Try asking yourself if you ever regretted having forgiven... How do you feel now at the idea of having forgiven and the thought of having been forgiven?

Now, step into your Compassionate Self [give a brief Compassionate Self induction]. *Try to imagine these two beings, in their human vulnerability, navigating through hurt and trying to defend themselves from it as best they can. Also contemplate their courage to deal with suffering in a different way... to choose, as best as they can, the way of connection, not of revenge and closing off... consider how this choice has impacted their mind, their lives...*

Then, when you feel ready, gently come back to the room, and open your eyes.

Therapist Script 11.4: Compassionate Forgiveness (10 minutes)

For this practice you will need a pen and paper to write a letter. You will also need to have an empty chair in front of you. Alternatively, this practice can be done in pairs.

Let us start this practice by closing our eyes or softening our gaze and feeling how we sit in our chair right now. Give yourself some time to settle into your compassionate posture with your back straight and shoulders in line with your hips while letting your breath get progressively longer, allowing your chest to expand in all directions as you breathe in and softening as you breathe out.

With each slower and deeper breath, you can try saying, slowly and in a friendly tone, "mind slowing down" and then, "body slowing down," alternatively – gradually getting that sense of grounding and opening of the heart and mind space at the same time. Notice your presence starting to change; maybe you feel more grounded, maybe you feel more at ease in the space your are inhabiting. Gradually, let your posture take the form of your Compassionate Self – transform your back and heart to bring wisdom, courage, and solidity into the body. Connect with the intention to help.

From this position, gently open your eyes and think about someone who has hurt you in some way but whom you would like to forgive. Think back to the actual event where you were treated badly by the other person. With the eyes of your Compassionate Self, try retracing your relationship with this person before the situation. Then recall how you felt during the event and after. As best you can, and to the extent that you feel comfortable with at this time, connect with the pain you felt in that moment. What needs were frustrated, what expectations disappointed, what things were lost?... Connect with how understandable and normal all the pain and anger you experienced in that moment is... Compassionate wisdom helps you understand why you suffered so much from what happened. How much it makes sense that your sadness and anger are so intense in this moment.

Now try to connect to the wish to help yourself in that pain... what would your Compassionate Self wish for your hurt self? What would they want for them?

Now, if you feel it ok for you, bring your compassionate gaze to the other person. Imagine how the other person felt during the situation and why they might have felt that way. What was going on in their life to act in such a hurtful way? What needs were they trying to have met? What insecurities and fears did they have? Maybe, with the wisdom and courage of your Compassionate Self, you can glimpse something behind the behaviour of the person who has hurt you.

Now, from the perspective of your Compassionate Self, begin writing a "forgiveness letter" to the person you are willing to forgive. Maybe you want to clarify what the intention of your letter is – it is not to make the other person feel bad, admit guilt, or say I'm sorry. The motivation of this letter is to affirm your understanding of the situation, and declare what needs have been hurt by the behaviour of the other person, but, at the same time, express your willingness to move on and be free. If you feel that you are not ready to say, "I forgive you," you can start with something else, e.g. "I have the intention to forgive you," or "I'm willing to forgive you because I want to be free and I'm willing to move on".

Once you have finished writing the letter, gently close your eyes again and imagine that the person you are willing to forgive is sitting on the chair in front of you. Remember that the intention is to "set yourself free" of unnecessary anger that prevents you from living the life that you want to live. From the compassionate position, read the letter to this person.

An alternative approach would be to read this letter aloud while looking at yourself in the mirror.

If doing this exercise in pairs, one person reads their letter to the other, imagining that the person in front of them is the person they wish to forgive.

Notice how you feel after having written and read this letter. How does the other person feel?

This procedure can be repeated with progressively more difficult situations (higher up the hurt ladder), but it is important to bear in mind the intention with which it is done, i.e., to be free from unnecessary resentment, which ultimately intoxicates our existence and limits us in some way.

Therapist Script 11.5: Deepening Self-Empathy (8 minutes)

Find a comfortable seated position and then gently close your eyes, letting your gaze turn inwards.

Take some time to settle in your body and your breathing, letting your attention softly move from one sensation to the next, from one in-breath to one out-breath. Let your breathing support you in connecting to your Compassionate Self through the body, creating a posture that you feel is courageous, strong, wise, and deeply helpful.

Now, from this posture, go back to a moment when you think you have hurt someone (or yourself) through something you did or did not do. This could be a memory of an argument you had with someone, when you got very angry at the other person; perhaps today you judge this anger almost as being an excessive reaction. It can be something that has happened recently or something that happened long ago. Or it might be a moment in which you behaved in a way that you are now ashamed of – and you "can't forgive yourself" for.

Recreate the scene, imagine observing the two people interacting. Dwell on yourself from the outside, on the verge of doing that action or gesture that you can't forgive yourself for now...try to look at yourself with the curious eyes of the Compassionate Self.... feel the posture of the Compassionate Self and the desire to peer deeply into what was happening to you at that moment...

Now, from this perspective, what do you notice? If you look at your own face while you are in that situation, what emotions can you discern? What needs drove you to do what you did? What fears? If you could look at this person (you) with the awareness that they didn't choose their needs, they didn't choose their emotions... and that like everyone else on this earth, they just want to be happy and not suffer, what would you understand about their behaviour? What insights did taking the other person's perspective bring you? Might adopting the other person's point of view help us cultivate not only empathy towards them, but also ourselves?

When you feel ready, come back to the present moment, and gently open your eyes.

Client Handouts

Client Handout 11.1: Compassionate Weekly Reflection

Let's do a curious, friendly reflection on this past week:

Which part of the self-practice did I do and why?

Which part of the self-practice did I not do?

Was this due to any anxieties or block regarding the practice or the path? Which ones can you identify?

We extend gratitude, respect, and compassion to resistances: What would make you and your resistances feel safer in going forward on this path?

Client Handout 11.2: My Hurt Ladder

It can be difficult to list the hurts we have created or suffered in life, and this practice can, therefore, trigger strong emotions. Do it while respecting your limits – don't force yourself: the purpose is not to feel guilt or feel victimised

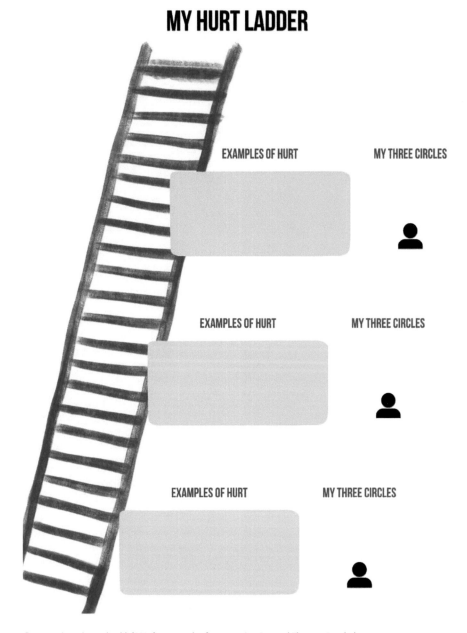

again, but to open up and embrace the stream of "hurts" in which we are all, willingly or unwillingly, immersed. It is not necessary to be exhaustive – you can point out only the most recurrent or most significant hurts.

Reflection questions after the practice:

What emotions did this exercise generate?

Did you notice connections between the three streams? Are there any similarities?

How does it make you feel to realise that everyone has reported all three types of hurt, that we are all, willingly or unwillingly, creators, and receivers of hurt?

Client Handout 11.3: What Forgiveness is and is Not

Forgiveness **is**:

- A deliberate, personal intentional choice to release feelings of anger, resentment, and vengeance and experience a greater sense of freedom
- An opportunity we offer ourselves
- A process
- Emotionally challenging, as it brings us into contact with feelings of loss and grief
- Done for ourselves, not for others

Forgiveness **is not**:

- An outcome
- Condoning or approving a harmful behaviour
- Forgetting
- Reconciliation with another person (it could be safer to maintain distance, or the other person might not be alive any more)
- An invitation for friendship
- Something we do for others (either because others expect us to forgive or because we do not like to be seen as people who still hold grudges)

Would you add anything to this list?

Which of these distinctions struck you the most? Why?

Which of these distinctions helps you the most?

Client Handout 11.4: Flows of Hurt

FLOWS OF HURT

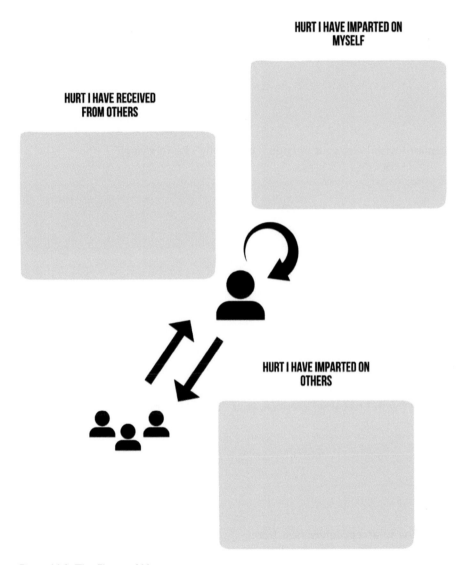

HURT I HAVE IMPARTED ON
MYSELF

HURT I HAVE RECEIVED
FROM OTHERS

HURT I HAVE IMPARTED ON
OTHERS

Figure 11.2 The Flows of Hurt.

Client Handout 11.4: Why Practise Forgiveness?

Reflect on what the potential benefits of forgiveness are for you. Why would you want to engage in the process of forgiveness of others, from others and of the self?

I'm willing to forgive _____ for:

because I wish I (set your intention, your "why" for forgiving):

I'm willing to forgive MYSELF for:

because I wish I (set your intention, your "why" for forgiving):

I'm willing to accept forgiveness from _____ for:

because I wish I (set your intention, your "why" for accepting forgiveness):

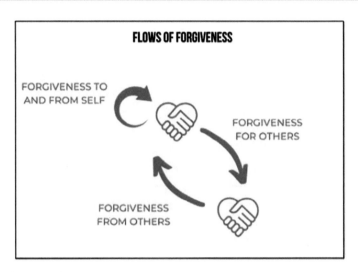

Figure 11.3 Flows of Forgiveness.

Represent how your body feels when holding on to resentment; use colours, textures, and different line thicknesses to represent your physical sensations. Choose whether to represent a state of resentment towards someone else or towards yourself.

Represent how your body feels when opening up to forgiveness or when you imagine opening up to forgiveness; use colours, textures, and different line thicknesses to represent your physical sensations. Choose which flow of forgiveness feels most relevant to you at this time.

Client Handout 11.6: Stories of Forgiveness

Try reflecting on the following situations and inquiring whether you would be willing to forgive.

Vignette #1

Sally is 54 years old and married to Neil. Sally finds out Neil has been cheating on her for the last five years.

How willing would you be to forgive Neil if you were Sally?

Does anything change for you if we provide additional information, such as the fact that Sally has also been cheating on Neil for the past three years? Would you be less or more willing to forgive him? What might be the possible benefits of forgiving?

Vignette #2

Joanne is 34 years old and is a stay-at-home mother; she is married to Andrew, who is 36 years old and is a retail worker. They have three children, Alicia, Oliver, and Jeannette.

Joanne got really angry at Andrew for arriving home late, but she feels badly about it, she was just stressed.

As Andrew, how willing would you be to forgive Joanne? What might the benefits of forgiving be? As Andrew, under what circumstances would you be willing to forgive? What would you need?

Vignette #3

Tom is 34 years old and works in an office. A colleague at work, Paul, accidentally runs into him, and Tom spills his coffee all over himself. Paul apologises and says sorry.

As Tom, how willing would you be to forgive Paul? Why or why not? What might the benefits of forgiving be? Under what circumstances would you be willing to forgive? What would you need?

Vignette #4

Rachael and Kate are good friends. Kate recently found out that Rachael lied to her about something that she was embarrassed about.

Kate forgave Rachael because she understood.

If you were Rachael, would you forgive yourself for lying to Kate? Why or why not? What might the benefits of forgiving be? Under what circumstances would you be willing to forgive? What would you need?

These brief vignettes highlight how there are many different nuances to forgiveness; try to reflect on how these different factors of forgiveness influence your willingness to forgive. Of course, the combinations of these ingredients are endless, making it really difficult to have just a single rule for how and when to forgive.

Factors that Influence Forgiveness

- Severity of Hurt
- Intentionality

- The person
- Time
- Empathy
- Self-Identity

Think of a person you have been able to forgive in your life. Which of these factors have been important to you in facilitating the process of forgiveness?

Now think of a person who is currently difficult for you to forgive. Which of these factors are influencing your choice to forgive?

Client Handout 11.7: My FBRs to Forgiveness

What fears might come up when opening up to forgiveness? How do you feel about openly expressing these fears?

What fears might come up when you think of releasing your resentment/desire for revenge?

Connect with your Compassionate Self – create your open, solid but not rigid posture and connect with the wisdom, strength, and desire to be helpful of this part of yourself. The Compassionate Self knows how important it is to acknowledge and give space to your anger – while at the same time, it wishes you could live a life that is not dominated by resentment. It wishes for you to be free.

What would this Compassionate Self tell you regarding to your fears? What would it advise you? Would it advise you to take the path of forgiveness?

Client Handout 11.8: Compassionate Forgiveness Letter

Before writing this letter, let your breathing support you in connecting to your Compassionate Self through the body, creating a posture that you feel is courageous, strong, wise, and deeply helpful.

Connect to your Compassionate Self, who fully understands the wounds that have been inflicted on us, the validity of the pain and anger we have experienced, but also the desire for freedom and peace, which we wish to employ as we approach the forgiveness process.

Dear _____

I am writing this letter about the situation/time where/when (What happened? Who was involved? When/Where did this happen? What was said?)

I feel this way because (What and why this issue is so meaningful to you):

However, having these emotions came at a price for me…

And now I feel that continuing to hold on to them might be harmful to me because (write down what resentment might generate in our future/might block; refer to what purposes/desires/needs you feel are hindered by not forgiving):

© Petrocchi, Kirby and Baldi (2025), *Essentials of Compassion Focused Therapy*, Routledge

The fears I have in letting go of these feelings are:

However, today I decided to write this letter to you because I intend to begin the process of forgiveness. I am doing this because (write the intention of the letter – whether you are seeking a sense of closure or seeking reconciliation, or any other purposes of the letter):

Set your intention for the future. What is your wish for yourself? What emotions would you like to nurture, which mental states do you want to train, which behaviours do you want to adopt? What do you wish for the person who harmed you?

Conclude the letter as you best see fit:

Signature

Client Handout 11.9: Self-Forgiveness and Multiple Selves

Focus on something that you are having a hard time forgiving yourself for. Go back to the situation (what you did or did not do, in terms of actions, thoughts, and emotions). Try to reflect on what each one of your selves might have been feeling, thinking, sensing in that situation, and that might have brought you to act in the way that you do not forgive yourself for at the present moment.

Table 11.2

ANGRY SELF	ANXIOUS SELF
Motives	Motives
Thoughts:	Thoughts:
Body:	Body:
Actions:	Actions:
Needs	Needs
SAD SELF	COMPASSIONATE SELF
Motives	*Motives*
Thoughts:	*Thoughts:*
Body:	*Body:*
Actions:	*Actions:*
Needs	*Needs*

What words of wisdom would your Compassionate Self offer, encouraging you to open up to self-forgiveness? What fears would you have in forgiving yourself?

How do you imagine self-forgiveness would feel in the body? How do you imagine yourself if you were free from this anger and resentment towards yourself? What would you do differently? What would you do that you are not allowing yourself to do now?

Client Handout 11.10: Self-Forgiveness Letter

As with the forgiveness letter above, before writing this letter, let your breathing support you in connecting to your Compassionate Self through the body, creating a posture that you feel is courageous, strong, wise, and deeply helpful.

The Compassionate Self fully understands the wounds we have inflicted on ourselves, the validity of the pain and anger we have experienced and still experience, often the sense of shame and guilt if what we want to forgive ourselves for involves someone else, but also the desire for freedom and peace with which we wish to approach the forgiveness process.

Dear _____ (write your name)

I am writing this letter about the situation/time where/when (What happened? Who was involved? When/Where did this happen? What was said?)

What happened/what you did/did not do has caused me (write the consequences of the behaviour and the emotions that were linked to that behaviour):

I feel this way because (write why your behaviour/way of being impacted you so much – which values/needs did it compromise/which part of you was invalidated/mistreated):

However, continuing not to forgive you and feeling anger and resentment towards you has cost me dearly, in fact (write everything in the past that was blocked or hindered by your lack of self-forgiveness):

Now I feel that continuing to dwell on those feelings might be harmful for me because (write down what resentment might generate in your future/might block; write down what purposes/desires/needs you feel are hindered by not forgiving yourself):

The fears I have in letting go of these feelings of resentment towards myself are:

However, today I chose to write this letter to you because I intend to begin the process of forgiveness. I do so because.................*(*write the intention of the letter – what purpose/value/needs self-forgiveness could facilitate you to achieve/embrace):

From now on, my intention is... (set your intention for the future. What is your wish for yourself; what emotions you wish to cultivate, what mental states you will try to train, what behaviours do you want to adopt?):

Conclude the letter as you best see fit:

Signature

Client Handout 11.11: Flows of Forgiveness

FLOWS OF FORGIVENESS

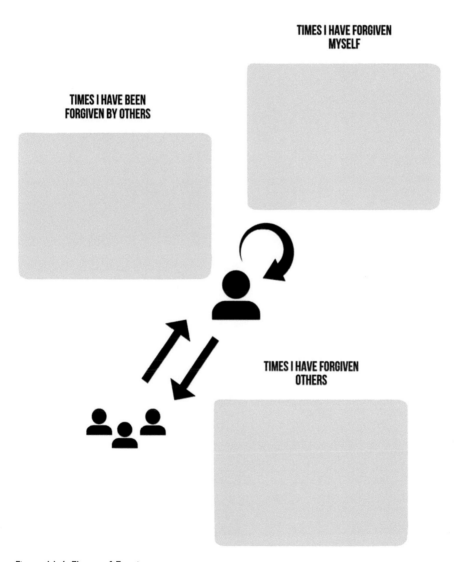

Figure 11.4 Flows of Forgiveness.

It can be useful to reflect on how the three flows of forgiveness are intertwined in our lives – has forgiving ourselves facilitated the forgiveness of others? Do we notice that we tend to feel obliged to forgive others for things for that we have also had to forgive ourselves for? What do you notice when you focus attention on this idea of flows of forgiveness?

Chapter 12

Module 12

Envisioning a Compassionate Future

Aims

- To revisit our compassionate journey, identifying what was useful along the way and exploring the emotions linked its conclusion
- To identify some prevention and emergency strategies for future difficulties
- To envision what a compassionate future might involve
- To connect to a sense of gratitude (both for others and for the self) through experiential practice

---

 Deepen Your Knowledge

In Gilbert, P. & Simos, G. (Eds). (2022). *Compassion Focused Therapy: Clinical Practice and Applications*. Routledge, please refer to:

Chapter 8. Compassionate Mind Training: Key Themes

In Gilbert, P. (Ed.). (2005). *Compassion: Conceptualisations, Research and Use in Psychotherapy*, please refer to:

Chapter 2: Compassion and Cruelty

DOI: 10.4324/9781003436058-14

Summary of Key Processes

Table 12.1 Module 12: Envisioning a Compassionate Future

Phase		Main Touch Points	Therapist Scripts	Client Handouts
1	Introduction	**1a)** Compassionate landing **1b)** Revision of personal practice and recap of previous session	□ **Script 12.1**: Compassionate Landing	□ **Handout 12.1**: Compassionate weekly reflection
2	Prevention and emergency strategies	**2a)** Dealing with distress and setbacks **2b)** Creating portals to compassion		□ **Handout 12.2**: Compassionate prevention and emergency strategies □ **Handout 12.3**: My portals to compassion
3	Looking back to look forwards: envisioning a compassionate future	**3a)** Reflecting on the journey **3b)** The Compassionate Future Self	□ **Script 12.2**: My Compassionate Future Self	□ **Handout 12.4**: My take home messages □ **Handout 12.5**: Letter to Compassionate Future Self □ **Handout 12.6**: Compassionate forecasting
4	Compassionate flourishing	**4a)** Cultivating gratitude **4b)** Metta and Mudita (optional)	□ **Script 12.3**: Metta and Mudita	□ **Handout 12.7**: Expressing gratitude □ **Handout 12.8**: Gratitude to the self
5	Wrap-up	**5a)** Compassionate wishes circle **5b)** Closing practice	□ **Script 12.4**: Closing practice	□ **Handout B**: Personal practice diary

Phase 1: Introduction

Main Touch Points

Therapist Script 12.1 – Compassionate Landing
Client Handout 12.1 – Compassionate Weekly Reflection

1a) Compassionate Landing

    Therapist Task

As a final welcome to the group, guide them through a Compassionate Landing (**Therapist Script 12.1**).

Before practicing the landing, you could guide them through a short Three-Circle Check-In.

Three-Circle Check-In

If participants had been keeping track of their Three-Circle Check-Ins during the various sessions, they can now reflect on their progress. Have they changed? If so, in what ways? How does the end of this journey impact their three circles? What do they notice? Can they notice the dynamic nature of the three circles? It is possible that the red system has not changed (the purpose was not to eliminate it) but is now balanced by increased activity of the green system.

We have now reached the end of this journey through Compassion Focused Therapy, and for some it can feel like we have only just scratched the surface of what a compassionate life can offer. However, we might now have a clearer picture of the direction we wish to give our lives and the motivation we can cultivate from now on in our relationships with ourselves and others. To soften this closure, we will engage in practices that strengthen the bonds that have been formed, that reconnect us to the shared experience of our unchosen human nature and we will envision together a compassionate future for ourselves and others.

1b) Revision of personal practice and recap of the previous session

    Therapist Task

Invite clients to use **Client Handout 12.1** to reflect on the past week/weeks; then get them into pairs or small groups and invite them to share (if they would like to do so) anything relevant about their past week, including any compassion episodes or fear, blocks, and resistances (FBRs) they might have experienced.

- Did they think about or try to practice forgiveness in their everyday life?
- What did they notice when considering/practicing forgiveness?
- How did forgiving or considering the idea of forgiveness influence their relationship with others?
- How did it influence their relationship with themselves?
- Did the Compassionate Self help them be more forgiving?
- Did they encounter any FBRs when wanting to be forgiving?

Before moving on, the therapist can provide a brief recap of the last session, in which the main points were:

- What forgiveness is and is not
- How a compassionate motivation can sustain the process of forgiveness
- FBRs to forgiveness
- Forgiveness as a flow

This can also be a space to set the scene for the current module; the main themes that are going to be explored are:

- Identifying some prevention and emergency strategies for future difficulties
- Revisiting the journey we have been on
- Envisioning what a compassionate future might involve
- Learning to practice gratitude

Phase 2: Prevention and Emergency Strategies

In this phase of the module we will focus on creating prevention strategies and think about possible emergency strategies we can use in difficult moments. We will try to provide applicable solutions to transfer the wisdom of compassion and the lessons learned in the previous modules to our everyday lives.

Main Touch Points

Client Handout 12.2 – Compassionate Prevention and Emergency Strategies
Client Handout 12.3 – My Portals to Compassion

2a) Dealing with Future Distress and Setbacks

 Therapist Task

As we have experienced throughout the modules, working with compassion not only involves training the various skills of compassion (e.g., becoming more proficient in visualisations and mindfulness), but also working with the FBRs that prevent us from accessing our Compassionate Self in moments of need. For many, constantly extending compassion to the critical part of the self and the fear from which it stems, as well as to the other blocks and resistances to compassion, is at the heart of compassionate mind training.

Adopting a compassionate perspective allows us to see distress and setbacks as part of the natural process of life: and we can be supportive and encouraging during those moments. During these periods of distress or setback, it si important to remember that compassion acts as a compass, and perhaps all we need to do to find our direction again.

It is useful to mention that on every journey there are many "lapses" (momentary deviations from the course), and that they become" "full relapses" when we criticise ourselves and do not embrace with compassion the bumpy nature of the path. If compassion is a direction, we can always let the system "recalculate the route" in the direction we have decided to take.

After this CFT journey formally ends, there can be a feeling of wanting to 'stay on track' and the fear of not being able to do so. But what do we mean by 'staying on track'? This can be an interesting moment for a shared reflection with the group or the client, asking them what they envision when they speak of "staying on track". What do these tracks look like? How wide are they? Most importantly, we can discuss how we commonly react when we feel we are getting off track.

After having shared and reflected what we mean by "staying on track", we can ask ourselves how our Compassionate Self can be of help when we feel we are losing direction, as well as in order to prevent forgetting that direction in the first place.

 Therapist Tips

Some people might hold a belief that they are only deserving of help or care when things are at their worst. Therefore, developing preventative strategies might be seen as weak or unnecessary. We must then reorient to the definition of compassion, which entails not only alleviating suffering when it occurs, but also preparing oneself and preventing suffering when possible.

Now that we have reaffirmed that "lapses" and how we relate to them are the core essence of this path, and that compassion is not meant to eliminate all pain from our lives, invite clients to engage with their Compassionate Self (you could lead them in a brief Compassionate Self induction) and then ask them to write down (**Client Handout 12.2**) some activities or prompts that can help them take care of themselves in moments of distress and prevent, to the best of their abilities, further distress.

The wisdom of the Compassionate Self recognises that we cannot fully control all moments of distress (it's not our fault); however, we are able to regulate those reactions and respond to them with a compassionate orientation (responsibility is seen as an "ability to respond" or a "skilful response"). It might be important to remind the client/s that compassion entails three flows, and our strategies can involve all three flows as well.

After the exercise, the strategies can be shared in groups or in pairs, so that people can be inspired by each other's compassionate wisdom.

You can provide some prompts for reflection:

- Is it easier to come up with ideas about one of the flows of compassion in particular?
- Is it easier them to come up with strategies for emergency rather than prevention?
- Are there any fears regarding those prevention or emergency strategies?
- How do you recognise signs of distress?

Ask if there is any shame around still experiencing at times the same distress they had at the beginning of the journey; how would they have reacted to that difficulty before starting the journey? How would they go about it now? It is important to emphasise that compassion and therapy is about embracing the possibility of not 'staying on track'. Distress and setbacks are part of our shared human experience. Our Compassionate Selves might encourage us to ask for help quicker than we would have before, and help us to not get stuck in self-critical and shameful mental loops.

2b) Creating Portals to Compassion

 Therapist Task

Compassion is a motivation that we can choose and apply as a direction to many activities in our lives, from work, to education, to raising our children, to romantic relationships. Although we all have the potential to be compassionate, it is certainly something that requires training. In fact, the extremely competition-driven context we live in constantly exposes us to triggers that are opposite to those that would help us develop more compassion. We must, therefore, remember the usefulness of accessing this motivation and find our own ways to access it more and more often. Throughout this manual, we have explored several ways of exposing and training our compassionate motivation, however, there are endless portals to compassion. Portals are anything that helps us connect with our compassionate motivation.

For some people this might be listening to specific music, which increases their feelings of empathy and connectedness. For others it may be creative activities, which we know are connected to the activation of the parasympathetic system; or hiking in the mountains, an activity which increases their feelings of connectedness and compassion toward the natural world and living beings; or even choosing to take an hour out of their week to volunteer at an animal shelter or community service. Even travelling and immersing yourself in a culture that is very different from your own can help develop a greater sense of interconnectedness, even with something that is new to us. You can refer to the acts of kindness and compassion done in Module 9: Deepening Self-Compassion.

The important point here is that every person has their own unique ways that help them access their compassionate motivation. A question that often helps clients make some room for compassion and avoid the "all or nothing" trap is: If I added 3% more compassion into my day today, how would it change? What would I do? What I not do? Or: what activity would add 3% more compassion to my day/week?

Invite clients to come up with alternative portals to compassion, ones that have not yet been explored during the previous sessions. Invite them to brainstorm and write down their ideas (**Client Handout 12.3**), then share them with you or the group. You could also invite clients to wonder if there are any portals to compassion that they are actively avoiding; why is this? Is it something that they are OK with, or would they like to access those portals but feel they cannot do so?

Phase 3: Looking Back to Look Forwards: Envisioning a Compassionate Future

The goal of this phase is to reflect on what useful teachings/experiences the programme has left us with, and how those have fostered change. We then encourage reflection on how those teachings can help us to create a compassionate future for ourselves.

Main Touch Points

Therapist Script 12.2 – Compassionate Future Self
Client Handout 12.4 – My Take-Home Messages
Client Handout 12.5 – Compassionate Future Self Letter
Client Handout 12.6 – Compassionate Forecasting

3a) Reflecting on the Journey

 Therapist Task

As the Compassion Focused Therapy programme comes to a close, it can be a good idea to reflect on the insights and learnings that each person will take home from the experience that was shared. We suggest that the therapist provide some time to briefly touch on all the themes that were presented in each module, perhaps by asking clients to share the one key point that they remember or that in some way changed their perspective. These are not necessarily theoretical insights that they learned, but may be intuitions, or light-bulb moments that they reached during that phase of the programme. They can also write down one key take-away for each module in **Client Handout 12.4**.

This may be a time where some participants might want to share their feelings about the end of the journey, or a poem they wrote, or a song they found captured the journey they took together, or a drawing.

Therapist Tips

When working with a group, this activity can be done in pairs, in small groups or with the group at large; it is important to emphasise that every person might have had a different experience of this programme and how normal this is. Sometimes people are afraid of having made some mistakes along the way or of not having applied the exercises as they 'should' have. This happens especially when many people share "major progress" that they have made, which can activate feelings of loneliness and shame for those who feel they have not had these major changes.

When and if clients share something similar, encourage them to take a compassionate stance on these anxieties, and reluctances, thanking them for the courage to show this authentic part of them. It is possible to reflect, ironically, that this disclosure might itself be a sign that the person is now more able to embrace parts of themselves that they would perhaps have hidden before. We are always trying to reconnect to a non-judgemental curiosity of our experience, to be compassionate with our fears.

3b) The Compassionate Future Self

Therapist Task

The Compassionate Future Self is an imagery practice which encourages us to imagine how we will appear in five years' time if we fully embrace our compassionate motivation. First, lead clients through the guided meditation (**Therapist Script 12.2**).

Therapist Tips

This practice can be problematic if you are working with patients with chronic health problems or in the terminal stages of an illness. However, it has been found anecdotally, that for some terminally ill patients this practice has allowed them to re-imagine the moment of their departure (what it would be like if it was my Compassionate Self going through it, or I was in the company of my compassionate image), thereby significantly reducing the anxiety that that phase of our lives induces. In fact, the brain is continually engaged in some form of future thinking – it can, therefore, be helpful for them to help imagine how their Compassionate Self would cope with whatever future stage the person is facing. For this reason, it is, therefore, important for the therapist to use caution with this type of clinical population.

Following the meditation, you can encourage them to engage with their compassionate future in several ways: for example, they could write a letter (**Client Handout 12.5**) or an email from the point of view of their future self, imagining that the person talking is a version of them five or ten years from now. How has compassion changed their lives? How do they embody the qualities of compassion in their daily lives? What have these qualities enabled them to do? You could also use an online service that allows people to write an email to themselves and to schedule the arrival date one, three or five years from the current date. This is often an exciting and moving experience for clients.

Another way to connect with their Compassionate Future Self is to create a vision board; what images, words, and colours would they want to see in their compassionate future vision board? This can be done either on a cardboard or digitally – either way, encourage them to take their time when collecting the images they want to use and when actually creating the visual representation of the felt sense of their compassionate future. Can they make space for all three circles in this compassionate future? Has their configuration changed compared to what it was before the training?

Finally, it is important to carve out space for some compassionate forecasting (**Client Handout 12.6**). This is a time to reflect on any FBRs that they might still want to work on in their future journey. Openly recognising that we might still have many FBRs at the end of the programme is de-shaming and an act of courageous vulnerability. We begin to radically accept that fears and resistances have a place in our compassionate narrative, but that they no longer inhibit us from accessing our compassionate future – they are actually a portal to it.

Phase 4: Compassionate Flourishing

In this final phase, we focus on practices that can help us connect to other types of positive affect that are part of a compassionate life. To cultivate positive affect, we introduce the practices of gratitude, metta, and mudita.

Main Touch Points

Therapist Script 12.3 – Metta and Mudita
Therapist Script 12.4 – Mudita
Client Handout 12.7 – Expressing Gratitude
Client Handout 12.8 – Gratitude to the Self

4a) Cultivating Gratitude

    Therapist Task

Gratitude is an emotion that is closely related to compassion. In fact, gratitude arises from noticing and appreciating the benefits that one has received, and very often that is what we feel when we turn on the flow of compassion. Genuine gratitude is to feel indebted for a gift that is appraised as costly to provide, valuable, and altruistically offered, and that can never be fully repaid. Thus, gratitude involves a "willingness to remain indebted," and a sense of safeness in acknowledging dependency on the benefactor. Therefore, it is an emotion that reminds us of our constant inter-connectedness, and it is connected to reduced levels of shame and self-criticism. It also helps us balance our negativity bias (threat system), allowing us to connect with the things in life that are already going well, so that we can experience contentment (soothing system).

Just like compassion, it follows three flows. These experiential exercises allow us to focus on offering gratitude to each other and to ourselves. You can invite clients to follow **Client Handout 12.7 and 12.8** to write two letters of gratitude.

    Optional Practice

4b) Metta and Mudita (optional practices)

    Therapist Background Knowledge

Metta and Mudita are two practices that originate from the Buddhist tradition, which are aimed at cultivating positive affect and attitudes towards the self and others. Metta and Mudita are part of the Brahmaviharas, also known as the four abodes or four immeasurables: they are the sublime attitudes that, according to Buddhist tradition, allow us to experience more joy and lightness. The other two Brahmaviharas are Upekkha (equanimity) and, of course, Karuna (compassion).

Metta, frequently referred to as loving-kindness or friendly-kindness meditation, involves directing thoughts of kindness towards the self, loved ones, acquaintances, strangers and even those with whom we share difficult relationships.

Mudita is usually translated as sympathetic joy or appreciative joy – it means being happy because others are happy. This concept is also expressed by the German word *Freudenfreude*, which describes the enjoyment and bliss that we feel when someone else succeeds, even if this does not directly involve us. Thus, it is thus a practice that can powerfully counterbalance the rank-based self-focus that often leads us to experience envy for the success of others.

Therapist Task

Therapist Script 12.3 offers a brief practice integrating the qualities of Metta and Mudita (**Therapist Script 12.4**) to cultivate positive affect.

Phase 5: Wrap-Up

The final phase of the module and the programme is focused on setting the intention to continue developing one's own personal journey of compassion. An ending exercise and practice provide closure.

Main Touch Points

Therapist Script 12.5 – Closing Practice
Client Handout B – Personal Practice Diary

5a) Compassionate Wishes Circle

Therapist Task

This practice is ideally done in a group; if working with a client individually, it can still be done through visualisation, connecting to the various parts of the self and to others.

Invite people to create a circle; in turn, each of the participants (including the therapist) say their name and then close their eyes. Everyone connects with their Compassionate Self and sends good wishes (usually in silence, for the duration of about 30 seconds) to the person who just spoke. The person with their eyes closed absorbs this stream of compassionate wishes. It is not necessary to create words, because the compassionate wish can take the form of a look that captures the compassionate intention toward the person; people might also imagine a compassionate colour reaching out and enveloping the person. Some examples of compassionate wishes are:

- May you have all the compassion you need to navigate the ups and downs of life
- May you continue to flourishing
- May you remember that you, like all of us, found yourself thrown into the flow of life and that like all of us you simply long for happiness – you are not alone in this journey
- May your compassion give you the courage to embrace and pursue your deepest desires
- May you feel safe, may you feel happy, may you be healthy, and may you live with ease
- May you be at peace with all the parts of yourself. May you treat them with compassion from now on
- May your compassion help others and set them free

 Optional Practice

Whether in person or online, you can ask people to write down, on a shared sheet or the chatbox, the greetings they created and exchanged during the practice so that everyone can have this list and can silently repeat the phrases once the group is finished.

5b) Closing Practice

 Therapist Task

Invite clients to share in one word their experience of this journey they have set out on.

Then, guide them through one last, short closing practice using **Therapist Script 12.5**.

Therapist Scripts

Therapist Script 12.1: Compassionate Landing (5 minutes)

(Refer to therapist Script 2.1.)

You can add the following elements to prepare for the present module:

As this supportive breath moves your the body, imagine it transforming your posture, maybe also your facial expression, softly creating a friendly facial expression.

If we feel it is right for us, we can reconnect to the idea we addressed last week....forgiveness, in its many forms...and the many resistances each of us has to undertaking this difficult yet transformative process...

This difficulty is not our fault...yet if we feel it is OK we can set the direction of our path...perhaps by simply repeating to ourselves...I'm opening to forgivenesss...I'm willing to start the process of forgiveness", and simply noticing what emerges.

Therapist Script 12.2: Compassionate Future Self (10 minutes)

To begin this practice, close your eyes, connect with the posture of your Compassionate Self, slow down your breathing until you reach your soothing rhythm breathing today, whatever that looks like.

Let your mind be visited by an image of you in the future at a time where you feel you have reached the balance you wish to achieve between your three systems and you have allowed compassion to change your life in the way you feel is best for you.

In this image your threat system is active and useful, you are capable of protecting yourself, of protecting those you love and who are close to your heart when needed. All the "negative" emotions that nature has created to help us protect ourselves and stay alert can be activated in useful ways, allowing you to stay alert, and giving you all the safety you need to navigate the most difficult times, and you know how to regulate them as best you can.

At the same time, your drive system is also active and responsive, and you are in touch with your desires, with the things that are dearest to you in your life, and the goals that you want to achieve...and you feel the necessary energy flowing into your body that pushes you to achieve your goals...you feel active and driven to achieve the things that are really important to you, that are really close to your heart.

You also see that in this future version of you, even the soothing system is finally active and helpful in your life. Imagine being able to slow down and rest, giving yourself the breaks you need, respecting your needs...experiencing a sense of contentment, fulfilment, and connection with others.

The most important thing is that this person in front of you, the person you will be in 5 years, is deeply infused with and nourished by compassion. This being has developed all the wisdom of compassion, of "it's nobody's fault that we all found ourselves here, with a body and a brain that we didn't choose"...they have developed the courage, the strength, and the serenity to accept those things that could only be accepted. But they have also developed a deep desire to be of help to themselves and others on this journey of life.

Your future self has developed full compassion towards others. They feel compassion for all the parts of themselves, especially those parts that are most in need and that are in darker places, that are lonelier. But your Compassionate Self is also finally able to feel the connection and compassion coming from others, and to open up to it.

You see yourself having harmoniously and gradually developed these three streams of compassion. How do you see yourself? What facial expression do you have? What clothes are you wearing? Are you in a particular place/location? What and who surrounds you? How do you relate to yourself and others?

Imagine you can capture an internal picture of this scene, registering all the sensations that you feel as your Compassionate Future Self.

Then, when you feel ready, begin to let go of that image and come back to the room. You may write down or draw your Compassionate Future Self if you feel called to do so.

 Optional Practice

Invite clients to represent through a shape, colour, or words what they saw.

Therapist Script 12.3: Metta (10 minutes)

Begin by finding a comfortable seated position, with your back straight but relaxed, letting it take its natural curved form; your shoulders open. If you feel comfortable doing so, close your eyes and let your inner gaze settle on your breathing and you let the air to flow in through the nose, exhaling through the mouth. Now, slow down until finding your soothing rhythm breathing. Rest your hands on your lap, palms facing up or down, whichever feels more comfortable for you. Continue to take a few deep breaths, feeling the rise and fall of your chest.

As you let your breath find its natural, calming, and soothing rhythm, bring your open awareness to your heart space, imagining your breath filling it with wisdom, courage, and desire to be helpful. Take a moment to set your intention for this meditation practice. Today, we will focus on cultivating feelings of loving-kindness and joy towards ourselves and others.

Begin by directing loving-kindness towards yourself. Visualise yourself sitting in front of you. Observe this being in front of you, who is on the journey of life, with all its highs and lows...certainly, there have been difficult moments...but with this being you have also experienced beautiful moments, maybe moments of joy, fun, or moments of deep peace and presence... let these moments come to your awareness...just like everyone else on this planet, this being desires only to be well and to experience these moments. Now, repeat the following phrases silently to yourself, with a friendly, kind inner tone of voice: "May you be happy. May you be healthy. May you be safe. May you live with ease".

Allow yourself to receive these words of friendliness... if there are other good wishes that spontaneously reach your heart whisper them to this being, in the way they would like to receive them.... maybe by imagining that this flow of wishes envelopes them...or by imagining that you get close and whisper them to their ear... if you like imagine them smiling...or their face relaxing at these words.

Next, bring to mind to someone you feel positive emotions for, a person or a being (or even an animal) that naturally brings a smile to your face. Visualise them sitting in front of you...observe them, remember the most beautiful moments you spent with this being... connect to the fact that this being too, simply wishes to be well and repeat the following phrases silently to yourself: "May you be happy. May you be healthy. May you be safe. May you live with ease". Allow yourself to feel the warmth of these words.... if there are other wishes that spontaneously reach your heart, whisper them to this being in the way they would like to receive them.

Finally, feel the presence of all the people here, of all those who have shared this journey with you. All these people who have committed to cultivating compassion, opening up to their difficult parts. Connect with these travel companions, who are on the journey of life...perhaps contemplate the visions, words, or beautiful moments that you have expected on this journey...these companions who, exactly like you, only wish to be well...then imagine wishing them well... As you inhale, silently repeat the phrase "May you be happy". As you exhale, silently repeat the phrase "May you be healthy". Repeat these phrases a few times, allowing yourself to feel a sense of kindness and compassion towards all these beings. If there are other wishes that spontaneously arrive to your heart, share them with the group, imagining that each person may receive and absorb them in the way that is most helpful. And while you are sending your wishes they are sending theirs to you....

Therapist Script 12.4: Mudita (10 minutes)

Next, we will be focusing on immersing ourselves in the joy that exists in this world; on allowing ourselves and others to experience this joy fully.

Take a moment to call to mind someone in your life who has recently experienced success or good fortune. It could be a friend, family member, or even someone you admire from a distance. Picture their face, their smile, the sound of their voice. As you inhale, silently repeat the phrase "May your happiness and success continue to grow". As you exhale, silently repeat the phrase "May your joy and good fortune be helpful to others". Repeat these phrases a few times, allowing yourself to feel a sense of joy and happiness for this person.

If you feel called to do so today, you might then choose to bring to mind someone who has experienced success or good fortune in a similar area as you. Perhaps a colleague who received a promotion, or a friend who achieved a goal you've been working towards. As you inhale, silently repeat the phrase "May your happiness and success continue to grow". As you exhale, silently repeat the phrase "May your joy and good fortune be helpful to others and to myself". Repeat these phrases a few times, allowing yourself to feel a sense of admiration and inspiration.

Now, shift your focus to yourself. Think about something positive that has happened in your life recently, no matter how small. It could be a compliment you received, a task you accomplished, or a moment of joy. As you inhale, silently repeat the phrase "May my happiness and success continue to grow". As you exhale, silently repeat the phrase "May my joy and good fortune be helpful to others". Repeat these phrases a few times, allowing yourself to feel a sense of joy and happiness for yourself.

Take these last breaths to contemplate the abundance of joy – someone who is rejoicing is not taking joy away from you... when you rejoice to the fullest in your successes and wish yourself even more good fortune, you are not taking away the possibility that others experience the same.

Take a few more deep breaths, and when you are ready, slowly open your eyes. Take a moment to notice how you feel, and carry this sense of Mudita with you on your journey.

Therapist Script 12.4: Closing Practice (8 minutes)

Now that we have developed our practices and compassionate-self let us take one final moment to consciously re-visit our intention to develop our compassionate mind and pattern.

Let's start by closing our eyes or looking down and feeling how we sit in our chair right now. Settle into your compassionate posture with your back straight and shoulders in line with your hips while letting your chest be free to expand in all directions. Now slow your breathing, and with each slower and deeper breath mentally repeat in a friendly tone of voice, "mind slowing down", "body slowing down" gradually getting that sense of grounding and widening of your awareness.

Now start tuning into your inner compassionate mind and pattern. Let us connect to the wisdom that we have developed: that we all just find ourselves here with a very tricky brain and certain life experiences that have shaped how our minds and bodies work – shaping the version of ourselves that we are. This very same mind has incredible potential to learn how to change and make choices. This body and mind we experience have an incredibly capacity for strength, courage and commitment to help ourselves and others address and deal with life and our inner difficulties.

Briefly acknowledge yourself for simply being here; with all your doubts, all your resistances, and all your difficulties, but also with the courage and the willingness to go on and to undertake this path of learning; whatever the current situation is. Acknowledge yourself for giving yourself the opportunity to experience this new learning, for having the courage to stretch your boundaries even when it's difficult *and tricky, and maybe scary. Connect to the breath of all those other people here, recognising that they, too, are facing very similar fears.*

If you hear a part of you telling you that you have not done enough, that you are still not compassionate enough...try sending compassion to the fear that generates this voice...remind them that compassion is a direction and that you will do everything to continue to cultivate compassion in more and more parts of your life...respecting your time...your nature...and your fears...

Gently ask yourself: [your name], what do you take home from today's session and from this journey you've begun (because you feel it's going to be helpful)?" And just listen to whatever arises with curiosity.

As we sit here, may we encourage each other to continue along this path, knowing that we are never truly alone in walking it. And as you send encouragement to others, you feel the encouragement of other people is reaching you right now...in a flow of mutual support.

Then, when we feel ready, we can open our eyes, and come back to the room.

Client Handouts

Client Handout 12.1: Compassionate Weekly Reflection

Let's do a curious, friendly reflection on this past week:

Which part of the self-practice did I do and why?

Which part of the self-practice did I not do?

Was this due to any anxieties or blocks regarding the practice or the path? Which ones can you identify?

We extend gratitude, respect, and compassion to resistances: What would make you and your resistances feel safer in going forward on this path?

Client Handout 12.2: Compassionate Prevention and Emergency Strategies

Get in touch with your Compassionate Self and then respond to the following prompts:

What are some of the future difficulties I might face?

What are some compassionate strategies that could be helpful in **preventing** harm to myself and to others?

What are some compassionate strategies that could be helpful in **alleviating suffering** and **regulating distress** in myself and in others?

Are there any **FBRs** that might make it difficult for you to enact these prevention and emergency strategies?

Client Handout 12.3: My Portals to Compassion

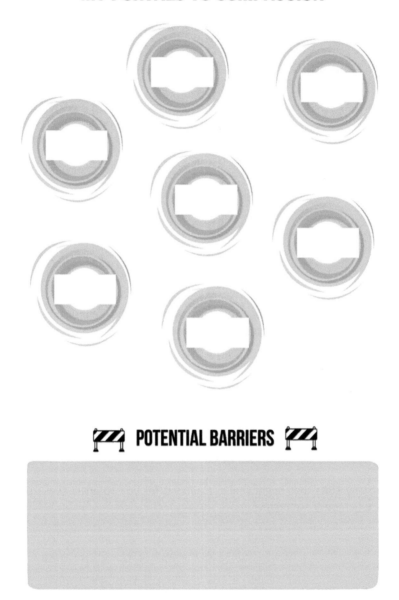

Figure 12.1 My Portals to Compassion.

Client Handout 12.4: My Take-Home Messages

Module	Take-Home Message/Intuition
Introduction to CFT and the Tricky Brain	
Three Functions and Forms of Emotion	
Mindfulness	
Safety and Safeness; Receiving Compassion from Others	
The Compassionate Self	
The Multiple Selves	

Module	Take-Home Message/Intuition
Self-Criticism	
Shame and Guilt	
Deepening Self-Compassion	
Assertiveness	
Forgiveness	
Envisioning a Compassionate Future	

Client Handout 12.5: Letter to my Compassionate Future Self

Five years have passed since the Compassionate Focused Therapy and now...

Describe in as much detail as you wish what you imagine your life will be like five years from now after this training is over...and after you have developed the three streams of compassion to the extent that you feel them to be right and useful for you...

You can be as detailed as you wish...you may describe the room you live in, what your days are like... how you eat... how you relate to others and to yourself... how you relate to your life...

Client Handout 12.6: Compassionate Forecasting

Think about some FBRs that you feel are still alive in you at this point in your journey and write them down. Notice whether you experience shame and self-criticism for these FBRs. Remember that they can be the most powerful gateway to experiencing more compassion in our lives.

What do you think would be compassionate in facing and addressing those FBRs? If you wanted to approach them with greater compassion, what would you do?

It might be something like "giving myself more time", "changing my standards", "remembering that all human beings are experiencing this or have experienced this in some form"....or maybe "connecting with a weekly practice group".

Table 12.3

My Fear, Block or Resistance	What would be helpful for me to be comfortable and work with this FBR?

Client Handout 12.7: Expressing Gratitude

Let's start by closing our eyes or looking down and feeling how we are sitting in our chair right now. Settle into your compassion posture ...Now, slow your breathing, and with each slower and deeper breath, mentally repeat in a friendly tone of voice, simply begin whispering several times, slowly, the words "thank you"..."thank you"..."thank you".... Let your mind expand in all directions and be curious about what emerges when you mentally repeat these words... perhaps you see images of people...faces...situations...in which you felt that someone did something important for you...let these images come while you continue repeating these words...

Now, let your mind land, and recollect someone who has done something for you, towards whom you feel extremely grateful, but with whom you've never had a chance to share your gratitude. Someone who, in this flow of life in which we all find ourselves, in some way has helped you with the real intention to do it...

Now write a letter to this person:

- Write as if you were speaking directly to this person (Dear...)
- Don't worry about using correct grammar or vocabulary
- Write why you are writing this letter, what your intention is
- Describe what this person has done using specific terms: why you are grateful to this person, how the behaviour and choices that this person has made have influenced your life in a positive way. Try to be as concrete as possible.
- Describe what you are doing with your life now as a result of this person's gift, this person's presence and energy, and how happy you are when remembering what this person has done for you
- If you want, finish with a wish

 Optional Practice

You might want to send the letter, or, if possible, make a "gratitude visit" – that is, choose to visit the person you wrote the letter to and read it to them.

Client Handout 12.8: Gratitude Letter to the Self

Let's start by closing our eyes or looking down, and feeling how we are sitting in our chair right now. Settle into your compassion posture ...Now, slow your breathing, and with each slower and deeper breath, mentally repeat with a friendly tone of voice the words "thank you [your name]"..."thank you [your name]" ..."thank you [your name]" .... Let your mind expand in all directions and be curious about what emerges when you mentally repeat these words... perhaps you get images of situations in which you have committed yourself to doing something that has had a positive effect in your life, or a time when you have had the courage to undertake something new (like this compassionate mind training).

Close your eyes, settle again into your compassion posture, and connect to the version of you that, in spite of the flaws, difficulties, or mistakes, had the courage to stand up to adversity....the version of you that made choices that led you to improve some aspects of your life. Speak to that part of you that brought you here, in spite of everything.

Now, write a letter to yourself:

- Write as if you were speaking directly to yourself (Dear....)
- Don't worry about grammar and vocabulary
- Write why you are writing this letter, what your intention is
- Accurately describe what you have done, why you are grateful to yourself and how your behaviour and your choices have influenced your life in a positive way. Try to be as specific as possible.
- Describe what you are doing right now in your life that is a result of your efforts and how you are sorry that you have never stopped before to recognise these efforts
- If you want, finish with a wish

 Optional Practice

If you wish, you can read the letter to yourself using a mirror – remaining curious and open to any resistances that might arise (see Module 9 for mirror practices).

Or, you can use a chair to represent the part of you that you wish to send these words of gratitude to, and read the letter aloud to the empty chair.

Appendix

In this section you will find handouts and materials that are repeated throughout the entire 12 modules. Feel free to photocopy these handouts and give them to clients for each session or as often as you believe is necessary.

Client Handout A: My Three Circles

MY THREE CIRCLES IN THIS MOMENT

Notes:

Client Handout B: Personal Practice Diary

We invite you to decide how many practices you can easily sustain in a week. Try to set wise goals, keeping these questions in mind:

- Am I being specific enough with my goals?
- Are my goals within my scope of reach?
- Why am I working towards this goal?
- How will I know I have reached my goal? How can I measure it?

We suggest you aim for at least three practices a week; if you reach three, that's 100 percent, if you do six practices, that's 200 percent, if you do one practice, that's 33% of your goal – these are all wins!

You can choose which ones of the meditation recordings provided you use as a guide.

Below is a weekly planner where you can tick off whether you have been able to do your practice each day. There is also space to provide some extra details on things you noticed, or possibly reactions to the practices.

What helped support your practice on the days you did get to do it and what got in the way on those days you were not able to practice? Were these internal or external hindrances? Did you feel them as imposed? Did you feel guilty when you did not do a practice (as if it was homework)? How could you change these practices so that they are truly helpful to you?

Also continue to try and notice your own loops in the mind.

On the following page, you will find a daily planner that you can print out for each day of the week to have more space for self-reflection about how your practice went.

WEEKLY PLANNER

DATES: _____

SUNDAY	MONDAY	TUESDAY	WEDNESDAY	THURSDAY	FRIDAY	SATURDAY
●	●	●	●	●	●	●

NOTES:

DAILY PLANNER

DATE :

PRACTICE FOR TODAY

ONE WORD TO SUMMARIZE MY PRACTICE

WHAT I NOTICED DURING THE PRACTICE

WHAT SUPPORTED MY PRACTICE AND WHAT DID NOT

NOTES :

References

Craig, C., Hiskey, S., & Spector, A. (2020). Compassion Focused Therapy: a systematic review of its effectiveness and acceptability in clinical populations. *Expert Review of Neurotherapeutics*, 20(4), 385–400.

Gilbert, P. (1992). *The evolution of powerlessness*. Psychology Press.

Gilbert, P. (Ed.). (2005). *Compassion: Conceptualisations, research and use in psychotherapy*. Routledge. doi:10.4324/9780203003459.

Gilbert, P. (2009). *The Compassionate Mind*. London: Constable & Robinson; and Oaklands, CA: New Harbinger.

Gilbert, P. (2009b). Evolved minds and compassion-focused imagery in depression. In L. Stopa (Ed.), *Imagery and the Threatened Self: Perspectives on Mental Imagery and the Self in Cognitive Therapy* (pp. 206–231). London: Routledge.

Gilbert, P. (2010). *Compassion Focused Therapy: Distinctive Features* (1st ed.). Routledge. doi:10.4324/9780203851197.

Gilbert, P. (Ed.). (2017). *Compassion: Concepts, research and applications*. Routledge/ Taylor & Francis Group. doi:10.4324/9781315564296-1.

Gilbert, P. (2018). *Living Like Crazy*, Annwyn House.

Gilbert, P. & Simos, G. (Eds). (2022). *Compassion focused therapy: Clinical practice and applications*. Routledge. doi:10.4324/9781003035879.

Millard, L. A., Wan, M. W., Smith, D. M., & Wittkowski, A. (2023). The effectiveness of compassion focused therapy with clinical populations: A systematic review and meta-analysis. *Journal of affective disorders, 326,* 168–192. https://doi.org/10.1016/j. jad.2023.01.010.

Petrocchi, N., Ottaviani, C., Cheli, S., Matos, M., Baldi, B., Basran, J. K., & Gilbert, P. (2023, December 7). The Impact of Compassion-Focused Therapy on Positive and Negative Mental Health Outcomes: Results of a Series of Meta-Analyses. *Clinical Psychology: Science and Practice*. Advance online publication. https://dx.doi.org/10.1037/cps0000193

Vidal, J. & Soldevilla, J. M. (2023). Effect of compassion-focused therapy on self-criticism and self-soothing: A meta-analysis. *British Journal of Clinical Psychology*, 62(1), 70–81.

Yalom, I. D. & Leszcz, M. (2005). *The theory and practice of group psychotherapy* (5th ed.). Basic Books/Hachette Book Group.

Index